Building an Intelligent Web
THEORY AND PRACTICE

Contains IBM® DB2® Express-C 9

Java™
COMPATIBLE

RAJENDRA AKERKAR
Technomathematics Research Foundation

PAWAN LINGRAS
Saint Mary's University

JONES AND BARTLETT PUBLISHERS

Sudbury, Massachusetts

BOSTON   TORONTO   LONDON   SINGAPORE

World Headquarters

Jones and Bartlett Publishers
40 Tall Pine Drive
Sudbury, MA 01776
978-443-5000
info@jbpub.com
www.jbpub.com

Jones and Bartlett Publishers
Canada
6339 Ormindale Way
Mississauga, Ontario L5V 1J2
CANADA

Jones and Bartlett Publishers
International
Barb House, Barb Mews
London W6 7PA
UK

Jones and Bartlett's books and products are available through most bookstores and online booksellers. To contact Jones and Bartlett Publishers directly, call 800-832-0034, fax 978-443-8000, or visit our website, www.jbpub.com.

Substantial discounts on bulk quantities of Jones and Bartlett's publications are available to corporations, professional associations, and other qualified organizations. For details and specific discount information, contact the special sales department at Jones and Bartlett via the above contact information or send an email to specialsales@jbpub.com.

Production Credits
Acquisitions Editor: Timothy Anderson
Production Director: Amy Rose
Marketing Manager: Andrea DeFronzo
Editorial Assistant: Melissa Elmore
Manufacturing Buyer: Therese Connell
Composition: Northeast Compositors, Inc.
Cover Design: Kristin E. Ohlin
Cover Image: top honeycomb image © Andrey Prakharov/ShutterStock, Inc.; bottom globe image
   © Norebbo/ShutterStock, Inc.
Printing and Binding: Malloy, Inc.
Cover Printing: Malloy, Inc.

Library of Congress Cataloging-in-Publication Data
Lingras, Pawan.
  Building an intelligent Web : theory and practice / Pawan Lingras and Rajendra Akerkar.
    p. cm.
  Includes bibliographical references and index.
  ISBN-13: 978-0-7637-4137-2
  ISBN-10: 0-7637-4137-X
  1. Expert systems (Computer science) 2. Data mining. 3. Web databases. 4. Web usage mining. I. Akerkar, Rajendra. II. Title.
  QA76.76.E95L557 2007
  006.3'3—dc22
                    2007011156

6048

Printed in the United States of America
11 10 09 08 07   10 9 8 7 6 5 4 3 2 1

To our families

Contents

Preface

In recent years we have witnessed an ever-growing flood of information, culminating in the advent of massive digital libraries. The *World Wide Web* has become a very popular way of publishing information and distributing electronic resources. The *World Wide Web* is an immense success, helping everyone from preschoolers to IT professionals share information, simplify research, and conduct business online. Though the Web is rich with information, collecting and making sense of this data is difficult because publication on the Web is relatively unorganized. Thus, data mining applied to the Web has the potential to be quite beneficial. Web mining is the application of data mining techniques to the *World Wide Web*. These techniques are mainly derived from Artificial Intelligence (AI) and Information Retrieval (IR). The application of these AI and IR techniques can be very useful in the development of the next generation of intelligent websites—the websites that adapt to users' information needs.

The objective of this book is to present web intelligence techniques in an organized, in-depth, yet very clear manner that is accessible to students, researchers, and a wide range of web technology developers. This is one of the most active and exciting areas among the web technology research community. Many researchers in areas such as artificial intelligence, data visualization, statistics, and machine learning are contributing to this field. The breadth of the field makes it difficult to comprehensively grasp its recent development. Most material is scattered in research papers and a few good books on some of the topics. We present the material in an organized and readable manner, which makes the book appropriate as a course textbook, yet at the same time it can be used as a reference for Web Intelligence.

This book has evolved from our lectures on data mining, information retrieval, and Web Intelligence delivered over a couple of years. The material was classroom tested for graduate courses. Dr. Cory Butz from the Department of Computer Science at the University of Regina class tested the book, in addition to class testing done at Saint Mary's University.

The material in this book is presented with the expectation that it can be read independently or used as part of a course that incorporates active and cooperative learning methodology. To accomplish this, the chapters are lucid and comprehensive so as to be easy to understand and to encourage readers to prepare by reading before class meetings.

Features and Benefits

Instructors will find it useful for teaching a course on Web Mining, Web Intelligence, or Web Information Retrieval at an advanced undergraduate level or first year graduate level. The detailed guide to the book is given in Section 1.7 of Chapter 1. Each chapter contains theoretical bases, which are also illustrated with the help of simple numeric examples, followed by practical implementations. Every chapter ends with a set of exercises, suitable as assigned homework. Adopters of this book may consult the Jones and Bartlett's website for on-line locations of PowerPoint lecture slides and hints to some exercises in the book: http://computerscience.jbpub.com/cs_resources.cfm.

The book is accompanied by one CD-ROM and DVD. The CD-ROM contains links to various public domain software packages and datasets used in the textbook. The software linked from the CD-ROM will enable students to carry out all relevant data mining, web mining, and information retrieval tasks. Java source code for a complete information retrieval system written and tested by the authors will help students understand, modify, and extend information retrieval systems. The readers can experiment with XML queries and simple Semantic Web using the XQEngine written by Howard Katz, which is linked from the CD-ROM under the GNU General Public License (GPL). The CTreeinExcel software written by Angshuman Saha allows us to perform moderate size classification tasks. A freely available software toolkit called PAFI for finding frequent patterns in diverse datasets is linked from the CD-ROM, and used to illustrate association and sequence mining. We have implemented Kohonen self-organizing maps and k-Means Algorithm in Java that can be used by readers to experiment with clustering. Analog software available under the GPL and linked from the CD-ROM is used to analyze web logs. More detailed session analysis is done using public domain software called Pathalizer. Pathalizer provides a graphical birds-eye view of user navigation on a website. Statviz is another software that provides graphical representation of aggregate navigation as well as individual sessions. Statviz is linked from the CD-ROM under the MIT open source license. We wrote a Java based crawler for the CD-ROM, which can be used to develop a more sophisticated web crawler. A link to Wget for Windows, a public domain crawler, can also be found on the CD-ROM. The book also contains the DB2 Discovery DVD™ that contains DB2 Express-C 9™ install images for Windows. It also has the DB2 Developer Workbench for Windows™, the DB2 Information Center™, as well as documentation, flash demos, and many useful links. The DB2 will help students learn and practice basic database operations as part of their data mining exercises. The instructor should master the software included on the CD-ROM because it facilitates the answers to "what if" questions that make it very interesting to learn the topics discussed in the text. Students should also learn the software so that they can run examples independently, work out the problems at the end of the chapters, and apply newly acquired knowledge to projects.

Acknowledgments

We would like to gratefully acknowledge the support and encouragement of Jones & Bartlett Publishers, Saint Mary's University, American University of Armenia and Technomathematics Research Foundation. We would like to express our appreciation to our sponsoring editor Tim Anderson, and the staff of Jones & Bartlett, who received our proposal for a textbook and supported us throughout its development. Similar gratitude is also due to reviewers who have greatly enhanced the quality of the manuscript:

Ricardo Campos, Teacher at Tomar Polytechnic Institute and researcher at Centre for Human Language Technology and BioInformatics (University of Beira Interior)
Gaël Dias, University of Beira Interior, Portugal
Kemal Efe, University of Louisiana at Lafayette
Jiming Liu, University of Windsor
Debajyoti Mukhopadhyay, West Bengal University of Technology
Vijay Raghavan, University of Louisiana at Lafayette
Biren Shah, University of Louisiana at Lafayette

We would like to thank Dr. Cory Butz for class testing the text. We acknowledge the students who have taken a course based on this text and given us exceedingly valuable feedback on the text and exercises. Our special thanks goes to Rucha Lingras for her work with the book, CD-ROM, and proofreading. We regret forgetting to express our gratitude to anyone else who has contributed to this book.

Finally, it is hoped that the students will find this textbook a useful companion for their course of study.

Rajendra Akerkar
Pawan Lingras

Introduction to Web Intelligence

1.1 Historical Perspective

When the Chinese pounded linen to make paper, they unwittingly provided a medium for spreading and storing knowledge. Then five and a half centuries ago, a German goldsmith named Gutenberg invented the printing press. Who could have predicted the impact of the printing press, which was initially devoted to publishing religious books, to be so great? Who could have imagined that books, once owned by the few and treasured as symbols of wealth and power, would one day be accessible to everyone? The Gutenberg press, with its wooden movable-type printing, brought down the price of printed material, making it affordable for the masses. Many newer printing technologies, such as offset printing, were developed based on Gutenberg's press. It remained the standard medium for the dissemination of knowledge until the twentieth century.

Now we are living in extraordinary times again. The modern world is being turned upside down before our very eyes. The electronic phenomenon of the last 50 years has matured very quickly into an online revolution that has fundamentally changed our world. But there is a huge difference between what happened in Gutenberg's time and now. We are dealing with an accelerated rate of change—change that is happening not only quickly, but also pervasively.

In 1834 British mathematician, economist, and engineer Charles Babbage conceived the first general-purpose programmable computer, the Analytical Engine. It was a mechanical device designed to be constructed out of thousands of precisely machined metal parts. Because it would have been enormously costly to build, and there was no urgent need for such a computer in Babbage's day, the Analytical Engine was never completed; only small portions of it were built from Babbage's engineering drawings after his death. This did, however, mark the beginning of the computer era, even though computers didn't become an integral part of our lives until only relatively recently. Consider for a moment that the Internet is about 40 years old, the microelectronics explosion happened only 30 years ago, the desktop computer appeared only about 25 years ago, the World Wide Web is really only a little more than a decade old, and that ubiquitous wireless Internet access is only now becoming a reality. Despite only relatively recent developmental history, we are facing an information explosion on the World Wide Web, making it necessary to build a better Web—an Intelligent Web—that will help users easily realize their information and commercial needs.

1.2 Toward an Intelligent Web

The past few years have produced an enormous amount of written information, resulting in the advent of massive digital libraries. With the advent of the World Wide Web, publishing is no longer the domain of a small number of elite scholars. Now almost anyone who has something to say can publish it on the Web. Search engines guarantee that readers around the world will be made aware of these publications. But despite the best efforts of today's search engines, the abundance of information on the Web is mostly unorganized; thus making sense of such available data is a very difficult task. Nowadays, data-mining techniques are used extensively to get required information from different databases, so why not use the same techniques to extract implicit and unknown information from the massive collection of documents available on the Web, which, in a sense, can be viewed as one large database? In order to extract useful information from the Web, we may use existing data-mining techniques, as well as new techniques designed specifically for the Web. Web mining—data mining applied to the Web—can be said to include the following techniques:

- Clustering: Finding natural groupings of users or pages
- Classification and prediction: Determining the class or behavior of a user or resource
- Associations: Determining which URLs tend to be requested together
- Sequence Analysis: Studying the order in which URLs tend to be accessed

In reality, the techniques such as clustering, classification, and association may be combined to obtain more sophisticated web mining applications.

In this text we will identify the essential features of web mining. We will discuss conventional searching techniques along with the emerging field of the Semantic Web. The standard data-mining techniques will be illustrated using the Web as the application platform. Finally, techniques that are specifically applicable to the Web, such as web usage, content, and structure mining, are presented to extract previously unknown information from the Web.

Kosala and Blockeel (2000) identified the following purposes for our interaction with the Web:

1. Learning new knowledge from the Web: We already have a collection of web data, and now we want to extract useful knowledge from it.

2. Searching for relevant information: Normally, when we wish to find specific information on the Web, we use either a search service or simply browse through the Web by following links. In the much-favored search option, we provide a list of keywords and get a list of pages as a result. Pages are ranked based on their similarity to the query. This can be called a query-triggered approach. However, there are two drawbacks of search tools: During a keyword search, we frequently observe that many pages of information are not relevant to our query. On the other hand, since some of the relevant pages are not properly indexed, we may not get those pages by using any of the search engines available today.

3. Personalized web pages: Individuals have their own preferences for how the content is presented while interacting with the Web. We may wish to synthesize a different web page for each individual from the available set of web pages or data.

4. Learning about individual users: Understand what the customers need and what they do. This knowledge helps organizations customize the information to the intended consumers, increasing the chances of a sale.

web mining provides a set of techniques to tackle the previously-mentioned problems. Such techniques may help create direct solutions for the problems. They can also be used as a part of a bigger application that addresses a wider issue. Web intelligence is an area of growing research and development. The Web Intelligence Consortium (WIC 2006) is an organization dedicated to the research on and education about Web intelligence. Readers may want to visit http://wi-consortium.org/ for more information.

1.2.1   Information Retrieval

While the Information Retrieval (IR) community has been tackling querying issues for several decades, we are just beginning to see the appearance of text-based knowledge-discovery systems. Therefore, it is important to study the relationship between areas such as information retrieval, information extraction, and computational linguistics with text-data mining. IR is concerned with finding and ranking documents that match the users' information needs. Most search engines are adept at information retrieval, which brings to the user's attention a list of documents that may contain the desired information. It is the user's responsibility to go through these documents to extract the information. Automatic information extraction, a research area of considerable interest, will extract the relevant information for the user in a concise form.

Figure 1.1 shows a comprehensive evolution of information and retrieval produced by (Fielden 2002). The Y axis shows the timeline from 9000 BCE to 1900 CE, but it is to scale from only 500 BCE. The scale on the X axis is exponential. Fielden observes several interesting facts from the data. With the development of written languages, the accumulation of information gathered momentum. Despite the fact that the invention of the printing press with movable type by Gutenberg had obvious effects on the amount of available information, the Library at Alexandria was an extraordinary phenomenon, and also an anomaly. While seriously damaged with considerable loss of documents at least twice, it set a standard of size that was not equalled in the Western world for over 1600 years (Fielden 2002).

Although information accumulation was a positive development, searching for the relevant information became an important issue. Vannevar Bush is credited with an early vision of information retrieval and hypertext. Bush proposed an imaginary information retrieval machine called *Memex* in a famous paper called "As We May Think" in 1945. Information retrieval soon flourished in the 1960s and '70s. Gerard Salton, one of the prominent personalities in information retrieval, developed SMART—the System for the Manipulation and Retrieval of Text (Salton, G. 1971). SMART was first developed at Harvard and matured at Cornell. Interest in information retrieval has been further rekindled with the advent of the World Wide Web. The foundations of information retrieval, established in the early years, are still applicable today.

The IR process, including digital libraries and Internet searching, consists of retrieving desired information from textual data. However, a single generic IR solution cannot be applied to every website. In order to facilitate navigation through their site, web developers will need to understand the fundamentals of information retrieval, including document representation, retrieval models, and analysis of retrieval performance. A well-thought-out IR solution using various fundamental components of information retrieval will enhance the browsing experience; therefore, this book begins with an introduction to the essentials of information retrieval. Keyword-based document representation is one of the primary ways in which the IR community

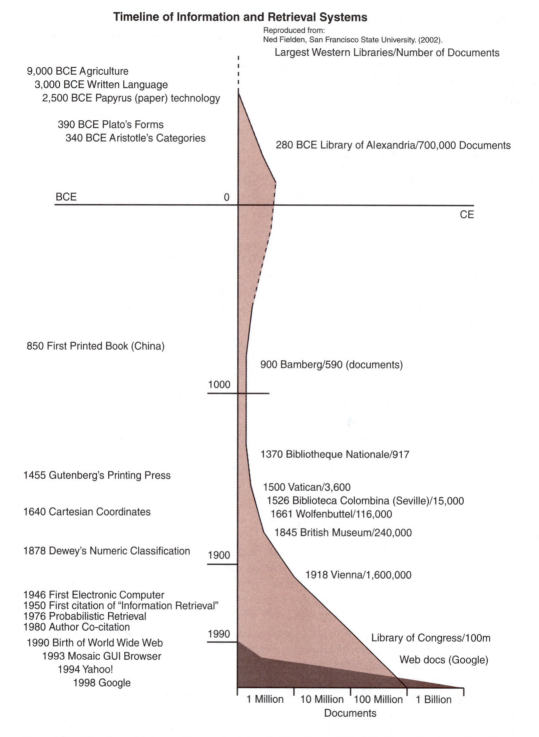

Timeline of Information and Retrieval Systems

Reproduced from:
Ned Fielden, San Francisco State University. (2002).

Largest Western Libraries/Number of Documents

9,000 BCE Agriculture
3,000 BCE Written Language
2,500 BCE Papyrus (paper) technology

390 BCE Plato's Forms
340 BCE Aristotle's Categories

280 BCE Library of Alexandria/700,000 Documents

BCE   0

CE

850 First Printed Book (China)

900 Bamberg/590 (documents)

1000

1370 Bibliotheque Nationale/917

1455 Gutenberg's Printing Press

1500 Vatican/3,600
1526 Biblioteca Colombina (Seville)/15,000
1661 Wolfenbuttel/116,000

1640 Cartesian Coordinates

1845 British Museum/240,000

1878 Dewey's Numeric Classification

1900

1918 Vienna/1,600,000

1946 First Electronic Computer
1950 First citation of "Information Retrieval"
1976 Probabilistic Retrieval
1980 Author Co-citation

1990

1990 Birth of World Wide Web

Library of Congress/100m

1993 Mosaic GUI Browser

Web docs (Google)

1994 Yahoo!
1998 Google

1 Million   10 Million   100 Million   1 Billion
Documents

Figure 1.1 Timeline of information and retrieval (Courtesy of Ned Fielden, San Francisco State University)

processes textual information. A document is summarized by identifying unique words and their frequency of occurrence. A "stemmer" is then used to identify the list of unique words and determine the root of a written word form. For example, words such as *cats, catlike,* and *catty* are essentially derived from the word or stem, *cat.* Occurrences of these words should not be separately listed in a document representation and would all fall under *cat.* A stemming algorithm will be presented in Chapter 2, which will include an illustration of its execution. The use of stemmer software will help readers create a term-document matrix (TDM) as a representation of a document collection. Every user query—also represented as a list of keywords—is matched with the term-document matrix by using a retrieval model. The Vector Space Model (VSM), one of the most popular retrieval models, will be presented in this text in great detail. An implementation of the VSM will be presented using the term-document matrix for several standard document collections. Variations of the VSM and probabilistic retrieval models will also be presented. A web developer should accept an IR system only after testing its retrieval performance. If the performance is not acceptable, the IR system should either be modified or replaced by another one. A periodic evaluation and fine-tuning of the IR system should be an essential part of website maintenance. In order to assist web developers with the evaluation task, this book includes a detailed discussion on measurements of retrieval performance such as precision/recall, F-measure, and mean average precision.

1.2.2   Semantic Web

The Semantic Web is the brainchild of Tim Berners-Lee, the developer of the World Wide Web. His vision of the Semantic Web will soon become a part of our everyday life. It is expected that intelligent-software agents will assist us with a suitable solution to our real-world problem. The Semantic Web will help these intelligent-software agents by making it possible for a computer to process available information. The World Wide Web Consortium (W3C) has provided a definition for the Semantic Web as follows:

> *The Semantic Web is the representation of data on the World Wide Web. It is a collaborative effort led by W3C with participation from a large number of researchers and industrial partners. It is based on the Resource Description Framework (RDF), which integrates a variety of applications using XML for syntax and URIs (Uniform Resource Identifiers) for naming.*

The formation of the Semantic Web is being realized by developing languages, tools, and so on. Berners-Lee envisaged the Semantic Web as a layered composition with resource-identifying systems such as Unicode and Uniform Resource Identifiers (URI) at its foundation. The subsequent layers compose the XML schema to depict resources and resource description framework (RDF) to match different descriptions used to depict web resources. Furthermore, ontologies identify the concept and the relationships between those concepts. In Chapter 3 we will study the basics such as URIs, XML, and components like RDF.

1.3   Knowledge

In today's computer world, we frequently observe data as a string of bits, numbers, and symbols, or objects, which are meaningful when sent to a program in a given format. Data can be defined as a collection of mere symbols. When data is processed with semantic considerations, we get information. Knowledge can be further defined as organized information. In other words, knowledge can be considered as data at a higher level of abstraction and generalization. Knowledge discovery is nothing but extracting valuable knowledge from a huge pool of data; that is, the process of detecting valid, innovative, useful, and understandable patterns in data.

1.3.1   Data Mining Applied to the Web

Data mining is a component of knowledge discovery. Under certain satisfactory computational efficiency limitations, data mining finds patterns or models in data and is typically used primarily by trade, financial, communication, and marketing organizations with a sound consumer focus. It enables these companies to determine relationships among "internal" factors, such as price, product positioning, or staff skills, and "external" factors, such as economic indicators, competition, and customer demographics. It enables them to determine the impact on sales, customer satisfaction, and corporate profits.

Data needs to be cleaned prior to mining a data set in order to eliminate errors and guarantee consistency. Data cleaning usually involves the use of straightforward statistical techniques, but sometimes may need highly sophisticated data analysis.

The World Wide Web has become an incredibly common medium for publishing. Clearly the Web provides a rich repository of data for mining. However, searching, comprehending, and using the semistructured information stored on the Web poses a significant challenge, because this data is more sophisticated and dynamic than the information contained in structured commercial databases.

Chapters 4 and 5 describe the features and particulars of the data-mining techniques necessary for building an intelligent Web.

To enhance keyword-based indexing—the basis for web search engines—researchers have applied data mining to web-page ranking. In this context, data mining helps search engines find high quality web pages. Web services and their usability must be improved and made more comprehensible in order to reach their full potential. As researchers continue to develop data-mining techniques, this technology will play a significant role in meeting the challenges of developing an intelligent Web. The Web is an immense and dynamic collection of data that includes countless hyperlinks and huge volumes of access and usage information. It provides a rich and exceptional data-mining source.

1.4   Web Mining

As seen earlier, it has become increasingly essential to utilize automated tools for required information resources and to track and analyze their usage patterns. The Web can be regarded as the largest database available and presents a challenging task for efficient design and access. Web mining can be defined as the discovery and analysis of useful information from the World

Wide Web. In web mining, data can be collected at the server-side, client-side, or proxy servers or acquired from an organization's database. Each type of data gathering varies not only in the location of the data source, but also in the characteristics of the data, the segment of the population from which the data is collected, and its method of implementation. There are many kinds of data that can be used in web mining. A survey paper on web-usage mining (Srivastava et al. 2000) classified collected data into the following types:

- Content: The real data in web pages, such as textual, image, audio, video, hyperlinks, and metadata.
- Structure: Data that illustrates the organization of content. This includes the arrangement of various HTML or XML tags within a given page. The primary kind of interpage structure information is hyperlinks connecting one page to another.
- Usage: Secondary data, which includes data from web-server access logs, proxy server logs, user profiles, cookies, and so on, derived from users' interactions on the Web.
- User Profile: Data that imparts demographic information, such as registration data and customer profile details, regarding users of a website.

The Web mining classification is shown in **Figure 1.2**.

Data mining originated from a need for mining unknown regular information from customers' baskets in a market. Many classical mining methods were invented to achieve this goal, such as association rules, sequential pattern analysis, classifiers, and clustering methods. Data mining can now help people know what is hidden behind a huge data resource by reducing the information capacity and complexity. It is normally defined as finding hidden information in a database and involves several algorithms to accomplish various tasks.

With the variety and quantity of information, the Web is creating new challenges for data-mining technology. The Web is a new resource for data mining that has a different data format embodied in the semantics, organization, structure, and storage of data. Thus, newer mining methods designed for the Web are needed.

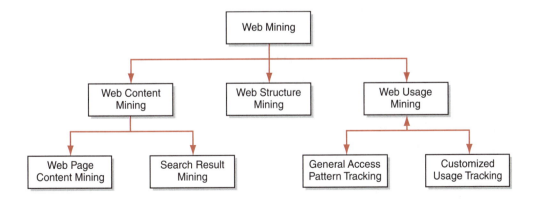

Figure 1.2   Web mining classifications (Courtesy of O. Romanko, 2002)

1.4.1 Web-Usage Mining

Web-usage mining is the study of data generated by the web surfer's sessions or behaviors. As pointed out earlier, web-usage mining works with the secondary data resulting from the user's communications with the Web. The Web servers accumulate the secondary data in web-access logs. Analysis of these logs from various Web sites can help in understanding user behavior and web structure.

As mentioned earlier, the secondary data utilized in web-usage mining include web logs, proxy-server logs, browser logs, and so on. A Web-access log is an inventory of page-reference data. It is at times referred to as *clickstream* data, as each entry corresponds to a mouse click. Logs can be observed from two angles:

- Server: It can be used to advance the design of a website.
- Client: The information about the user is found by assessing a client's sequence of clicks. This information could be used to carry out the caching of pages. This makes the loading of Web pages efficient.

Ultimately, such analysis helps organizations efficiently market their products on the Web. It can also supply essential information on how to restructure a website. A high level web-usage mining process (Srivastava et al. 2000) is shown in **Figure 1.3**.

Web logs or web-usage mining can be used to enhance server performance, improve website navigation, target customers for electronic commerce, and identify potential prime advertisement locations. Web-analysis tools offer the means for reporting user activity in the servers and various forms of data filtering. Such tools can be used to find out the number of accesses to the server and to individual files, the times of visits, and the locations of users. However, these tools are designed to manage low-to-medium traffic servers. Moreover, these tools also are limited in their abilities to provide analysis of data relationships. The diagrammatic representation of web-usage mining applications are given in Srivastava (2000). We have shown

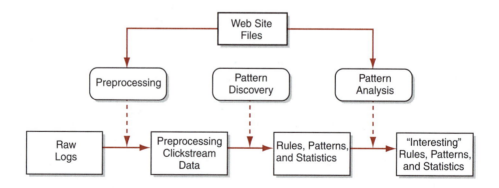

Figure 1.3   High level web usage mining process (Courtesy of Srivastava *et al.*, 2000)

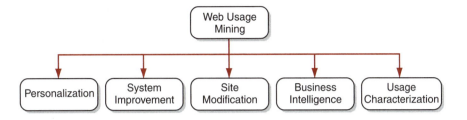

Figure 1.4   Applications of web usage mining (Courtesy of O. Romanko, 2002; Courtesy of Srivastava *et al.*, 2000)

the same in **Figure 1.4**. Complete details of web-usage mining, including applications, will be elaborated on in Chapter 6.

1.4.2   Web-Content Mining

Web-content mining deals with primary data on the Web; that is, the contents of web pages. This content could encompass an extremely broad variety of data from a broad variety of sources, such as digital libraries, government information portals, and e-commerce sites; more applications and systems are migrating to the Web all the time. Some of the content data are generated dynamically as a result of queries and also hidden data; and such data are normally not indexed.

As mentioned earlier, web content consists of various types of data, such as textual, images, video, audio, metadata, and hyperlinks. Researchers have paid much more attention to mining the contents of text and hypertext documents. Textual data are comprised in unstructured data, for instance free texts: semistructured data, such as HTML documents, and structured data, such as HTML pages form databases and data in tables. For the most part, web-content data is unstructured, therefore text-mining techniques play a major role in web-content mining. We will study Web-content mining in Chapter 7.

1.4.2.1   Overview of Crawlers

A "crawler" is a program that navigates the hypertext structure of the Web. This is used in web-content mining by search engines.

Here we will briefly explain the functioning of a crawler (for a more detailed discussion, see Chapter 7). A crawler starts with an original URL, also called a "seed," and starts recording and collecting all the links. It collects information from every page it visits in the form of keywords. **Figure 1.5** describes the use of crawlers in a search engine (Romanko 2006). Crawlers can be categorized as

- periodic: triggered periodically;
- incremental: updates an index;
- focused: visits pages associated with specific topics.

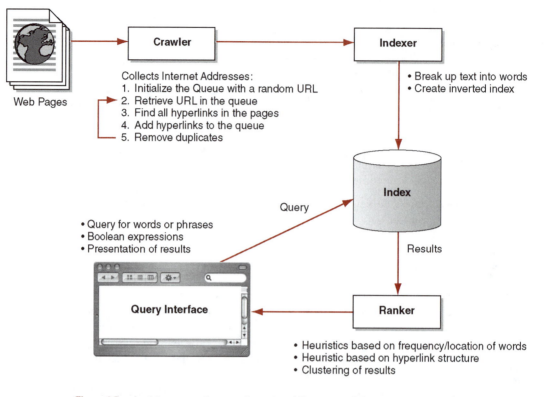

Figure 1.5 Architecture of a search engine (Courtesy of O. Romanko, 2002)

1.4.3 Web-Structure Mining

Web-structure mining consists of finding the model underlying the link structures of the Web, which can be utilized to classify web pages. It is also beneficial for producing information, such as the similarity and relationship between various websites. Web-structure mining analyzes the structures of documents within the Web. Various algorithms have been proposed to model web topology, for instance PageRank, HITS, and CLEVER. These models are primarily useful as a technique for computing the rank of every web page. Some of the techniques that are useful in modeling web topology will be presented in Chapter 8, along with the concept of social network analysis, which uses an exponentially varying damping factor. Web-structure mining applies social-network analysis to model the underlying link structure of the Web. The primary assumption is that if one web page points to another web page, then the former is approving the significance of the latter.

1.5 Building Better Web Sites Using Intelligent Technologies

Website development is becoming increasingly more complex; and with the rising flood of sites, it is essential to make sure that user needs are fulfilled to the best of a site's abilities.

Even if a site has the information required by a user, ineffective navigation facilities will make a user drift to an alternate site. Some websites offer generic search facilities, which are not always useful to surfers. A better understanding of the various components of information retrieval discussed in this book will enable web developers to put together a search engine that is applicable to their sites. Moreover, the discussion in this book will also help developers evaluate the quality of search results. Such an evaluation can lead to better site organization, as well as improved retrieval process.

Traditional information retrieval is based on keyword matching. Users construct an appropriate combination of keywords that may or may not provide documents relevant to their needs. The Semantic Web attempts to address this shortcoming. It will use embedded tags that do not affect the way a document is displayed and will help provide more meaningful answers to user queries. In addition to considering the semantics of a document, the Semantic Web can also be used to provide more specific information in response to user queries. Although the Semantic Web is currently in its infancy, over the last decade we have seen the proliferation of its standards, applications, and approaches.

The World Wide Web has become an important commercial vehicle. Serving a customer in the world of e-commerce is now even more critical than the physical supermarkets. A cyber shopper can hop from one store to the next and back in a matter of seconds. Understanding the customers and presenting them with products that best suit their desires is essential for survival in the world of e-commerce. Web-usage mining will help developers not only monitor the usage of websites but also improve customer satisfaction. This text illustrates a complete data-mining process, including data preparation and application of data-mining techniques.

Although multimedia information retrieval, which attempts to incorporate audio and visual (still pictures and movies), is still young, ignoring the information contained in these multimedia components can seriously hamper the quality of retrieval. The web-content mining discussion in Chapter 7 may be helpful in incorporating multimedia information in the retrieval process. Web crawlers, which are also discussed under Web-content mining, will not only help client software to explore the Web, but also help web developers keep track of their own dynamically growing sites.

Web-structure mining includes the analysis and reorganization of the structure of a site. There are many ways of organizing a website. Many sites provide different home pages for different types of users. Usually these classes are predefined; for example, a University site may have different pages for faculty, students, prospective students, staff, and the general public. The clustering of web users and documents accessed by users described under web-usage mining may help developers uncover different groups of users as well as their interests. Site maps and static indexes represent other efforts at restructuring the look of a website. Understanding the underlying information-retrieval process will enable developers to dynamically create index pages to facilitate site navigation, as demonstrated in Chapter 8 on web-structure mining.

1.6   Benefits of Intelligent Web

In this section, we will look at some of the benefits one can gain from web mining (Megaputer 2006).

Matching existing resources to a visitor's interests

There can be various types of resources such as products, information fragments, or e-mail fragments from a mailing list that is circulated online. The metadata from these resources are accumulated in a database. Web-mining software helps study visitor interests by collecting and analyzing information produced by interactions with a website, such as clickstream data, search requests, and cookies. Web-mining software can use this knowledge to rank the resources by their importance to a user. This helps create a higher visitor-to-customer conversion rate for a company's e-business.

Boost the value of a visitor

Using collaborative filtering, one can envisage what type of information a visitor may be interested in. Such predictions can be used to offer related products and resources to a visitor. Collaborative filtering may also result in a rise in sales.

Enhance the visitor's experience on the website

With the help of data- and text-mining techniques, one can study a visitor's interaction with a website to find out user interests. This helps the website to act proactively and deliver largely personalized resources to the visitor.

Achieve targeted resource management

Buying behavior varies from person to person. Whereas some are potential customers, others are searching for information and familiarizing themselves with company products at the same time. Such probable customers may become profitable customers in the future.

Test the significance of content and website architecture

With the help of log analyzers, one can envisage the frequently traversed paths through the website. This analysis will further increase the usability of the site, or at least optimize the site to improve the experience for promising prospects.

1.7   Guide to Using the Book

This book is divided into eight chapters. Readers can select the appropriate chapters based on their interests. For instance, a graduate student in Computer Science studying a course on Information Retrieval may be interested in Chapters 1, 2, 3, 7, and 8. The tree-like structure for specific use of this textbook is presented in **Figure 1.6**. This book can be used as a textbook for a course on Web Mining, Web Intelligence, or Web Information Retrieval at an advanced undergraduate level or first-year graduate level in Computer Science. At the same time, the book can be used to teach a web-mining curriculum in mathematics or statistics. Each chapter contains theoretical bases, which are also illustrated with the help of simple numeric examples followed by practical implementations. Datasets and programs included on or linked to the CD that accompanies this book will enable students to experiment with some of the concepts discussed in each chapter. Those who are not familiar with Java programming and not interested in mathematical details can ignore the sections denoted by the icon ☕. Every chapter ends with a set of exercises, suitable for assigned homework.

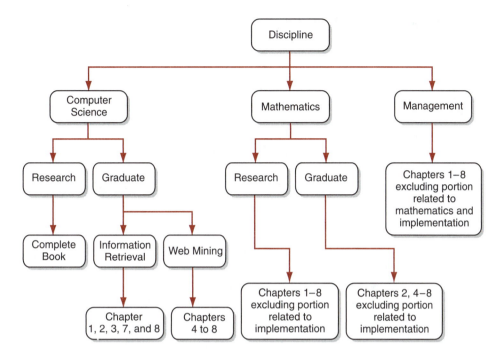

Figure 1.6   Decision tree-like structure

1.8 What Is on the CD?

The CD that accompanies this book is divided according to the chapters in the book. **Figure 1.7** shows the home page for the CD. The software demonstrations given in each chapter refer to the resources listed under that chapter on the CD. Readers will be able to run these demonstrations by following instructions given in the corresponding chapters.

The resources on the CD consist of demo programs, open-source software, as well as datasets. The demonstration programs are usually simple implementations of algorithms described in the book. The main purpose of these demo programs is to help readers see how the theory can be implemented. More technically minded readers can also use these programs as a starting point for developing more elaborate and sophisticated tools. The open-source software and freeware included on the CD provide a greater degree of functionality and can be used to create intelligent websites. A brief outline of the contents of the CD follows.

Chapter 2 addresses various issues in traditional information retrieval (IR), two of which are document representation and retrieval. The chapter describes an algorithm that stems similarly spelled words to a common base form. For example, *learner, learning,* and *learned* will all stem from the same word, *learn.* The CD includes the code of one of the publicly available stemmers. A document is typically represented by the frequency of various stemmed words. A term-document matrix represents a document collection. These term-document matrices are used for retrieving documents relevant to a user query. The CD contains a set of Java classes

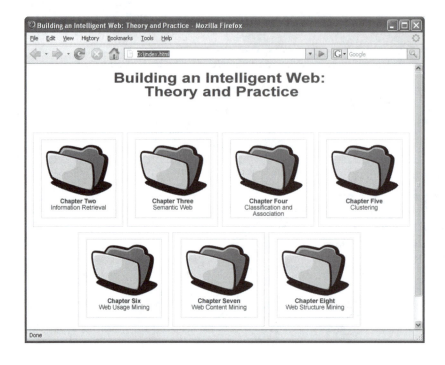

Figure 1.7   Home page for the CD-ROM

illustrating the implementation of a popular retrieval model called the Vector Space Model (VSM).

Chapter 3 deals with the Semantic Web, which enables users to look for more specific information. A description of the Semantic Web building process as well as a small application to illustrate how to build a Semantic Web is included in the chapter.

Database manipulations are a precursor to any data-mining process. The description of database theory in Chapter 4 is based on the assumption that the users will have access to a publicly available MySQL server. If the readers do not have access to such a server, clicking on a link under Chapter 4 will take users to a MySQL server that will allow them to experiment with smaller databases. Chapter 4 also includes a number of web and e-commerce datasets that can be used to test two of the techniques described in the chapter: classification and association. Public-domain software for these two techniques is linked from the CD along with instruction on its use.

Clustering, another important data mining technique, is discussed in Chapter 5. The CD contains simple implementations of $k-$means clustering algorithms and Kohonen self-organizing maps, along with datasets used for demonstrating their uses.

The web logs used in Chapter 6 can also be found on the CD. A simple program to process these logs, along with software that facilitates the web-log analysis, are also included.

A simple implementation of a web crawler and multimedia information retrieval software can be found under Chapter 7 on the CD.

Java classes for two popular web-structure mining algorithms, PageRank and HITS, are available on the CD under Chapter 8.

EXERCISES

1. Define knowledge discovery in databases.

2. Briefly describe the steps of knowledge discovery in databases.

3. What is the role of visualization techniques in data mining?

4. What is the difference between information retrieval and information extraction?

5. Explain the need for web mining.

6. What major research issues are dealt with in web-mining tasks?

7. How does Web mining differ from traditional data mining?

8. What are major components of web mining?

9. List important data-mining techniques.

References

Berners-Lee, T. 2000. Semantic Web – XML 2000. http://www.w3.org/2000/Talks/1206-xml2k-tbl/.

Bush, V. As we may think. Atlantic Monthly, July 1945. 101–108. http://sloan.stanford.edu/mousesite/Secondary/Bush.html.

Fielden, N. 2002. History of information retrieval systems & increase of information over time. http://online.sfsu.edu/~fielden/hist.htm.

Kosala R. and H. Blockeel. 2000. Web mining research: A survey. ACM SIGKDD, 2(1): 1–15.

Megaputer. 2006. Benefits of Web data mining. http://www.megaputer.com/products/wa/benefits.php3.

Romanko, O. 2006. Web mining. http://www.cas.mcmaster.ca/~cs4tf3/romanko_slides.pdf .

Salton, G. (1971): The SMART retrieval system—experiments in automatic document processing, Prentice-Hall.

Srivastava, J., R. Cooley, M. Deshpande, and P. Tan. 2000. Web usage mining: Discovery and applications of Web usage patterns from Web data. ACM SIGKDD explorations, 1(2): 12–23.

WIC. 2006. Web Intelligence Consortium. http://wi-consortium.org/.

W3C. 2001. Semantic Web. http://www.w3c.org/2001/sw/.

Further Reading

Agrawal, R., Srikant, R. (1994): Fast algorithms for mining association rules. In Proc. of the 20th VLDB Conference, Santiago, Chile, pp. 487–499.

ASI, (2006): American Society of Indexers, How Information Retrieval Started, http://www.asindexing.org/site/history.shtml.

Buckland, M. (1992): Emanuel Goldberg, electronic document retrieval, and Vannevar Bush's Memex. Journal of the American Society for Information Science, 43, pp. 284–294.

Brown, C. M., Danzig, B. B., Hardy, D., Manber, U., Schwartz. M. F. (1994): The harvest information discovery and access system. In Proc. 2nd International World Wide Web Conference.

Chen, M.S., Park, J.S., Yu, P.S. (1996): Data mining for path traversal patterns in a Web environment. In Proc. of the 16th International Conference on Distributed Computing Systems, pp. 385–392.

Cooley, R., Tan, P-N., Srivastava. J. (1999): Discovery of interesting usage patterns from Web data. Technical Report TR 99–022, University of Minnesota.

Cooley, R., B. Mobasher and J. Srivastava. Web Mining: Information and Pattern Discovery on the World Wide Web, In Proc. of International Conference on Tools with AI, pp. 558–567, 1997.

Cooley, R., B. Mobasher, and J. Srivastava. Grouping Web page references into transactions for mining World Wide Web browsing patterns. Technical Report TR 97–021, University of Minnesota, Dept. of Computer Science, Minneapolis, 1997.

Deogun, J.S., V.V. Raghavan, A. Sarkar, and H. Sever. Data mining: Research trends, challenges, and applications, in Rough Sets and Data Mining: Analysis of Imprecise Data (Lin, T. Y. & Cercone, N., eds.), Boston, MA: Kluwer Academic Publishers, pp. 1–28, 1996.

Dunham, M. Data mining: Introductory and Advanced Topics, Pearson Education, 1998.

Efe, K., V. Raghavan, and A. Lakhotia, (2004): "Content and Link Structure Analysis for Searching the Web," Computational Web Intelligence: Intelligent Technology for Web Applications, Y-Q. Zhang, A. Kandel, T. Y. Lin and Y. Y. Yao (Editors), World Scientific, pp. 431–448.

Etzioni, O. The World Wide Web: Quagmire or Gold Mine. Communications of the ACM, 36(11), pp. 65–68, 1999.

George. P. (2006): Web Mining and Pattern Discovery. Department of Computer Science, Southern Methodist University, http://engr.smu.edu/~mhd/8331f04/george.doc

Hammond, K., Burke, R., Martin, C., Lytinen. S. (1995): Faq-finder: A case-based approach to knowledge navigation. In Working Notes of the AAAI Spring Symposium: Information Gathering from Heterogeneous, Distributed Environments. AAAI Press.

Han J., Kamber, M. (2001): Data Mining: Concepts and Techniques, Morgan Kaufmann Publishers.

Houtsma, M. A. W., Swami, A. N. (1995): Set-oriented mining for association rules in relational databases. In Proc. of the 11th Int'l Conf. on Data Eng., Taipei, Taiwan, pp. 25–33.

Konopnicki, D., Shmueli, O. (1995): W3qs: A query system for the World Wide Web. In Proc. of the 21th VLDB Conference, Zurich, pp. 54–65.

Liu, B., Ma, Y., Yu, P. S. (2001): Discovering Unexpected Information from Your Competitors' Web Sites, In Proc. of the seventh ACM SIGKDD international conference on Knowledge discovery and data mining.

Madria, S.K., Rhowmich, S. S., Ng, W.K., Lim, F.P. (1999): Research issues in Web data mining. In Proceedings of Data Warehousing and Knowledge Discovery, First International Conference. DaWaK'99, pp. 303–312.

Man, L. (2002): Hypertext and information retrieval and Web mining. http://www.cyberartsWeb.org/cpace/ht/lanman/wm1.htm

Mannila, H., Toivonen, H., Verkamo. A. I. (1995): Discovering frequent episodes in sequences. In Proc. of the First Int'l Conference on Knowledge Discovery and Data Mining, Montreal, Quebec, pp. 210–215.

Mehta, M., Agrawal, R., Rissanen, J. (1996): SLIQ: A fast scalable classifier for data mining. In Proc. of the Fifth Int'l Conference on Extending Database Technology, Avignon, France.

Merialdo P., Atzeni, P., Mecca, G. (1997): Semistructured and structured data in the Web: Going back and forth. In Proceedings of the Workshop on the Management of Semistructured Data (in conjunction with ACM SIGMOD).

Mobasher B. (1995): WEBMINER: A System for Pattern Discovery from World Wide Web Transactions. http://maya.cs.depaul.edu/~mobasher/Research-01.html

Pitkow. J. (1997): In search of reliable usage data on the www. In Sixth International World Wide Web Conference, Santa Clara, CA, pp. 451–463.

Pirolli, P., Pitkow, J., Rao, R. (1996): Silk from a sow's ear: Extracting usable structures from the Web. In Proc. of 1996 Conference on Human Factors in Computing Systems (CHI-96), Vancouver, British Columbia, Canada.

Shah, B., V. Raghavan, P. Dhatric, X. Zhao, (2006): "A Cluster-Based Approach for Efficient Content-Based Image Retrieval using a Similarity-preserving Space Transformation Method," Journal of the American Society for Information Science and Technology, 57 (13). (to appear)

Shepherd, M., Watters, C., Kennedy. A. (2004): Cybergenre: Automatic Identification of Home Pages on the Web. Journal of Web Engineering, 3(3&4), pp. 236–251.

Srikant, R., Agrawal, R. (1995): Mining generalized association rules. In Proc. of the 21th VLDB Conference, Zurich, Switzerland, pp. 407–419.

Srikant, R., Agrawal, R. (1996): Mining sequential patterns: Generalizations and performance improvements. In Proc. of the Fifth Int'l Conference on Extending Database Technology, Avignon, France.

Weiss, R., Velez, B., Sheldon, M. A., Namprempre, C., Szilagyi, P., Duda, A., Gifford, D. K. (1996): Hypursuit: a hierarchical network search engine that exploits content-link hypertext clustering. In Hypertext'96: The Seventh ACM Conference on Hypertext.

Zhong, N., Liu, J., Yao Y. (2003): Web Intelligence, Springer.

Information Retrieval

2.1 Introduction

An essential requirement for any website is the provision of appropriate navigation facilities, which may include well-designed hyperlink structure, menus, and site maps. However, it is difficult to predict all possible navigational patterns and provide corresponding navigation paths. The problem is even more complicated for a dynamically growing website in which several people deposit documents. Any site of sufficient complexity should provide a search facility to simplify the navigation. There are many generic commercial and noncommercial search engines. Sometimes installation of these generic search engines will satisfy the requirements of a website; other times it may be necessary to develop a site-specific search engine, which can be developed from scratch or assembled using various software components tuned to satisfy the needs of the site. Either way, it is important to evaluate a search engine's retrieval performance on a regular basis. This chapter provides a detailed introduction to Information Retrieval (IR), which can be useful for the development, implementation, and evaluation of a search engine. Knowledge of the IR process may also help web developers create innovative navigation tools, such as dynamically changing search engines.

For over 4000 years humans have been designing tools to improve information storage and retrieval. The table of contents and the index of a book are examples of some of the early efforts. With the increasing collection of documents, various databases have been created for the summarization, searching, and indexing of these documents. Vannevar Bush visualized an imaginary IR machine called *Memex* in his 1945 paper "As We May Think" (Bush 1945), which is credited as the foundation of modern information retrieval. SMART (the System for the Manipulation and Retrieval of Text), which was conceived at Harvard University and flourished at Cornell University under the leadership of Gerard Salton (Salton 1971), provided the first practical implementation of an IR system. The basic theoretical foundations of SMART still play a major role in today's IR systems. The four major components of an IR process are

- document representation,
- query representation,
- ranking the documents by comparing them against a query using a retrieval model, and
- evaluation of the quality of retrieval.

This chapter will discuss the theoretical foundations of these four components, along with algorithms, their implementations, and descriptions of noncommercial information retrieval software.

2.2 Document Representation

Documents on the Web consist of a variety of different formats, and the information may consist of text, graphics, audio, and video. This chapter deals with traditional text-based information retrieval. Multimedia information retrieval is still in its infancy (some initial attempts are discussed in Chapter 7). The IR process described here will be based on text extracted from different types of documents. We will look at some of the tools that make it possible for us to retrieve text from various document formats. Traditional IR represents documents using keywords, which in some cases may consist of multiple words. Reducing text to a list of keywords is a simplistic representation of a document, as it ignores the semantics in the document.

Figure 2.1 shows the typical steps involved in transforming a document into a list of keywords with associated frequencies or weights. The first step in the transformation of a document is simply listing all the words in a document by removing spaces, tabs, new-line characters, and other special characters such as commas, periods, exclamation points, and parentheses. The second step is the removal of some of the most commonly occurring words. Words that appear in, for example, more than 80% of documents will not be very useful in discriminating documents. These words are usually referred to as "stopwords." Natural candidates for stopwords are articles, prepositions, and conjunctions, which are filtered out from the list of potential keywords. Another advantage of eliminating stopwords is the reduction in the size of the document representation. The third and fourth steps from Figure 2.1 are discussed in Sections 2.2.1 and 2.2.2.

Figure 2.2 gives a partial list of typical stopwords in the English language. A more complete list can be found on the CD under Chapter 2. **Figure 2.3** shows an example of a document collection with four documents that will be used for illustrating the theory and implementation of information retrieval systems.

The CD contains Java classes that will help create a simple information retrieval system. Clicking on the "Simple Information Retrieval System" link will reveal various other links related to the IR system. One of the folders, "java," contains Java classes (source and class files) used for development of the system. Let us look at the first class called `TokenizedDoc`.

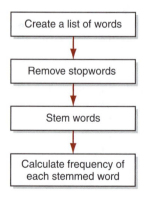

Figure 2.1   Transforming a text document to a weighted list of keywords

I	how	was
a	in	were
about	is	what
an	it	when
are	la	where
as	of	who
at	on	why
be	or	will
by	that	won't
com	the	with
de	their	within
en	there	without
for	this	und
from	to	www

Figure 2.2   A partial list of stopwords

The class is used for creating a list of words (also referred to as terms, index terms, or tokens) from a file. The words are listed in alphabetical order and exclude stopwords.

The link javadoc provides documentation for all the Java classes used in Chapter 2. **Figure 2.4** shows the information about the constructor and methods of the TokenizedDoc class. The class has only one constructor, which takes three parameters. The first parameter is a document represented as a string, the second parameter is the list of characters in addition to the white spaces that may be used as word or token separators, and the third parameter is the name of the file containing stopwords. The function getTokens returns the vector of words/tokens in the document. The main function in the class shows an example of how to call the constructor. The main program can be used to make stand-alone use of the class.

Before testing the class, let us copy all the relevant files to a directory or folder called IR. We will assume basic understanding of using command-line interface under Windows and Linux. We will use the Linux conventions for directory specifications. Windows users should substitute / with \ whenever it is appropriate. At the command prompt, change your directory to IR/fig2.3. This directory contains electronic copies of four documents from Figure 2.3. The first document from Figure 2.3 is called d1.txt. The class TokenizedDoc can be run for the file d1.txt using the following command:

```
java -cp ../java TokenizedDoc d1.txt "\!\?\[\].,;-" ../misc/stopwords.txt
```
(Command 2.1)

Data Mining has emerged as one of the most exciting and dynamic fields in computing science. The driving force for data mining is the presence of petabyte-scale online archives that potentially contain valuable bits of information hidden in them. Commercial enterprises have been quick to recognize the value of this concept; consequently, within the span of a few years, the software market itself for data mining is expected to be in excess of $10 billion. Data mining refers to a family of techniques used to detect *interesting* nuggets of relationships/knowledge in data. While the theoretical underpinnings of the field have been around for quite some time (in the form of pattern recognition, statistics, data analysis and machine learning), the practice and use of these techniques have been largely ad-hoc. With the availability of large databases to store, manage and assimilate data, the new thrust of data mining lies at the intersection of database systems, artificial intelligence and algorithms that efficiently analyze data. The distributed nature of several databases, their size and the high complexity of many techniques present interesting computational challenges.

This course will expose the students to research in applied sciences. The objectives of the course will be achieved through various active learning sessions that involve critical review of papers from scholarly journals and conferences. The activities will also include the preparation and presentation of annotated bibliographies, literature reviews, thesis abstracts, and research project outlines. Students are also required to provide feedback to their colleagues. It is hoped that students will refine their own presentation skills through critically reviewing other presentations. In addition to the regular class activities, students must attend and submit written reports for a total of six (three per semester) external seminars.

This course is designed to extend the student's knowledge of, and provide additional hands-on experience with, the programming language encountered in CSC 226, in the context of the structured data types provided by that language, and within the larger contexts of abstract data types and more complex problem-solving situations. Techniques for managing file input and output in the current language will also be studied. A number of classical algorithms and data structures for the storage and manipulation of information of various kinds in a computer's internal memory will be studied. The student will acquire the knowledge that comes from actually implementing a non-trivial abstract data type and the experience that comes from having to make use, as a client programmer, of an abstract type that has already been implemented.

This course consists of a study of general language design and evaluation. The course will include examination of the design issues of various language constructs, design choices for these constructs in various languages, and comparison of design alternatives. Students will program in a variety of programming languages (FORTRAN, Pascal, C, C++, Java, C#, Lisp, and Prolog) to gain a better understanding of the theoretical discussion. In addition, students will get exposure to other languages ranging from Algol-60 to Ada-95.

Figure 2.3   A sample document collection $= \{d_1, d_2, d_3, d_4\}$

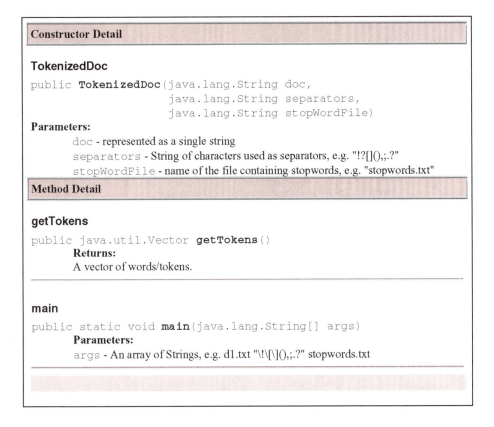

Figure 2.4   Methods for `TokenizedDoc` class (Suitable for Java programmers)

The command java is used to run a java class file.

- The option `-cp` is used to specify the class path; that is, where the java class files can be found. In our case, the class path of `../java` (second argument) is a subdirectory `java` under the main directory `IR`.
- The third argument `TokenizedDoc` specifies the name of the class.
- The fourth argument gives the name of the document to be `d1.txt`.
- The fifth argument specifies the additional (nonwhite) characters that should be used as word separators. A backslash, used before !, [, and], ensures that these characters are not treated as special characters.
- The sixth argument, `../misc/stopwords.txt`, mentions that the file containing stopwords is called `stopwords.txt` and is located in the subdirectory `misc` under the main directory `IR`.

ad	Data	field	mining	relationships
algorithms	data	fields	mining	scale
analysis	data	force	mining	science
analyze	data	form	mining	size
archives	data	hidden	mining	software
artificial	database	high	mining	span
assimilate	databases	hoc	nature	statistics
availability	databases	information	nuggets	store
billion	detect	intelligence	online	systems
bits	distributed	interesting	pattern	techniques
challenges	driving	interesting	petabyte	techniques
commercial	dynamic	intersection	potentially	techniques
complexity	efficiently	large	practice	thrust
computational	emerged	largely	presence	time
computing	enterprises	learning	present	underpinnings
concept	excess	lies	quick	valuable
data	exciting	machine	recognition	years
data	expected	manage	recognize	
data	family	market	refers	

Figure 2.5   List of words in d_1 after deleting stopwords

The list of tokens or words using (Command 2.1) will be printed on the screen. If you wish to store the tokens in a file, you should redirect the output as shown here:

`command > output-file-name`

For example, appending `> Tokenized-d1.txt` to the (Command 2.1) as

`java -cp ........... > Tokenized-d1.txt`

will allow storage of the list of tokens from `d1.txt` into a file called `Tokenizedd1.txt`. The file `Tokenized-d1.txt` is in the `IR/fig2.3` directory on the CD and is also shown in Figure 2.5. The list is alphabetically sorted to make it easy to count the frequency of each word. It also underscores the fact that keyword-based retrieval tends to ignore the semantic structure of documents. The files `d2.txt`, `d3.txt`, `d4.txt` under the subdirectory `fig2.3` can be used to create a similar list of words for the rest of the documents from Figure 2.3 (see Exercise section).

2.2.1   Stemming

A given word may occur in a variety of syntactic forms, such as plurals, past tense, or gerund forms (a noun derived from a verb). For example, the word *connect,* may appear as *connector, connection, connections, connected, connecting, connects, preconnection,* and *postconnection.* A stem is what is left after its affixes (prefixes and suffixes) are removed. In our example, *ed, s, or, ed, ing,* and *ion* are suffixes, while *pre* and *post* are prefixes that will be removed to form the stem *connect.* It can be argued that the use of stems will improve retrieval performance. Users rarely specify the exact forms of the word they are looking for. Moreover, it seems reasonable to retrieve documents that contain a word similar to the one included in a user request. For example, a document containing the word *connection* may be relevant to a user request that includes the word *connect*. Reducing words to stems also reduces the storage required for a document representation by reducing the number of distinct index terms.

Researchers have conflicting opinions about the value of stemming in an information retrieval process. Some of the search engines do not use stemming in their document representations. Nevertheless, stemming is an important part of document preparation in information retrieval, and hence, we should study it in more detail.

There are several stemming strategies; for example, one can simply maintain a table of all the words and corresponding stems. In that case, stemming will involve a simple table lookup. This strategy will require significant storage, assuming that data on every word in the language is available. Other strategies include the successor variety based on structural linguistics, or N-grams based on term clustering. These strategies can be relatively complex. Affix removal is one of the simplest stemming strategies because it is intuitive and can be easily implemented. We will study affix removal in greater detail. It may be desirable to combine affix removal with table lookup for those words that cannot be easily stemmed.

Although affixes mean prefixes and suffixes, suffixes appear more frequently than prefixes. There are a few suffix-removal algorithms. Martin Porter (1980) proposed the most popular algorithm, the Porter algorithm, which is known for its simplicity and elegance. Even though it is simple, the stemming results from the Porter algorithm compare favorably to more sophisticated algorithms. The following is a detailed description of the Porter algorithm.

2.2.1.1 Porter's Stemming Algorithm

Martin Porter maintains an official page for the algorithm at http://www.tartarus.org/~martin/PorterStemmer/index.html. The information in this section includes verbatim descriptions of the five steps of the algorithm (Figures 2.6–2.10) from Porter's website. The explanation used here is also provided from the website.

In order to understand the algorithm, we need to define a few terms. Letters A, E, I, O, and U are vowels. A consonant in a word is a letter other than A, E, I, O, or U, with the exception of Y. The letter Y is a vowel if it is preceded by a consonant, otherwise it is a consonant. For example, Y in *synopsis* is a vowel, while in *toy,* it is a consonant. A consonant in the algorithm description is denoted by c, and a vowel by v. A list ccc... of length greater than 0 will be denoted by C, and a list vvv... of length greater than 0 will be denoted by V. Any word, or part of a word, therefore has one of the four forms:

$$
\begin{aligned}
&\text{CVCV} \ \ldots \ \text{C}\\
&\text{CVCV} \ \ldots \ \text{V}\\
&\text{VCVC} \ \ldots \ \text{C}\\
&\text{VCVC} \ \ldots \ \text{V}
\end{aligned}
\tag{2.1}
$$

Square brackets are used to denote the optional presence of a sequence. Therefore, the four forms shown in Eq. (2.1) can be represented by the single form:

$$
\text{[C]VCVC} \ \ldots \ \text{[V]}
\tag{2.2}
$$

```
Step 1a

    SSES -> SS                      caresses  ->  caress
    IES  -> I                       ponies    ->  poni
                                    ties      ->  ti
    SS   -> SS                      caress    ->  caress
    S    ->                         cats      ->  cat

Step 1b

    (m>0) EED -> EE                 feed      ->  feed
                                    agreed    ->  agree
    (*v*) ED  ->                    plastered ->  plaster
                                    bled      ->  bled
    (*v*) ING ->                    motoring  ->  motor
                                    sing      ->  sing
```

If the second or third of the rules in Step 1b is successful, the following is done:

```
    AT -> ATE                       conflat(ed)  ->  conflate
    BL -> BLE                       troubl(ed)   ->  trouble
    IZ -> IZE                       siz(ed)      ->  size
    (*d and not (*L or *S or *Z))
       -> single letter
                                    hopp(ing)    ->  hop
                                    tann(ed)     ->  tan
                                    fall(ing)    ->  fall
                                    hiss(ing)    ->  hiss
                                    fizz(ed)     ->  fizz
    (m=1 and *o) -> E               fail(ing)    ->  fail
                                    fil(ing)     ->  file
```

The rule to map to a single letter causes the removal of one of the double letter pair. The -E is put back on -AT, -BL and -IZ, so that the suffixes -ATE, -BLE and -IZE can be recognised later. This E may be removed in step 4.

```
Step 1c

    (*v*) Y -> I                    happy     ->  happi
                                    sky       ->  sky
```

Figure 2.6   First step in the Porter algorithm (http://www.tartarus.org/∼martin/)

The braces {} are used to represent repetition; for example, (VC){m} means VC repeated m times, therefore, Eq. (2.1) or (2.2) can also be written as

[C](VC){m}[V]   (2.3)

Here, m will be called the "measure" of any word or word part. For a "null" word m = 0. The following are some of the examples of various values of the measure:

m = 0 TR, EE, TREE, Y, BY.
m = 1 TROUBLE, OATS, TREES, IVY.
m = 2 TROUBLES, PRIVATE, OATEN, ORRERY.

```
Step 2

    (m>0) ATIONAL ->   ATE        relational      ->   relate
    (m>0) TIONAL  ->   TION       conditional     ->   condition
                                  rational        ->   rational
    (m>0) ENCI    ->   ENCE       valenci         ->   valence
    (m>0) ANCI    ->   ANCE       hesitanci       ->   hesitance
    (m>0) IZER    ->   IZE        digitizer       ->   digitize
    (m>0) ABLI    ->   ABLE       conformabli     ->   conformable
    (m>0) ALLI    ->   AL         radicalli       ->   radical
    (m>0) ENTLI   ->   ENT        differentli     ->   different
    (m>0) ELI     ->   E          vileli          - >  vile
    (m>0) OUSLI   ->   OUS        analogousli     ->   analogous
    (m>0) IZATION ->   IZE        vietnamization  ->   vietnamize
    (m>0) ATION   ->   ATE        predication     ->   predicate
    (m>0) ATOR    ->   ATE        operator        ->   operate
    (m>0) ALISM   ->   AL         feudalism       ->   feudal
    (m>0) IVENESS ->   IVE        decisiveness    ->   decisive
    (m>0) FULNESS ->   FUL        hopefulness     ->   hopeful
    (m>0) OUSNESS ->   OUS        callousness     ->   callous
    (m>0) ALITI   ->   AL         formaliti       ->   formal
    (m>0) IVITI   ->   IVE        sensitiviti     ->   sensitive
    (m>0) BILITI  ->   BLE        sensibiliti     ->   sensible
```

Figure 2.7   Second step in the Porter algorithm (http://www.tartarus.org/~martin/)

```
Step 3

    (m>0) ICATE ->   IC          triplicate      ->   triplic
    (m>0) ATIVE ->               formative       ->   form
    (m>0) ALIZE ->   AL          formalize       ->   formal
    (m>0) ICITI ->   IC          electriciti     ->   electric
    (m>0) ICAL  ->   IC          electrical      ->   electric
    (m>0) FUL   ->               hopeful         ->   hope
    (m>0) NESS  ->               goodness        ->   good
```

Figure 2.8   Third step in the Porter algorithm (http://www.tartarus.org/~martin/)

The strings for m = 0 match [C][V]. The strings for m = 1 have only one occurrence of (VC) between [C][V], and so on. The rules for removing a suffix in Figures 2.6–2.10 are given in the form

```
(condition) S1 -> S2
```

The condition is usually given in terms of m. If the stem before S1 satisfies the condition, then replace S1 by S2. For example, in the rule

```
(m > 1) EMENT ->
```

```
Step 4

    (m>1) AL     ->                revival       -> reviv
    (m>1) ANCE   ->                allowance     -> allow
    (m>1) ENCE   ->                inference     -> infer
    (m>1) ER     ->                airliner      -> airlin
    (m>1) IC     ->                gyroscopic    -> gyroscop
    (m>1) ABLE   ->                adjustable    -> adjust
    (m>1) IBLE   ->                defensible    -> defens
    (m>1) ANT    ->                irritant      -> irrit
    (m>1) EMENT  ->                replacement   -> replac
    (m>1) MENT   ->                adjustment    -> adjust
    (m>1) ENT    ->                dependent     -> depend
    (m>1 and (*S or *T)) ION ->    adoption      -> adopt
    (m>1) OU     ->                homologou     -> homolog
    (m>1) ISM    ->                communism     -> commun
    (m>1) ATE    ->                activate      -> activ
    (m>1) ITI    ->                angulariti    -> angular
    (m>1) OUS    ->                homologous    -> homolog
    (m>1) IVE    ->                effective     -> effect
    (m>1) IZE    ->                bowdlerize    -> bowdler
```

Figure 2.9   Fourth step in the Porter algorithm (http://www.tartarus.org/~martin/)

```
Step 5a

    (m>1) E        ->             probate       -> probat
                                  rate          -> rate
    (m=1 and not *o) E ->         cease         -> ceas

Step 5b

    (m > 1 and *d and *L) -> single letter
                                  controll      -> control
                                  roll          -> roll
```

Figure 2.10   Fifth step in the Porter algorithm (http://www.tartarus.org/~martin/)

S1 is "EMENT" and S2 is null. The previously mentioned rule would, for example, map *replacement* to *replac,* because *replac* is a word part for which m = 2. The condition part may also contain the following expressions:

```
*S - the stem ends with S (and similarly for the other letters).
*v* - the stem contains a vowel.
*d - the stem ends with a double consonant (e.g., -TT, -SS).
*o - the stem ends cvc, where the second c is not W, X, or Y (e.g., -WIL, -HOP).
```

Finally, the condition part may also contain expressions with logical operators **and, or,** and **not.** For example,

```
(m > 1 and (*S or *T))
```

matches a stem with $m > 1$ ending in S or T. Similarly, in the condition

```
(*d and not (*L or *S or *Z))
```

a stem will end with a double consonant other than L, S, or Z.

In a set of rules that follow each other, only the one with the longest matching S1 for the given word is obeyed. For example, consider the following sequence of rules (with null conditions):

```
SSES -> SS
IES  -> I
SS   -> SS
S    ->
```

The word *caresses* stems to *caress*, because *sses* is the longest match for S1. Similarly, *caress* stems to itself (S1= *ss*) and *cares* to *care* (S1= *s*).

Now we are ready to look at the five steps of the Porter algorithm. Figures 2.6–2.10 show the rules used in the Porter algorithm in every step. Applications of the rules are given on the right in lowercase. Step 1 given in Figure 2.6 deals with plurals and past participles. The subsequent steps 2–4, given in Figures 2.7 to 2.9, show the relatively straightforward stripping of suffixes. Step 5 (Figure 2.10) is used for tidying up. Complex suffixes are removed in several stages. For example, *generalizations* is stripped as follows:

Step 1: GENERALIZATION

Step 2: GENERALIZE

Step 3: GENERAL

Step 4: GENER

Similarly, OSCILLATORS is stripped as follows:

Step 1: OSCILLATOR

Step 2: OSCILLATE

Step 4: OSCILL

Step 5: OSCIL

The algorithm does not remove a suffix when the length of the stem, given by its measure (m), is small. For example, consider the following two lists:

```
List A        List B
------        ------
RELATE        DERIVATE
PROBATE       ACTIVATE
CONFLATE      DEMONSTRATE
PIRATE        NECESSITATE
PRELATE       RENOVATE
```

The words from List A have small measures, hence *-ate* is not removed. However *-ate* is removed from the words from List B, which have larger measures.

```
Number of words reduced in step 1:     3597
              "                  2:      766
              "                  3:      327
              "                  4:     2424
              "                  5:     1373
Number of words not reduced:           3650
```

Figure 2.11   Suffix stripping of a vocabulary of 10,000 words (http://www.tartarus.org/~martin/)

In an experiment reported on Porter's site, a vocabulary of 10,000 words reduced the words in various steps, as shown in **Figure 2.11**. After reduction, there were 6370 stems left in the list; that is, the suffix-stripping process using Porter's algorithm reduced the size of the vocabulary by 36%. Figure 2.16, on page 33 (details of the figure will be discussed later) shows the list of stems left after eliminating the stopwords and stripping the words from document d₁ in Figure 2.3. The original document contained 184 words. After the elimination of stopwords and duplicate stems, there were 73 distinct words found in Figure 2.3. The aforementioned document was a summary course description. A longer document would have resulted in additional reductions. The two numbers after each stem in Figure 2.16 represent the frequency and normalized frequency of the stem in the document (discussed later).

2.2.1.2   Stemmer Software

The Porter algorithm has been implemented in a variety of programming languages. The original implementation of the algorithm was in BCPL, an ancestor of C. The official site of the Porter Stemming Algorithm (http://www.tartarus.org/~martin/PorterStemmer/) provides links to its implementation in C, Java, Perl, PHP, C#, Python, Common Lisp, Visual Basic, Ruby, and Javascript. The links to these versions can be found under Chapter 2 on the CD. A Java version (Stemmer.java) and its class file (Stemmer.class) are also available on the CD. The compilation and execution of the stemmer can be done at the command prompt (Windows, UNIX, or MacOS). First, change the directory to IR/porter. The Java file can then be compiled using the command

```
javac Stemmer.java
```

This command will produce the class file that can be run using the command

```
java Stemmer input.txt
```

It is assumed in the previous command that you have a file with a list of words. The program will go through the list and output the stemmed versions of the word. The file voc.txt contains a sample of vocabulary from the official site of the Porter algorithm. The corresponding output is given in vocoutput.txt. The files Stemmer.java, Stemmer.class, voc.txt, and vocoutput.txt are stored under a subdirectory called porter in the IR directory. Duplicate copies of files Stemmer.java and Stemmer.class are also stored in the java subdirectory.

Readers should see the effects of running the Stemmer on `Tokenized-d1.txt` from the subdirectory `fig2.3` by typing the following command:

```
java cp ../java Stemmer Tokenized-d1.txt
```
(Command 2.2)

The results of redirecting the output from (Command 2.2) appear in the file `Stemmedd1.txt` in the subdirectory `fig2.3`.

2.2.2   Term-Document Matrix

Term-document matrix (TDM) is a two-dimensional representation of a document collection. The rows of the matrix represent various documents, and the columns correspond to various index terms. The values in the matrix can be either the frequency or weight of the index term (identified by the column) in the document (identified by the row). **Figure 2.12** shows an abstract representation of a document collection. It is assumed that the document collection contains 7 documents: D0 to D6. These documents are represented by 7 keywords: K0 ... K6. We use the C-array convention for numbering lists. For a list of n items, the numbering starts at 0 and ends at n-1. The cell values denote the frequency of the keywords in the documents. For example, in Figure 2.12, the keyword K2 appears in document D0 five times. Similarly, the keyword K3 appears seven times in document D3.

Usually the number of keywords is large. For example, in our document collection from Figure 2.3 with four very short documents, the number of keywords is 172. Most of the documents do not contain every one of these keywords. Hence, the term-document matrix is usually sparse; that is, many of its entries are zeroes. In general, in order to save storage only nonzero entries are stored. One of the popular representations of a sparse matrix uses triplets (row, column, value) for nonzero entries. For example, the term-document matrix from Figure 2.12 will be represented using the triplet as shown in **Figure 2.13**. There were 49 entries in Figure 2.12; only 24 of those entries need to be stored in Figure 2.13. In this example, because we are storing three values for each nonzero entry, we end up storing 72 numbers. If we had created separate storage for each document, we could have eliminated the need to store the first number corresponding to the document number. Each nonzero entry in this case will be represented using a pair (column, value). We can use a line character to distinguish the

	K0	K1	K2	K3	K4	K5	K6
D0	0	0	5	2	0	1	2
D1	4	1	1	0	0	0	0
D2	0	3	0	0	4	2	7
D3	2	2	0	7	1	0	0
D4	0	0	0	5	2	1	1
D5	7	0	2	0	0	0	3
D6	0	0	0	0	2	3	0

Figure 2.12   An abstract term-document matrix

$$
\begin{array}{lll}
(0,2,5) & (2,4,4) & (4,4,2) \\
(0,3,2) & (2,5,2) & (4,5,1) \\
(0,5,1) & (2,6,7) & (4,6,1) \\
(0,6,2) & (3,0,2) & (5,0,7) \\
(1,0,4) & (3,1,2) & (5,2,2) \\
(1,1,1) & (3,3,7) & (5,6,3) \\
(1,2,1) & (3,4,1) & (6,4,2) \\
(2,1,3) & (4,3,5) & (6,5,3)
\end{array}
$$

Figure 2.13   Representation of sparse term-document matrix using triplets

$$
\begin{aligned}
&(2,5)(3,2)(5,1)(6,2) \\
&(0,4)(1,1)(2,1) \\
&(1,3)(4,4)(5,2)(6,7) \\
&(0,2)(1,2)(3,7)(4,1) \\
&(3,5)(4,2)(5,1)(6,1) \\
&(0,7)(2,2)(6,3) \\
&(4,2)(5,3)
\end{aligned}
$$

Figure 2.14   Representation of sparse term document matrix using pairs

rows/documents. This will give us the representation of our document collection as shown in **Figure 2.14**. In this case, we store 48 numbers to represent 49 values from our original matrix. Our abstract example does not illustrate the reduction in storage very well. For the document set from the four short documents in Figure 2.3, with 173 keywords, we will require 172*4=688 entries in the term-frequency matrix. However, there are only 195 nonzero entries. If we use a triplet (row, column, value), we will need 195*3=585 numbers. The savings correspond to 103 integers or 14.97%. If we use a pair, we will need 195*2=390 numbers. In this case, the savings will be 298 numbers or 43.31%. The savings are even more noticeable in larger and more diverse document collections.

Usually the raw frequency values are not useful for a retrieval model, many of which prefer normalized weights, usually between 0 and 1, for each term in a document. Dividing all the keyword frequencies by the largest frequency in the document is a simple method of normalization. Mathematically, we can write the equation for calculating the weight of a term in a document as

$$
w_{ij} = \frac{freq_{ij}}{\underset{k=1}{\overset{m}{\mathrm{MAX}}} freq_{ik}},
\tag{2.4}
$$

where w_{ij} is the weight, and $freq_{ij}$ is the frequency of the jth keyword in i^{th} document. It is assumed that there are m terms in a document collection; that is, the number of columns in the TDM is m. **Figure 2.15** shows the normalized version of the term-document matrix from Figure 2.12. Whenever necessary, we will qualify the term-document matrix with either frequency or weight. For example, the matrix given in Figure 2.12 is the term-document frequency matrix, while the one in **Figure 2.15** is the term-document weight matrix.

	K0	**K1**	**K2**	**K3**	**K4**	**K5**	**K6**
D0	0	0	1	0.4	0	0.2	0.4
D1	1	0.25	0.25	0	0	0	0
D2	0	0.43	0	0	0.57	0.29	1
D3	0.29	0.29	0	1	0.14	0	0
D4	0	0	0	1	0.4	0.2	0.2
D5	1	0	0.29	0	0	0	0.43
D6	0	0	0	0	0.67	1	0

Figure 2.15 Normalized term document weight matrix

The `java` subdirectory under the `IR` directory contains a class called `DocVector,` which can be used to create each row of a term-document matrix. Each element of the row is represented as a triplet (word, frequency, normalized frequency). It should be noted that the class creates a representation that takes a little more space than an efficient implementation requires. For example, a word could be stored by its index similar to Figure 2.14, and only frequency or normalized frequency needs to be stored for a given IR model. In fact, the Boolean retrieval model requires neither the frequency nor the normalized frequency, only the presence or absence of a term, which can lead to a very efficient storage. However, the document representation created by `DocVector` is more readable and easy to use in simple implementations of a variety of information retrieval models. The class `DocVector` is run essentially the same way as the class `TokenizedDoc.`

```
java -cp ../java DocVector d1.txt "\!\?\[\].,;-" ../misc/stopwords.txt   (Command 2.3)
```

The redirected output from (Command 2.3) is stored in the file `Vector-d1.txt`, also shown in **Figure 2.16**. Readers are encouraged to run the same command for the other three text files from

```
ad 1 0.125              drive 1 0.125        larg 2 0.25        recognit 1 0.125
algorithm 1 0.125       dynam 1 0.125        learn 1 0.125      refer 1 0.125
analysi 1 0.125         effici 1 0.125       li 1 0.125         relationship 1 0.125
analyz 1 0.125          emerg 1 0.125        machin 1 0.125     scale 1 0.125
archiv 1 0.125          enterpris 1 0.125    manag 1 0.125      scienc 1 0.125
artifici 1 0.125        excess 1 0.125       market 1 0.125     size 1 0.125
assimil 1 0.125         excit 1 0.125        mine 5 0.625       softwar 1 0.125
avail 1 0.125           expect 1 0.125       natur 1 0.125      span 1 0.125
billion 1 0.125         famili 1 0.125       nugget 1 0.125     statist 1 0.125
bit 1 0.125             field 2 0.25         onlin 1 0.125      store 1 0.125
challeng 1 0.125        forc 1 0.125         pattern 1 0.125    system 1 0.125
commerci 1 0.125        form 1 0.125         petabyt 1 0.125    techniqu 3 0.375
complex 1 0.125         hidden 1 0.125       potenti 1 0.125    thrust 1 0.125
comput 2 0.25           high 1 0.125         practic 1 0.125    time 1 0.125
concept 1 0.125         hoc 1 0.125          presenc 1 0.125    underpin 1 0.125
data 8 1.0              inform 1 0.125       present 1 0.125    valuabl 1 0.125
databas 3 0.375         intellig 1 0.125     quick 1 0.125      year 1 0.125
detect 1 0.125          interest 2 0.25      recogn 1 0.125
distribut 1 0.125       intersect 1 0.125
```

Figure 2.16 Vector representation of document d$_1$

Figure 2.3 (see the Exercise section). Unlike Figure 2.14, the triplets from a document vector appear as one per line. In order to store the entire term-document matrix, we need separators. Following the convention from the SMART collections, we will use a line starting with ".I" followed by document ID to identify the beginning of the file. In fact, the file `Vector-d1.txt` begins with the line `.I d1.txt`. The vector representations of the remaining three documents from Figure 2.3 can be created similarly using a variation of (Command 2.3). The concatenation of resulting files can then be used as a term-document matrix (see the Exercise section).

Figure 2.17 shows information about the constructor and methods of the `DocVector` class. The class has two constructors. One of them is a default constructor that does not initialize any fields. The other constructor takes two parameters: `Vector` of the words in the document, and the document's ID. The constructor then uses two private functions to

- stem the word,
- eliminate duplicates, and
- calculate frequency and normalized frequency of the stemmed words.

One member function, `getVector()`, returns the vector representation of the documents as a `Vector` of objects of type `Term`, a triplet (word, frequency, normalized frequency). The class `Term` is discussed at the end of this paragraph. The other member function `getID()` returns the ID of the document. The functions starting with "`set`" make it possible to set the values of the two fields in the class. The constructor expects the file processing is done elsewhere (`TokenizedDoc` class). The main function in the class shows an example of how to use the `TokenizedDoc` class before calling the constructor of the `DocVector` class. The main program can be used to make stand-alone use of the class. **Figure 2.18** shows relevant portions of the main function. The program segment between the `try` and `catch` block reads a document as a string. The string representing a document is then passed along with another string containing separators and the name of the stopwords file to construct an object of the type `TokenizedDoc`. The `Vector` of words/tokens from the `TokenizedDoc` is then used to construct the vector representation of documents using the triplet (word, frequency, normalized frequency). The triplet is represented using a Java class called `Term`. It consists of three fields:

- `word`: A string representing the actual term.
- `freq`: The number of times the term appears in the document.
- `normalizedFreq`: Given by Eq. (2.4).

Figure 2.19 shows the summary of constructors and various methods to access the fields of the class `Term`. The constructor needs the value of `word` in order to construct an object of type `Term`. The functions beginning with "`get`" are used to get the value of a field. Similarly, functions beginning with "`set`" are used to change the value of a field.

Constructor Detail

DocVector

public **DocVector**()
      Default Constructor

DocVector

public **DocVector**(java.util.Vector wordVector,
                java.lang.String initID)
      Creates a vector of Term using the words/tokens from the wordVector.
Parameters:
      wordVector - A Vector of words
      initID - A string used to identify the document
See Also:
      Term

Method Detail

getVector

public java.util.Vector **getVector**()
      Returns:
      A vector of Term: a triplet consisting of stemmed words, frequency, and normalized
      frequency.
      See Also:
      Term

---

getID

public java.lang.String **getID**()
      Returns:
      A string identifying the document

---

setVector

public void **setVector**(java.util.Vector initVector)
      See Also:
      Term

---

setID

public void **setID**(java.lang.String initID)
      Parameters:
      initID - A string identifying the document

---

main

public static void **main**(java.lang.String[] args)
      Parameters:
      args - An array of Strings, e.g. d1.txt "\!\[\](),;.?" stopwords.txt

Figure 2.17 Methods for the **DocVector** class (Suitable for Java programmers)

```
try
{
                    ......
    String s = in.readLine();
    while(s != null)
    {
        test += s + "\n";
        s = in.readLine();
    }
}catch(IOException e){}

Vector wordVector = new TokenizedDoc
                    (test, args[1], args[2]).getTokens();

DocVector documentVector = new DocVector(wordVector, args[0]);

Vector cdv = documentVector.getVector();

System.out.println(".I "+documentVector.getID());

for(int i = 0; i < cdv.size(); i++)
    System.out.println(cdv.get(i));
```

Figure 2.18   Code snippet from the main of the **DocVector** class (Suitable for Java programmers)

Constructor Summary	
Term(java.lang.String initWord)	

Method Summary	
int	**getFreq**()
double	**getNormalizedFreq**()
java.lang.String	**getWord**()
void	**setFreq**(int f)
void	**setNormalizedFreq**(int n)
void	**setWord**(java.lang.String w)
java.lang.String	**toString**()

Figure 2.19   Methods for the **Term** class (Suitable for Java programmers)

2.2.3   Standard Document Collections

The experiments described so far are based on a document set with four very short documents given in Figure 2.3. For any significant experimentation, one needs to work with a larger number of documents with more significant contents. This section describes some of the standard document collections that are available for experimentation. These collections are widely used by IR researchers and provide a good means of conducting comparative studies. Many of these document collections are too large to be provided on the CD accompanying this textbook; therefore, the URLs for these collections appear both on the CD as well as in this section. Additionally, the CD contains smaller document collections that can be used for preliminary experimentation.

2.2.3.1   TREC Collections

In 1992, under the auspices of the first Text Retrieval Conference (TREC), one of the most prominent document collections was made available as part of the TIPSTER Text program. The homepage for TREC can be found at http://trec.nist.gov/. The TREC is co-sponsored by the National Institute of Standards and Technology (NIST) and the U.S. Department of Defense. The TREC supports research in information retrieval by providing the infrastructure necessary for large-scale evaluation of text retrieval methodologies. The goals of the TREC workshop series as listed on the TREC website are as follows:

- to encourage research in information retrieval based on large test collections;
- to increase communication among industry, academia, and government by creating an open forum for the exchange of research ideas;
- to speed up the transfer of technology from research labs into commercial products by demonstrating substantial improvements in retrieval methodologies on real-world problems; and
- to increase the availability of appropriate evaluation techniques for use by industry and academia, including the development of new evaluation techniques more applicable to current systems.

Preparations for every TREC competition begin with a document collection and queries provided by NIST. A list of documents ranked by their relevance to the queries using competing retrieval systems are returned to NIST. A program committee consisting of representatives from government, industry, and academia judges the retrieved documents for correctness and evaluates the results. The participants discuss their experiences at the end of the TREC in a workshop. The TREC participation has increased significantly with 93 groups from 22 countries participating in TREC 2003. Their website justifiably claims success in meeting its dual goals of improving the state of the art in information retrieval and of facilitating technology transfer. The TREC website reported a twofold increase in retrieval system effectiveness over the first six years of TREC.

The TREC test-collections and evaluation software are available for anyone to evaluate the retrieval effectiveness of their systems at any time (not just at TREC). In addition to English text documents, TREC is sponsoring evaluations of the retrieval of Spanish and Chinese documents, retrieval of recordings of speech, as well as retrieval across multiple languages. Furthermore, TREC has provided evaluation platforms for question answering and content-based

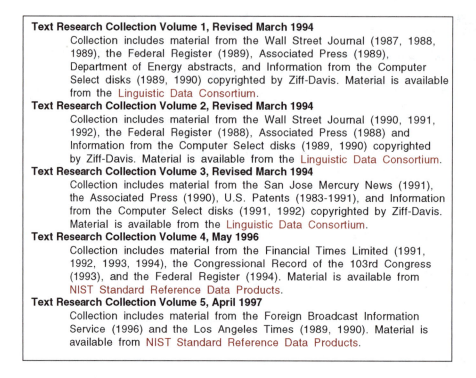

Text Research Collection Volume 1, Revised March 1994
Collection includes material from the Wall Street Journal (1987, 1988, 1989), the Federal Register (1989), Associated Press (1989), Department of Energy abstracts, and Information from the Computer Select disks (1989, 1990) copyrighted by Ziff-Davis. Material is available from the Linguistic Data Consortium.
Text Research Collection Volume 2, Revised March 1994
Collection includes material from the Wall Street Journal (1990, 1991, 1992), the Federal Register (1988), Associated Press (1988) and Information from the Computer Select disks (1989, 1990) copyrighted by Ziff-Davis. Material is available from the Linguistic Data Consortium.
Text Research Collection Volume 3, Revised March 1994
Collection includes material from the San Jose Mercury News (1991), the Associated Press (1990), U.S. Patents (1983-1991), and Information from the Computer Select disks (1991, 1992) copyrighted by Ziff-Davis. Material is available from the Linguistic Data Consortium.
Text Research Collection Volume 4, May 1996
Collection includes material from the Financial Times Limited (1991, 1992, 1993, 1994), the Congressional Record of the 103rd Congress (1993), and the Federal Register (1994). Material is available from NIST Standard Reference Data Products.
Text Research Collection Volume 5, April 1997
Collection includes material from the Foreign Broadcast Information Service (1996) and the Los Angeles Times (1989, 1990). Material is available from NIST Standard Reference Data Products.

Figure 2.20   An example of TREC data collection (http://trec.nist.gov/data/docs_eng.html)

retrieval of digital video. The large size of the TREC collections makes them suitable for the real-world testing of retrieval systems. The TREC website claims that most of the existing commercial search engines include technology first developed in TREC. Their collections have grown in size to several gigabytes; information on how to obtain the collection can be found on the TREC website. **Figure 2.20** shows a description of ad hoc test collections from the website as an example of the type of data provided by TREC.

2.2.3.2   CACM and CISI Collections

TREC collections are very useful for realistic testing of IR systems before deploying them for general use. However, they require significant efforts in preprocessing (Baeza-Yates and Ribeiro-Neto 1999). The testing process is quite involved and time-consuming. For a relatively rapid testing of an IR model, one can use smaller collections. Two of the most popular IR collections are called CACM and CISI (or ISI). These collections were created as part of the SMART project at Cornell University (Salton 1971).

The CACM collections (ftp://ftp.cs.cornell.edu/pub/smart/cacm/) consist of abstracts from the Communications of the ACM (CACM) from the first issue in 1958 to the last issue in 1979. The CACM served as an important periodical during the formative years of computing science and, as such, contains a broad spectrum of articles. In addition to the text from the abstracts, the collections provide structured information about the document such as names of authors, date of publication, cross-references, and so on. The CACM collections are provided

```
.I 20
.T
Accelerating Convergence of Iterative Processes
.W
A technique is discussed which, when applied
to an iterative procedure for the solution of
an equation, accelerates the rate of convergence if
the iteration converges and induces convergence if
the iteration diverges.   An illustrative example is given.
.B
CACM June, 1958
.A
Wegstein, J. H.
.N
CA580602 JB March 22, 1978  9:09 PM
.X
20   5    20
20   5    20
```

Figure 2.21 An example of a document from the CACM collection (ftp://ftp.cs.cornell.edu/pub/smart/cacm/)

on the CD in this book. If you have copied the IR directory to your hard drive, you will find the CACM collections in the subdirectory IR/cacm. The file cacm.all contains the actual documents. **Figure 2.21** shows an example of a document entry in the CACM collections.

A line beginning with a period specifies the type of field. ".I" stands for identification of the document. The number following ".I" is the document ID. The document given in Figure 2.21 has the ID of 20. ".T" corresponds to the title of the document, specified on the following line. The lines following ".W" contain the abstract of the document. The date of publication is on the line following ".B", while author names follow ".A". ".N" corresponds to the date of the entry, while ".X" corresponds to reference information. We will only focus on the ".I", ".T", ".W", and ".A" fields. While all the 3204 documents have IDs and titles, only 3120 have authors, and 1587 documents have abstracts; therefore, caution needs to be exercised while processing the CACM collections. The file **SMARTparser.java** contains a parser that will help in the processing of a SMART collection such as CACM or CISI.

The CISI (ftp://ftp.cs.cornell.edu/pub/smart/cisi/) collections use the same convention as the CACM collections. They consist of the 1460 most cited documents in information sciences. The CISI collections use ".A", ".B", ".T", ".W", ".X". Every one of the 1460 documents have the ".A", ".T", ".W", ".X" fields. Only 24 documents have the ".B" (date of publication) field. Moreover, the type of information in the ".B" field is not consistent; therefore, it will be prudent to ignore the ".B" field in the CISI collections. The multiple authors in the CISI collections are treated differently. In most cases, multiple authors appear on multiple lines (one line per author) after a single ".A" entry; in other cases, there is a separate ".A" entry for each of the authors.

The class `SMARTparser` can be used to parse a SMART document collection and to create an array of SMART documents. We can see how the `SMARTparser` class works by first changing the directory to `IR/cacm` and then typing

```
java -cp ../java SMARTparser cacm.all 3204
```
(Command 2.4)

The first parameter following the class name `SMARTparser` is the name of the file containing a document collection. The second parameter specifies the number of documents in the collection. Therefore, (Command 2.4) is used to parse 3204 documents from the collection `cacm.all`. Because the output is long, it scrolls rather quickly. You can either redirect the output to a file or examine the tail of the output as it appears on the screen.

Our simple IR system uses a class called `SMARTdoc` consisting of five fields:

- ID: A string used to identify the document.
- authors: A string used to store author names.
- title: A string used to store title.
- contents: A string used to store contents.
- date: A string used to store date of publication.

Figure 2.22 shows the methods of the `SMARTdoc` class. Methods beginning with the word "`get`" return the values of various fields in the class. Similarly, functions beginning with "`set`" are used to change the value of a field. The method `toString()` provides a concatenation of the field's authors, title, contents, and date. Other classes, such as `SMARTparser`, use the `SMARTdoc` class for processing documents from SMART collections. **Figure 2.23** shows the methods for the class `SMARTparser`. The constructor builds an array of document collections using the name of the document collection and the number of documents. The array can be accessed by using the method `getDocArray()`. A snippet of the constructor from **Figure 2.24** shows how the document collection is processed. If the line that is read starts with ".I", the array index is incremented and then the ID of the document is recorded. The following code segment shows how the processing proceeds after a line beginning with ".A" is read. First, the program checks if we already have an author for the document, otherwise the author field is initialized to an empty string. The program keeps on appending authors from subsequent lines until a line beginning with a period is read. The rest of the fields are processed in a similar fashion. The complete source for all the classes including `SMARTparser` is available on the CD.

The class `SMARTtdmMaker` allows us to build a TDM for a SMART document collection. Assuming we are in the directory `IR/cacm`, execute the following command:

```
java -cp ../java SMARTtdmMaker cacm.all 3204 "\!\[\]().;,-?" ../misc/stopwords.txt
```
(Command 2.5)

Because the output is very long, it scrolls quickly on the screen. You should redirect the output to a file called `cacm.tdm`. **Figure 2.25** shows the twentieth row of the term-document matrix for the CACM collections. This row corresponds to the document shown in Figure 2.21.

Method Summary	
java.lang.String	getAuthors()
java.lang.String	getContents()
java.lang.String	getDate()
java.lang.String	getID()
java.lang.String	getTitle()
void	setAuthors(java.lang.String initAuthors)
void	setContents(java.lang.String initContents)
void	setDate(java.lang.String initDate)
void	setID(java.lang.String initID)
void	setTitle(java.lang.String initTitle)
java.lang.String	toString()

Figure 2.22   Methods for the SMARTdoc class (Suitable for Java programmers)

To improve readability, each element in the row appears on a single line. In addition to the cacm.all the subdirectory IR/cacm contains another file called query.text, which contains a query collection for the CACM documents. The query collection is formatted similar to the document collection. There are 64 queries in the collection. You can create a term-document matrix for a query collection by running the following command:

```
java -cp ../java SMARTtdmMaker query.text 64 "\!\[\]().;,-?" ../misc/stopwords.txt
```
(Command 2.6)

You should redirect the output from (Command 2.6) to a file called query.tdm for future use.

SMARTparser

```
public SMARTparser(java.lang.String fileName,
                   int sizeDocs)
```
Parameters:
        fileName - Name of the file containing a SMART document collection.
        sizeDocs - Number of documents in the collection.

Method Detail

getDocArray

```
public SMARTdoc[] getDocArray()
```
        Returns:
        An array of SMARTdoc
        See Also:
        SMARTdoc

---

main

```
public static void main(java.lang.String[] args)
```
        Parameters:
        args - An array of Strings, e.g. cacm.all 3204

Figure 2.23   Methods for the **SMARTparser** class (Suitable for Java programmers)

```
........
if(line.startsWith(".I"))
{
    i++;
    if(i >= docArray.length) return;
    docArray[i] = new SMARTdoc();
    docArray[i].ID = line.substring(3);
    line = in.readLine();
}
else if(line.startsWith(".A"))
{
    if(!docArray[i].authors.equals(""))
    {
        docArray[i].authors += "\n";
    }
    line = in.readLine();
    while(line != null && !line.startsWith("."))
    {
        docArray[i].authors += line;
        docArray[i].authors += "\n";
        line = in.readLine();
    }
}
........
```

Figure 2.24   Code snippet from the constructor of the **SMARTparser** class (Suitable for Java programmers)

```
.I 20
acceler 2 0.5
appli 1 0.25
cacm 1 0.25
converg 4 1.0
discuss 1 0.25
diverg 1 0.25
equat 1 0.25
illustr 1 0.25
induc 1 0.25
iter 4 1.0
june 1 0.25
procedur 1 0.25
process 1 0.25
rate 1 0.25
solut 1 0.25
techniqu 1 0.25
wegstein 1 0.25
```

Figure 2.25 A row corresponding to a document from the CACM collection (ftp://ftp.cs.cornell.edu/pub/smart/cacm/)

Figure 2.26 shows the methods for the **SMARTtdmMaker** class. The class contains only the main function. The examples of parameters passed to the main function are shown in Figure 2.26 or (Command 2.4) and (Command 2.5). The **SMARTtdmMaker** class uses all of the previously discussed classes to create a term-document matrix from a SMART document or a query collection. **Figure 2.27** shows the essence of the main program that does the conversion. The first step in Figure 2.27 (before the *for* loop) creates an array of **SMARTdoc** using **SMARTparser**. The first step in the loop creates a **Vector** of words in the document using the **TokenizedDoc** class. The **Vector** of words is used to create an object of the type **DocVector** in the second step in the loop. The third step gets the **Vector** of **Term** objects using the object of the type **DocVector**. The fourth step in the *for* loop prints the document ID after ".I". Finally, the nested loop prints the **Term** objects from the Vector.

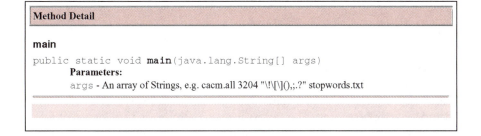

Figure 2.26 Method for the **SMARTtdmMaker** class (Suitable for Java programmers)

```
.........
SMARTdoc [] docs = new SMARTparser(args[0],
                new    Integer(args[1]).intValue()).getDocArray();

for(int i = 0; i < docs.length; i++)
{
    Vector wordVector = new TokenizedDoc
            (docs[i].toString(), args[2], args[3]).getTokens();

    DocVector documentVector = new DocVector
                            (wordVector, docs[i].getID());

    Vector cdv = documentVector.getVector();

    System.out.println(".I "+ documentVector.getID());

    for(int j = 0; j < cdv.size(); j++)
        System.out.println(cdv.get(j));

}
.........
```

Figure 2.27   Code snippet from the main of the **SMARTtdmMaker** class (Suitable for Java programmers)

2.2.4   Linguistic Model for Document Representation

In this chapter we focus on simple statistical information for indexing a document. Raghavan and colleagues (2004) provide an excellent summary of various indexing techniques as well as linguistic methods (briefly described in this section), which can be categorized as term-phrase formation and thesaurus-group generation. A term phrase consists of terms that tend to occur close to each other in the same sentence. Use of term phrases is expected to improve precision. The thesaurus-group generation, on the other hand, is designed to improve recall. A thesaurus consists of a list of words with similar meaning. Each list of synonymous words is called a thesaurus group. This enables a retrieval system to broaden the scope of search. For example, *writer* and *author* may belong to the same thesaurus group. A query specifying the keyword *author* may retrieve documents that include *writer* as well as the *author*.

2.2.5   Handling HTML and Other Document Formats

Information retrieval concepts discussed in this chapter are solely text based. They can be easily extended to documents in other formats. For most of the document formats, there usually exists a utility for converting it to machine-readable text; but these conversions usually do not retain all the formatting features. The text conversion also leads to a loss of other embedded objects, such as pictures or mathematical equations. However, the objective of the conversion is to use the resulting text as an alternative display format. We are interested only in creating a vector representation consisting of a triplet (word, frequency, normalized frequency) of the document, as discussed earlier in this section. **Figure 2.28** gives a list of various converters that

Type of file	Linux	Windows
Adobe pdf	ps2text	commercial
postscript	ps2text	commercial
html	html2text	commercial
Microsoft powerpoint	catppt	catppt.exe
Microsoft word	catdoc	catdoc.exe
Microsoft Excel	xls2csv	xls2csv.exe

Figure 2.28 Utilities for converting various document formats to text (non-commercial versions are available on the CD-ROM)

are available for converting different document formats to text. The figure lists utilities for Adobe portable document format (pdf), postscript files, html files, Microsoft Word, Microsoft Excel, and Microsoft PowerPoint. Most of these utilities are readily available for Linux. Copies of these utilities can be found on the CD. Freeware for converting Microsoft Word, Microsoft Excel, and Microsoft PowerPoint so that they can run under DOS are also included on the CD. However, these DOS utilities do not support long filenames under Windows. Readers may be able to search the Web for various commercial utilities that run under Windows.

2.3 Retrieval Models

The Boolean, Vector Space, and probabilistic are three classic IR models (Baeza-Yates and Ribeiro-Neto 1999). In this section we will discuss the theoretical foundations of these three models, as well as some of their prominent theoretical extensions. The Vector Space Model (VSM) is arguably the most popular model in information retrieval (Salton and McGill 1986). In fact, many existing search engines use VSM as an important component of their retrieval process. This section describes the detailed workings of the Vector Space Model, including a simple implementation in Java.

During the discussions of these models, we will assume that we have represented a document collection as a term-document matrix. The information contained in a term-document matrix is sufficient, but not always necessary for the application of each model. For example, the Boolean model needs to know only the presence or absence of a term in a document. The frequency of the document is not relevant to the basic Boolean retrieval model.

2.3.1 The Boolean Retrieval Model

Based on set theory and Boolean algebra, the Boolean retrieval model provides one of the simplest and most efficient retrieval mechanisms. Let us adopt the conventional numeric representations of *false* as 0 and *true* as 1 for the remainder of the discussion. The Boolean model is interested only in the presence or absence of a term in a document. Thus, the term-document matrix from Figure 2.12 can be represented simply as shown in **Figure 2.29**. We have replaced all the nonzero values from Figure 2.12 with 1.

	K0	K1	K2	K3	K4	K5	K6
D0	0	0	1	1	0	1	1
D1	1	1	1	0	0	0	0
D2	0	1	0	0	1	1	1
D3	1	1	0	1	1	0	0
D4	0	0	0	1	1	1	1
D5	1	0	1	0	0	0	1
D6	0	0	0	0	1	1	0

Figure 2.29   A Boolean term document matrix

The Boolean retrieval model uses the standard *and*, *or*, and *not* Boolean operators. If a user is interested only in documents that have both the keywords K0 and K4, the user needs will translate to the query "K0 *and* K4". The set of documents that have keyword K0 is {D1,D3,D5}. Let us call this set DocSet(K0). The set of documents that have keyword K4 will be DocSet(K4)={D2,D3,D4,D6}. The *and* operation corresponds to the intersection of these two sets, which is equal to DocSet(K0) $\cap$ DocSet(K4) = {D3}; that is, D3 is the only document that has both the keywords K0 and K4 in the document collection described by Figure 2.29. Therefore, the Boolean retrieval model will return document D3. On the other hand, if the query were "K0 *or* K4", then the user is looking for documents that have either of the two keywords K0 or K4. We will use the union of the sets DocSet(K0) and DocSet(K4); that is,

$$\text{DocSet(K0)} \cup \text{DocSet(K4)} = \{D1,D2,D3,D4,D5,D6\}.$$

More complicated Boolean queries are also possible; for example, a user could ask for "K0 *or* (*not* K3 *and* K5)". We can translate such a Boolean query to the set theoretic operation $\text{DocSet(K0)} \cup \left(\overline{\text{DocSet(K3)}} \cap \text{DocSet(K5)}\right)$, where $\overline{\text{DocSet(K3)}}$ is the set theoretic complement of DocSet(K3) for the query component "*not* K3". We can find out the resulting set of documents as follows:

$$\text{DocSet(K0)} = \{D1,D3,D5\},$$
$$\text{DocSet(K3)} = \{D0,D3,D4\},$$
$$\overline{\text{DocSet(K3)}} = \{D1,D2,D5,D6\},$$
$$\text{DocSet(K5)} = \{D0,D2,D4,D6\},$$
$$\left(\overline{\text{DocSet(K3)}} \cap \text{DocSet(K5)}\right) = \{D2,D6\},$$
$$\text{DocSet(K0)} \cup \left(\overline{\text{DocSet(K3)}} \cap \text{DocSet(K5)}\right) = \{D1, D2, D3, D5, D6\}.$$

Therefore, the Boolean query "K0 *or* (*not* K3 *and* K5)" will lead to the retrieval of the document set {D1,D2,D3,D5,D6}. Studies of Boolean queries submitted by users have found that the queries generally do not involve very complicated Boolean expressions. In any case, a Boolean query can be represented in a "disjunctive normal form" (DNF). The term "disjunction" corresponds to the *or* operation, while "conjunction" refers to the *and* operation.

DNF consists of a disjunction of conjunctive Boolean expressions. For example, the expression "(K0 *or* (*not* K3 *and* K5))" is in DNF, because it corresponds to two expressions "K0" and "(*not* K3 *and* K5)"; both the expressions are conjunctive because they are connected only by an *and* operation. The advantage of accepting queries in a DNF is that the processing can be very efficient. If any one of the conjunctive expressions is true, the entire DNF will be true. This fact can be used to short-circuit the expression evaluation. We can stop matching the expression with a document as soon as we find a conjunctive expression that matches the document and label the document as relevant to the query. If none of the conjunctive expressions match a given document, that document is considered nonrelevant to the query. Implementing a Boolean retrieval model wherein expressions are provided in DNF is left for readers as a programming project (see the Exercises). The implementation of the Vector Space Model discussed in the following section will be useful as guidance for such a programming project.

The Boolean retrieval model received considerable attention in the early years. Its advantages are the simplicity and efficiency of implementation. The binary values can be stored using bits, which will reduce storage requirements. Moreover, the retrieval will involve bitwise operations that can be executed rather efficiently. For these reasons, the Boolean retrieval was adopted by many commercial bibliographic systems. Boolean queries are akin to database queries with precise pattern-matching requirements. Hence, it is more appropriate to call these bibliographic systems document database systems, instead of information retrieval systems. The Boolean retrieval model suffers from many drawbacks:

- A document is either relevant or nonrelevant to the query; it is not possible to assign a degree of relevance. For example, let us consider our earlier query "K0 *and* K4". The document D1, which contains K0 but not K4, is considered to be at the same level of relevance as document D0, which contains neither K0 nor K4. Clearly, D1 should be more relevant than D0 to the query "K0 *and* K4".
- The precise semantics of Boolean queries can be problematic for a user, who is often not comfortable with complicated Boolean queries.
- Boolean queries often retrieve too few or too many documents. The two queries we considered earlier, "K0 *and* K4" and "K0 *or* K4", are good illustrations of this drawback. The query "K0 *and* K4" retrieved only one out of six documents, while "K0 *or* K4" retrieved five out of a possible six documents.

Because of these shortcomings, modern IR systems tend to prefer a more flexible model such as the Vector Space Model, which will be discussed in the next section.

2.3.2   The Vector Space Model

The Vector Space Model (VSM) circumvents the problems associated with binary-term weights by creating a weight based on the frequency in the document. The simplest way to compute the weight was given by Eq. (2.4) in Section 2.2. Later in this section, we will study more sophisticated weighting schemes. The VSM treats both the documents and queries as vectors. Let us assume that there are m terms and N documents in our document collection. That means the number of columns in the term-document matrix is m and the number rows is N.

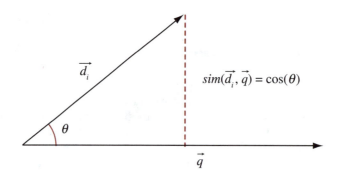

Figure 2.30   A graphical representation of Vector Space Model

Let $\overrightarrow{d_i} = (w_{i1}, w_{i2}, \cdots, w_{im})$ be a document vector corresponding to one of the rows in a term-document matrix. For example, the vector $\overrightarrow{d_0} = (0, 0, 1, 0.4, 0, 0.2, 0.4)$ could represent the document D0 in our abstract document collection given by Figure 2.15. A similar vector $\overrightarrow{q} = (w_{q1}, w_{q2}, \cdots, w_{qm})$ will also represent a query. **Figure 2.30** shows a graphical representation of the document and query vectors, as well as the similarity function $sim(\overrightarrow{d_i}, \overrightarrow{q})$, used to measure similarity between the two vectors. The similarity function is given by

$$sim(\overrightarrow{d_i}, \overrightarrow{q}) = \frac{\overrightarrow{d_i} \bullet \overrightarrow{q}}{\left|\overrightarrow{d_i}\right| \times \left|\overrightarrow{q}\right|}$$

$$= \frac{\sum\limits_{j=1}^{m} w_{ij} \times w_{qj}}{\sqrt{\sum\limits_{j=1}^{m} w_{ij}^2} \times \sqrt{\sum\limits_{j=1}^{m} w_{qj}^2}} \qquad (2.5)$$

$\overrightarrow{d_i} \bullet \overrightarrow{q}$ is the dot product of the document and query vectors. $\left|\overrightarrow{d_i}\right|$ and $\left|\overrightarrow{q}\right|$ are the norms of the document and query vectors, respectively. Because $\overrightarrow{d_i} \bullet \overrightarrow{q} = \left|\overrightarrow{d_i}\right| \times \left|\overrightarrow{q}\right| \times \cos(\theta)$, where θ is the angle between the query and document vectors, the similarity function $sim(\overrightarrow{d_i}, \overrightarrow{q})$ is in fact the *cosine of the angle* between the document and query vectors as shown next:

$$sim(\overrightarrow{d_i}, \overrightarrow{q}) = \frac{\overrightarrow{d_i} \bullet \overrightarrow{q}}{\left|\overrightarrow{d_i}\right| \times \left|\overrightarrow{q}\right|}$$

$$= \frac{\left|\overrightarrow{d_i}\right| \times \left|\overrightarrow{q}\right| \times \cos(\theta)}{\left|\overrightarrow{d_i}\right| \times \left|\overrightarrow{q}\right|}$$

$$= \cos(\theta).$$

Let us illustrate how the similarity function can be used to retrieve documents from a document collection. Let the collection be represented using a term-document weight matrix from Figure 2.15. Let us further consider a hypothetical query $\vec{q} = (0, 0.2, 0.6, 0, 0.2, 0.3, 0)$. The user is interested in the keywords K1, K2, K4, and K5, with the weights of 0.2, 0.6, 0.2, and 0.3, respectively.

$$sim(\vec{d_0}, \vec{q}) = \frac{0 \times 0 + 0 \times 0.2 + 1 \times 0.6 + 0.4 \times 0 + 0 \times 0.2 + 0.2 \times 0.3 + 0.4 \times 0}{\sqrt{0^2 + 0^2 + 1^2 + 0.4^2 + 0^2 + 0.2^2 + 0.4^2} \times \sqrt{0^2 + 0.2^2 + 0.6^2 + 0^2 + 0.2^2 + 0.3^2 + 0^2}}$$

$$= \frac{0.66}{\sqrt{1.36} \times \sqrt{0.53}}$$

$$= \frac{0.66}{1.166 \times 0.728}$$

$$= 0.7774.$$

We can also calculate the similarity between the rest of the document vectors from Figure 2.15 and the query vector to yield the following:

$$sim(\vec{d_1}, \vec{q}) = 0.2590,$$

$$sim(\vec{d_2}, \vec{q}) = 0.3123,$$

$$sim(\vec{d_3}, \vec{q}) = 0.1084,$$

$$sim(\vec{d_4}, \vec{q}) = 0.1727,$$

$$sim(\vec{d_5}, \vec{q}) = 0.2122,$$

$$sim(\vec{d_6}, \vec{q}) = 0.4953.$$

If we sort the documents using the values of similarity functions, we will get the following order: D0 (0.7774), D6 (0.4953), D2 (0.3123), D1 (0.2590), D5 (0.2122), D4 (0.1727), D3 (0.1084). Here, the numbers in the parentheses represent the similarity values for the document with respect to the given query. Based on the previous calculations, one can conclude that the VSM considers D0 to be the most relevant to the query $\vec{q} = (0, 0.2, 0.6, 0, 0.2, 0.3, 0)$, while D3 is the least relevant document. The example presented here illustrates how the VSM overcomes some of the shortcomings of the Boolean retrieval model. The advantages of VSM over the Boolean retrieval model are as follows:

- The queries are easier to express and allow users to attach relative weights to terms. Moreover, a descriptive query can be transformed to a query vector, using the same technique used for transforming documents to their vector representations.
- The matching between a query and a document is not precise. Every document that has one of the terms mentioned in the query is allocated a degree of similarity.
- Instead of classifying documents as relevant and nonrelevant, the documents are ranked based on their similarity scores. The users can go through the ranked list until their information needs are met.

The following section describes how the theoretical description of VSM can be implemented in practice.

2.3.2.1   Simple Implementation of the VSM and its Application to a Standard Document Collection

The class **VSMranker** can be used to rank the documents for a query. The class provides various functions that will enable programmers to develop different user interfaces for their retrieval system. The class can also be run stand-alone to find matches—from a document collection that is represented as a TDM—for a query collection that is also stored as a TDM. First, we will explore the stand-alone use of the class. Later on we will create additional utilities that will help us retrieve documents for keyword-based queries. Change to the directory **IR/cacm**. Assuming that you have executed the (Command 2.5) (redirecting the output to **cacm.tdm**) and (Command 2.6) (redirecting the output to **query.tdm**), type the following command:

```
java -cp ../java VSMranker cacm.tdm query.tdm 7
```
(Command 2.7)

The first argument following the class name **VSMranker** in (Command 2.7) is the name of the file containing the document collection, which is represented as a TDM. The second argument is the name of the file containing the query collection, which is also represented as a TDM. The third argument specifies how many top-ranked documents should be listed in the output. The retrieval process is rather slow, and the output is rather long. Redirect the output to a file called **cacmranked.txt**. **Figure 2.31** shows the top ten lines from the file **cacmranked.txt**. The first number represents the query ID, followed by the document ID, and its score. For example, **cacmranked.txt** tells us that for query 1, document 1071 received a score of 0.552, while document 1938 received a score of 0.545, and so on. In order to find out the contents of queries and documents, we can use another Java class called **SMARTfetcher**. Let us make sure that we are in the directory **IR/cacm**. The following three commands will enable us to obtain the contents of query 1 and documents 1071 and 1938, respectively.

```
java -cp ../java SMARTfetcher query.text 64 1
```
(Command 2.8)
```
java -cp ../java SMARTfetcher cacm.all 3204 1071
```
(Command 2.9)
```
java -cp ../java SMARTfetcher cacm.all 3204 1938
```
(Command 2.10)

The first argument after the class name **SMARTfetcher** specifies the document collection, the second argument specifies the total number of documents in the collection, and the third

```
1 1071 0.552422157047008
1 1938 0.5447670420505112
1 2371 0.5421393180573578
1 2319 0.5084751798731267
1 1680 0.503681768861609
1 1572 0.4854680364376411
1 1591 0.4784116216161057
2 356 0.12909944487358055
2 740 0.12909944487358055
2 136 0.11785113019775793
......
```

Figure 2.31   First ten lines of **cacmranked.txt**

specifies which document we wish to view. The results of (Commands 2.8–2.10) can be found in **Figure 2.32**. The query wishes to retrieve documents related to time-sharing systems. The top two documents refer to the time-sharing systems. Therefore, using keyword matching as the criteria, we can conclude that our simple implementation of the VSM seems to provide reasonable retrieval performance.

Query 1:

What articles exist which deal with TSS (Time Sharing
System), an operating system for IBM computers?

Document number 1071:

Rosenberg, A. M.

Computer-Usage Accounting for Generalized Time-Sharing
Systems

The current development of general time-sharing
systems requires a revision of accounting procedures
for computer usage. Since time-sharing system users
operate concurrently, it is necessary to be more
precise as to the amount of computer time and storage
space that a user actually utilizes. The various
cost factors which should be considered for computer usage
accounting in generalized time-sharing systems
are discussed.

CACM May, 1964

Document number 1938:

Stimler, S.

Some Criteria for Time-Sharing System Performance

Time-sharing systems, as defined in this article,
are those multiaccess systems which permit
a terminal user to utilize essentially the full resources
of the system while sharing its time with other
terminal users. It is each terminal user's ability
to utilize the full resources of the system that
makes quantitative evaluation of time-sharing systems
particularly difficult. Six criteria are described
which have been successfully used to perform first-level
quantitative time-sharing system performance
evaluation.

CACM January, 1969

Figure 2.32 Query 1 and its two top ranked documents (CACM collection)

Figure 2.33 shows the methods for the **VSMranker** class. The class has three public methods in addition to the main function. The function **sim** provides the similarity between two document/query vectors as given by Eq. (2.5). The method **readTDM** can be used for reading a

---

Method Detail

sim

```
public static double sim(DocVector d,
                              DocVector q)
```
    Parameters:
    d - of the type DocVector
    q - of the type DocVector
    Returns:
    similarity score between d and q as a double
    See Also:
    DocVector

---

readTDM

```
public static java.util.Vector readTDM(java.lang.String fileName)
```
    Parameters:
    fileName - A String repesenting a file containing the TDM
    Returns:
    A term document matrix (TDM) represented as a Vector of DocVector
    See Also:
    DocVector

---

rank

```
public static java.util.Vector rank(java.util.Vector docTDM,
                                          DocVector q)
```
    Parameters:
    docTDM - A term document matrix (TDM) represented as a Vector of DocVector
    q - of the type DocVector
    Returns:
    A Vector of IDscore sorted according to scores
    See Also:
    IDscore, DocVector

---

main

```
public static void main(java.lang.String[] args)
```
    Parameters:
    args - An array of Strings, e.g. cacm.tdm query.tdm 7

Figure 2.33   Methods for the **VSMranker** class (Suitable for Java programmers)

TDM stored in a file. The method **rank** is used to rank documents in a given TDM based on their similarity with a given query. The main function allows us to retrieve documents for a given query collection as illustrated by (Command 2.7). **Figure 2.34** shows the code for the **sim** function. The *while* loop in the function calculates the numerator. If the term in the query is matched with the term in a document, multiplications of their normalized weights are accumulated in the numerator. The two *for* loops are used to calculate the norms of document and query vectors. **Figure 2.35** shows the **rank** method, which essentially calls the **sim** function for each document in the TDM. The result is a **vector** of document IDs and corresponding scores, sorted by score. The method uses two other classes: **IDscore** and **ScoreComparator**.

```java
public static double sim(DocVector d, DocVector q)
{
    double num = 0, den1 = 0, den2 = 0;

    int i = 0, j = 0;
    while(i < d.vec.size() && j < q.vec.size())
    {
        Term dTerm = (Term) d.vec.get(i);
        Term qTerm = (Term) q.vec.get(j);
        if(dTerm.word.equals(qTerm.word))
        {
            num += dTerm.normalizedFreq*qTerm.normalizedFreq;
            i++;
            j++;
        }
        else if(dTerm.word.compareTo(qTerm.word) < 0)
            i++;
        else
            j++;
    }

    for(int k = 0; k < d.vec.size(); k++)
    {
        Term dTerm = (Term) d.vec.get(k);
        den1 += dTerm.normalizedFreq*dTerm.normalizedFreq;
    }
    for(int k = 0; k < q.vec.size(); k++)
    {
        Term qTerm = (Term) q.vec.get(k);
        den2 += qTerm.normalizedFreq*qTerm.normalizedFreq;
    }
    double denominator = Math.sqrt(den1)*Math.sqrt(den2);
    if(denominator != 0)
        return num/denominator;
    else
        return 0;
}
```

Figure 2.34 Calculation of similarity between two document vectors (Suitable for Java programmers)

```
public static Vector rank(Vector docTDM, DocVector q)
{
    Vector vecIDscore = new Vector();
    for(int i = 0; i < docTDM.size(); i++)
    {
        DocVector doc = (DocVector)docTDM.get(i);
        IDscore pair = new IDscore();
        pair.ID = doc.ID;
        pair.score = sim(doc,q);
        if(pair.score != 0)
          vecIDscore.add(pair);
    }
    ScoreComparator c = new ScoreComparator();
    Collections.sort(vecIDscore,c);
    return vecIDscore;
}
```

Figure 2.35   Ranking documents for a given query (Suitable for Java programmers)

```
Vector vecIDscore = new Vector();
Vector docTDM = readTDM(args[0]);
Vector qTDM = readTDM(args[1]);
int toPrint = Integer.parseInt(args[2]);
for(int i = 0; i < qTDM.size(); i++)
{
    DocVector q = (DocVector)qTDM.get(i);
    Vector rankedDoc = rank(docTDM,q);
    for(int j = 0; j < rankedDoc.size() && j < toPrint; j++)
        System.out.println(q.ID + ": " + rankedDoc.get(j));
}
```

Figure 2.36   Code snippet of main function from the **VSMranker** class (Suitable for Java programmers)

IDscore has two fields: ID and score. The **ScoreComparator** is used for comparing objects of the type **IDscore**, based on the values of score. Finally, the essence of the **main** function is shown in **Figure 2.36**. The **main** reads both the document collection and query collection. Then the function **rank** is called to rank the document collection for every query and print top ranked documents.

While the stand-alone use of the class **VSMranker** is only applicable to a query collection, the class provides a number of member functions that makes it possible to develop an interactive search engine. The class **VSMinteract** is an example of a command-line-based search engine.

Let us make sure that we are in the directory **IR/cacm**. The following command will allow us to run the class **VSMinteract**:

```
java -cp ../java VSMinteract cacm.all 3204 cacm.tdm
```
(Command 2.11)

The first argument following the class name **VSMinteract** in (Command 2.11) is the name of the file containing a document collection. The second argument is the number of documents in the collection. The third argument specifies the file that contains the term-document representation of the document collection. **Figure 2.37** shows a sample session using the class

```
****************************************************
* Please input your query:                         *
* '.q' followed by <ENTER> to quit.                *
****************************************************
parallel algorithm
****************************************************
***   Total number of documents retrieved: 66   ***
****************************************************
***   Document ID: 2664 Ranked 1 out of 66      ***
****************************************************
Even, S.

Parallelism in Tape-Sorting

Two methods for employing parallelism in tape-sorting
are presented.  Method A is the natural
way to use parallelism. Method B is new.  Both approximately
achieve the goal of reducing the processing
time by a divisor which is the number of processors.

CACM April, 1974


****************************************************
* Press <ENTER> to see the next document          *
* '.n' followed by <ENTER> to start a new query *
* '.q' followed by <ENTER> to quit.               *
****************************************************


****************************************************
***   Document ID: 1262 Ranked 2 out of 66      ***
****************************************************
Opler, A.

Procedure-Oriented Language Statements to Facilitate
Parallel Processing

Two statements are suggested which allow a programmer
writing in a procedure-oriented language
to indicate sections of program which are to be executed
in parallel.  The statements are DO TOGETHER
and HOLD.  These serve partly as brackets in establishing
a range of parallel operation and partly to
define each parallel path within this range.  DO TOGETHERs
may be nested.  The statements should be particularly
effective for use with computing devices capable of
attaining some degree of compute-compute overlap.

CACM May, 1965

****************************************************
* Press <ENTER> to see the next document          *
* '.n' followed by <ENTER> to start a new query *
* '.q' followed by <ENTER> to quit.               *
****************************************************
```

Figure 2.37 An interactive information retrieval session (CACM collection)

VSMinteract. The session includes typing the query consisting of two keywords, *parallel* and *algorithm.* The order of the keywords is important. The keywords that appear earlier in the list are weighed higher than those that appear later. The results show that our simple VSM-based retrieval model identified 66 documents from the collection as possibly relevant to the query. The documents are ordered based on their relevance to the query. The program displays the highest ranked document and gives users a choice to either view the next relevant document by simply pressing the <ENTER> key, start a new query (by typing ".n" followed by <ENTER>), or quit (by typing ".q" followed by <ENTER>). The top two ranked documents are related to parallel processing, which seems to suggest that the retrieval process again yielded reasonable results. Later in the chapter, we will discuss formalisms for evaluating retrieval performance.

Figures 2.38–2.40 show the programming details for the **VSMinteract** class. The methods are shown in Figure 2.38. The method **createQueryVector** (Figure 2.39) shows how the keywords are converted to a query. The first keyword is assigned a normalized weight of 1.0, the second keyword is assigned a normalized weight of 0.9, and so on. Each subsequent keyword gets a normalized weight, which is 0.1 less than the previous one. The tenth keyword and all the subsequent ones will have a normalized weight of 0.1. The **main** function, shown in Figure 2.40, receives the name of the document collection, size of the collection, and corresponding TDM as arguments. The function prompts the user for a query and then retrieves ranked documents using the **VSMranker.rank** method. The documents are displayed until user enters an ".n" or ".q". ".n" would lead to a new query. ".q" terminates the search session.

Method Detail

createQueryVector

```
public static DocVector createQueryVector(java.lang.String line)
```
      Parameters:
      line - A string containing keywords of a query
      Returns:
      query represented as a document vector
      See Also:
      DocVector

main

```
public static void main(java.lang.String[] args)
```
      Parameters:
      args - An array of Strings, e.g. cacm.all 3204 cacm.tdm

Figure 2.38   Methods for the **VSMinteract** class (Suitable for Java programmers)

```java
public static DocVector createQueryVector(String line)
{
    DocVector qVec = new DocVector();
    qVec.ID = "";
    qVec.vec = new Vector();
    double normalizedWeight = 1.0;
    int weight = 10;
    try
    {
        StreamTokenizer tok = new StreamTokenizer
                    (new StringReader(line));
        while(tok.nextToken() != tok.TT_EOF)
        {
            if(tok.ttype == tok.TT_WORD)
            {
                Stemmer s = new Stemmer();
                String word = tok.sval;
                for(int j = 0; j < word.length(); j++)
                {
                    char ch = word.charAt(j);
                    s.add(ch);
                }
                s.stem();
                Term t = new Term(s.toString());
                t.setFreq(weight);
                t.setNormalizedFreq(normalizedWeight);
                if(weight > 1)
                {
                    weight--;
                    normalizedWeight -= 0.1;
                }
                qVec.vec.add(t);
            }
        }
    }catch(IOException e){}
    return qVec;
}
```

Figure 2.39   Creating an interactive query (Suitable for Java programmers)

```
BufferedReader in = new BufferedReader(new
InputStreamReader(System.in));
SMARTdoc [] docs = new SMARTparser(args[0],
      new Integer(args[1]).intValue()).getDocArray();
Vector docTDM = VSMranker.readTDM(args[2]);
String line = prompt1(in);
while(!line.startsWith(".q"))
{
    DocVector q = createQueryVector(line);
    Vector rankedDoc = VSMranker.rank(docTDM,q);
    int j = 0;
    int totalRetrieved = rankedDoc.size();
    display1(totalRetrieved);
    while(j < totalRetrieved && !line.startsWith(".n")
          && !line.startsWith(".q"))
    {
        IDscore dv = (IDscore)rankedDoc.get(j);
        int i = new Integer(dv.ID).intValue();
        display2(i,j,totalRetrieved);
        System.out.println(docs[i-1]);
        line = prompt2(in);
        j++;
    }
    if(!line.startsWith(".q"))
        line = prompt1(in);
}
```

Figure 2.40   Code snippet of main function from the **VSMinteract** class (Suitable for Java programmers)

2.3.3   Variations of the VSM

The VSM is one of the most studied information retrieval models. Researchers have suggested various modifications to improve its performance (Salton and McGill 1986). We will briefly look at some of the prominent efforts in this area. Salton and Buckley (1988) discussed several variations of the normalized frequency given by Eq. (2.4).

In particular, the retrieval performance has been shown to improve by using an additional factor called *inverse document frequency*, idf_j, for the jth term given by

$$idf_j = \log \frac{N}{n_j}, \tag{2.6}$$

where N is the number of documents in the collection, and n_j is the number of documents that contain the jth term. The modified weights

$$w'_{ij} = w_{ij} \times idf_j = \frac{freq_{ij}}{\underset{k=1}{\overset{m}{\text{MAX}}} freq_{ik}} \times \log \frac{N}{n_j} \tag{2.7}$$

have provided better retrieval performance with various collections, such as the CACM and the CISI collections.

The previous weighting scheme proposed for documents was found to be inappropriate for weights of query terms. After extensive experimentation and with some theoretical justification, Salton and Buckley (1988) suggested a different formulation for weights of query terms:

$$w'_{qj} = (1 + w_{qj}) \times 0.5 \times idf_j = \left(0.5 + \frac{0.5 \times freq_{qj}}{\underset{k=1}{\overset{m}{\mathrm{MAX}}} freq_{qk}} \right) \times \log \frac{N}{n_j}, \qquad (2.8)$$

where $freq_{qj}$ is the frequency of the jth term in the query q. The query weights given by Eq. (2.8), in conjunction with the document weights given by Eq. (2.7), have been reported to provide better retrieval performance. Term-weighting strategies based on the inverse document frequencies are called *tf-idf* schemes.

For the document collection represented in Figure 2.15, we can see that $idf_0 = idf_1 = idf_2 = idf_3 = \log \frac{7}{3} = 0.368$, and $idf_4 = idf_5 = idf_6 = \log \frac{7}{4} = 0.243$. The modified TDM is shown in **Figure 2.41**. If we run our original query $\overrightarrow{q} = (0, 0.2, 0.6, 0, 0.2, 0.3, 0)$ against the new term-document matrix, we will get the following similarity scores. (We did not modify our query using the inverse document frequency, because the query was not represented using frequencies, but by actual weights.)

$$sim(\overrightarrow{d_0}, \overrightarrow{q}) = 0.7867,$$

$$sim(\overrightarrow{d_1}, \overrightarrow{q}) = 0.2590,$$

$$sim(\overrightarrow{d_2}, \overrightarrow{q}) = 0.3361,$$

$$sim(\overrightarrow{d_3}, \overrightarrow{q}) = 0.0969,$$

$$sim(\overrightarrow{d_4}, \overrightarrow{q}) = 0.1208,$$

$$sim(\overrightarrow{d_5}, \overrightarrow{q}) = 0.2215,$$

$$sim(\overrightarrow{d_6}, \overrightarrow{q}) = 0.4953.$$

	K0	K1	K2	K3	K4	K5	K6
D0	0	0	0.368	0.1472	0	0.0486	0.0972
D1	0.368	0.092	0.092	0	0	0	0
D2	0	0.15824	0	0	0.13851	0.07047	0.243
D3	0.10672	0.10672	0	0.368	0.03402	0	0
D4	0	0	0	0.368	0.0972	0.0486	0.0486
D5	0.368	0	0.10672	0	0	0	0.10449
D6	0	0	0	0	0.16281	0.243	0

Figure 2.41 Term document matrix using inverse document frequencies

If we sort the documents using the values of similarity functions, we will get the following order: D0 (0.7867), D6 (0.4953), D2 (0.3361), D1 (0.2590), D5 (0.2215), D4 (0.1208), D3 (0.0969). The new similarity scores are in parentheses. In this case, the document ranking remains unchanged.

Calculations of idf_j with static document collections are a feasible programming exercise (left to the readers as a project in the Exercise section). If the document collection is constantly changing, it is not easy to obtain the values of N and n_j. One of the possibilities is to estimate these values based on a sample document collection.

Raghavan and Wong (1986) as well as Wong and colleagues (1987) proposed one of the prominent theoretical extensions of the VSM. Referred to as the Generalized Vector Space Model, it questions the independence or orthogonality assumption in the VSM. It is assumed that the index terms used in the model are not related to each other. In practice, this is not true; some of the terms are in fact related to each other; for example, the terms *computer* and *microprocessor* are related. If the term *computer* were described in detail, it is likely that *microprocessor* would be used in the description. In the VSM, this assumption corresponds to the orthogonality assumption; that is, if we had a document represented by the vector $\vec{d}_{computer}$ that contained only the term *computer,* and another document represented by the vector $\vec{d}_{microprocessor}$ that contained only the term *microprocessor,* the dot product between these two vectors $\vec{d}_{computer} \bullet \vec{d}_{microprocessor} = 0$. That assumption also implies that there is no similarity between these two documents. Clearly, such an assumption is incorrect. Wong and colleagues (1987) proposed an elaborate formulation that would overcome this theoretical shortcoming. Various concepts introduced by the Generalized VSM are of importance from a theoretical standpoint.

2.3.4   Probabilistic Information Retrieval

In 1976 Sparck-Jones introduced the classical probabilistic retrieval model, also known as the binary independence retrieval model (Sparck-Jones and Willet 1997; Croft and Harper 1979; van Rijsbergen 1999; van Rijsbergen 2005; Robertson et al. 1981). As the name suggests, the probabilistic information retrieval formulates the information retrieval problem within a probabilistic framework. It is assumed that for a given user query $\vec{q}$, there is, as yet unknown, a set, R, of relevant documents. Its set theoretical complement, called the set of nonrelevant documents, is denoted by $\overline{R}$. The similarity between a document $\vec{d}_i$ and $\vec{q}$, $sim_{prob}(\vec{d}_i, \vec{q})$, is given by

$$sim_{prob}(\vec{d}_i, \vec{q}) = \frac{P(R|\vec{d}_i)}{P(\overline{R}|\vec{d}_i)}. \tag{2.9}$$

Here, $P(R|\vec{d}_i)$ is the probability that a document $\vec{d}_i$ is relevant to the query $\vec{q}$; that is, $\vec{d}_i \in R$. Similarly, $P(\overline{R}|\vec{d}_i)$ is the probability that the document $\vec{d}_i$ is not relevant to the query $\vec{q}$, i.e., $\vec{d}_i \in \overline{R}$. By using the Bayes rule, probabilistic independence assumptions, probabilistic additivity axiom, and eliminating factors that are the same for all the documents, Sparck-Jones provided the following approximation for $sim_{prob}(\overrightarrow{d}_i, \overrightarrow{q})$:

$$sim_{prob}(\overrightarrow{d}_i, \overrightarrow{q}) \sim \sum_{j=1}^{m} w_{ij} \times w_{qj} \times \left(\log \frac{P(k_j|R)}{1 - P(k_j|R)} + \log \frac{1 - P(k_j|\overline{R})}{P(k_j|\overline{R})} \right). \qquad (2.10)$$

Here, w_{ij} and w_{qj} are the weights of the jth term in i^{th} document and query, respectively. Similar to the Boolean retrieval model, these weights are assumed to be binary. It is also assumed that there are m terms in a document collection; that is, the number of columns in the term-document matrix is m. $P(k_j|R)$ is the probability that the jth term appears in a document randomly chosen from the set of relevant documents R, and $P(k_j|\overline{R})$ is the probability that the jth term appears in a document randomly chosen from the set of nonrelevant documents $\overline{R}$. Because the sets of relevant and nonrelevant documents are not known, the following initial values can be used:

- $P(k_j|R) = 0.5$ for all the terms, and,
- $P(k_j|\overline{R}) = \dfrac{n_j}{N}$, where N is the number of documents in the collection, and n_j is the number of documents that contain the jth term.

The initial guesses of $P(k_j|R)$ and $P(k_j|\overline{R})$ are modified after retrieving an initial set of documents. Let us assume that based on a predefined criteria r, top-ranked documents are retrieved. We will also assume that these r documents are relevant and the rest are nonrelevant. Further, let r_j be the number of documents from the r retrieved documents that contain the jth term. These values are used to recalculate the values of $P(k_j|R)$ and $P(k_j|\overline{R})$ as follows:

$$P(k_j|R) = \frac{r_j + \frac{n_j}{N}}{r + 1} \qquad (2.11)$$

$$P(k_j|\overline{R}) = \frac{n_j - r_j + \frac{n_j}{N}}{N - r + 1} \qquad (2.12)$$

The formulations described in (Eq. 2.11) and (Eq. 2.12) are based on experimental results and a certain amount of theoretical reasoning. Researchers have also suggested other formulations for calculating $P(k_j|R)$ and $P(k_j|\overline{R})$.

The use of a probabilistic framework for retrieval may provide a semantically attractive approach to information retrieval. However, the probabilistic model is criticized for its two-stage retrieval approach for computing $P(k_j|R)$ and $P(k_j|\overline{R})$. Moreover, the use of binary weights tends to ignore the relative frequency of various terms in the document. The probabilistic independence assumption used in the model is akin to the orthogonality assumption in VSM. It is not clear if the probabilistic independence assumption will actually affect the retrieval performance.

There is some disagreement between the relative retrieval performance of the classical probabilistic retrieval model and the VSM. However, it is generally believed that the VSM tends to provide more accurate and efficient retrieval (Baeza-Yates and Ribeiro-Neto 1999).

The probabilistic approach discussed previously can also be looked at as an alternate way of calculating weights of index terms from those calculated in Sections 2.3.2.1 and 2.3.3. In that case the probabilistic model can also be seen as a variant of the VSM. Moreover, the class-conditional probabilistic independence assumption corresponds to the orthogonality assumption from VSM, and hence can be overcome by using GVSM.

2.4   Evaluation of Retrieval Performance

Every system must be tested before it is made available for general use. However, there is no guarantee that such an initial testing will include the usage of all of the system once it is in production. Software system developers generally employ beta testing of products before releasing the final version. Beta testing usually involves a select group of potential users. Even after such an extensive initial testing, regular feedback from users is part of most software maintenance and upgrade processes.

Some of the common performance measures for software systems include functionality, response time, and space requirements. First and foremost, a software system must provide all the functions that the system was developed for. There is usually a trade-off between time and space requirements. Developers tend to aim for an acceptable compromise between the two. Other measures include the quality of human-computer interaction. In addition to these traditional measures of performance, an information retrieval system needs to evaluate the quality of retrieval, which is especially difficult because user information needs are inherently vague.

In the early days of information retrieval systems, the evaluation of the quality of retrieval was based on laboratory experiments for batch processing. For example, a collection of queries was tested against a given document collection. The stand-alone use of the `VSMranker` class given by (Command 2.7) is an example of such a batch processing. The (Command 2.7) made it possible for us to find the ranking of the documents from the CACM collections stored in the file `cacm.all` for the query collections stored in `query.text`. Both files are stored in the directory `IR/cacm`. Although modern IR systems pay more attention to interactive testing of the retrieval process, the off-line/batch laboratory experiments are still commonly used. Among the reasons is that such experiments make it possible to establish standard benchmarks, and other researchers and developers can repeat the testing independently. In this section, we will discuss frequently used retrieval measures.

2.4.1   Precision and Recall

Precision and recall are complementary measures most commonly used by information retrieval theorists and practitioners. These performance measures are based on the assumption that the set of documents relevant to a given query is known. Using previously used notations, we will denote such a set of relevant documents as R. Let A be the set of documents retrieved by an information retrieval system. **Figure 2.42** shows a graphical representation of these sets. The precision and recall are given by

$$precision = \frac{|R \cap A|}{|A|}, \tag{2.13}$$

$$recall = \frac{|R \cap A|}{|R|}. \tag{2.14}$$

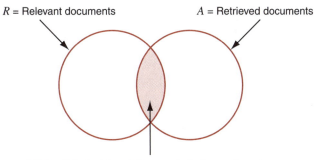

R = Relevant documents

A = Retrieved documents

$R \cap A$ = Set of retrieved documents that are relevant

Figure 2.42   Illustration of precision and recall measures

Here, $|R|, |A|,$ and $|R \cap A|$ are the cardinalities (or size) of the sets $R, A,$ and $R \cap A$. Precision is a measure of the accuracy of our retrieval. Higher precision implies that the probability of a retrieved document being relevant is high. The recall, on the other hand, tells us what percentage of documents was actually retrieved. If the recall value is closer to 1.0, we have most of the relevant documents from the collection. Usually precision and recall complement each other. One can increase the recall by increasing the number of retrieved documents; however, that would increase the chances of retrieving nonrelevant documents and can reduce the precision. Let us recall our earlier example illustrating the VSM, where we ranked the documents from the TDM given in Figure 2.15 for a query $\vec{q} = (0, 0.2, 0.6, 0, 0.2, 0.3, 0)$ as

1. D0*   2. D6   3. D2*   4. D1   5. D5*   6. D4   7. D3*

Let us assume that based on semantic analysis, the user has identified documents marked with an asterisk as relevant to her information needs. Let us further assume that based on a predetermined criteria, we retrieved the three top-ranked documents. In that case, the set of relevant documents is $R = \{$D0, D2, D5, D3$\}$, and the set of retrieved documents is $A = \{$D0, D6, D2$\}$. The intersection is $R \cap A = \{$D0, D2$\}$. We can calculate precision and recall based on these observations as

$$precision = \frac{|R \cap A|}{|A|} = \frac{|\{D0,D2\}|}{|\{D0,D6,D2\}|} = \frac{2}{3} = 0.67$$

$$recall = \frac{|R \cap A|}{|R|} = \frac{|\{D0,D2\}|}{|\{D0,D2,D5,D3\}|} = \frac{2}{4} = 0.5$$

2.4.2   Other Performance Measures

Although precision and recall are the most popular measures, one of their shortcomings is that we have to deal with two different values. Information retrieval practitioners have proposed various measures derived from the concept of precision and recall. A critical review of these performance measures can be found in (Raghavan et al. 1989). One of the measures, called F-measure, involves simply taking the harmonic mean of the two values. The harmonic mean of two numbers is the ratio of multiplication of the two numbers, and their arithmetic mean. Therefore, the F-measure is given by

$$F = \frac{precision \times recall}{\left(\dfrac{precision + recall}{2}\right)} = \frac{2 \times precision \times recall}{precision + recall}. \tag{2.15}$$

The F-value for our example of the seven-document collection represented by Figure 2.15, and the query $\vec{q} = (0, 0.2, 0.6, 0, 0.2, 0.3, 0)$ will be

$$F = \frac{2 \times precision \times recall}{precision + recall} = \frac{2 \times 0.67 \times 0.5}{0.67 + 0.5} = \frac{0.67}{1.17} = 0.57.$$

Another measure, called average precision, is based on the changing values of precision from an algorithm that provides ranked retrieval. We assumed that we retrieved the three top-ranked documents. The number three was somewhat arbitrary. If we change this number, we will get different precision and recall values as shown next.

Rank retrieved	Precision	Recall
1	1.00	0.25
2	0.50	0.25
3	0.67	0.50
4	0.50	0.50
5	0.60	0.75
6	0.50	0.75
7	0.57	1.00

While precision seems to go up and down with rank, it is clear that the maximum precision for a given recall level decreases with the increase in recall. This fact is represented graphically in **Figure 2.43**. The change in recall takes place at a rank when there is a relevant document. Based on this observation, the average precision is given as follows:

$$\text{Average Precision} = \frac{\displaystyle\sum_{i=1}^{N} precision(i) \times relevance(i)}{|R|}$$

Here, $precision(i)$ is the precision at the ith rank, and $relevance(i)$ has a value of 1 if the ith document is relevant, and 0 otherwise. R is the set of relevant documents. For our example, the average precision will be given by

$$\text{Average Precision} = \frac{1.00 \times 1 + 0.50 \times 0 + 0.67 \times 1 + 0.50 \times 0 + 0.60 \times 1 + 0.50 \times 0 + 0.57 \times 1}{4}$$

$$= \frac{2.84}{4}$$

$$= 0.71$$

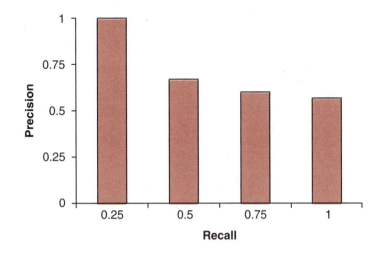

Figure 2.43 Relationship between precision and recall

Both the CACM and CISI collections provide a list of relevant documents to each query. The file `qrels.text` contains the list of relevant files for each query. **Figure 2.44** shows the first ten lines from the file. The first number on each line is the query ID and the second number corresponds to the document ID. The third and fourth numbers are always zero. For example, the list of relevant documents to the query 01 is 1410, 1572, 1605, 2020, and 2358. It should be noted that these relevant documents have been identified based on the manual semantic analysis of the documents. Keyword-based queries do not take into account the semantics, and hence, will rarely be able to provide very high precision and recall values. Assuming that you are in the `IR/cacm` directory and have redirected output from (Command 2.7) to a file called `cacmranked.txt`, we can compare the list of relevant documents from `qrels.text` with

```
01 1410  0 0
01 1572  0 0
01 1605  0 0
01 2020  0 0
01 2358  0 0
02 2434  0 0
02 2863  0 0
02 3078  0 0
03 1134  0 0
03 1613  0 0
......
```

Figure 2.44 First ten lines from `qrels.text`

`cacmranked.txt`. Our IR package contains a utility class called `PrecisionRecallCalc`, which can be run as follows:

```
java -cp ../java PrecisionRecallCalc qrels.text cacmranked.txt 64        (Command 2.12)
```

The first argument following the class name `PrecisionRecallCalc` in (Command 2.12) is the name of the file containing information about relevant documents. The second argument is the name of the file that contains information about retrieved documents. The third specifies the number of queries. Note that the file `cacmranked.txt` contains only the top seven documents for each query, ranked by our simple implementation of the VSM. The output provides the precision and recall for each query, as well as the overall average for the query collection. When we retrieved a maximum of seven documents for each query, the average precision was 0.20 and average recall was 0.14. If we increase the number of retrieved documents in (Command 2.7) to 100, the average precision and recall values change to 0.052 and 0.44, respectively. These values experimentally support our earlier observation: as the number of retrieved documents increases, the precision tends to decrease and the recall tends to increase.

2.5 Public Domain Information Retrieval Systems

The simple information retrieval system described earlier in this chapter illustrates how theoretical concepts can be translated into practical implementation. However, our IR system will not work with a document collection of significant size. This section looks at publicly available IR software that can be used with large document collections. We will focus mainly on general-purpose IR systems, which do not necessarily support web search; however, they can be used for developing a search engine. In addition to providing searching abilities, web search engines include crawlers, software agents that travel through the World Wide Web collecting information that can be used by the information IR component. We will discuss web crawlers, search engines, and related software under web-content mining in Chapter 7.

Figure 2.45 shows a list of IR systems and their URLs. The first system listed in Figure 2.45 is the System for the Manipulation and Retrieval of Text (SMART) that has already been discussed extensively in this chapter. SMART provides the first implementation of the

SMART Early IR engine from Cornell University
(ftp://ftp.cs.cornell.edu/pub/smart/)

Lemur Language Modelling IR Toolkit
(http://www.lemurproject.org/)

Xapian Open source IR platform based on Muscat
(http://www.xapian.org/)

MG full-text retrieval system
(http://www.nzdl.org/html/mg.html)

Figure 2.45 Public domain information retrieval software

VSM. The ftp site listed in the Figure provides a complete implementation of SMART in C. In addition, many datasets are also available for testing an IR system. The next system listed in Figure 2.45 is the Lemur Toolkit. It was developed at Carnegie Mellon University and the University of Massachusetts at Amherst. It is intended for researchers in language modeling and IR. The theoretical foundations of the Lemur toolkit are probabilistic. It can support a variety of research, including cross-language information retrieval, summarization, filtering, and classification. The toolkit is written in C and C++ and is designed to run primarily under the UNIX operating systems; however, it can also be used under Windows. The third listing in Fig 2.45 corresponds to Xapian, which is an IR system also based on a probabilistic framework. While it is written in C++, it provides bindings that make it possible to use its features from other languages such as Perl, Python, PHP, Java, and TCL. Developers can use Xapian as an adaptable toolkit to add indexing and search abilities to any application. Finally, the fourth listing, *MG* (the name stemming from the book *Managing Gigabytes* by Witten, Moffat, and Bell (Witten et al. 1999), is a free full-text retrieval system. MG attempts to reduce the storage requirements by storing the index, while the corresponding text is stored in compressed form. Readers are encouraged to explore these publicly available IR systems.

EXERCISES

1. Create a list of words/tokens for documents d2.txt, d3.txt, d4.txt from Figure 2.3 using the Java class TokenizedDoc.

2. Pick 7–10 interesting words from documents given in Figure 2.3. Follow the Porter algorithm and find out how the words will be stemmed. Check your answers using the Stemmer program.

3. Consider the term-document matrix given next:

	K0	K1	K2	K3	K4	K5	K6
D0	4	3	5	0	0	0	5
D1	0	1	4	7	0	0	0
D2	1	2	0	0	4	2	7
D3	2	0	3	3	0	8	0
D4	0	0	0	0	2	1	1
D5	3	0	0	0	0	0	2
D6	0	0	8	5	2	3	0

Calculate the normalized weights as well as the tf-idf weights. Rank these documents using the VSM-based similarity measure (show all the similarity values) for the following queries:

	K0	K1	K2	K3	K4	K5	K6
q0	0.5	0	0.65	0	0.25	0	0
q1	0	0.51	0.31	0	0	0.25	0
q2	0	0.34	0	0	0	0	0.75

4. Represent the documents from the previous exercise as pairs (column, value). Calculate the savings in storage by using such a representation.

5. Create a term-document matrix for the four document collections from Figure 2.3. You should

   - use the Java class `DocVector` to create a document vector for each document,
   - concatenate all four files together to form the term-document matrix.

6. Create a term-document matrix for the CISI collections, which are located under the subdirectory `IR/cisi`. The document collections can be found in `cisi.all,` and the query collections are stored in the file `query.text`. The list of relevant documents is reported in the file `qrels.text`. Run the classes `VSMranker` and `VSMinteract` and report on the retrieval performance using the class `PrecisionRecallCalc`.

7. Create a TDM for the MEDLAR collections, which is located under the subdirectory `IR/med`. The document collections can be found in `med.all` and query collections are stored in the file `query.text`. The list of relevant documents is reported in the file `qrels.text`. Run the classes `VSMranker` and `VSMinteract` and report on the retrieval performance using the class `PrecisionRecallCalc`.

8. Under the `IR` directory on the CD, there is an additional collection in the subdirectory `time`. The collection contains *Time* magazine stories from 1963 in a file called `doc.text`. The queries are in a file called `query.text`. Convert both the document and query collections to standard SMART collection format. You need use only the ".I" and ".W" fields. The list of relevant documents is reported in the file `qrels.text`. Run the classes `VSMranker` and `VSMinteract` and report on the retrieval performance using the class `PrecisionRecallCalc`.

9. For one of the SMART collections (CACM, CISI, or MEDLAR), run the class `VSMranker` by changing the number of retrieved documents from 10, 20, 30, ... , 100. Plot the values of precision versus recall.

10. Modify the weights for one of the SMART collections using inverse document frequency, and report the precision and recall values with the modified TDM.

11. Create a term-document frequency matrix for a collection of nontext files using text converters supplied with the CD or accessible through your Linux system. Implement an interactive utility similar to `VSMinteract` for such a collection.

12. Using `VSMinteract` as a model, write a class called `BooleanRetriever`. The class should accept Boolean expressions in DNF. Each conjunctive normal form should be entered on a separate line. A special word such as ".e" can be used to end the expression. Test the retrieval effectiveness of your implementation for a SMART collection.

13. Using `VSMinteract` as a model, write a class called `ProbabilisticRetriever` based on the probabilistic model discussed in this chapter. Test the retrieval effectiveness of your implementation for a SMART collection.

14. Install and test one of the publicly available IR systems and report on its retrieval performance.

15. In addition to the three IR models discussed in this chapter, researchers have proposed a number of other retrieval models. Write a research paper on one of these models.

References

Baeza-Yates, R., and B. Ribeiro-Neto. (1999): *Modern information retrieval.* Boston: Addison-Wesley.

Bush, V. As we may think. Atlantic Monthly, July 1945. 101–108. http://www.theatlantic.com/doc/194507/bush

Croft, W.B., and D.J. Harper. (1979): Using probabilistic models of document retrieval without relevance information. *Journal of Documentation* 35:285–95.

Porter, M.F. (1980): An algorithm for suffix stripping. *Program* 14 (3): 130–37.

Raghavan, V.V., P. Bollmann, and G. Jung. (1989): A Critical investigation of recall and precision as measures of retrieval system performance. ACM *Transactions on Information Systems* 7 (3): 205–29.

Raghavan, V.V., N. Gudivada, Z. Wu, and W. Grosky. (2004): Information retrieval. In *The Practical handbook of internet computing,* ed. Munindar P. Singh, Part 2, Chapter 12. Boca Raton, FL: Chapman and Hall/CRC Press.

Raghavan, V.V., and S.K.M. Wong. (1986): A critical analysis of vector space model for information retrieval. *Journal of the American Society for Information Sciences* 37 (5): 279–87.

Raghavan, V. V., and Yu, C. T. (1979): Experiments on the determination of the relationships between terms, ACM Transactions on Database Systems, 4(2), pp. 240-260.

Robertson, S.E., C.J. van Risjbergen, and M. Porter. (1981): Probabilistic models of indexing and searching. In *Information retrieval research.* eds. S.E. Robertson, C.J. van Risjbergen, and P. Williams, 35–56.

Salton, G. (1971): *The SMART retrieval system—Experiments in automatic document processing.* Upper Saddle River, NJ: Prentice-Hall.

Salton, G. (1988): *Automatic text processing: The transformation, analysis, and retrieval of information by computer.* Boston: Addison-Wesley.

Salton, G., and Buckley, C. (1988): Term weighting approaches in automatic text retrieval. Information Processing and Management, 24(5), pp. 513-523.

Salton, G., and M.J. McGill. (1986): *Introduction to modern information retrieval.* New York: McGraw-Hill.

Sparck-Jones, K., and P. Willet, eds. (1997): *Readings in information retrieval.* San Francisco: Morgan Kaufmann.

van Rijsbergen, K. (1999): Information retrieval. http://www.dcs.gla.ac.uk/~iain/keith/.

van Rijsbergen, K. (2005): The Geometry of Information Retrieval, Cambridge University Press.

Witten, I.H., Moffat, A., and Bell T.C. (1999): Managing Gigabytes: Compressing and Indexing Documents and Images, San Francisco: Morgan Kaufmann.

Wong, S.K.M., W. Ziarko, V.V. Raghavan, and P.C.N. Wong. (1987): On modeling of information retrieval concepts in vector spaces. ACM *Transactions on Database Systems* 12 (2): 299–321.

Semantic Web

3.1 Introduction

Tim Berners-Lee, the inventor of the World Wide Web (WWW), introduced the idea of the Semantic Web. One of the major shortcomings of the existing Web is that machines can semantically understand only a limited segment of the available information. Nowadays there is a shift of spotlight from humans as the direct users of the information highway to viewing computers as entry points. Instead of humans searching through a large amount of data, computers will roam through the information highway to collect, understand, and summarize information for humans. The Semantic Web provides a common framework that allows data to be shared and reused across application, enterprise, and community boundaries. Semantic Web technology helps associate different types of information to enable broader and more affluent information discovery and exchange.

While the World Wide Web taught us to link pages and documents electronically, the Semantic Web lets us link smaller elements of data and information and further assign meaning to the links between data elements. Berners-Lee's dream of the Semantic Web is that in the future we will have intelligent software agents that will analyze a given situation and present us with the best possible alternatives. The connectivity that is initiated manually on PCs today will become a part of our everyday life through a wide variety of appliances.

Most of today's web content is suitable for human use. Even web content that is generated automatically from databases is usually offered exclusive of the original structural information found in databases. Standard usages of the Web include looking for and making use of information, searching for and getting in touch with other people, reviewing catalogs of online stores and ordering products by filling out forms, and viewing adult material. There are few web technologies currently available, such as parsers, that can validate web documents by checking for syntactical errors; however, until now, computers have been unable to understand the semantics underlying the documents. For instance, a computer cannot recognize that a particular web page is the homepage of a person. The idea behind the Semantic Web is to nurture the technologies that make the information more meaningful for the machines. Ultimately it will lead to more effective search and retrieval of information for human consumption.

Although there have been many enhancements in search engine technology, the usage difficulties remain essentially the same. Even if a search is successful, it is the person who must browse selected documents to extract the information; therefore, the term *location finder* sometimes replaces *information retrieval.* In contrast, the Semantic Web technology is expected to automatically extract the relevant information nugget from a document, saving the user from the onerous task of browsing through the located documents.

Search activities are not particularly well supported by software tools. Apart from the existence of links that establish connections between documents, the main valuable tools are search engines. Keyword-based search engines, such as AltaVista, Yahoo, and Google, are the primary tools for using today's Web. Today's search engines are reasonably rigorous, given the type of information they have to work with; however, they return either unduly long or inadequate lists of hits, resulting in either lower precision or lower recall or both. Berners-Lee has suggested supplementing the existing information on the Web with machine-processible information. This additional information will enhance the quality of extraction. Machine-processible information can point the search engine to not only a relevant page but to the appropriate part within the page. This will help improve both precision and recall. Consider a case in which the only explicit information stored in a university database is the relationships between people and the courses they attended, and between courses and the topics they cover. This information in itself is of limited value; however, one can formulate a link between these two tables by using the following semantic rule: people who attended a course that was about a certain topic have knowledge about that topic. Such a rule will boost the quality of information that will be made available to the user.

From the previous discussion, one can conclude that the main obstacle to providing better aid to web users is that machines do not understand the semantics of web content. There are tools that can retrieve text, break it into parts, check the spelling, and count the word frequencies, but when it comes to understanding sentences and obtaining useful information for users, the existing software is hardly effective.

One approach to understanding sentences is to represent web content in a form that is more easily processed by machines and to use intelligent techniques to take advantage of these representations. This transformation of the Web is called the Semantic Web initiative. It should be emphasized that the Semantic Web will not be a new global information highway analogous to the current World Wide Web. Instead, it will gradually evolve out of the existing Web.

The Semantic Web is not an application; it is an infrastructure on which many different applications will develop. E-commerce and knowledge management on the Web can take advantage of this semantic infrastructure. There can be two methodologies to the application of the Semantic Web:

- Semantic Web applications for organizations that involve the development of ontology-based marketplaces for business-to-business e-commerce. Another potential application can be a bioinformatics knowledge lattice in which biological data and knowledge bases are interconnected.
- Semantic Web applications for users such as an intelligent personal assistant who accumulates and classifies suitable information based on user preferences. The information is further structured in a logical way for convenient browsing.

The Semantic Web is still under development. The following steps show the direction in which it is moving:

1. Providing a common syntax for machine-understandable statements.

2. Establishing common vocabularies.

3. Agreeing on a logical language.

4. Using the language for exchanging proofs.

This chapter is based on the rich repository of the World Wide Web Consortium (W3C) http://www.w3c.org. The W3C is an international consortium headed by Tim Berners-Lee. It's member organizations, along with a full-time staff, work with the public in developing standards for the World Wide Web. The official mission statement of the W3C as stated on its website (http://www.w3.org/Consortium/) is

> To lead the World Wide Web to its full potential by developing protocols and guidelines that ensure long-term growth for the Web.

In addition, the W3C is involved in education and outreach as well as software development. It also serves as an open forum for discussion about the Web.

In the next section, we briefly discuss the layered-language model suggested by Berners-Lee. Section 3.3 discusses the concepts of metadata and ontologies. Further, ontology languages for the Web, such as XML, XML Schema, and RDF, are introduced in Section 3.4. Topic maps and their workings are presented in subsection 3.4.3. Finally, some issues associated with URIs, which may influence the building of the Semantic Web, are presented.

3.2   The Layered-Language Model

Berners-Lee suggested a layered structure for the Semantic Web consisting of Unicode/URI, XML/Name Spaces/ XML Schema, RDF/RDF Schema, ontology vocabulary, logic, proof, and trust. We will discuss these terms in subsequent sections in this chapter. First, let us try to understand the Layered-Language Model. This structure for the Semantic Web, shown in **Figure 3.1**, reflects the steps listed previously. It follows the understanding that each step alone will already provide added value, so that the Semantic Web can be realized incrementally.

First, two layers provide a common syntax. *Uniform Resource Identifiers* (URIs) is a standard way to refer to entities, while *Unicode* is a standard for exchanging symbols. The

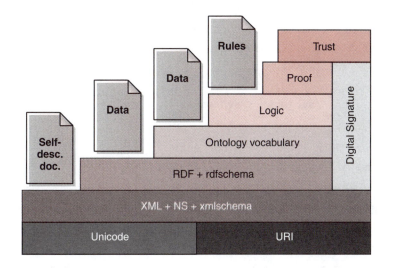

Figure 3.1   The layer language model for the Web (Courtesy of W3C, 2001)

Extensible Markup Language (XML) specifies a notation for describing labeled trees, and XML Schema is used for defining the grammars of XML documents. XML documents may use different *namespaces* to explicitly state the context of different tags. The formalizations of these two layers are now more widely accepted, and the number of XML documents is rapidly increasing. The *Resource Description Framework* (RDF) can be seen as the first layer that is part of the Semantic Web.

According to the W3C recommendations, the RDF is a foundation for processing metadata. It provides interoperability between applications that exchange machine-understandable information on the Web. RDF documents consist of three types of entities: resources, properties, and statements. Resources may be web pages, parts or collections of web pages, or any real-world objects that are not directly part of the WWW.

In RDF, URIs always address resources. Properties are specific attributes, characteristics, or relations describing resources. A resource together with a property having a value for that resource forms an RDF statement. A value is a literal, a resource, or another statement. Statements can thus be considered as object–attribute–value triples.

Let us try to understand some terms mentioned in the previous model before we proceed further.

Definition 3.1   Markup is text that is added to the data of a document in order to convey information about it.

Example 3.1   Suppose we have the sample text, "I would not sell the house just for $1,000,000, says John." Different kinds of markup of the text can be written as

a) markup of syntactic structures (XML syntax),

```
<sentence><subclause><subject> I
</subject> <predicate> would not sell
</predicate> <object> house</object> for just
$1,000,000</subclause>,
<predicate> says</predicate>
<subject> John </subject>.</sentence>
```

b) markup of entities (LATEX syntax),

```
\person[ref="John"]{ I} would not sell
\dog{ house} for just $1,000,000, says
\person{ John}.
```

c) markup of rendering attributes (HTML syntax).

```
<i><b>I</b> would not sell house for just
$1,000,000,</i> says John.
```

Definition 3.2 Unicode is a character set that provides a unique number to every character irrespective of the platform, program, and the language.

Assigned characters of the Unicode standard (v4.1, 03/2005) can be found at http://www.unicode.org/charts/. Unicode also specifies character classes for each character as letters (capital and lowercase), digits, punctuation, and control characters.

The foremost difficulty in accessing web resources is the inconsistency of the resources. Sometimes a user ends up with the *Page not found* message. This could be because of various reasons, such as the change in location of the web page, change in location of the server hosting the resource, and so on. Another significant problem with web resources is identifying them. For the vision of the Semantic Web to be fulfilled, one of the most essential prerequisites would be identifying a resource uniquely and globally. The same identifier, irrespective of its location or availability in various formats, should know a resource universally.

Definition 3.3 Uniform Resource Identifiers (URIs) are used to identify resources.

Generic URI syntax

$$<URI> := <scheme> : <scheme-specific-part>$$

The syntax of a URI is a scheme name followed by a colon, which in turn is followed by a path that follows the specifications of the given scheme.

Example 3.2   Typical parts of URIs are

```
http://www.tmrf.org.in:8080/secret/top.jsp?id=10&from=3
```

|-Scheme--|------- host----------------| -port --|---------path------------|------query--------|

            |-------------------------scheme-specific part ----------------------------------|

Remark 3.1 A URI is called *hierarchical* if and only if

```
<scheme-specific-part> := ( // <authority > [ <path> ] | <path>)
[ ? <query> ] [ # <fragment> ]
                <path> := ( / <path-segment> )+
```

otherwise it's called *opaque*.

The path-segments . and .. have special meaning: context path and parent path.

A hierarchical URI is called *server-based* if and only if

```
<authority> := [ <userinfo> @ ] <host> [ : <port> ]
```

otherwise it is called *registry-based*.

The notation used in the grammar shown above is called *Extended Backus-Naur Form* (EBNF). It is an extension of *Backus-Naur Form* (BNF), which is a formal notation to describe the grammar of a language. Many programming-language standards use a variant of EBNF to define the grammar of the language. It is also used in other standards; namely, definition of protocol and data formats, and markup languages such as XML. In addition to BNF operators, EBNF has a few more operators:

?:   means that the symbol (or group of symbols in parentheses) to the left of the operator is optional (it can appear zero or one times).

#:   the number of leading zeros in the # form is insignificant.

*:   means that something can be repeated any number of times.

+:   means that something can appear one or more times.

Remark 3.2 Fragment identifiers are used to identify parts of the resource identified by a URI.
    In a URI, only some characters may be used literally in nonsyntactic parts (data). All other characters have to be escaped using their code (in some character encoding):

```
<dataChars> := <alphanum> | - | _ | . | ! | ~ | * |  | ( | )
        <escapedChar> := % <hexDigit> <hexDigit>
```

The specifications given for URIs are applicable to all its subsets.

Definition 3.4 Uniform Resource Names (URNs) are special kinds of URIs that

- *map other namespaces* into URN-space
- are required to remain *globally unique and persistent* (even when the resource ceases to exist or becomes unavailable)
- can be specified in a single line of text
- have the scheme urn

```
<URN> := urn: <namespace> : <namespace-specific-part>
```

Example 3.3   `urn:isbn:0-395-36341-1`

`urn:newsml:reuters.com:20000206:IIMFFH05643_2004-08-03_17-54-01_L06154`

A book or a news item (identified by a URN) may be retrieved from different locations (URLs).

A *Uniform Resource Locator* (URL), another special type of URI, is the term used to identify an Internet resource and can be specified in a single line of text. In summary, the URI specifies a generic syntax. It consists of a generic set of schemes that identify any document/resource like URL, URN (Uniform Resource Name), URC (Uniform Resource Characteristic), and so on. The following example shows the difference between URL, URN, and URI:

URL `http://www.tmrf.org/kpr/issue1.htm`

URN `www.tmrf.org/kpr/issue1.htm#one`

URI `http://www.tmrf.org/kpr/issue1.htm#one`

A URL refers to a web page. It includes the scheme (http in this case), but may not include a name location. A URN does not include the scheme, but may include the location of a code fragment as shown by "#one". Just like a URN, a URI refers to a web page, including the location of the code fragment. In addition, a URI consists of the scheme. For more information on Internet terminology, readers may refer to Pierobon (2005) and RFC2396 <URL: http://ds.internic.net/rfc/rfc2396.txt>.

3.3   Metadata and Ontologies

As we have discussed previously, the Semantic Web is an emerging field. At the moment, most efforts are required in the areas of integration, development of tools, standardization, and adoption by users. Semantic Web technologies are used for information retrieval, extraction, and integration. In the following subsections, we will outline a few technologies that are necessary for achieving these functionalities.

3.3.1   Explicit Metadata

Currently, web content is formatted for human readers rather than for programs. HTML is the predominant language in which web pages are written (directly or using tools).

A typical web page of a Student Service Center is shown in **Figure 3.2**. Humans will easily understand the information in this figure, but machines will have problems interpreting it. Keyword-based searches will identify the words *student service* and *office hours*. And an intelligent agent might even be able to identify the personnel of the center; but it will have

```
<h1>Student Service Centre</h1>

Welcome to the home page of the Student Service Centre.

The centre is located in the main building of the University.

You may visit us for assistance during working days.

<h2>Office hours</h2>

Mon to Thu 8am - 6pm<br>

Fri 8am - 2pm<p>

But note that centre is not open during the weeks of the

<a href=". . .">State Of Origin</a>.
```

Figure 3.2   Example of a web page of a Student Service Center

trouble distinguishing the director from the secretary and have even more trouble finding the exact office hours.

The Semantic Web approach to solving these problems does not consist of developing superintelligent agents that process natural languages; instead, it intends to tackle the problem from the web page side. If other proper languages substitute HTML, then the web pages could wear their contents on their sleeves. In addition to containing formatting information aimed at producing a document for human readers, they could contain information about their content. In our example, the information might be represented as shown in **Figure 3.3**.

```
<organization>

      <serviceOffered>Admission</serviceOffered>

      <organizationName>Student Service Centre</organizationName>

      <staff>

         <director>John Roth</director>

         <secretary>Penny Brenner</secretary>

      </staff>

</organization>
```

Figure 3.3   Example of a web page of a Student Service Center

The representation from Figure 3.3 is far easier to process by machines. The term *metadata* refers to such information: data about data. Metadata capture part of the meaning of data, thus the term *semantic* in the Semantic Web.

Let us relate the situation today to the early days of the Web. The first users decided to adopt HTML because it had started to establish itself as a standard. They were expecting benefits from being early adopters. Similarly, many organizations are embracing the Semantic Web to derive benefits from early adoption.

Although XML is not enough in itself for the fulfillment of the Semantic Web vision, it is a vital initial measure. Organizations interested in knowledge management and Business-to-Business (B2B) e-commerce are adopting XML and RDF, the current Semantic Web-related W3C standards. This is a crucial stage in the development of the Semantic Web; however, getting general web developers to adopt XML is a challenge. Other challenges include getting industries to agree on a common vocabulary (XML tags) and converting existing web documents to include relevant XML tags. In short, the real challenge to the establishment of the Semantic Web is not scientific but rather one of technology adoption.

3.3.2   Ontologies

Ontologies capture data relationships and their associated meaning. A paper by Noy and McGuiness (2001), entitled "Ontology Development 101: A Guide to Create Your First Ontology," presents details of ontologies and how to construct an ontology. This section provides a brief summary of the paper.

Generally speaking, an ontology is a specification of a conceptualization. It is an arrangement of concepts that signifies an outlook of the world that can be used to shape information. Ontologies can be mined from hierarchical pools of documents, such as those in Yahoo! or the Open Directory Project, which is the most widely distributed database of web content classified by humans. It can be used as a freely available hierarchical arrangement of concepts and associated web pages.

Artificial-intelligence literature contains various (sometimes conflicting) definitions of an ontology. It originates from the concept of a semantic network used in artificial intelligence.

Definition 3.5 An *ontology* is a precise narrative of concepts in a field of discourse (classes or concepts), properties of each concept narrating various features and attributes of the concept (slots, roles, or properties), and restrictions on slots (facets or role restrictions).

Semantic Web ontologies defer to a taxonomy. Taxonomies are a way of referring to concepts in a hierarchical fashion, including parent-child relationships or general-specific cases. For instance, a car is a general concept, whereas a Honda Civic is a specific instance of the concept. An ontology can capture hierarchies as well as more complex definitions, relationships, and classifications.

A few other researchers (Uschold and Gruninger 1996) have described ontologies in the following ways:

- An ontology is a common, shared, and formal description of important concepts in a specific domain.
- An ontology is a theory that uses a specific vocabulary to describe entities, classes, properties, and related functions with a certain point of view.

An ontology, jointly with a set of individual *instances* of classes, constitutes a *knowledge base*.

In reality, there is a fine line between where an ontology ends and a knowledge base begins. Classes are the focus of most ontologies and classes describe concepts in the domain. We will illustrate two simple ontologies in the following examples.

Example 3.4   This example summarizes a Semantic Web project called Wine Agent (http://onto.stanford.edu:8080/wino/index.jsp). A detailed explanation of the Wine Agent can be found at: http://www.ksl.stanford.edu/projects/wine/explanation.html. A class called `wines` represents all wines. Specific wines are instances of this class. The Bordeaux wine is an instance of the class of Bordeaux wines. A class can have subclasses that represent concepts that are more precise than the superclass. That means we can divide the class `wines` into red, white, and rosé wines. Furthermore, we can divide the class `wines` into sparkling and nonsparkling wines.

Here, slots describe properties of classes and instances: Château Lafite Rothschild Pauillac wine has a full body; it is produced by the Château Lafite Rothschild winery. We have two slots describing the wine in this example: the slot body with the value *full* and the slot maker with the value *Château Lafite Rothschild winery*. At the class level, we can say that instances of the class `wine` will have slots describing their flavor, body, sugar level, and the maker of the wine.

All instances of the class `wine`, and its subclass `Pauillac`, have a slot maker, the value of which is an instance of the class `Winery`. All instances of the class `Winery` have a slot that refers to all the wines (instances of the class `wine` and its subclasses) that the winery produces.

In practical terms, developing an ontology includes

- defining classes in the ontology,
- arranging the classes in a taxonomic (subclass–superclass) hierarchy,
- defining slots and describing allowed values for these slots,
- filling in the values of slots for instances.

We can then create a knowledge base by defining individual instances of these classes and by filling in specific slot value information and additional slot restrictions.

Figure 3.4 shows some of the classes, instances, and relations among them in the wine domain. Hollow rectangles are used for representing classes and filled rectangles for their instances. Direct links represent slots and internal links, such as instance-of and subclass-of.

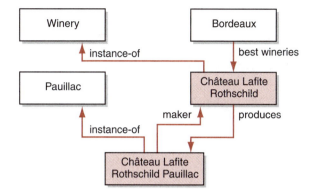

Figure 3.4   Representing classes and instances (Noy and McGuiness, 2001)

Ontologies are beneficial for the organization and navigation of websites. Today, many websites expose the top levels of a concept hierarchy of terms, on the lefthand side of the page. The user may click on one of them to expand the subcategories. In addition, ontologies are convenient for improving the correctness of web searches. Search engines can try to find pages that refer to a precise *concept* in an ontology, rather than collecting all pages in which certain keywords occur. Thus, discrepancies in vocabulary between web pages and the queries can be overcome. If a query does not succeed in obtaining any relevant documents, the search engine may propose to the user a more general query. It is possible for the engine to run such queries proactively and reduce the reaction time, in case the user adopts a suggestion. If too many answers are retrieved, the search engine may propose to the user certain specializations. In Artificial Intelligence (AI), it is traditional to develop and use ontology languages, which are also the foundation for Semantic Web research.

An ontology construction has some resemblance with the development of object-oriented programs. The classes and objects in a program are concerned with data structures, whereas classes and objects in ontologies are about the domain. An ontology is said to be the definition of entities and their relationship with each other.

The following are reasons why ontologies are created:

- to distribute common understanding of the information structure between individuals or software agents
- to facilitate reuse of domain knowledge
- to formulate exact domain assumptions
- to split domain knowledge from operational knowledge
- to analyze domain knowledge

The creation of an ontology is analogous to defining a set of data and their structure for other programs to use. A few researchers have suggested a methodology to develop ontologies for declarative frame-based systems. It consists of phases such as the definition of classes, organizing them in a hierarchical structure, the specification of slots and the assignment of valid values, and the elaboration of classes. Another approach to building an ontology was proposed by Arpírez and colleagues (1998) and Gómez-Pérez (1998). It follows the set of principles given next.

- *Clarity and objectivity*: An ontology should provide precise and objective definitions in natural language form.
- *Completeness*: Definitions should be expressed by necessary and sufficient conditions.
- *Coherence*: An ontology should allow for consistent inferences with definitions.
- *Maximal monotonic extendibility*: Inclusion of new general or specific terms in the ontology without revision of existing definitions.
- *Minimal ontological commitment*: Make as few axioms as possible about the modeled world.
- *Ontological distinction principle*: Classes with different identity criteria must be disjoint.

A good practice to support the ontology building process is to produce an ontology specification document written in natural language with information, such as the purpose of the ontology, its end users, use case scenarios, degree of formality used to codify the ontology, and its scope.

There are other types of ontologies, which take into consideration measures such as the formality of the language or the level of dependence on a particular task or point of view.

- *Top-level ontologies* depict broad concepts similar to space, time, object, event or action, which do not depend on a particular domain.
- *Domain ontologies* and *task ontologies* depict the vocabulary for a generic domain (such as bioinformatics), a task or activity, by means of specific terms.
- *Application ontologies* depict concepts that rely on a specific domain and task. The concepts react to roles performed by domain entities while doing certain tasks.

3.4 Ontology Languages for the Web

The World Wide Web Consortium established two standards—Resource Description Framework (RDF) and the Web Ontology Language (OWL)—which define how developers specify these relationships. These standards define how data text and facts are linked and how to define relationships between elements. The syntax used to make semantic associations is called an RDF triple. The triple definition lets information describe itself. Applications can interpret RDF triples without knowing many details about the source or schema of the data. Self-description reduces the coding and data mapping needed to exchange information between applications.

Presently, the most important ontology languages for the Web are the following:

- **XML** presents syntax for structured documents but enforces no semantic constraints on the meaning of these documents.
- **XML Schema** is a language for limiting the structure of XML documents.
- **RDF** is a data model for objects and relations between them. It provides simple semantics for the data model. These data models can be represented in XML syntax.

- **RDF Schema** is a vocabulary description language for describing properties and classes of RDF resources, with semantics for generalization hierarchies of such properties and classes.
- **OWL** is a richer vocabulary description language for describing properties and classes, such as relations between classes, cardinality, equality, richer typing of properties, characteristics of properties, and enumerated classes.

Ontologies are principally classified as general and domain-specific. They can be built using XML and RDF; however, nowadays there are specific ontology development languages. The *Defense Advanced Research Projects Agency* (DARPA) is an agency of the United States Department of Defense responsible for the development of new technology for use by the military. DARPA initiated a project called DAML (Distributed Agent Markup Language). Another effort from European researchers with the support of the European Commission resulted in OIL—Ontology Interface Layer. These two languages have now been merged into a single ontology language, DAML+OIL. In late 2001 the W3C set up a working group called "WebOnt" to define an ontology language for the Web, based on DAML+OIL. It is called the OWL (Web Ontology Language) project. These ontology languages intend to offer developers a way to properly define a common conceptualization of a domain. They encompass both a means of representing the domain and of reasoning the representation by means of a formal logic. For instance, DAML+OIL language uses the Description Logic, which provides a formal logical foundation for frame-based systems such as ontologies.

3.4.1 Extensible Markup Language (XML)

This section gives a brief introduction to XML and shows how it can be used for the portable representation of data. The essential background provided here might be useful while reading more comprehensive material on XML. *An Introductory Tutorial on Web Services, Java and XML* (Armstrong et al. 2002) is an excellent source for more information. The examples and description in this section are adopted from this book.

XML (Extensible Markup Language) is an industry-standard, system-independent way of representing data. Like HTML (HyperText Markup Language), XML encloses data in tags; but there are major differences between the two markup languages. XML tags can relate to the meaning of the enclosed text (we have seen this in Section 3.3.1), whereas HTML tags specify how to display the enclosed text. Kinsman and McManus (2002) list the following advantages of XML over other data formats:

- *XML Documents are clearly readable and self-explanatory*: An XML document holds tags that indicate data types of every element.
- *XML Documents can be hierarchical*: It is straightforward to insert related data to a node in an XML document without formatting the cumbersome document.
- *XML is interoperable*: There is nothing about XML that binds it to a specific operating system or technology. Numerous XML parsers exist for almost every operating system.
- *No need to write the parser*: There are numerous object-based parsers available for XML. XML parsers work in a similar manner on practically every platform.

```
<priceList>
    <tea>
        <name>Lipton</name>
        <price>40.15</price>
    </tea>
    <tea>
        <name>Brook Bond</name>
        <price>36.20</price>
    </tea>
</priceList>
```

Figure 3.5   An XML document `tea.xml`

Example 3.5   **Figure 3.5** shows an XML example of a price list with the name and price of two types of tea. The <tea> and </tea> tags tell a parser that the information between them is about a type of tea. The two other tags inside the <tea> tags specify that the enclosed information is the tea's name and its price per pound. Because XML tags indicate the content and structure of the data they enclose, they make it possible to do things like archiving and searching.

Example 3.6   We illustrate the following XML syntax in the form of an ordered labeled tree (or data model).

```
<location name=Innsbruck>
   <college name=College of Engineering>
      <deptcode>CIS</deptcode>
   </college>
</location>
```

The ordered labelled tree is shown in **Figure 3.6**.

Another major difference between XML and HTML is that XML tags are extensible, allowing you to write your own XML tags to describe your content. With HTML, you are limited to using only those tags that have been predefined in the HTML specification.

With the extensibility that XML provides, you can create the tags you need for a particular type of document. You define the tags using the XML schema language. A schema describes the structure of a set of XML documents and can be used to constrain the contents of the XML documents. The most widely used schema language is the Document Type Definition schema language, because it is an integral part of the XML 1.0 specification. A schema written in this language is called Document Type Definition (DTD).

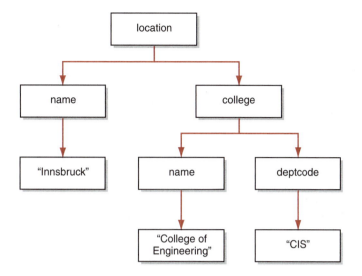

Figure 3.6 An ordered labeled tree

The DTD defines the tags used in the price list XML document. It specifies four tags (elements) and further specifies which tags may occur (or are required to occur) in other tags. The DTD also defines the hierarchical structure of an XML document, including the order in which the tags must occur.

Example 3.7

```
<!ELEMENT priceList (tea)+>
<!ELEMENT tea (name, price) >
<!ELEMENT name (#PCDATA) >
<!ELEMENT price (#PCDATA) >
```

The first line in the example gives the highest level element, `priceList`, which means that all the other tags in the document will come between the `<priceList>` and `</priceList>` tags. The first line also says that the `priceList` element must contain one or more `tea` elements (indicated by the plus sign). The second line specifies that each `tea` element must contain both a name element and a price element, in that order. The third and fourth lines specify that the data between the tags `<name>` and `</name>` and between `<price>` and `</price>` is character data, signified by the term `#PCDATA`, which should be parsed. The name and price of each `tea` are the actual text that makes up the price list.

Another popular schema language is XML Schema, which is currently being developed by the W3C. Once fully developed, XML Schema is predicted to be a significantly more powerful language than DTD.

3.4.1.1   XML Schema

The DTDs have their place and offer many benefits when combined with XML. However, there are also many limitations:

1. DTD syntax is different from XML syntax. Thus we cannot process using XML tools. For instance, if we use DTD syntax as `<!ELEMENT Date (#PCDATA)>` then ''!'' means all the element definitions are just comments to an XML parser.

2. DTDs offer poor support for XML namespaces.

3. DTDs offer limited data typing.

4. DTDs offer limited content model descriptions. Extra information about data formats or constraints have to be included in dedicated comments, which then have to be coded by users or solution providers.

5. Components in DTDs can be declared global only with unique names.

The XML Schema overcome many of these limitations. It has richer capabilities than a DTD and can describe the possible arrangement of tags and text in a valid document. There are more than 44 datatypes (as opposed to 10 in DTDs). XML Schemas allow attribute grouping and also support the use of namespaces. They can also support object-oriented design; that is, "custom" data types can be derived from other data types and inherit their attributes. It can specify element constraints and valid values. The comments in XML Schemas are really comments (documentation), not specifications.

There are four important constructs in an XML Schema: simple type definitions, complex type definitions, and attribute and element declaration. Simple and complex type definitions describe a group of Unicode text strings and a set of requirements for elements and attributes, respectively. An attribute declaration links an attribute name with a simple type, and element declarations link an element name with a simple or complex type. We will take one simple example to illustrate the schema. In our XML Schema in **Figure 3.7**, we present one element declaration `course` and two attribute declarations called `num` and `credit`. Further, we can add a simple type definition `Credit` and complex type definition `CourseType`.

In Figure 3.7, the XML Schema's elements are recognized by the namespace `http://www.w3.org/2001/XMLSchema`. Here, `schema` is the root element of an XML Schema document. This root element has a `target Namespace` attribute. It specifies that the schema illustrate the namespace. In order to refer to our specific definitions in the schema, we have declared the namespace c. That will allow us to use the prefix ''c'' for our definitions. Notice that two elements or two types should have distinct names within one schema. The `element` asserts the element name `course` and links `course` to the type `CourseType`. The `complexType` defines the type `CourseType` as two attribute references. The `simpleType` describes a type `credit` and presents the permissible values of the `credit` attribute

3.4.1.2   Portability of XML

A schema gives XML data its portability. The `priceList` DTD, discussed earlier, is a simple example of a schema. If an application is sent a `priceList` document in XML format and has the `priceList` DTD, it can process the document according to the rules specified in the DTD.

```
<xsd:schema xmlns:xsd ="http://www.w3.org/2001/XMLSchema"

     xmlns:s="http://www.tmrf.org/college"

     targetNamespace="http://www.tmrf.org/college">

     <xsd:element name="course" type="c:CourseType"/>

     <xsd:attribute name="num" type="xsd:string"/>

     <xsd:attribute name="credit" type="c:Credit"/>


     <xsd:complexType name="CourseType">

          <xsd:attribute ref="c:num" use="required"/>

          <xsd:attribute ref="c:credit" use="required"/>

     </xsd:complexType>


     <xsd:simpleType name ="Credit">

          <xsd:restriction base="xsd:integer">

          <xsd:minInclusive value="2"/>

          <xsd:maxInclusive value="4"/>

          </xsd:restriction>

     </xsd:simpleType>

</xsd:schema>
```

Figure 3.7   Example of an XML schema

That means, given the `priceList` DTD, a parser will know the structure and type of content for any XML document based on that DTD. If the parser is a validating parser, it will know that the document is not valid if it contains an element not included in the DTD, such as the element `<juice>`, or if the elements are not in the prescribed order, such as having the price element precede the name element.

Other features also add to the recognition of XML as a method for data interchange. It is written in text format, so both humans and text-editing software can read it. Applications can parse and process XML documents. Moreover, humans can read them in case there is an error in processing. Because an XML document does not consist of formatting directions, it can be exhibited in various ways.

As Armstrong and colleagues (2002) point out, while XML enables document portability, it cannot do the job in a vacuum. Two applications that are communicating with each other must agree on a variety of issues, such as

- using XML for communication
- setting elements in the XML documents and their semantics
- Web services methods
    - the function of the methods
    - if and when more than one method is needed, the order in which they are invoked.

3.4.1.3   An Illustration of XML Communication

In *XML and SQL: Developing Web Applications* (2001), Appelquist provides strong arguments in favor of the use of XML. This section summarizes some of the key points from that book. Let us assume that we want to maintain a record of books by ISBN, which are suitable because they provide a unique numbering scheme for books. Let us take a look at references, notable by ISBN:

```
<document id="1">Hawkings <book isbn="0553103741">A brief history of
time</book> gives truly intimate glimpses into the intricacies of
both the universe and Hawking himself.</document>
```

We have added `<document id="1">` and `</document>` tags around the body of our document so each document can uniquely identify itself. Each XML document you write has an ID number, which you have designated. The ID number should be in a tag named "document" that wraps around the entire document.

For easy reference, we want to keep track of which ISBN numbers are referred to from which documents. We may design a relational table as given in Table 3.1. The attribute *doc_id* has referential integrity to a list of valid document ID numbers. Similarly, the ISBN attribute has referential integrity to a list of valid ISBN numbers.

Now the issue at hand is how this form of markup is superior to HTML (Appelquist 2001). Suppose we have thousands of documents, such as book reviews, articles, and bulletin board messages, and we want to determine which of them refer to a specific book. In the HTML, we can perform a textual search for occurrences of the book name. But what if we have documents that refer to Hawking's *Brief History of Time* and Hawkins's *Brief History of Palm?* If we search for the word "Hawking's Brief History," our search results will list both the books. However, if we have marked up all our references to books by ISBN and we have extracted this

doc_id	ISBN
1	0553103741
2	0552804325

Table 3.1   Database of books

information into a table in a database, we can use a simple SQL (Structured Query Language) query to get the information we need quickly and reliably:

```
select doc_id from doc_isbn where isbn = 0553103741
```

The search results are a set of document ID numbers. We can choose to display the title of each document as a hyperlink, clickable to the actual document, or we can concatenate the documents and display them to the user one after another on a page. If we bring together the power of XML machine-readable metadata and relational database, we can create a document retrieval tool (Appelquist 2001). In the following sections, we will see how the XML queries can be used for similar purposes.

3.4.1.4   Path Expressions

In relational databases, parts of a database can be selected and retrieved using SQL. On similar lines, part of an XML document can be selected and retrieved using an XML query language. The central concept of XML query languages is a path expression that specifies how a node or a set of nodes, in the tree representation of the XML document, can be reached. XPath is syntax for defining parts of an XML document. It uses path expressions to navigate XML documents. These path expressions look like the expressions you see when you work with a traditional file system. XPath includes almost 100 built-in functions and has been a W3C standard since 1999. A general path expression consists of a series of steps separated by slashes. A step in the path expression consists of a node test, an axis specifier, and zero or more filter expressions. An axis specifier (for instance, // is an axis specifier) determines the tree relationship between the nodes to be selected and the context node. A node test specifies which nodes are to be addressed. Many times element names are used as node tests. For example, "*" addresses all element nodes. The filter expressions are used to refine the set of addressed nodes and are optional. For instance, the expression [1] selects the first node; alternately, the expression [position() = first()] also selects the first node (Antoniou and van Harmelen 2004). The filter expressions are always embedded in square brackets. There are many query languages, such as Xpath, Xquery, XQL, and XML-QL. The language Xpath operates on the data model of XML and addresses part of an XML document.

Consider the XML document shown in **Figure 3.8**. We can represent the document from Figure 3.8 as a tree, as shown in **Figure 3.9**. The tree representation of an XML document is an ordered labeled tree containing exactly one root and no cycles. Each non-root node has exactly one parent. The order of elements is important, whereas the order of attributes is not important. In Figure 3.9, elements are highlighted in gray, while @ is added in front of attributes.

The following are some examples of path expressions in XPath query language:

Query 3.1   Select all lecturer elements.

```
/college/lecturer
```

The expression selects all lecturer elements, which are children of the college element node that resides immediately below the root node. The tree representation of this query is given in **Figure 3.10**.

```
<college location="Innsbruck">

     <lecturer name="Sam Hoofer">

          <course   title="Nonlinear   Analysis"/>

          <course   title="Modern   Algebra"/>

          <course   title="Discrete   Structures"/>

     </lecturer>

     <lecturer name="Daniela Frost">

          <course   title="Nonlinear   Analysis"/>

     </lecturer>

     <lecturer name="Edward Bunker">

          <course   title="Computational   Algebra"/>

          <course   title="Algorithms"/>

     </lecturer>

</college>
```

Figure 3.8   XML document `college.xml`

Query 3.2 Select all lecturer elements.

`//lecturer`

In this expression, // says that you must consider every element in the document and check whether they are of the type lecturer. This path expression selects all lecturer elements present anywhere in the document. The tree representation of this query is identical to the tree representation of Query 1 given in Figure 3.10.

Query 3.3 Select all courses with the title "Nonlinear Analysis".

`//course[@title=''Nonlinear Analysis'']`

Here, the test within square brackets restricts the set of selected nodes. The expression selects *course* elements with the *title* that satisfies a particular condition. The tree representation of this query is given in **Figure 3.11**.

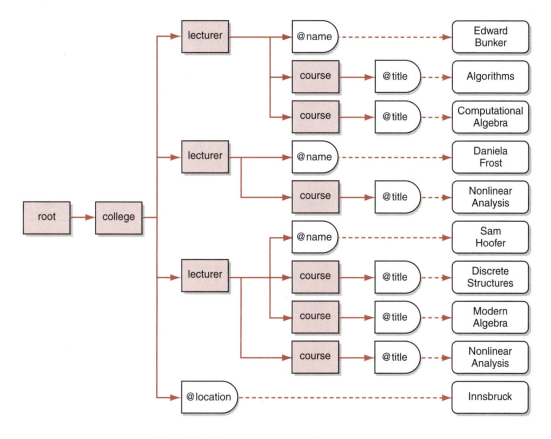

Figure 3.9 Tree representation for `college.xml`

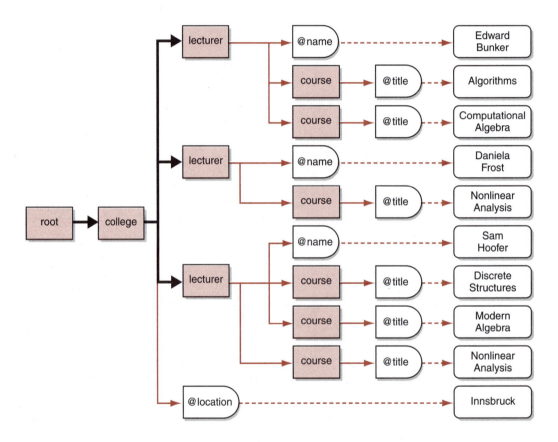

Figure 3.10 Tree representation for Queries 1 and 2

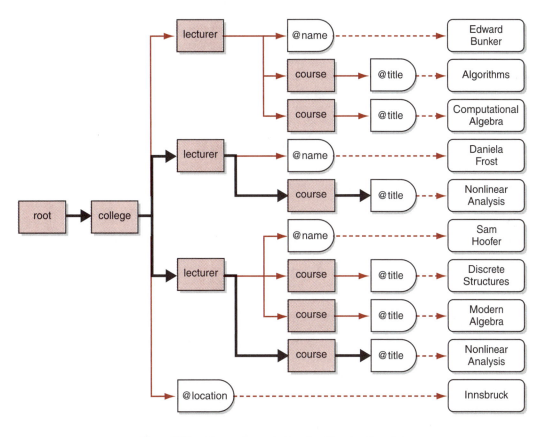

Figure 3.11   Tree representation for Queries 3 and 4

Query 3.4   Select all *title* attribute nodes within *course* elements, anywhere in the document, which have the value "Nonlinear Analysis."

```
//course[@title="Nonlinear Analysis"]/@title
```

This expression collects *title* attribute nodes of the *course* elements. The symbol @ denotes the attribute nodes. The tree representation of this query is identical to Query 3 given in Figure 3.11.

3.4.1.5   Use of Java Package XQEngine for Querying XML Documents

This section describes a Java package called XQEngine, which can be used for a full-text search through XML documents. The information and package in this section is obtained from http://xqengine.sourceforge.net/. The complete Java source is available from the website, which consists of a reasonably compact set of Java classes that can be embedded in any Java-based application. A copy of the XQEngine 0.69 is linked from the CD under Chapter 3. There is no stand-alone application associated with the package; however, it provides a SampleApp

Java class to demonstrate its use. This section also describes a small Java class to illustrate the use of the package. The developers suggest that the package may be useful as a personal productivity tool on a single desktop, part of a CD-based application, or an XML query engine on a server with low to moderate traffic. The developers also cite the following benefits of using the XQEngine as opposed to other XQuery and XPath implementations:

- XQEngine's ability to handle large collections of multiple XML documents from a variety of sources including local storage and web servers. The current maximum limit is 2,147,000,000 documents. Each document can contain up to 8,400,000 nodes (elements, attributes, and text nodes).
- XQEngine provides fast indexing of XML documents. (Documents need to be indexed before they can be searched.)
- XQEngine has fast query processing.
- XQEngine has an easy-to-use application programming interface (API). (We will demonstrate its use later in this section.) Most of the interaction with the query engine will likely consist of the invocation of two main APIs:

    1. setDocument(docName) for indexing a document

    2. setQuery(queryString) for running a query

- XQEngine is an open-source software. See the website http://xqengine.sourceforge.net/ for licensing details.
- The primary focus of XQEngine is full-text retrieval. The *contains-word* function is useful for specifying search terms. Developers believe that the function will be part of standard XML query processing. We will see its use while working with our small demo program a little later in this chapter.
- In addition, XQEngine supports a variety of other convenient query and document source specifications. Refer to http://xqengine.sourceforge.net/ for more details.

Under Chapter 3 on the CD, you will be able to see a link called XQEngine. This will take you to a directory/folder named XQEngine. Create a directory called chapter3 on your hard disk. Copy the XQEngine subdirectory to the newly created directory chapter3. In the same directory, download and unzip the XQEngine from http://sourceforge.net/projects/xqengine. Once you have unzipped the software you will have the Java jar file `XQEngine.jar`. The directory has a Java class called TryXMLQ. The directory also contains a number of XML files. Let us run the Java class for the `college.xml` file, which is shown in Figure 3.8 and used in the previous section for learning the XPath queries. The class TryXMLQ can be run using the following command:

```
java -cp XQEngine.jar:. TryXMLQ college.xml <CMND>
```
(Command 3.1)

(Command 3.1) uses the Java archive or .jar file called XQEngine.jar, which contains the classes from the XQEngine package. We use the –cp option (first argument after java) to indicate that all the necessary classes are to be found in directories or .jar files given by the following argument. If we have to specify multiple .jar files or directories, we separate them using a colon. Therefore, the third argument XQEngine.jar:. tells us that the Java classes are either in the file XQEngine.jar or in the current directory (signified by the period after the

```
Please input your query ("quit" to end the program):
/college/lecturer
<lecturer name="Sam Hoofer">
                <course title="Nonlinear Analysis"/>
                <course title="Modern Algebra"/>
                <course title="Discrete Structures"/>
        </lecturer>
<lecturer name="Daniela Frost">
                <course title="Nonlinear Analysis"/>
        </lecturer>
<lecturer name="Edward Bunker">
                <course title="Computational Algebra"/>
                <course title="Algorithms"/>
        </lecturer>

Please input your query ("quit" to end the program):
//lecturer
<lecturer name="Sam Hoofer">
                <course title="Nonlinear Analysis"/>
                <course title="Modern Algebra"/>
                <course title="Discrete Structures"/>
        </lecturer>
<lecturer name="Daniela Frost">
                <course title="Nonlinear Analysis"/>
        </lecturer>
<lecturer name="Edward Bunker">
                <course title="Computational Algebra"/>
                <course title="Algorithms"/>
        </lecturer>

Please input your query ("quit" to end the program):
//course[@title="Nonlinear Analysis"]
<course title="Nonlinear Analysis"/>
<course title="Nonlinear Analysis"/>

Please input your query ("quit" to end the program):
//course/@title="Nonlinear Analysis"/@title
<course title="Nonlinear Analysis"/>
<course title="Nonlinear Analysis"/>

Please input your query ("quit" to end the program):
quit
```

Figure 3.12 An XQEngine query session

semicolon). The fourth argument TryXMLQ specifies the Java class we are going to run. The following argument is the name of the XML file, `college.xml`. Now we can type the queries from the previous section to see the results. The session will end when we type quit. **Figure 3.12** shows the session for the four queries from the earlier section. The first three queries display the relevant portions from the XML file.

The XQEngine also provides a useful function called *contains-word* to search the information using partial match on single or multiple words. For example, we may be interested

```
Please input your query ("quit" to end the program):
contains-word(//course/@title,"Analysis")
@title="Nonlinear Analysis"
@title="Nonlinear Analysis"

Please input your query ("quit" to end the program):
contains-word(//course/@title,"Algebra")
@title="Modern Algebra"
@title="Computational Algebra"

Please input your query ("quit" to end the program):
quit
```

Figure 3.13 Use of *contains-word* in XQEngine

in titles that contain the word "Analysis" or "Algebra." **Figure 3.13** shows examples of queries involving the function *contains-word*. The first query,

```
contains-word(//course/@title,"Analysis")
```

displays two titles, both are "Nonlinear Analysis." The second query,

```
contains-word(//course/@title,"Algebra")
```

displays a title "Modern Algebra" and another one "Computational Algebra."

The Java class TryXMLQ is designed to work with any number of XML files. For example,

```
java -cp XQEngine.jar:. TryXMLQ book.xml bib.xml<CMDN>
```
(Command 3.2)

will allow you to query two XML files, `book.xml` and `bib.xml`. Readers are welcome to experiment with sample XML files in the folder and any other sample files obtained from the Web. The sample file `news.xml` may be of particular interest in the context of the Semantic Web. The file is an RSS feed—a simplified version of an RDF. **Figure 3.14** shows the news feed from the Times of India related to cricket, a popular sport in the Indian subcontinent. We can query an RSS feed such as `news.xml` using the XQEngine package as follows:

```
java -cp XQEngine.jar:. TryXMLQ news.xml <CMDN>
```
(Command 3.3)

Figure 3.15 shows a sample session resulting from (Command 3.3). The figure illustrates how one can get titles or descriptions of news stories from an RSS feed involving a name, in this case "Dhoni."

The XQEngine package is available in its entirety as XQEngine.zip under Chapter 3 on the CD. The expanded version of the package supplemented by the class TryXMLQ (Java and class files) can be found in the folder XQEngine. Complete documentation for the Java classes in

```
<?xml version="1.0"?>
  <rss version="0.91">
    <channel>
      <title>
          Cricket - News
      </title>
      <link>
          http://cricket.indiatimes.com
      </link>
      <description>
          The long and the shot of cricket news on and by
          India's number one website
      </description>
      <language>
          en-gb
      </language>
      <lastBuildDate>
          Mon, 20 Mar 2006 22:08:59+0530
      </lastBuildDate>
      <copyright>
          Copyright: Times Internet Limited,
          http://info.indiatimes.com/terms/tou.html
      </copyright>
      <docs>
          http://syndication.indiatimes.com/
      </docs>
      <image>
          <title>
              The Times of India- Cricket
          </title>
          <url>
              http://cricket.indiatimes.com/images/Cricket/logo.gif
          </url>
          <link>
              http://cricket.indiatimes.com/
          </link>
      </image>
      <item>
          <title>
              Had I stayed on, it would've been different: Dhoni
          </title>
          <description>
              The controversial dismissal of Mahendra Singh Dhoni
              could prove to be the turning point of the match with
              the wicketkeeper-batsman stating that had he stayed
              a little longer.
          </description>
          <link>
              http://cricket.indiatimes.com/articleshow/1457202.cms
          </link>
      </item>
      <item>
          <title>
              Was Dhoni out?
          </title>
          <description>
              In a decision that may have a crucial bearing on the match,
              K Hariharan, the third umpire, dealt a big blow to the
              Indian team by declaring Dhoni run out.
          </description>
          <link>
              http://cricket.indiatimes.com/articleshow/1457191.cms
          </link>
      </item>
```

Figure 3.14   Example of an RSS feed (http://cricket.indiatimes.com/)

```
Please input your query ("quit" to end the program):
contains-word(//title,"Dhoni")
<title>
                Had I stayed on, it would've been different: Dhoni
        </title>
<title>
                Was Dhoni out?
        </title>

Please input your query ("quit" to end the program):
contains-word(//description,"Dhoni")
<description>
                The controversial dismissal of Mahendra Singh Dhoni
                could prove to be the turning point of the match with
                the wicketkeeper-batsman stating that had he stayed
                a little longer.
        </description>
<description>
                In a decision that may have a crucial bearing on the match,
                K Hariharan, the third umpire, dealt a big blow to the
                Indian team by declaring Dhoni run out.
        </description>

Please input your query ("quit" to end the program):
quit
```

Figure 3.15 Query session for an RSS feed

XQEngine can be found under the subfolder doc. If clicking on the subfolder doc does not bring up the documentation, click on the index.html. We will try to understand the essential part of the application-programming interface (API) of XQEngine using the file TryXMLQ.java found directly under the folder XQEngine. As mentioned before, two important methods that a Java programmer needs to be aware of while using the XQEngine package are

1. setDocument(docName) for indexing a document,

2. setQuery(queryString) for running a query.

Figure 3.16 shows the data member and constructor of the class TryXMLQ. The class contains a handler called engine for objects of the type XQEngine. The constructor creates an object of the type XQEngine and calls the private method installSunXMLReader to install Sun's utilities for parsing XML. **Figure 3.17** shows the main method of the class TryXMLQ. After constructing an object of the type TryXMLQ, the method calls readDocument and passes the entire list of parameters to it. The readDocument method (Figure 3.17) in turn opens all the XML documents by using the XQEngine API method setDocument. The main method then calls the query method. The query method, shown in **Figure 3.18**, reads queries from the user and calls the XQEngine API method setQuery to get an object of the type ResultList. The class ResultList has a method called emitXml to display the results in XML format. The method query keeps on repeating until the user types quit. In order to compile the file TryXMLQ.java, you need to use the file XQEngine.jar as

```
javac -classpath XQEngine.jar <CMDN>TryXMLQ.java
```

(Command 3.4)

```
public class TryXMLQ
{
    XQEngine    engine;
    private void installSunXMLReader() throws Exception
    {
        SAXParserFactory spf = SAXParserFactory.newInstance();
        SAXParser parser = spf.newSAXParser();
        XMLReader reader = parser.getXMLReader();
        engine.setXMLReader( reader );
    }

    public TryXMLQ() throws Exception
    {
        engine = new XQEngine();
        installSunXMLReader();
    }
    ..............
```

Figure 3.16   Data member and constructor of TryXMLQ

```
public static void main( String[] args )
{
    try
    {
        TryXMLQ t = new TryXMLQ();
        t.readDocuments( args );
        t.query();
    }
    catch( Exception e )    { System.err.println( e ); }
}
```

Figure 3.17   `main` method of TryXMLQ

```
public void readDocuments(String [] args) throws Exception
{
    for(int i = 0; i < args.length; i++)
        engine.setDocument( args[i] );
}
```

Figure 3.18   `readDocument` method of TryXMLQ

The folder XQEngine also contains a Java class **SampleApp.java** that demonstrates the use of the XQEngine package through a graphical user interface (**Figure 3.19**).

```
void query( ) throws Exception
{
    String q;
    BufferedReader in = new BufferedReader
                 (new InputStreamReader(System.in));
    System.out.println("Please input your query ……
    q = in.readLine();
    while(q.compareTo("quit") != 0)
    {
        ResultList results = engine.setQuery( q );
        if ( results.getNumValidItems() ==  0 )
        {
            System.out.println( "No hits!" );
        }
        else
        {
            System.out.println( results.emitXml(true) );
        }
        System.out.println
            ("Please input your query ……
        q = in.readLine();
    }
}
```

Figure 3.19   `query` method of TryXMLQ

3.4.1.6   Microsoft Support for XML Queries

This section provides a brief introduction to Microsoft support for XML queries through a tutorial from http://www.w3schools.com/. W3Schools is the largest and most popular web developers' resource in the world. The tutorial for the XQuery can be found through http://www. w3schools.com/xquery/default.asp. Readers may want to browse through the tutorial to get additional information on XML queries. We will go directly to some of the examples that illustrate the Microsoft XMLDOM object, which is used to load the XML document. The selectNodes() function is used to select nodes from the XML document `bookstore.xml`. The document `bookstore.xml` from the W3Schools website is shown in **Figure 3.20**. The W3Schools site allows you to experiment with the queries as shown in **Figure 3.21** obtained from

http://www.w3schools.com/xpath/tryit.asp?filename=try_xpath_select_pricenodes_35

The query in Figure 3.21 is /bookstore/book[price>35]/price, which displays all the books with prices greater than \$35. The URI provides a unique opportunity to learn about the XMLDOM without creating an elaborate website. Readers can make changes to the queries and observe the results. For example, **Figure 3.22** shows the results of tweaking the previous query to obtain the titles of the books with a price less than \$35. The modified query is /bookstore/book[price>35]/title. Readers can visit the previous URI and experiment with the queries.

```
<?xml version="1.0" encoding="ISO-8859-1"?>
<bookstore>
<book category="COOKING">
  <title lang="en">Everyday Italian</title>
  <author>Giada De Laurentiis</author>
  <year>2005</year>
  <price>30.00</price>
</book>
<book category="CHILDREN">
  <title lang="en">Harry Potter</title>
  <author>J K. Rowling</author>
  <year>2005</year>
  <price>29.99</price>
</book>
<book category="WEB">
  <title lang="en">XQuery Kick Start</title>
  <author>James McGovern</author>
  <author>Per Bothner</author>
  <author>Kurt Cagle</author>
  <author>James Linn</author>
  <author>Vaidyanathan Nagarajan</author>
  <year>2003</year>
  <price>49.99</price>
</book>
<book category="WEB">
  <title lang="en">Learning XML</title>
  <author>Erik T. Ray</author>
  <year>2003</year>
  <price>39.95</price>
</book>
</bookstore>
```

Figure 3.20   The document `bookstore.xml`

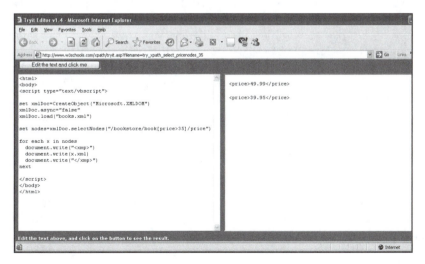

Figure 3.21   Querying XML documents using Microsoft.XMLDOM
(http://www.w3schools.com/xpath/tryit.asp?filename=try_xpath_select_pricenodes_35)

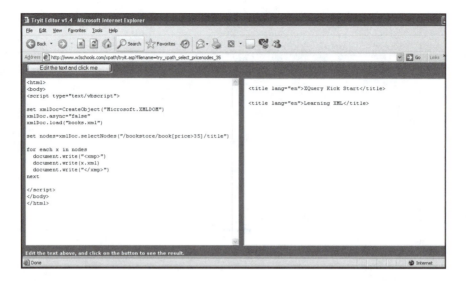

```
<html>
<body>
<script type="text/vbscript">

set xmlDoc=CreateObject("Microsoft.XMLDOM")
xmlDoc.async="false"
xmlDoc.load("books.xml")

set nodes=xmlDoc.selectNodes("/bookstore/book[price>35]/title")

for each x in nodes
  document.write("<xmp>")
  document.write(x.xml)
  document.write("</xmp>")
next

</script>
</body>
</html>
```

```
<title lang="en">XQuery Kick Start</title>

<title lang="en">Learning XML</title>
```

Figure 3.22   Experimenting with the query on W3Schools
(http://www.w3schools.com/xpath/tryit.asp?filename=try_xpath_select_pricenodes_35)

3.4.2   Resource Description Framework

Resource Description Framework is one of the most exciting new standards to emerge from the World Wide Web Consortium. RDF is all about metadata and addresses the problem with XML, which is that the same data can be described in various manners. For instance, you may use the element "Author" while another person uses "Writer," and so on. Both of them probably refer to the same object, but different tags that refer to the same thing can cause confusion when machines try to share data with each other. Conversely, preventing this kind of flexibility and extensibility will also result in lack of adequate resource description. Hence, there should be a common framework that can bridge the gap between these numerous schemas. It is at this stage that the RDF comes into the picture.

It is important to note that XML is not in fact a markup language in and of itself; it is a framework for creating markup. RDF is the same sort of being as XML, not a metadata standard. It is a means to develop metadata standards and signify metadata in XML form.

Definition 3.6   *Resource Description Framework* (RDF) is a framework that can be used in many different contexts to achieve different goals.

In general, an RDF model has three components:

1. Resource: Any entity that has to be described is known as Resource or Object. It can be a "web page" on the Internet or an "individual" in a society.

2. Property: Any characteristic of a Resource or its attribute that is used for the description of the same is known as Property (also called Predicate). For example, a web page may be

known by "Title" or an individual is recognized by his "Name." Thus, both are attributes for recognition of a Resource "web page" and "individual," respectively.

3. Value: A Property must have a value. For instance, the title of an Institution's web page is "College of Engineering," or the name of an individual is "Arthur."

An RDF goes one step beyond a standard representation of metadata: it is self-describing metadata.

Example 3.8 Let us see how we would deconstruct the sentence "John sold his apartment last week" as an RDF. First, break down the sentence into a number of assertions.

Rewrite the sentence as three simpler sentences:

- "John sold the apartment."
- "The apartment sold last week."
- "John had the apartment."

These assertions can be described by a graph, such as in **Figure 3.23**. The *directed labeled graph* indicates that there was a sell, which occurred last month; in which John was owner; and it was related to apartment, also owned by John. The ovals are objects, or *resources*, and the lines or *arcs* represent properties (aspects of the resources), which we refer to as a *predicate*.

Let us consider another example that is more appropriate for the Semantic Web. How can we use an RDF to describe this book you are reading right now? Using a directed labeled graph, a description of the title and author of this book might look like **Figure 3.24**. We have

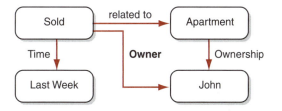

Figure 3.23 Anatomy of a sell of an apartment as a directed labeled graph

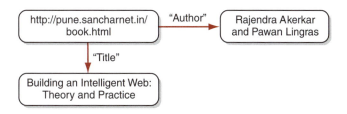

Figure 3.24 Using a graph to represent metadata

Figure 3.25   Metadata graph with URI references

used a URL to specify the object we are defining, but literal strings are used for all the other values. This graph accurately depicts the author and title of the article. However, in order to interpret the graph, you need to know what is meant by "Author" and "Title." This is where the power of an RDF really comes into play. If we replace the words "Author" and "Title" with URI references, the meaning of these relationships is much more clearly defined, as shown in **Figure 3.25**.

Unlike words, URIs are unambiguous. The word *title* has different meanings in different contexts; for example, a majestic title, professional title, or title to a piece of land. We understand what we are talking about when we say *title* because we have the context; however, machines cannot use such contextual information. They can compare only two strings and tell us whether they are the same. Hence, the main thing we get by replacing the literals with URI references is clarity, which lets a computer do elegant things with content by doing what it is good at. As an additional benefit, we can follow the URI reference to find documentation on that relationship. We will come back to this point later in the chapter.

Let us make this RDF example even more useful by substituting the author name with another URI reference:

```
http://pune.sancharnet.in/authors/author.asp?authorid=K24R9
```

The URI points to a specific author record or author description. Like the URI reference for the relationship, it is not important what it points to, as long as its use is internally consistent within our documents.

As we have seen so far, an RDF is just an abstract framework to depict metadata. It uses the XML syntax to offer semantics to the metadata. Due to the XML encoding, the RDF documents become almost interchangeable over the Web. An RDF uses the XML namespaces for describing the metadata schema being used. The syntax of declaring an XML namespace is

```
xmlns:namespace-prefix="namespace"
```

For example,

```
xmlns:myelements=http://www.example.com/elements/2.0/
xmlns:dc=http://purl.org/dc/elements/1.0/
```

In these examples, `myelements` and `dc` are the namespace prefixes. The actual namespaces are defined by their relevant URIs (in our example these URIs are in fact URLs). The elements and attributes of these namespaces are located and defined at these URLs. For example, in the namespace `myelements` URI, you can define elements of your own, "`author`," "`name_of_book`," and so on. In the namespace `dc` URI, the Dublin Core elements are defined. Some of the elements defined in `dc` include "`creator`", "`title`", and so on. Different namespaces can be used in the same RDF documents. For example,

```
<myelements:name_of_book>
      Building an Intelligent Web: Theory & Practice
</myelements:name_of_book>
<dc:creator>Rajendra Akerkar & Pawan Lingras</dc:creator>
```

These examples illustrate that it is because of the use of XML Namespaces that the RDF documents are able to synchronize between various metadata schemas.

We have already seen that an RDF makes it possible to specify the relationships between nodes using URI references. Now let us see its relation with XML. The fragment of an RDF shown in **Figure 3.26** takes the previous graph one step further, by describing the book you are reading in an RDF's XML syntax, using a specified RDF entity set called the *Dublin Core*. The first line of the previous RDF fragment is the XML declaration that indicates the following content is XML and the version of XML. The next line begins with an `rdf:RDF` element, which indicates the following XML content (up to the last line of the fragment) is intended to represent an RDF. On the same line, you will see an XML namespace declaration, which is an `xmlns` attribute of the `rdf:RDF` start tag. This declaration means all tags in this content prefixed with rdf: are part of the namespace identified by the URI `http://www.w3.org/1999/02/22-rdf-syntax-ns#`. An additional namespace declaration is given in line 3, which identifies the additional namespace `dc` used in the statement. The word

```
<?xml version="1.0"?>

<rdf:RDF xmlns:rdf="http://www.w3.org/1999/02/22-rdf-syntax-ns#"

    xmlns:dc="http://purl.org/dc/elements/1.1/">

  <rdf:Description rdf:about="">

    <dc:title>

          Building an Intelligent Web: Theory and Practice

     </dc:title>

    <dc:creator> Rajendra Akerkar and Pawan Lingras </dc:creator>

  </rdf:Description>

</rdf:RDF>
```

Figure 3.26 Fragment of an RDF

```
<rdf:RDF xmlns:rdf="http://www.w3.org/1999/02/22-rdf-syntax-ns#"
    xmlns:dc="http://purl.org/dc/elements/1.1/">
  <rdf:Description rdf:about="">
    <dc:language>en</dc:language>
  </rdf:Description>
</rdf:RDF>
```

Figure 3.27   RDF document

`dc` corresponds to Dublin Core, which is a set of properties for describing documents. We notice `dc:title` and `dc:creator` in lines 5, 7, and 8. Here the property "title" is a name given to the resource. Likewise, the property "creator" is an entity accountable for generating the content of the resource.

The RDF uses XML Namespaces syntax to tell us that the title and creator elements are from an XML namespace that "lives" at the URI `http://purl.org/dc/elements/1.1/`. The attribute `rdf:about=""` (with a blank value for the URI) in the description tag indicates that the RDF description refers to the enclosing resource—the book you are reading.

Vocabularies make a particular sort of metadata more significant by providing a predefined list of values that these elements can hold. Vocabularies are known by many different names: taxonomies, authority files, reference data, controlled vocabularies, and ontologies. Actually, a vocabulary is a list of predefined values. An RDF provides the ability to represent those lists through an RDF schema, even if the list has a complex structure as with an ontology.

Example 3.9   Let us consider a language as an example. The Dublin Core element language defines a language as "the intellectual content of the [given] resource." An RDF descriptor to define a language is shown in **Figure 3.27**. The Dublin Core recommendations for usage of this element direct you to some IETF and ISO documents (RFC 3066 and ISO 3166, respectively) that recommend a set of codes to use as the value of this element. The designation **en** stands for English, but if we wanted to be more specific we could have used **en-GB** for Great Britain English or **en-US** for United States English.

Example 3.10   We create an RDF model that contains at least three classes, three properties, and at least one instance of each class using properties like **type** and **subClassOf** in a correct way. Then we design an RDF model as an RDF/XML file and use the *W3C RDF Validator* to check that our RDF file is syntactically correct. The RDF model is given in **Figure 3.28**. Now we design an RDF model as an RDF/XML file, which is shown in **Figure 3.29**.

You can use the RDF parser provided at the W3C website (`http://www.w3.org/RDF/ Validator/`). It will show you that the previous RDF/XML file is in the proper RDF format.

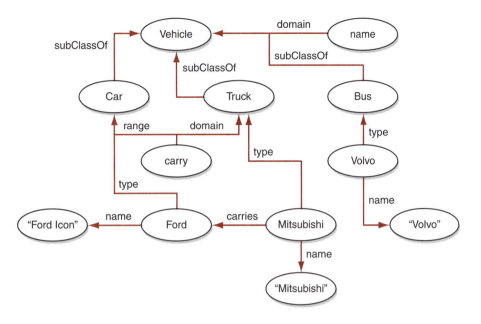

Figure 3.28 An RDF model for automobiles

An RDF is reasonably popular among the library and information-management society. Upcoming metadata standards such as PRISM, Dublin Core, RSS, and PICS are influencing RDFs to build domain-specific metadata standards. The Dublin Core has caught the attention of the publishing industry.

It is quite possible to use an RDF without knowing all the nitty-gritty details. Many organizations use RSS syntax, a simplified RDF grammar, to organize information on their sites. We saw an example of an RSS feed in Section 3.4.1.5. If you go to `http://news.com.com/2009-1090-980549.html`, you will find a set of RSS feeds for different `News.com` articles. The PRISM working group, which defines a metadata standard on top of RDF, is composed of such premier brands as Adobe, Time Inc., and Kodak.

An RDF is developed to be domain independent; but at the same time, it can be used to describe information about any domain. The RDF model replicates the class system of object-oriented programming. A collection of classes, as defined for a specific purpose or domain, is called a *schema* in an RDF. These classes are extensible through *subclass refinement*. In addition, RDFs support metadata reuse by permitting transmission or sharing between different schemas.

The developers of RDFs foresee them being applied

- in resource discovery to offer enhanced search engine capabilities;
- in describing pools of pages that denote a single logical "document";
- by intelligent software agents to assist knowledge sharing in content rating;
- in cataloging to explain the content and content relationships available at a particular website, web page, or digital library;

```
<?xml version="1.0"?>

<rdf:RDF

  xmlns:rdf="http://www.w3.org/1999/02/22-rdf-syntax-ns#"

  xmlns:rdfs="http://www.w3.org/2000/01/rdf-schema#"

  xmlns:my="http://www.myvehicle.com/vehicle-schema/">


  <rdfs:Class rdf:about="#Vehicle"/>


  <rdfs:Class rdf:about="#Car">

    <rdfs:subClassOf rdf:resource="#Vehicle"/>

  </rdfs:Class>


  <rdf:Property rdf:about="#name">

    <rdfs:domain rdf:resource="#Vehicle"/>

  </rdf:Property>


  <rdf:Description rdf:about="#Ford">

    <rdf:type rdf:resource="#Car"/>

    <my:name>Ford Icon</my:name>

  </rdf:Description>


  <my:Truck rdf:about="#Mitsubishi">

    <my:name>Mitsubishi</my:name>

    <my:carry rdf:resource="#Mitsubishi"/>

  </my:Truck>

</rdf:RDF>
```

Figure 3.29   An RDF/XML file for the automobile example

- for reciting intellectual property rights of web pages; and
- for conveying the confidentiality preferences of a user as well as the confidential strategies of a website.

There are some disadvantages to an RDF format:

1. You cannot design your XML in an arbitrary way. The RDF format restricts you on how you design your XML.

2. An RDF uses namespaces to uniquely identify types (classes), properties, and resources; thus, you must have a solid understanding of namespaces.

3. In order to use the RDF format, you have to learn the extensive RDF vocabulary.

3.4.3 XML Topic Map

Information inside any electronic data stores is diverse. A methodology to connect the diverse information resources is to alter the data into XML; then, the XML hierarchy and internal link classification can be used to offer information access. This approach has some disadvantages. It is unusually costly to transfer legacy data into XML. Further, we are restricted to a static hierarchical navigation within the document, and simple one-way links between documents. Such a nonflexible navigation mechanism happens to be uncontrollable. It is also problematic as the information base increases. Experience suggests that diverse inadequate links prevent users from finding the data they need. In addition, the available linking and navigation mechanisms do not let us plan our navigation policy. Navigation based upon the hierarchy, content, and links embedded in the data cannot easily be updated when another navigational approach is desired. In any case, the current linking and navigation mechanisms do not allow us to plan our navigation strategy; instead, we must follow links, blindly hoping they will take us to the information we so desperately seek. Ultimately, navigation based upon the hierarchy, content, and links entrenched in the data cannot be easily updated when another navigational tactic is desired. Topic Maps is an upcoming ISO standard (Rath and Pepper 1999; Garshol 2002; Durusau and Newcomb 2005), which offers a new paradigm for knowledge navigation and creation: it enables us to create virtual knowledge maps for the Web.

The birth of the topic maps paradigm took place in 1993, when it was first articulated as an operational document by the Davenport Group. The paradigm was explored later within the GCA Research Institute (now known as IDEAlliance) in an activity called *Conventions for the Application of HyTime*. Topic maps were officially adopted as an ISO Standard in 2000.

A topic map is a collection of topics and semantically significant relationships between these topics. That means it creates *semantic networks* that provide a meaningful description of the relationship between subjects. Topic maps link these topics with external references, such as resources behind URLs. The XML Topic Map (XTM) serves as an XML-based interchange format for topic maps. It is used to arrange information in a manner that can be optimized for navigation. Software such as *Ontopia* navigator is available for creating topic maps, which serve as a *knowledge interface layer* between storage devices like websites or databases and user interfaces such as web browsers.

We now present some facts about Topic Maps. The narrative here is based on the papers by (Garshol 2002; Pepper et al., 2005; Rath and Pepper, 1999). Topic maps are SGML (Standard Generalized Markup Language) or XML documents that describe what an information set is about. This is done by properly asserting topics and by linking the appropriate parts of the information set to the appropriate topics. They can be in separate documents. Topic maps operate without changing an information set; thus, one can say that Topic Maps can be applied from "above" the information set, rather than from "inside" them, meaning they are superimposed views. A topic map conveys someone's opinion about what the topics are and which components of an information set are relevant to which topics. There is no limit to the number of topic maps that can be created above the same information set. Topic maps help organize and retrieve online information in a way that can be mastered by information owners and information users. They play the same role as the index plays in a book.

To create a topic map, we need to define the *theme*, which should be covered. Then, we collect as many *topics* as we can find that are relevant for the theme, together with other external information resources, such as websites. This is called *occurrences*. And to conclude, we have to think about relationships between the collected topics. They are called *associations*.

As an example, we can discuss the setting of "topic map designing" and introduce essential concepts such as *topics*, *associations*, and *scope*. Let us prepare a partial XML Topic Map (XTM) document that gives information about our institution *Technomathematics Research Foundation.*

The Topic Map itself can be defined via an XML document containing all relevant information, as shown in **Figure 3.30**. Like any XML documents, a Topic Map document begins with a header indicating the version of XML, followed by the `topicMap` tag that asserts namespaces, which we ignore in this case. The <!-- .... --> can contain any comment the author would like

```
<?xml version="1.0"?>

<topicMap id="tmrf"

        xmlns       = 'http://www.topicmaps.org/xtm/1.0/'

        xmlns:xlink = 'http://www.w3.org/1999/xlink'>

<!--

    The map contains information about Technomathematics Research Foundation.

    We can include comment and narrative here…

-->

.... here my topics and my associations go ...

</topicMap>
```

Figure 3.30   A Topic Map document (Adopted from http://topicmaps.bond.edu.au/docs/6/1)

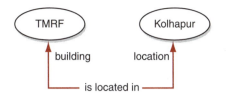

Figure 3.31   Topics with associations

to provide. Subsequently, any number of topics and associations can be added to this map. The sequence of these declarations does not matter.

Whenever someone has expertise in a particular area or *theme*, the author will denote their knowledge in the form of a so-called topic map, which may consist of as many topics as wanted. These topics may be important to the original theme, as well as others that are somewhat related to the theme. The number of topics will eventually influence the size and complexity of the topic map. Some of the topics within a topic map may be in a relationship (or associations) with each other. Moreover, topics can play distinct roles in distinct associations. Topics can also contain any number of external references, such as web pages, which supposedly elaborate on a specific topic.

Topics can have multiple relationships with each other. The trick is to find the most meaningful association between topics. That means you have to be explicit about which relationship two or more topics have to each other. Associations can be general such as *is located in, published by,* or *born in;* or they can be more specific: *is an academic organization within* or *requires to have property.* A simple example for an association could be "TMRF is located in Kolhapur" as shown in **Figure 3.31**.

To make clear who is who and who plays which role in the association, we should use some scheme; for instance, the topics involved in the association are called *members* and they play *roles*. Let us introduce a reference to a new topic: `topicRef xlink:href`, and define the topic as shown in **Figure 3.32**. Furthermore, associations can also connect more than two topics, for instance, "Rohan is the registrar of the TMRF." This example is shown in **Figure 3.33**. **Figure 3.34** shows the creation of the association property.

Similarly, we can create new associations. The *occurrences* can be further integrated in your document to specify a resource contributing additional information relevant to a topic. In Topic Map vocabulary, external resources are handled via `resourceRefs` while internal resources are depicted by `resourceData`. Hence, the distinctive feature between these two resources is that

- the `resourceRef` links to an external information resource,
- the `resourceData` is a tiny bit of information.

Following along these lines, we find the resource for our TMRF example as shown in **Figure 3.35**.

Each occurrence can have a type: `instanceOf` specifies the more general terms, which our resource belongs to. The `instanceOf` is optional within one occurrence. Because we have introduced two new topics, we have to define them as shown in **Figure 3.36**.

```
<association>
  <instanceOf>
    <topicRef xlink:href="#is-located-in"/>
  </instanceOf>
  <member>
    <roleSpec><topicRef xlink:href="#building"/></roleSpec>
    <topicRef xlink:href="#tmrf"/>
  </member>
  <member>
    <roleSpec><topicRef xlink:href="#location"/></roleSpec>
    <topicRef xlink:href="#kolhapur"/>
  </member>
</association>
```

Figure 3.32 XML file for topics with associations

Rohan
TMRF
holder
organization
position
registrar
holds position in organization

Figure 3.33 Three topics with associations

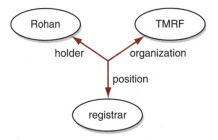

```
<association>

  <instanceOf>

    <topicRef xlink:href="#holds-position-in-organisation"/>

  </instanceOf>

  <member>

    <roleSpec><topicRef xlink:href="#holder"/></roleSpec>

    <topicRef xlink:href="#rohan"/>

  </member>

  <member>

    <roleSpec><topicRef xlink:href="#position"/></roleSpec>

    <topicRef xlink:href="#registrar"/>

  </member>

  <member>

    <roleSpec><topicRef xlink:href="#organisation"/></roleSpec>

    <topicRef xlink:href="tmrf"/>

  </member>

</association>
```

Figure 3.34   An association property

Likewise, we can include different information resources. Each individual `resourceRef` or `resourceData` is embedded in its own occurrence. It is generally advisable to not list several websites within one occurrence. Finally, show the *scope,* which validates a topic characteristic. A topic characteristic can be a base name, an occurrence, or an association. The assignment of such a characteristic can be considered to be valid only within a certain scope. Considering that not everybody is interested in everything or is supposed to have access to all information, the Topic Map author should be aware that the information in the topic map could be viewed under different contexts. To indicate this context, he has the option to scope either the *baseName* of a topic, an *occurrence* in a topic, or an *association.* With an illustration of *scoping a base name,* we could denote a language the base name is written in. Assume the topic *TMRF* should be covered in two languages, English and German, as shown in **Figure 3.37**.

```
<topic id="tmrf">

  <instanceOf><topicRef xlink:href="#institution"/></instanceOf>

  <baseName>

    <baseNameString>Technomathematics Research

Foundation</baseNameString>

  </baseName>

  <occurrence>

    <instanceOf><topicRef xlink:href="#journal"/></instanceOf>

    <resourceData>the online research article</resourceData>

  </occurrence>

  <occurrence>

    <instanceOf><topicRef xlink:href="#webpage"/></instanceOf>

    <resourceRef xlink:href="http://pune.sancharnet.in/kpr_tmrf"/>

  </occurrence>

</topic>
```

Figure 3.35   Example of occurrence

```
<topic id="journal">

  <baseName>

    <baseNameString>journal</baseNameString>

  </baseName>

</topic>


<topic id="webpage">

  <baseName>

    <baseNameString>webpage</baseNameString>

  </baseName>

</topic>
```

Figure 3.36   Defining two new topics in the document

```
<topic id="tmrf">

  <baseName>

    <scope>

      <subjectIndicatorRef

          xlink:href="http://www.topicmaps.org/xml/1.0/language.xtm#en"/>

    </scope>

    <baseNameString>Technomathematics Research Foundation</baseNameString>

  </baseName>

  <baseName>

    <scope>

      <subjectIndicatorRef

          xlink:href="http://www.topicmaps.org/xml/1.0/language.xtm#de"/>

    </scope>

    <baseNameString>Technomathematik Forschung Stiftung</baseNameString>

  </baseName>

</topic>
```

Figure 3.37   An illustration of *scoping a base name*

Scopes can be used to reduce the amount of information presented to a user. The more a system knows about the user's background (language, preferences, etc.), the more personalized the information can be.

3.5   Issues That May Affect the Development of Semantic Web

In the existing Web, URIs identify resources. Some of the issues associated with URIs are presented next, which may influence the building of the Semantic Web.

1. The URI structure is strongly decentralized (i.e., anyone can create a URI), which means there can be several URIs for the same resource.

2. It is hard to verify the context of what the URI identifies. This is a major problem both for locating and reasoning.

3. URIs are used for identifying "real-world" objects on the Web. Due to the decentralized nature of URI definition, there is no rule for identification. It will be very useful to have a normalized way to address an object without having to resort to a centralized resource.

4. The Web infrastructure is based on an old naming model. Names are not attached to concepts, and there can be several analogous models. The Semantic Web will not be limited to web resources but must cover real-world objects. Is it good to disconnect concept identifiers from concept names? People could then call particular concepts with different names depending on the context. The naming model of Topic Maps allows such facility. Adopting it to the Semantic Web languages may furnish specific solutions.

At the moment, Semantic Web activity is centered on the Internet, but individuals who build and manage business applications are starting to see its importance. Though practical uses of Semantic Web technology are just emerging, each successful implementation paves the way for others to follow.

EXERCISES

1. What is the difference between a URI, a URL, and a URN? Give an example for each.

2. Explain the concept of XML Namespaces. How are namespaces declared and used in XML?

3. How is namespace information represented in the XPath data model? What are namespaces used for?

4. What is an ontology? Name two different representations for ontologies. How do they differ?

5. A media store offers the following products:

```
1.  <?xml version="1.1"?>
2.  <products xmlns:xsi=http://www.w3.org/2001/XMLSchema-instance
3.  xsi:noNamespaceSchemaLocation=products.xsd>
4.  <book>
5.  <title>Learning XML</title>
6.  <author>EricRay</author>
7.  <price>30.00</price>
8.  </book>
9.  <cd>
10. <title>for you</title>
11. <interpret>Frank Chastenier</interpret>
12. <price>15.00</price>
13. </cd>
14. <dvd>
15. <title>Goldrush</title>
16. <director>Charly Chaplin</director>
17. <price>19.00</price>
18. </dvd>
19. </products>
```

Write a DTD for the previous XML document.

6. Construct an RDF model that contains at least four classes, four properties, and at least two instances of each class. You should use properties like `type` and `subClassOf` correctly. Write your design for an RDF model as an RDF/XML file and use the *RDF Validator* (see `http://www.w3.org/RDF/Validator/`) to verify that your RDF file is syntactically accurate.

7. Define an RDF description for your course website and some of the documents available on that site. Include a description of the exercises as a sequence in your RDF description.

8. In Table 3.2, you are given data records about persons. Write an XML document for these data records.

First Name	Middle Name	Last Name	City	Salary
Rudi	Armen	Buller	Montreal	$ 3500
James	John	Bruner	Vancouver	$ 5000
Rita	Mark	Calligan	Toronto	$ 6500
Roger	Ronald	Gibbon	Vancouver	$ 8000
Peter	Helmut	Fox	Montreal	$ 5000

Table 3.2

9. Define a DTD for any given XML document. What are the limitations of DTDs?

10. Express the fact that the "School of Computer Science belongs to TMRF" as an association, and give a corresponding XML Topic Map document.

11. Create a simple XTM document that gives information about your favorite theme.

References

Antoniou, G. and F. van Harmelen. (2004): *A Semantic Web primer.* MA: MIT Press.

Appelquist, D. (2001): *XML and SQL: Developing Web applications.* Boston: Addison-Wesley.

Armstrong, E., S. Bodoff, D. Carson, M. Fisher, D. Green, and K. Haase. (2002): *An introductory tutorial on Web services, Java and XML.* Boston: Addison-Wesley.

Arpírez, J., A. Gómez-Pérez, A. Lozano, and S.H. Pinto. (1998): (ONTO)[2]Agent: An ontology-based WWW broker to select ontologies; Workshop on application of ontologies and problem solving methods. ECAI '98. Brighton, UK. ECAI '98.

Durusau, P., and S. Newcomb. (2005): Topic maps: Reference model. http://www.isotopicmaps.org/rm4tm/RM4TM-official.html.

Fensel, D. (2001): Ontologies: a silver bullet for knowledge management and electronic commerce. Springer.

Garshol, L. (2002): What are topic maps. http://www.xml.com/pub/a/2002/09/11/topicmaps.html.

Gómez-Pérez, A. (1998): Knowledge sharing and reuse. In *The handbook on applied expert systems,* ed. Liebowitz. Boca Raton, FL: CRC Press.

Kinsman, C. and J. McManus. (2002): *Using XML.* Boston: Addison-Wesley.

Noy, N., and D. McGuinness. (2001): Ontology development 101: A guide to creating your first ontology. http://protege.stanford.edu/publications/ontology_development/ontology101-noy-mcguinness.html.

Pepper, S. et al (2005): A Survey of RDF/Topic Maps Interoperability Proposals. http://www.w3.org/TR/2005/WD-rdftm-survey-20050329/

Pierobon, J. M. (2005): Basic Internet definitions. http://www.pierobon.org/iis/index.htm.

Rath, H., and S. Pepper. (1999): Topic maps at work. In *XML handbook,* C. Goldfarb and P. Prescod eds. Upper Saddle River, NJ: Prentice-Hall.

RFC2396. Uniform resource identifiers (URI): Generic syntax. http://ds.internic.net/rfc/rfc2396.txt.

Uschold, M., and M. Gruninger. (1996): Ontologies: Principles, methods and applications. *Knowledge Engineering Review* 11 (2): 93–155.

Further Reading

Berners-Lee, T., Hendler, J., Lassila, O. (2001): The Semantic Web, Scientific American, May 2001.

Broekstra, J., Klein, M. C. A., Decker, S., Fensel, D., Harmelen, F. v. and Horrocks, I. (2001): 'Enabling knowledge representation on the Web by extending RDF schema' In *World Wide Web*, pp. 467-478.

Didier Courtaud. (2002): From gencode to xml: a history of markup languages.

Dumais, S. (1998): Using svms for text categorization, IEEE Intelligent Systems Magazine, Trends and Controversies, Marti Hearst, pp 21-23.

Eckstein, R., Eckstein, S. (2003): *XML und Datenmodellierung.* dpunkt.verlag.

Fensel, D., Hendler, J., Lieberman, H., Wahlster, W. (2003): Introduction to the Semantic Web. In: Spinning the Semantic Web. Bringing the World Wide Web to Its Full Potential. MIT Press, pp.. 1-25.

Goldfarb, C. F., Prescod, P. (2003): XML Handbook, Prentice Hall.

Katz, H. (2004): XQuery from the experts: a guide to the W3C XML query language. Addison-Wesley.

Patrick, J. D. (1991): Snob: A program for discriminating between classes, Technical Report 91/151, Department of Computer Science, Monash University, Victoria, Australia.

Rasmussen, E. (1992): *Clustering Algorithms*, In W. B. Frakes and R. B. Yates, (eds), Information Retrieval: Data structures and algorithms, Prentice Hall, pp. 419-442.

Rocchio, J. (1971): Relevance feedback in Information Retrieval. In The SMART Retrieval System: Experiments in Automatic Document Processing, Prentice Hall.

Salomon, J. (2001): Support vector machines for phoneme classification. Master of Science Thesis, School of AI, University of Edinburgh.

Wine Agent (2003): Wine Agent (Version 1.0). http://onto.stanford.edu:8080/wino/index.jsp

WIC (2006): World Wide Web Consortium http://www.w3c.org.

Classification and Association

4.1 Introduction

The evolution of data mining dates back to the time when business data was first stored in computers and technologies were generated to allow users to navigate through the data in real time. The core components of data mining technologies have been under development for decades. Recently the high-performance relational database engines and broad data integration efforts have made these data mining techniques practical. Data mining is a component of a wider process called *knowledge discovery* from databases. Data mining techniques range from simple statistical methods to highly complex data analysis. The field of data mining is of interest to disciplines such as statistics, computer science, and business management. There are three major areas of activities in this field: theory, algorithmic approach, and applications. In this chapter and in Chapter 5, we will attempt to establish the basic foundations of data mining—the theoretical background of the decision tree, association rules, clustering and other statistical techniques, as well as their implementations in the real world.

4.2 Data Preparation

Data mining is the process of discovering potentially useful and previously unknown information nuggets from huge data collections. In order to mine for the knowledge, one needs to manipulate the available data so that various mining techniques can be applied. In this section, we will study the essentials of database theory, including representation and retrieval.

4.2.1 Database Theory

Although scientific computations may have been one of the first applications of modern-day computers, business applications were not too far behind. Databases play a major role in the business applications of computers. One of the primary design issues in creating a database is the representation model, which is a theory or specification describing how a database is structured and used (Wikipedia 2006a). Early databases used somewhat unstructured hierarchical and network models. In 1970, E. F. Codd from IBM introduced the relational database model, which revolutionized the database world. Some of the newer models, such as Object-relational and Object database models, may be advantageous in some cases, however, relational database remains the most widely used model. We will use the relational model in all our discussions in this book.

Data in the relational model is represented as mathematical relations. The data is manipulated using relational calculus or algebra. The mathematical basis for the relational database

119

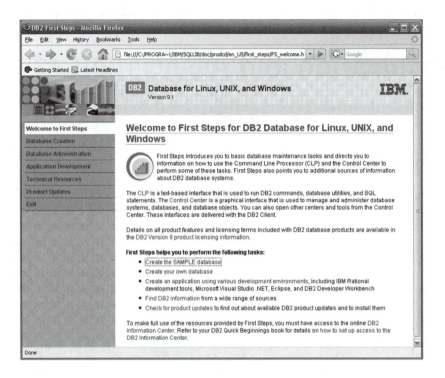

Figure 4.1   IBM DB2 First Steps Launchpad

model makes it possible to minimize data redundancy and verify data integrity. More informally, data in a relational database is stored in a table. Each row of the table, called a *tuple* in relational algebra, corresponds to a record or an object. Each field in the record is called an *attribute*. Let us look at an example of a database with the help of one of the premier and first relational database management software programs, called DB2 and developed by IBM. The book includes a CD consisting of IBM's DB2 express-C software. This trial version is available through IBM for educational use and can be used with moderate size databases.

Once you install the DB2 express-C, you can launch the first step, Launchpad window, as shown in **Figure 4.1**. Clicking on the first link on the left "Database Creation" will give you a choice of creating a sample database that can be used to learn the essentials of relational database theory. Once you click on the "Create SAMPLE Database" button, you will see a small window showing spinning gears. Whenever you see these spinning gears, please wait and let DB2 finish its task. Once DB2 has finished creating the sample database, click on the third link on the left "Database Administration," and picking the link "Basic administration tasks" will give you a button to launch the control center. After launching the control center, a dialogue box appears with a choice of views; choose the basic view.

Figure 4.2 shows the basic view of the control center; take a moment to familiarize yourself with it. There is a menu at the top, with icons underneath that act as buttons for frequently used tasks. There are two tabs under the icons: one for object views and the other for the command editor. We will go back and forth between these two tabs. Let us start with the object view. We see three panels: one on the left and two horizontal ones on the right. An

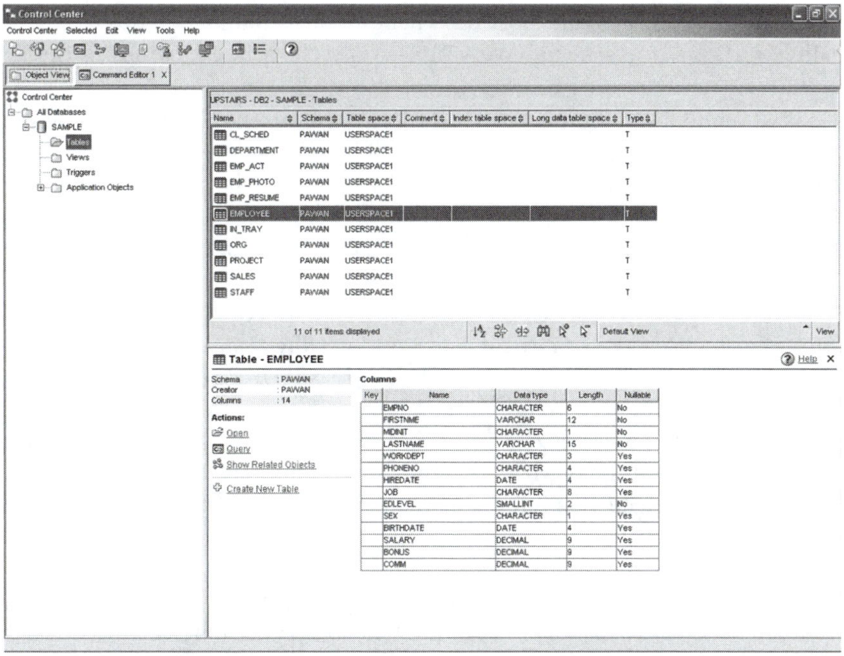

Figure 4.2 Attributes for Employee Table

object chosen in the left panel is expanded in the top right panel. More information and options for the top right panel appear in the bottom right panel. Please expand the "All Databases" folder, the SAMPLE database, and the Tables folder in the left panel. It will bring the list of tables in the SAMPLE database in the top right panel. A single click on the EMPLOYEE table will show more information about the table in the bottom right panel, as shown in Figure 4.2.

The bottom left panel in Figure 4.2 tells us that there are 14 columns or attributes in the table. For every column, the panel describes whether it is a key, its name, the type of data it can hold, its length, and whether its value can be missing in a record (i.e., nullable). If a column is a key, the table is optimized for searching using that column. In addition, the top right corner of the bottom left panel also tells us the creator and schema of the table. A schema is a unique identifier used to group a set of database objects (such as tables, views, indexes, and aliases); that is, if you were creating a table named EMPLOYEE, it would be tedious to have to search the database to find out whether some other user has already created a table with the same name. The name of each object needs to be unique only within its schema. Most database objects have a two-part object name: the first part being the schema name and the second part, the name of the object. When an object is created, you can assign it to a specific schema. If you do not specify a schema, it is assigned to the default schema, which is usually the user ID of the person who created the object. For example, a user named Pawan might have a table named PAWAN.EMPLOYEE. Similarly, we use a three part name for an attribute. For example, PAWAN.EMPLOYEE.WORKDEPT means we are referring to the WORKDEPT attribute from the EMPLOYEE table within the schema PAWAN. For simplicity we will drop the schema portion whenever possible in our discussion, as we will only be dealing with a single schema. We will use only the schema names in the actual DB2 commands.

Let us look at an additional table, DEPARTMENT, from the SAMPLE database by single clicking on it in the top right panel (see **Figure 4.3**). The bottom right panel tells us that it has five columns and also describes their properties. The bottom right panel gives us three options: Open, Query, and Show related objects. Click on the "Open" option. Another window pops up as shown in **Figure 4.4**. We can see all nine records from the table DEPARTMENT. You can resize the window and columns to improve your view.

Although the relationship between the two tables EMPLOYEE and DEPARTMENT is not explicitly stated in the SAMPLE database, they are logically related to each other through the columns EMPLOYEE.WORKDEPT and DEPARTMENT.DEPTNAME. A typical database is split into several tables in an attempt to minimize the redundancy and maintain integrity. For example, the information from the two tables EMPLOYEE and DEPARTMENT could have been joined in a single table with 18 columns (one column called either the DEPTNAME or WORKDEPT plus thirteen remaining columns from the EMPLOYEE table with four remaining columns from the DEPARTMENT table). However, doing so would mean that the information about a department such as the name, location, and manager would have to be repeated for every employee in the department. Moreover, if the location of the department were changed, the change would have to be made for every member of the department, lest

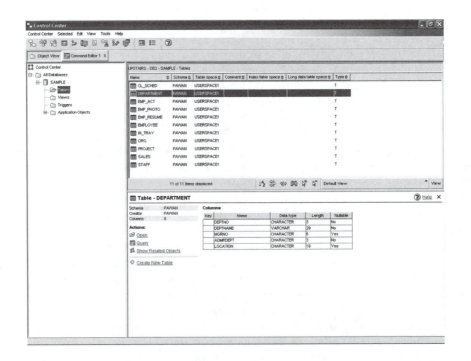

Figure 4.3   Attributes for Department Table

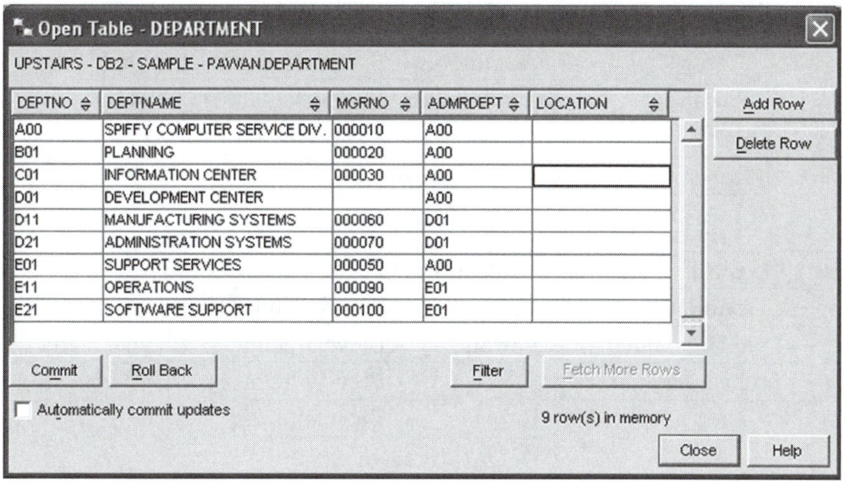

DEPTNO	DEPTNAME	MGRNO	ADMRDEPT	LOCATION
A00	SPIFFY COMPUTER SERVICE DIV.	000010	A00	
B01	PLANNING	000020	A00	
C01	INFORMATION CENTER	000030	A00	
D01	DEVELOPMENT CENTER		A00	
D11	MANUFACTURING SYSTEMS	000060	D01	
D21	ADMINISTRATION SYSTEMS	000070	D01	
E01	SUPPORT SERVICES	000050	A00	
E11	OPERATIONS	000090	E01	
E21	SOFTWARE SUPPORT	000100	E01	

Figure 4.4 Department Table

the integrity of the database be compromised. The process of splitting large tables into smaller tables is called *database normalization.*

A database is said to be in a normal form if the relationships between attributes is rigorously defined (Wikipedia 2006b). Originally, Codd (1970) specified three normal forms. The first normal form (1NF) states that an attribute can store only one value; for example, let us assume that we want to keep a list of products bought by a customer with two attributes: Customer and Product. If a customer, "Pawan," buys two products "Bicycle pump" and "Bicycle helmet," we cannot have a single record with "Customer = Pawan" and "Product = {Bicycle pump, Bicycle helmet}." Instead, we need two records, as shown in **Table 4.1**. The second and third normal forms deal with the functional dependency of non-key attributes on the primary key. Let us look at an example of how a database is turned into a 2NF, as shown in **Table 4.2**. Table 4.2(a) shows a database with four attributes for purchases made in a store: Customer, E-mail, Product, and Price. There are four records in the database. Clearly there is a functional relationship between the key attribute "Customer" and the non-key attribute "e-mail." Similar functional dependency can also be detected from the key attribute "Product" and a non-key attribute "Price." If we split the original database into three tables as shown in Table 4.2(b), we will not only save storage (not obvious in our example, because we have only a few

Customer	Product
Pawan	Bicycle pump
Pawan	Bicycle helmet

Table 4.1 Illustration of 1NF

Customer	e-mail	Product	Price
Pawan	pawan@yahoo.ca	Bicycle pump	$19.99
Pawan	pawan@yahoo.ca	Bicycle helmet	$24.99
Paul	paul@gmail.ca	Bicycle helmet	$24.99
Robert	robert@halifax.ca	Bicycle pump	$19.99

(a) **Original database**

Customer	e-mail
Pawan	pawan@yahoo.ca
Paul	paul@gmail.ca
Robert	robert@halifax.ca

Customer	Product
Pawan	Bicycle pump
Pawan	Bicycle helmet
Paul	Bicycle helmet
Robert	Bicycle pump

Product	Price
Bicycle pump	$19.99
Bicycle helmet	$24.99

(b) **Database in 2NF**

Table 4.2 Illustration of 2NF

records), but also maintain database integrity. For example, if we had to change the price of the bicycle helmets to $29.99, we would need to make the change for only one record. That means we would not make the mistake of changing the price of bicycle helmets in one place and not in the other. Please note that these three tables can be joined together to recover the original table; hence, the decomposition shown in Table 4.2 is lossless. We will see how two or more tables can be joined using queries in DB2 in the next section.

Since Codd's original proposal, database researchers have proposed additional normal forms, such as Boyce-Codd normal form (BCNF), as well as the fourth and fifth normal forms (4NF and 5NF). The sixth normal form (6NF) was also proposed for temporal databases. For a more detailed discussion on normal forms, browse Wikipedia (2006b). The DB2 Express-C CD contains various database resources related to IBM's DB2, which provide more information on database design based on normal forms. Date (2004) is also an excellent source for more information on theoretical and practical foundations of database systems.

4.2.2 SQL

We have seen how the data is stored in a relational database from the previous section. DB2 was used to view an entire table in a database. For more sophisticated manipulation and retrieval of data, one needs to use a database query language. The Structured Query Language (SQL) is the most commonly used in the relational database world.

SQL commands can be grouped into various categories: data retrieval, data manipulation, data transaction, data definition, and data control (Wikipedia 2006c). Data retrieval is the most frequently used function of SQL. The records are retrieved from a database using a SELECT statement. In a SELECT query, the user describes only the desired result set. A database management system such as DB2 optimizes the query into an efficient query plan. The following are commonly used keywords with a SELECT command:

- FROM indicates from which tables the data is to be taken.
- WHERE specifies which rows are to be retrieved.
- GROUP BY is used to combine rows with related values.
- HAVING functions much like a WHERE, but it operates on the results of the GROUP BY.
- ORDER BY is used to identify which columns are used to sort the resulting data.

Let us experiment with some simple SELECT statements using our sample database from DB2. Assuming that you are in the view shown in Figure 4.3, click on the query link in the bottom right panel. A "Command Editor" tab will be opened in your control center. (You can go back to the view from Figure 4.3 by clicking on the "Object View" tab.) The command editor will probably show the default query

SELECT * FROM PAWAN.DEPARTMENT;

The previous SELECT statement will essentially show us the entire DEPARTMENT table. The schema name "PAWAN" will almost definitely be different for you. Let us change the SELECT statement a bit as shown in **Figure 4.5**:

SELECT deptname FROM pawan.department;

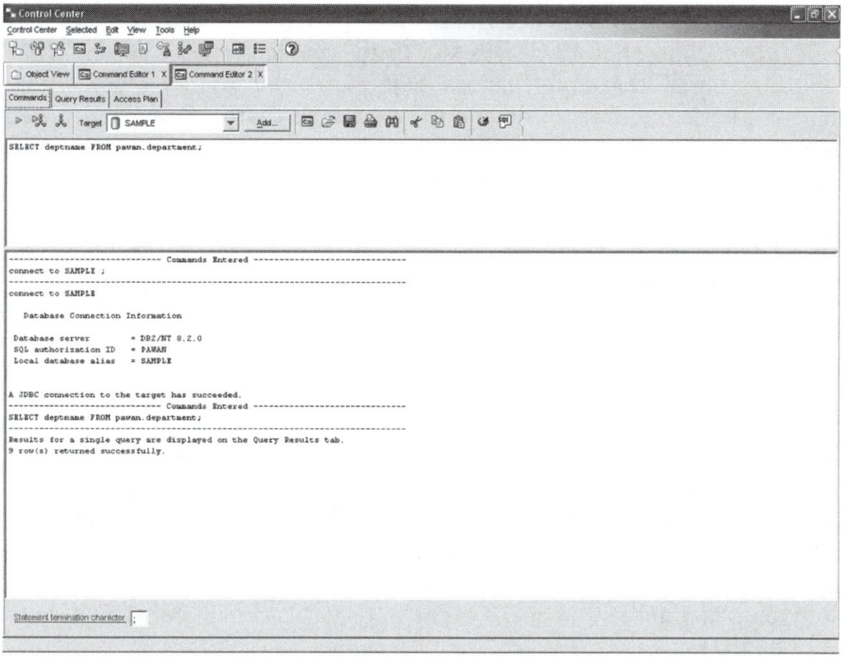

Figure 4.5 Simple SQL query

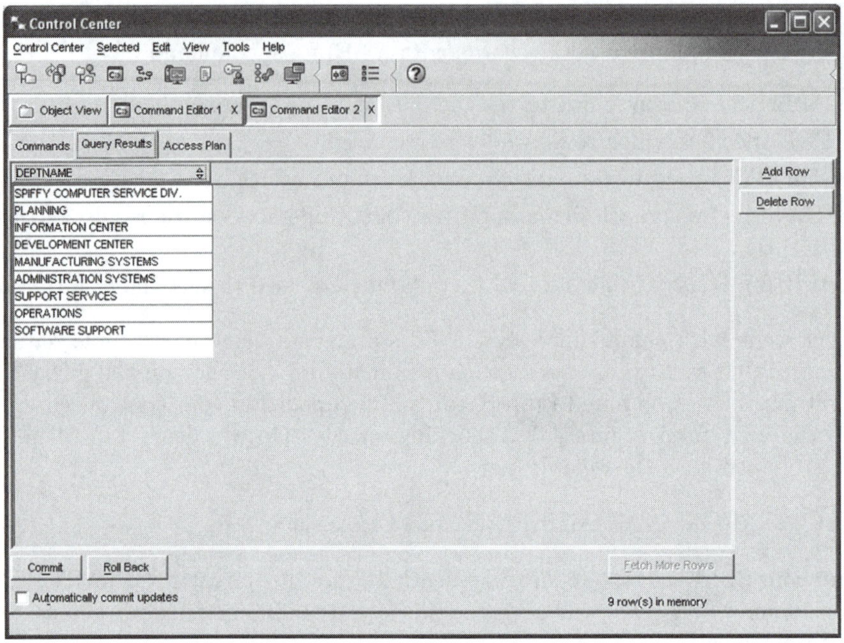

Figure 4.6 Results from the simple SQL query

After typing in this statement, click on the green play icon in the top toolbar. You will see the results of the query as shown in **Figure 4.6**. Again, you can adjust the size of the columns to get a complete view. Please note that the SQL statements are case insensitive. You may have also noticed the second level of tabs in the command center: Command, Query Results, and Access Plan. Click on the Command tab on the second level to go back to the SELECT statement. Let us try a more complicated query:

SELECT e.firstname,d.deptname

FROM pawan.department AS d, pawan.employee as e

WHERE e.workdept=d.deptno;

We want to see a list of employees (listed by their first names) and the department they are working in. The information resides in two tables: first name is in the "employee" table, while the name of the department is the "department" table. These two tables are logically linked through the department number, which is called "workdept" in the "employee" table and "deptno" in the "department" table. Therefore, the WHERE clause tells DB2 to ensure that the values for these two attributes match. In the previous query, we are using the alias "d" for the table pawan.department and "e" for pawan.employee. The use of aliases helps us save a bit of typing and makes the query easier to read. The results of the query can be seen in **Figure 4.7**.

We will return to the SELECT statement a little later in the chapter, when we start working with an e-Commerce database. Let us look at a summary of other SQL statements.

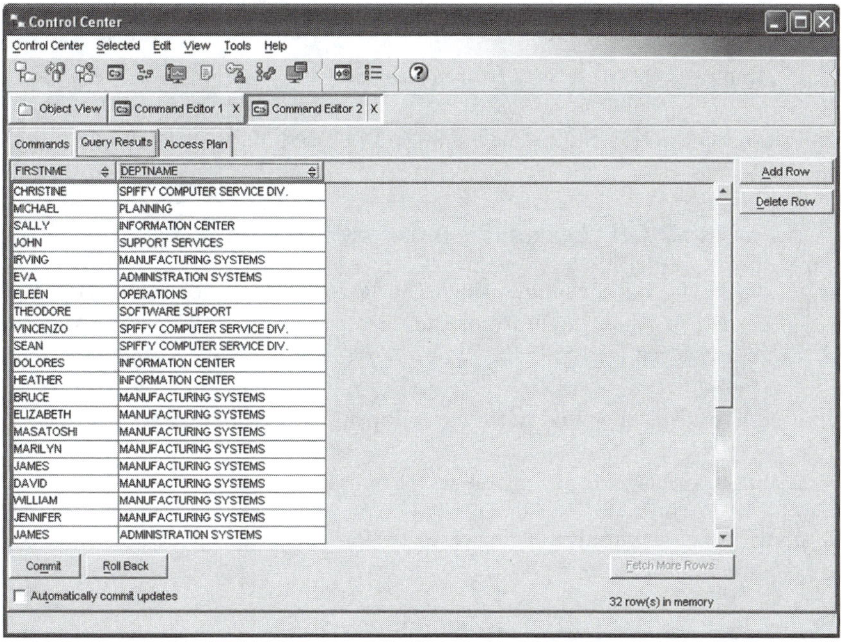

Figure 4.7 Results from the SQL query involving multiple tables

It should be noted that many of these statements are usually run through user interfaces such as the DB2 control center, so an average user usually does not have to explicitly type these statements. Nevertheless, we should be aware that these database operations could also be run through SQL statements. The following is a summary of these SQL statements obtained from Wikipedia (2006c). More details about these can be obtained through either Wikipedia or the DB2 documentation available on the CD.

The following data definition SQL commands are used to create, delete, and modify structures of tables in the database:

CREATE used for creating an object such as a table in the database.

DROP used for irretrievably deleting an object from the database.

ALTER permits modification of an existing object (for adding or deleting a column to an existing table).

The data manipulation statements add, update, and delete data.

INSERT Adds rows or tuples to an existing table.

UPDATE Used to modify the values of a set of existing table rows.

MERGE Used to combine the data of multiple tables.

TRUNCATE Deletes all data from a table.

DELETE   Removes existing rows from a table.

The following data transaction SQL statements can be used along with the data manipulation statements:

COMMIT   causes all data changes in a transaction to be made permanent.

ROLLBACK causes all data changes since the last COMMIT or ROLLBACK to be discarded, so that the state of the data is "rolled back" to the way it was prior to those changes.

The data control in SQL is specified with the following two statements:

GRANT   authorizes a user to perform a set of operations on an object.

REVOKE   restricts the capability of a user to perform a set of operations.

4.2.3   An E-Commerce Database

Let us try our database knowledge on a real-world dataset. The dataset that we will use was made available for the Knowledge Discovery from Databases (KDD) Cup Competition in 2000. The complete datasets can be downloaded only from the website: http://www.ecn.purdue. edu/KDDCUP/. You are required to sign a nondisclosure agreement in order to receive a password to access the data. The original restrictions were dramatically relaxed in April 2002 to allow wider use of the data. Basically, any use of the data is allowed as long as the proper acknowledgment is provided (Kohavi et al. 2000), and a copy of the work is provided to Blue Martini Software. The data consists of web clickstreams and purchase transactions collected by the Blue Martini Software application that ran at Gazelle.com (no longer operational), which sold legware and legcare products. **Figure 4.8** shows the homepage of Gazelle.com at the time of data collection in 2000. The data provided was collected directly at the store and is available with minimal cleaning.

We provide some processed data files that will make it easier for you to use the data for mining. We will focus our discussion around one dataset: http://www.ecn.purdue.edu/KDDCUP/ data/orders.zip

After you download the file and unzip it, you will see a folder called **order**, which contains two files: **question3.names** and **question3.data**. These two files were originally used to answer Question 3 from the KDD Cup 2000. Both the files are simple text files; however, the file **question3.data** is rather large. You can first open the file **question3.names**, which has the list of all the 232 attributes contained in the data stored in the file **question3.data**, using a text editor or word processor. The data file is best opened using a spreadsheet program such as Microsoft Excel. You should be able to use any other spreadsheet or database software as well. In Excel, choose the "Open" option from the "File" menu. Pick **question3.data** from the orders folder. You will see a text-import wizard as shown in **Figure 4.9**. Choose the "delimited" (see Figure 4.9) file type and click next. Choose "comma" as the delimiter as

Figure 4.8 Home page of Gazelle.com

shown in Figure 4.9 and click on the "Finish" button. The entire data should now be loaded in an Excel spreadsheet. The file is rather large, with 232 columns (going up to column HX in Excel) and 3465 rows.

In order to facilitate navigation, we have created an Excel file called `header.xls`, which you can find on the CD under Chapter 4, in a folder called "Support for KDD cup data." Open the file and select the first row by clicking on the button "1" for row 1, and copy it to the clipboard (by pressing "Ctrl-c"). Now go back to your `question3.data` file, choose "Insert/rows" and go to the newly created row and paste the header that was copied to the clipboard by pressing "Ctrl-v." Your file should now look as shown in **Figure 4.10**. Save the file as a Microsoft Excel document `question3.xls`. You can expand the columns to see their complete titles. Some of the titles are very long, and you may want to come up with shorter versions.

The file `question3.data` and other data from KDD Cup 2000 are a rich resource for data mining projects (see Exercises). We will focus on a small portion of the file in this chapter as well as in Chapter 5. The extracted file, shown in **Figure 4.11**, is available on the CD as `order15.xls`—under Chapter 4—in a folder called "Support for KDD cup data."

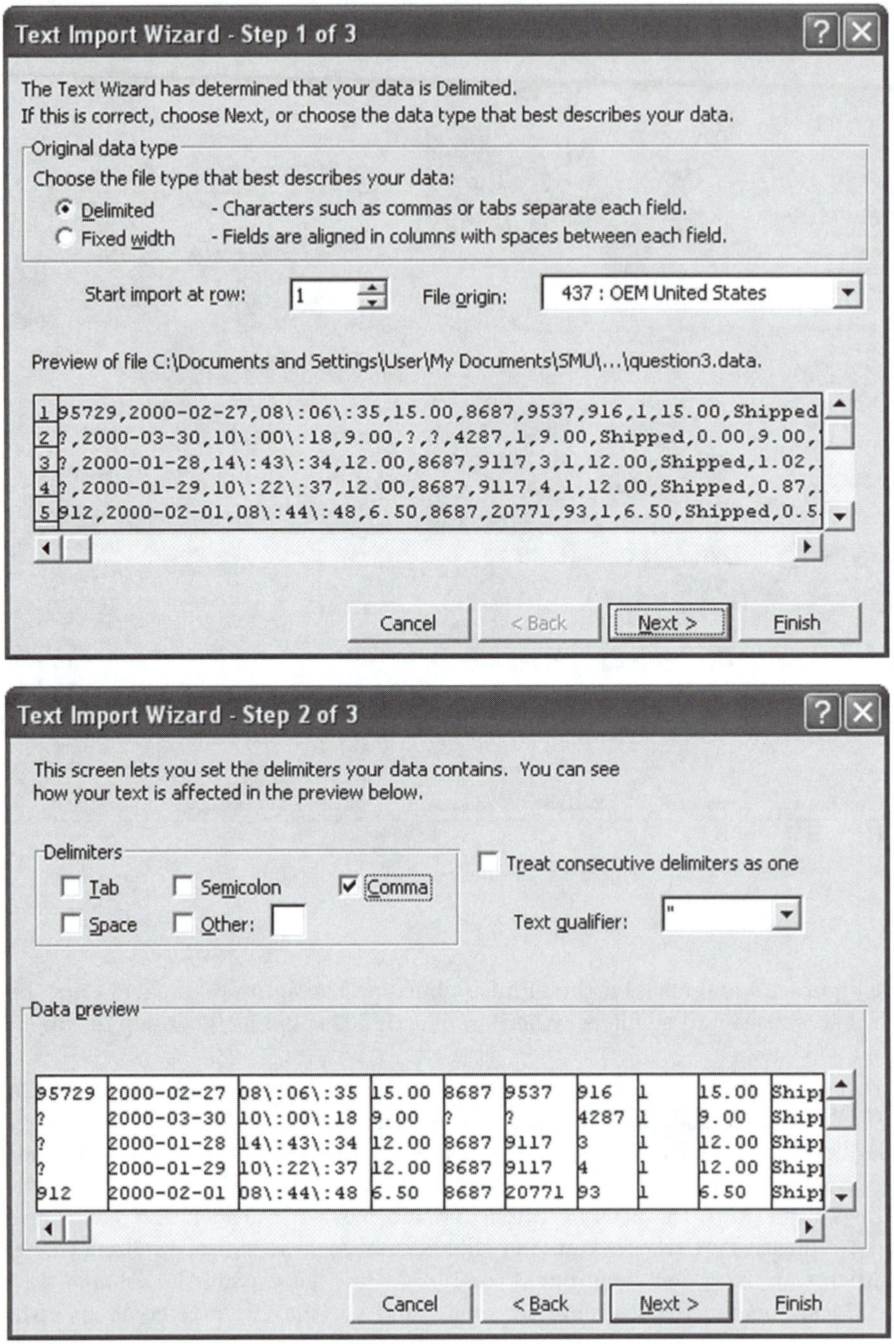

Figure 4.9 Importing KDD Cup data into Microsoft Excel

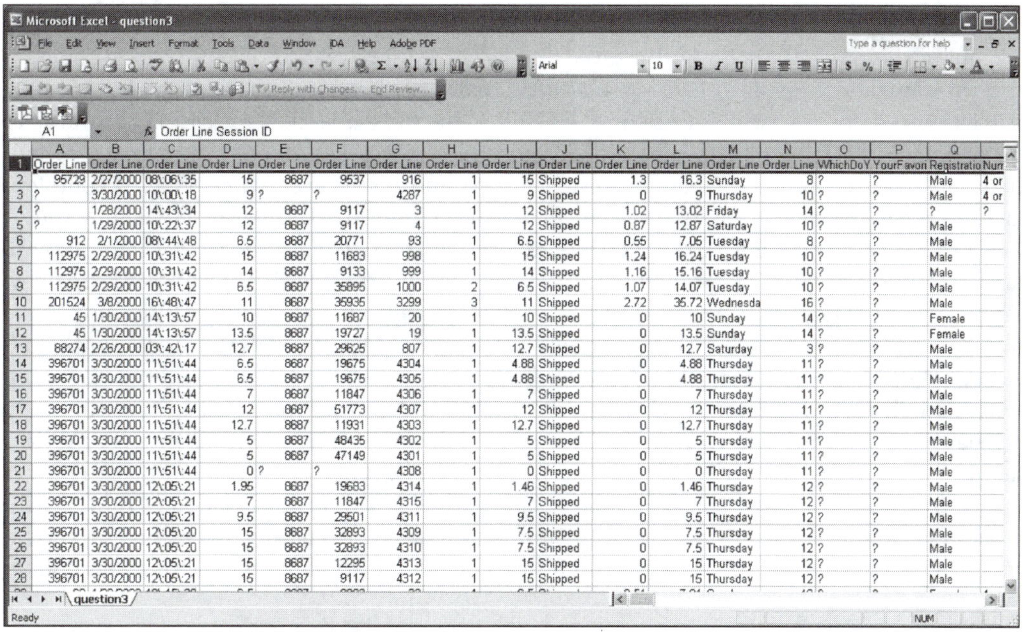

	A	B	C	D	E	F	G	H	I	J	K	L	M	N	O	P	Q	
1	Order Line	Order Line	Order Line	Order Line	Order Line	Order Line	Order Line	Order Line	Order Line	Order Line	Order Line	Order Line	Order Line	Order Line	WhichDoY	YourFavori	Registratio	Num
2	95729	2/27/2000	08\:06\:35	15	8687	9537	916	1	15	Shipped	1.3	16.3	Sunday	8	?	?	Male	4 or
3	?	3/30/2000	10\:00\:18	9	?	?	4287	1	9	Shipped	0	9	Thursday	10	?	?	Male	4 or
4	?	1/28/2000	14\:43\:34	12	8687	9117	3	1	12	Shipped	1.02	13.02	Friday	14	?	?	?	?
5	?	1/29/2000	10\:22\:37	12	8687	9117	4	1	12	Shipped	0.87	12.87	Saturday	10	?	?	Male	
6	912	2/1/2000	08\:44\:48	6.5	8687	20771	93	1	6.5	Shipped	0.55	7.05	Tuesday	8	?	?	Male	
7	112975	2/29/2000	10\:31\:42	15	8687	11683	998	1	15	Shipped	1.24	16.24	Tuesday	10	?	?	Male	
8	112975	2/29/2000	10\:31\:42	14	8687	9133	999	1	14	Shipped	1.16	15.16	Tuesday	10	?	?	Male	
9	112975	2/29/2000	10\:31\:42	6.5	8687	35895	1000	2	6.5	Shipped	1.07	14.07	Tuesday	10	?	?	Male	
10	201524	3/8/2000	16\:48\:47	11	8687	35935	3299	3	11	Shipped	2.72	35.72	Wednesda	16	?	?	Male	
11	45	1/30/2000	14\:13\:57	10	8687	11687	20	1	10	Shipped	0	10	Sunday	14	?	?	Female	
12	45	1/30/2000	14\:13\:57	13.5	8687	19727	19	1	13.5	Shipped	0	13.5	Sunday	14	?	?	Female	
13	88274	2/26/2000	03\:42\:17	12.7	8687	29625	807	1	12.7	Shipped	0	12.7	Saturday	3	?	?	Male	
14	396701	3/30/2000	11\:51\:44	6.5	8687	19675	4304	1	4.88	Shipped	0	4.88	Thursday	11	?	?	Male	
15	396701	3/30/2000	11\:51\:44	6.5	8687	19675	4305	1	4.88	Shipped	0	4.88	Thursday	11	?	?	Male	
16	396701	3/30/2000	11\:51\:44	7	8687	11847	4306	1	7	Shipped	0	7	Thursday	11	?	?	Male	
17	396701	3/30/2000	11\:51\:44	12	8687	51773	4307	1	12	Shipped	0	12	Thursday	11	?	?	Male	
18	396701	3/30/2000	11\:51\:44	12.7	8687	11931	4303	1	12.7	Shipped	0	12.7	Thursday	11	?	?	Male	
19	396701	3/30/2000	11\:51\:44	5	8687	48435	4302	1	5	Shipped	0	5	Thursday	11	?	?	Male	
20	396701	3/30/2000	11\:51\:44	5	8687	47149	4301	1	5	Shipped	0	5	Thursday	11	?	?	Male	
21	396701	3/30/2000	11\:51\:44	0	?	?	4308	1	0	Shipped	0	0	Thursday	11	?	?	Male	
22	396701	3/30/2000	12\:05\:21	1.95	8687	19683	4314	1	1.46	Shipped	0	1.46	Thursday	12	?	?	Male	
23	396701	3/30/2000	12\:05\:21	7	8687	11847	4315	1	7	Shipped	0	7	Thursday	12	?	?	Male	
24	396701	3/30/2000	12\:05\:21	9.5	8687	29501	4311	1	9.5	Shipped	0	9.5	Thursday	12	?	?	Male	
25	396701	3/30/2000	12\:05\:20	15	8687	32893	4309	1	7.5	Shipped	0	7.5	Thursday	12	?	?	Male	
26	396701	3/30/2000	12\:05\:20	15	8687	32893	4310	1	7.5	Shipped	0	7.5	Thursday	12	?	?	Male	
27	396701	3/30/2000	12\:05\:21	15	8687	12295	4313	1	15	Shipped	0	15	Thursday	12	?	?	Male	
28	396701	3/30/2000	12\:05\:21	15	8687	9117	4312	1	15	Shipped	0	15	Thursday	12	?	?	Male	

Figure 4.10 `question3.xls` file with column headers

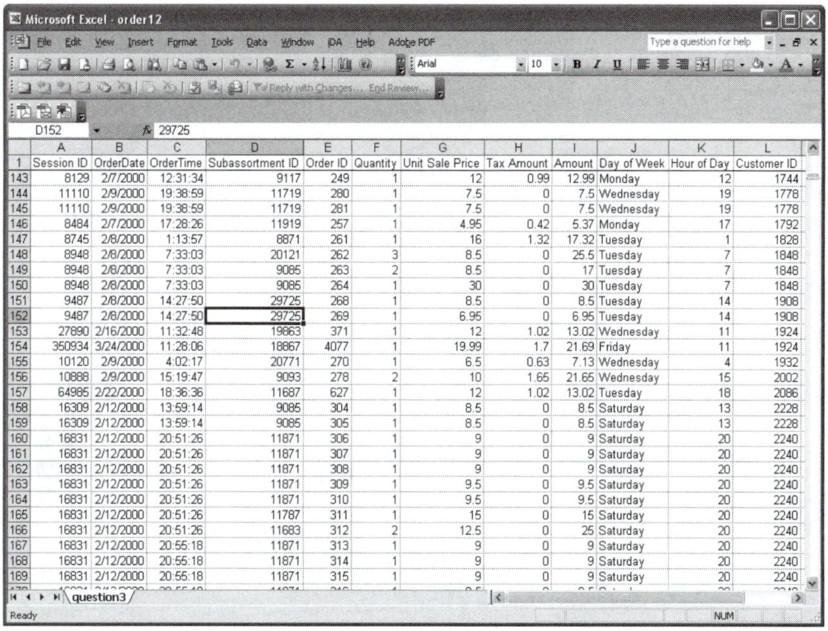

	A	B	C	D	E	F	G	H	I	J	K	L
1	Session ID	OrderDate	OrderTime	Subassortment ID	Order ID	Quantity	Unit Sale Price	Tax Amount	Amount	Day of Week	Hour of Day	Customer ID
143	8129	2/7/2000	12:31:34	9117	249	1	12	0.99	12.99	Monday	12	1744
144	11110	2/9/2000	19:38:59	11719	280	1	7.5	0	7.5	Wednesday	19	1778
145	11110	2/9/2000	19:38:59	11719	281	1	7.5	0	7.5	Wednesday	19	1778
146	8484	2/7/2000	17:28:26	11919	257	1	4.95	0.42	5.37	Monday	17	1792
147	8745	2/8/2000	1:13:57	8871	261	1	16	1.32	17.32	Tuesday	1	1828
148	8948	2/8/2000	7:33:03	20121	262	3	8.5	0	25.5	Tuesday	7	1848
149	8948	2/8/2000	7:33:03	9085	263	2	8.5	0	17	Tuesday	7	1848
150	8948	2/8/2000	7:33:03	9085	264	1	30	0	30	Tuesday	7	1848
151	9487	2/8/2000	14:27:50	29725	268	1	8.5	0	8.5	Tuesday	14	1908
152	9487	2/8/2000	14:27:50	29725	269	1	6.95	0	6.95	Tuesday	14	1908
153	27890	2/16/2000	11:32:48	19863	371	1	12	1.02	13.02	Wednesday	11	1924
154	350934	3/24/2000	11:28:06	18867	4077	1	19.99	1.7	21.69	Friday	11	1924
155	10120	2/9/2000	4:02:17	20771	270	1	6.5	0.63	7.13	Wednesday	4	1932
156	10888	2/9/2000	15:19:47	9093	278	2	10	1.65	21.65	Wednesday	15	2002
157	64985	2/22/2000	18:36:36	11687	627	1	12	1.02	13.02	Tuesday	18	2086
158	16309	2/12/2000	13:59:14	9085	304	1	8.5	0	8.5	Saturday	13	2228
159	16309	2/12/2000	13:59:14	9085	305	1	8.5	0	8.5	Saturday	13	2228
160	16831	2/12/2000	20:51:26	11871	306	1	9	0	9	Saturday	20	2240
161	16831	2/12/2000	20:51:26	11871	307	1	9	0	9	Saturday	20	2240
162	16831	2/12/2000	20:51:26	11871	308	1	9	0	9	Saturday	20	2240
163	16831	2/12/2000	20:51:26	11871	309	1	9.5	0	9.5	Saturday	20	2240
164	16831	2/12/2000	20:51:26	11871	310	1	9.5	0	9.5	Saturday	20	2240
165	16831	2/12/2000	20:51:26	11787	311	1	15	0	15	Saturday	20	2240
166	16831	2/12/2000	20:51:26	11683	312	2	12.5	0	25	Saturday	20	2240
167	16831	2/12/2000	20:55:18	11871	313	1	9	0	9	Saturday	20	2240
168	16831	2/12/2000	20:55:18	11871	314	1	9	0	9	Saturday	20	2240
169	16831	2/12/2000	20:55:18	11871	315	1	9	0	9	Saturday	20	2240

Figure 4.11 `order12.xls` file

We will use the processed data file to create a database for our experimentation. In order to simplify the process, we have also saved the data from `order12.xls` in a comma-separated form without the column headings in a file called `order12.csv` under the same folder, "Support for KDD cup data." We will discuss all the fields in the file while we are creating the database. Let us launch the DB2 control center. (Please exercise a certain amount of patience, as DB2 operations require significant computing resources, and hence need some time to complete). Choose "Basic View" for the control center, click on the "All Databases" folder in the left panel, and click on the link "Create new database" in the bottom right panel. Then type the name "orders" for the database and press the "Finish" button (as shown in **Figure 4.12**). It will take anywhere from 3 to 5 minutes as DB2 goes through all the required tasks involved in creating a database. Once it is done, you will see the newly created ORDERS database under the "All Databases" folder in the left panel. Expand the ORDERS database, open the Tables folder, and click on the "Create a New Table" link in the bottom right panel. You will get the table-creation dialogue box (**Figure 4.13**). You can keep the default schema name (PAWAN, in our case), and choose ORDERS12 as the table name. Clicking on "Next" will bring us to the next screen, which asks us to set up the structure of the table. Click on the "Add" button on the right and add the first attribute/column as shown in **Figure 4.14**. We will name the first attribute as SESSION_ID, and specify that it is a character attribute with a maximum length

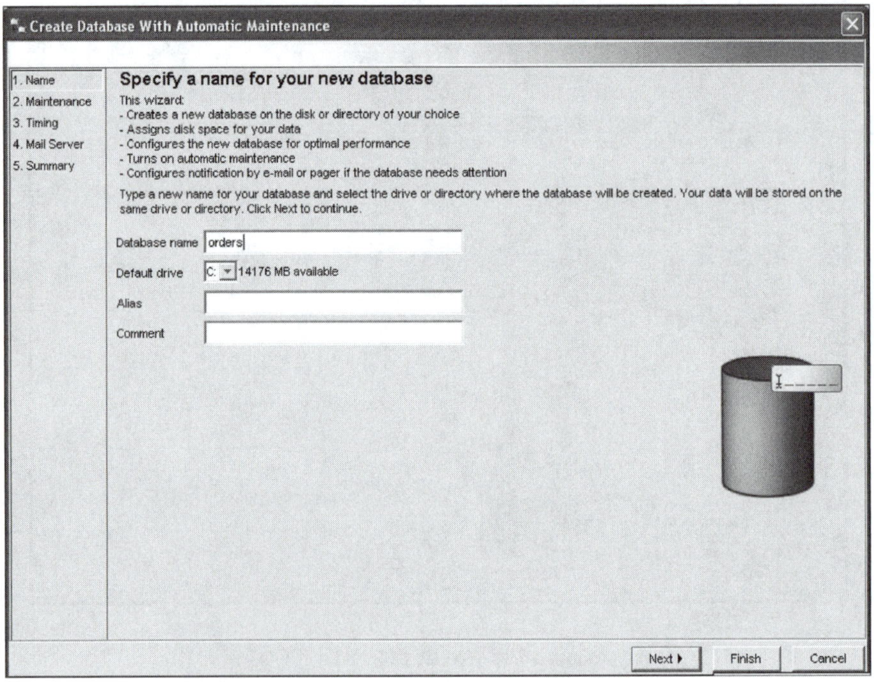

Figure 4.12 Creating ORDERS database in DB2

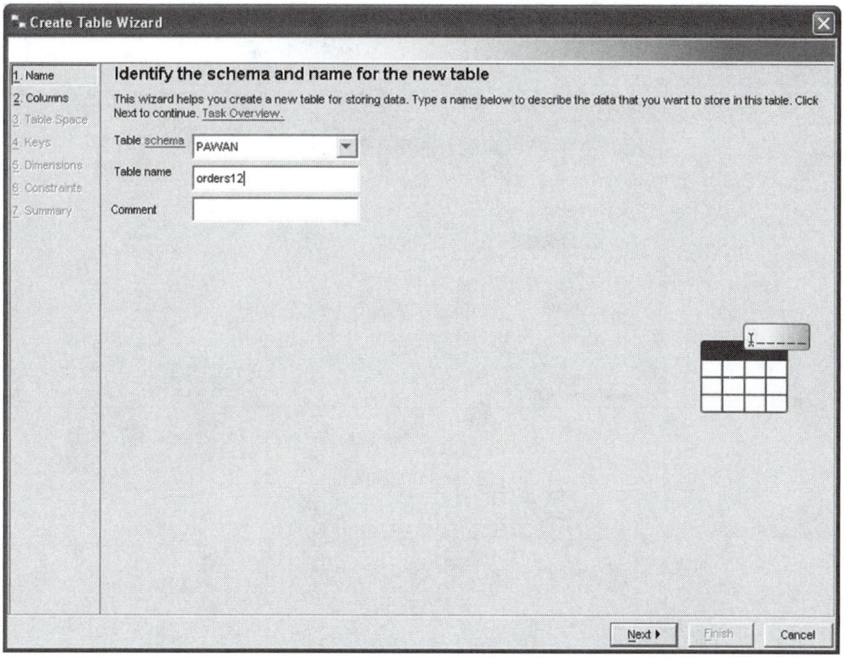

Create Table Wizard

Identify the schema and name for the new table

1. Name
2. Columns
3. Table Space
4. Keys
5. Dimensions
6. Constraints
7. Summary

This wizard helps you create a new table for storing data. Type a name below to describe the data that you want to store in this table. Click Next to continue. Task Overview.

Table schema   PAWAN

Table name   orders12

Comment

Next ▶   Finish   Cancel

Figure 4.13   Creating a table in the ORDERS database

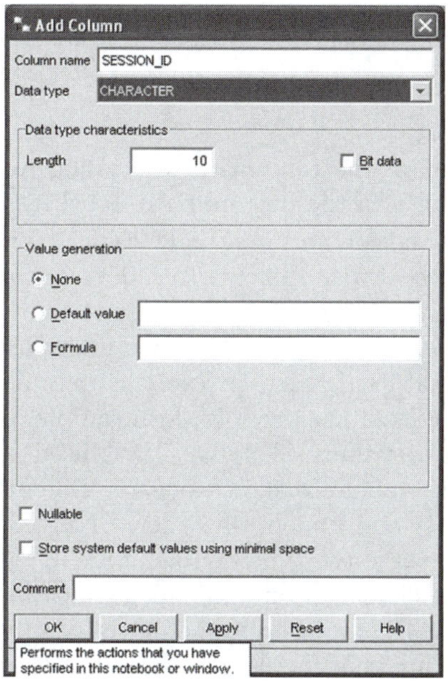

Add Column

Column name   SESSION_ID

Data type   CHARACTER

Data type characteristics

Length   10   ☐ Bit data

Value generation

◉ None

○ Default value

○ Formula

☐ Nullable

☐ Store system default values using minimal space

Comment

OK   Cancel   Apply   Reset   Help

Performs the actions that you have specified in this notebook or window.

Figure 4.14   Specifying attributes in the ORDERS12 table

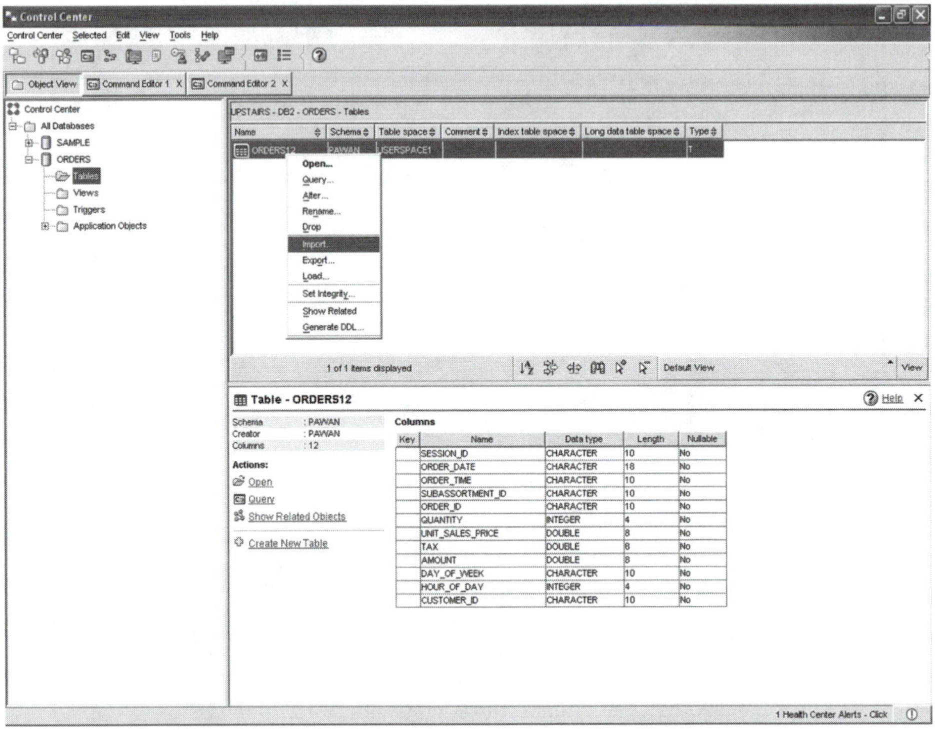

Figure 4.15   Structure of the ORDERS12 table and the menu of operations

of 10. Figure 4.15 shows the rest of the columns in the table. Add each one of the attributes using the type information shown in the bottom right panel from Figure 4.15.

Let us go through each of the columns and understand the information they contain. The following information might be a little difficult to follow, so we will follow it up with SQL queries, which will help our understanding. Every visit to the Gazelle.com website that concluded in purchase is a session, each session may have multiple orders, and there is a record for every order. Please note that each order corresponds to a unique product, but a customer may purchase multiple quantities of the product; for example, five bottles of the same lotion will have a single record. The attribute SESSION_ID is used to uniquely identify a session. All the unknown values in the table are shown by "?". The attributes ORDER_DATE and ORDER_TIME give us the date and time of the order. UNIT_LIST_PRICE is the price of the item stored as a real number using the type double. ASSORTMENT_ID and SUBASSORT-MENT_ID tell us the product classification and subclassification. Because most transactions have the same ASSORTMENT ID, we will retain only the SUBASSORTMENT_ID to identify the product. These are just numbers for us, so we really do not know what they actually mean. ORDER_ID gives us a unique transaction number per item purchased. Each session has multiple ORDER_IDs that are usually sequentially numbered. QUANTITY is an integer field that tells us how many items of that type were bought. TAX gives us the tax charged for that purchase. AMOUNT tells us the cost of the purchase. The meanings of DAY_OF_WEEK

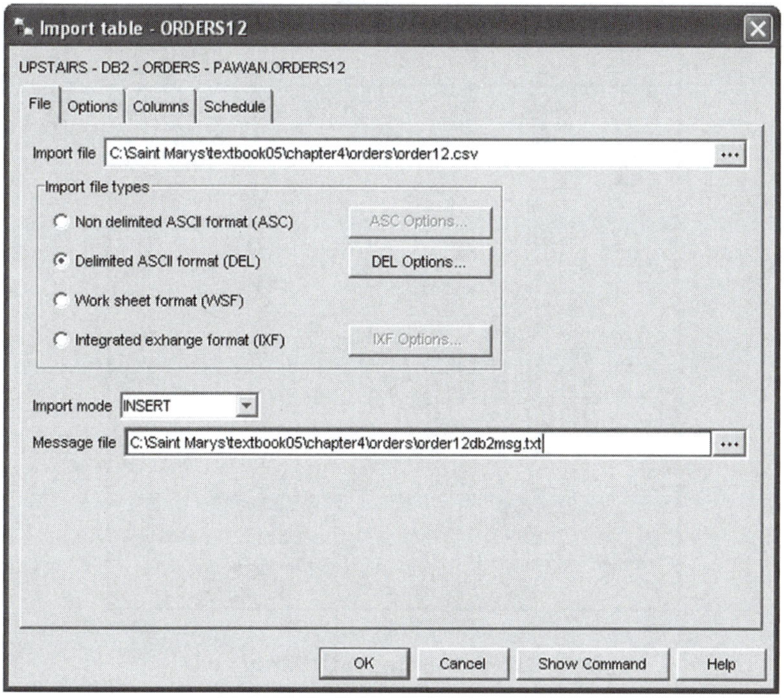

Figure 4.16 Importing data into the ORDERS12 table

and HOUR_OF_DAY are self-evident. Finally, CUSTOMER_ID allows us to uniquely identify a customer.

Now we are ready to populate the table with the records from the file `orders.csv`. Right clicking on the table ORDERS12 will give you a menu of operations. Pick "Import" as shown in Figure 4.15; it will bring up a dialogue box for importing (shown in **Figure 4.16**). Use the top browse button (marked " ... ") to specify where `orders12.csv` resides. You will also have to specify a filename, where DB2 will keep the log of error messages. Clicking on the "OK" button will start the importing process. Once the data is successfully imported, you can click on the table ORDERS12 in the top right panel of the control center, and then click on the "Open" link in the bottom right panel. You will see the table populated with the data similar to **Figure 4.17**.

Let us run some simple queries on ORDERS12 to understand the data. As before, click on the table ORDERS12 in the top right panel of control center, and then click on the "Query" link in the bottom right panel to launch the Command editor, and type the following query as shown in **Figure 4.18**:

SELECT   customer_id,SUM(amount) AS spending

GROUP BY customer_id

ORDER BY spending DESC;

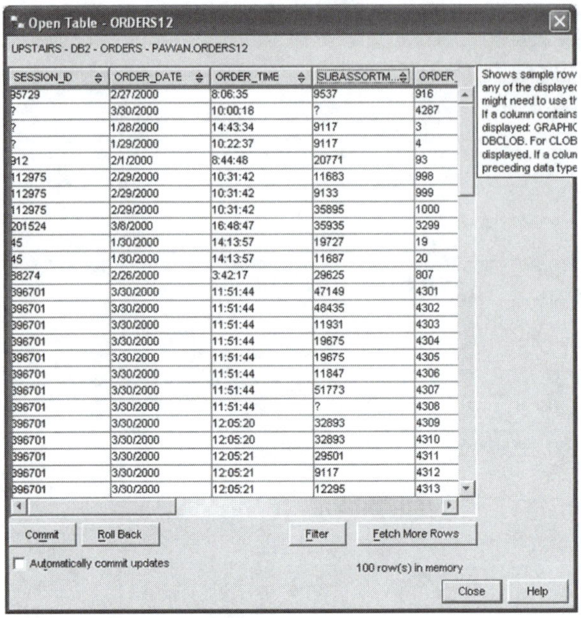

Figure 4.17 Populated ORDERS12 table

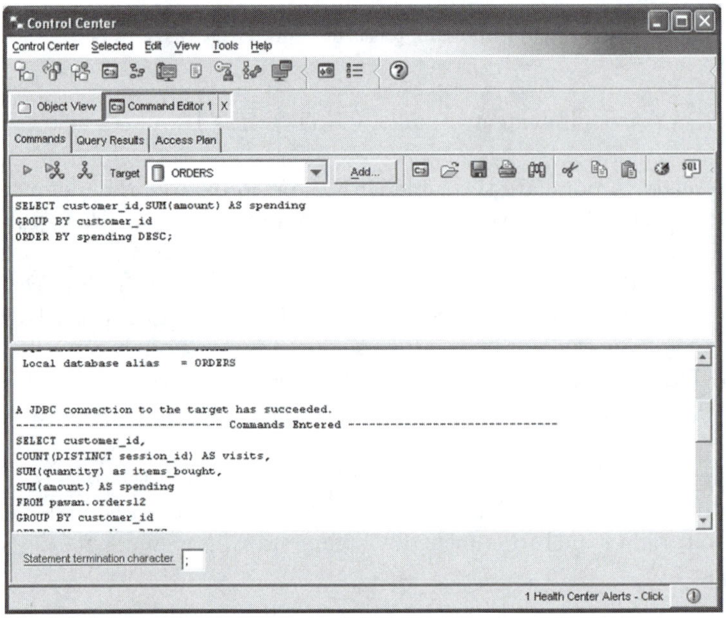

Figure 4.18 Query to get spending for each customer

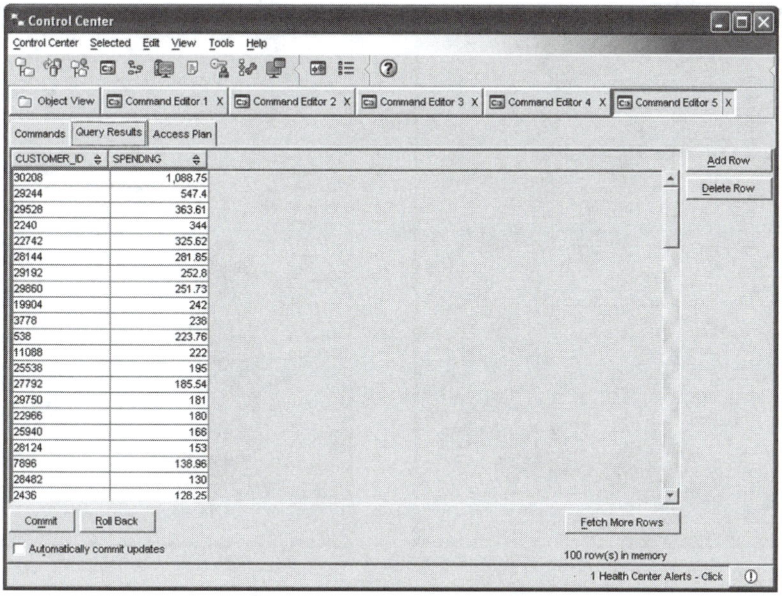

Figure 4.19 Spending for each customer

This query asks for a listing of CUSTOMER_ID and their total spending. The total spending is obtained by summing up the values of the column AMOUNT. "GROUP BY customer_id" tells DB2 how to perform the sum. "AS spending" gives an alias spending to the sum of amounts. Finally, "ORDER BY spending DESC" specifies that the results should be sorted in descending order based on spending. Clicking on the green "Play" button will execute the query, and another window will pop up as shown in **Figure 4.19**.

Let us try a few more queries, which will help us understand our database, as well as some additional SQL features. If you wish to find out how many customers are in the database, you can count distinct occurrences of customer_id as

SELECT count(DISTINCT customer_id)

FROM pawan.orders12;

If you type the previous query in your command editor, you should get 1831 as the result. Let us try to get a list of customers with their visits, number of items bought, and spending using the following query sorted in descending order by the spending:

SELECT   customer_id,

COUNT(DISTINCT session_id) AS visits,

SUM(quantity)   as items_bought,

SUM(amount) AS   spending

FROM   pawan.orders12

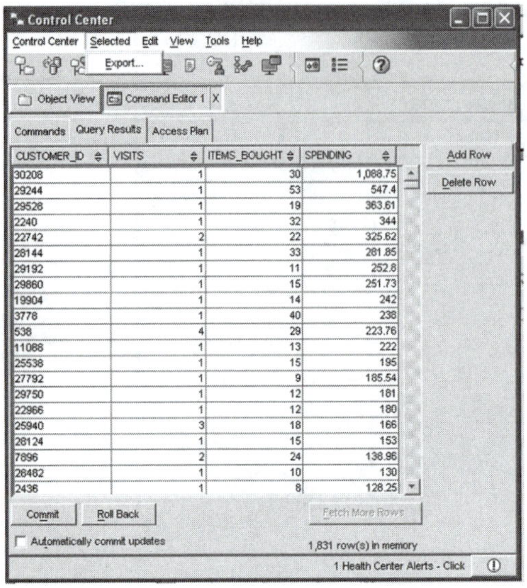

Figure 4.20 Listing of customer's visits, items, and spending

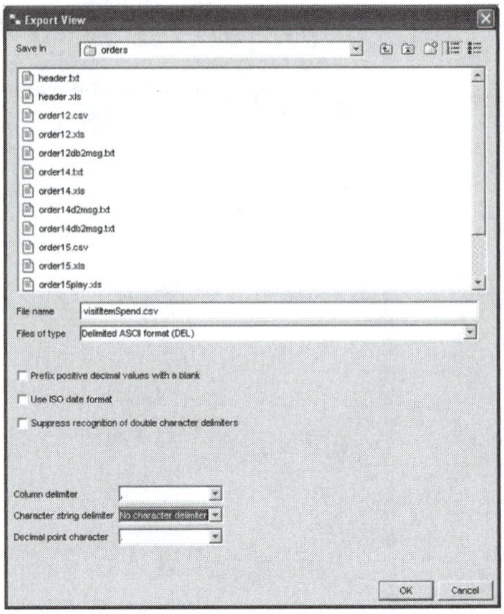

Figure 4.21 Export dialogue box in DB2

GROUP BY customer_id

ORDER BY spending DESC;

Type the previous query in your DB2 command editor to get the results as shown in **Figure 4.20**. By default, DB2 retrieves only the first 100 rows. If you keep on clicking "Fetch More Rows," you will get all 1831 rows. Once you have retrieved all the rows, export the results into a comma-separated file. Look at the top left corner in Figure 4.20 that shows how to call the "Export" option from the menu. When you choose the "Export" option, you will get the dialogue box as shown in **Figure 4.21**. Choose an appropriate directory (we recommend using the `orders` folder that was created before), and name the file `visitItemSpend.csv`. Make sure that you choose a comma for a column delimiter, not a character delimiter, and a period as the decimal point character, as the bottom portion of Figure 4.21 shows. Click on OK, and the results will be exported to a comma-separated text file that we can import into Excel for our data mining exercise. We will work on this file after we learn about classification in the next section.

4.3 Classification

The classification of large datasets is a very important problem in data mining. Classification decides which class a given record belongs to. Furthermore, classification is concerned with generating a description or a model for each class from the given dataset. Supervised classification is one of the most widely used classification paradigms. In supervised classification, we have a training dataset of records. The class for every record in the training dataset is known.

With the help of the training set, the classification process attempts to generate the description of the classes, which in turn helps to classify unknown records. A test dataset can also be used to determine the effectiveness of the classification. The classification tree or decision tree is one of several approaches to supervised classification.

Decision trees are powerful and popular tools for classification and prediction. The beauty of tree-based methods lies in their representation of *rules*, which can be readily expressed so that humans can understand them. They can also be expressed in a database language like SQL, so that records falling into a particular category may be retrieved.

In some applications, the accuracy of a classification or prediction is the only thing that matters. In certain circumstances, the ability to explain the reason for a decision is crucial; for example, in health insurance underwriting, there are legal prohibitions against discrimination based on certain variables. An insurance company could find itself in the position of having to demonstrate to the satisfaction of a court of law that it has not used illegal discriminatory practices in granting or denying coverage. There are a variety of algorithms for building decision trees that share the desirable trait of explicability. There are two specific requirements that should be taken into consideration while designing any decision tree algorithms for data mining. First, the method should efficiently handle very large databases. Moreover, the method should be able to handle categorical attributes. In this section, we will learn some basic features of decision tree construction and a generic algorithm for decision tree construction. We will also outline three important design considerations that should be taken into account while studying a particular algorithm. After a discussion on two useful measures, Entropy-based gain and the Gini Index, we shall study the method of determining splitting points for both numerical and categorical attributes.

4.3.1   ID3 Algorithm

ID3 (Quinlan 1986) represents concepts as decision trees. A decision tree is a classifier in the form of a tree structure where each node is either a *leaf node*, indicating a class of instances, or a *decision node*, which specifies a test to be carried out on a single attribute value, with one branch and a sub-tree for each possible outcome of the test. A decision tree can be used to classify an instance by starting at the root of the tree and moving through it down to a leaf node, which provides the classification of the instance.

As discussed earlier, the decision tree is a classification scheme that generates a tree and a set of rules, representing models of different classes, from a given dataset. The set of records available for developing such classification methods is generally divided into two disjoint subsets—a *training set* and a *test set*. The former is used for deriving the classifier, while the latter is used to measure the accuracy of the classifier, which is determined by the percentage of the test examples that are correctly classified.

One can categorize the attributes of the records into two different types. Attributes whose domain is numerical are called *numerical attributes,* and the attributes whose domain is not numerical are called *categorical attributes.* There is one distinguished attribute called the *class label.* The goal of the classification is to build a concise model that can be used to predict the class of the records whose class label is not known.

Example 4.1   In this popular example (Wikipedia 2006d), we will learn the concept of a decision tree. Let us consider two datasets, the training dataset (see **Table 4.3**) and the test dataset (see **Table 4.4**). The dataset has five attributes. There is a special attribute called *class*, which is the class label. The attributes *temp* and *humidity* are numerical attributes and the other attributes are categorical, which means they cannot be ordered. Based on the training dataset, we want to find a set of rules to know what values of *outlook, temperature, humidity,*

OUTLOOK	TEMP (F)	HUMIDITY (%)	WINDY	CLASS
Sunny	85	85	False	No play
Sunny	80	90	True	No play
Overcast	83	78	False	Play
Rain	70	96	False	Play
Rain	68	80	False	Play
Rain	65	70	True	No play
Overcast	64	65	True	Play
Sunny	72	95	False	No play
Sunny	69	70	False	Play
Rain	75	80	False	Play
Sunny	75	70	True	Play
Overcast	72	90	True	Play
Overcast	81	75	False	Play
Rain	71	80	True	No play

Table 4.3   Training dataset for playing golf

OUTLOOK	TEMP (F)	HUMIDITY (%)	WINDY	CLASS
Sunny	79	90	True	Play
Sunny	56	70	False	Play
Sunny	79	75	True	No play
Sunny	60	90	True	No play
Overcast	88	88	False	No play
Overcast	63	75	True	Play
Overcast	88	95	False	Play
Rain	78	60	False	Play
Rain	66	70	False	No play
Rain	68	60	True	Play

Table 4.4   Test dataset for playing golf

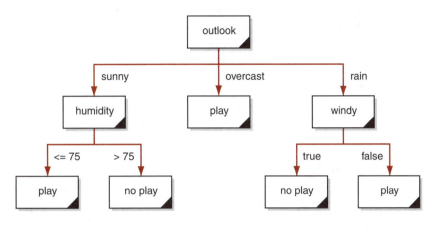

Figure 4.22 A sample decision tree

and *wind,* determine whether or not to play golf. **Figure 4.22** gives a sample decision tree for this description.

In Figure 4.22, we have five leaf nodes. In the decision tree, each leaf node represents a rule:

RULE 1 If it is sunny and the humidity is not above 75%, then play.

RULE 2 If it is sunny and the humidity is above 75%, then do not play.

RULE 3 If it is overcast, then play.

RULE 4 If it is rainy and not windy, then play.

RULE 5 If it is rainy and windy, then don't play.

Note that this may not be the best set of rules that can be derived from the given training dataset.

By traversing the tree from the root node to a leaf node, an unknown input vector is classified. A record enters the tree at the root node, where a test is applied to determine which child node the record will encounter next. This process is repeated until the record arrives at a leaf node. All the records that end up at a given leaf of the tree are classified in the same way. There is a unique path from the root to each leaf. The path is a rule that is used to classify the records. In the tree given in Figure 4.22, we can do the classification for an unknown record as follows.

Let us suppose that we know the values of the first four attributes for a record, but we do not know the value of the *class* attribute, as: Outlook = rain; temp = 70; humidity = 65; and windy = true.

Let us begin from the root node to verify the value of the associated attribute. This attribute is called the *splitting attribute.* In a decision tree, there is a splitting attribute associated with every node. In our example, *outlook* is the splitting attribute at the root. Because for the given record, *outlook = rain,* we go to the right-most child node of the root. At this node, the splitting attribute is *windy* and we find that for the record we want to classify, *windy = true.* Therefore, we move to the left child node to deduce that the class label is "no play." Here, each path from the root node to a leaf node signifies a rule.

Confidence in the classifier is determined by the percentage of the test dataset that is correctly classified. Consider the test dataset given in Table 4.4. We can see that for Rule 1, there are two records of the test dataset satisfying *outlook = sunny* and *humidity* ≤ 75, and only one of these is correctly classified as *play.* Thus, the confidence in this rule is 0.5 (50%). Similarly, the confidence in Rule 2 is also 0.5, and the confidence in Rule 3 is 0.66 (or 66%).

Example 4.2   Consider the training dataset given in **Table 4.5**. There are three attributes: *age, zip,* and *class.* The attribute *class* is used for the class label.

The attribute *age* is a numeric attribute, whereas *zip* is a categorical one. Even if the domain of *zip* is numeric, no ordering can be defined among ZIP values. You cannot derive any useful information if one ZIP code is greater than another. **Figure 4.23** gives a decision tree for this training dataset.

The splitting attribute at the root is *zip,* and the splitting criterion here is *zip* = 500046. Likewise, the splitting criterion is *age* < 48 (the splitting attribute is *age)* for the left child node. Although the right child node has the same attribute as the splitting attribute, the splitting criterion is distinct.

Many decision tree building algorithms start with finding the test that does the best job of splitting the records among the required categories. The tree continues to grow until it is no longer possible to find better ways to split up incoming records, or when all the records are in one class. In Figure 4.23, we see that at the root level we have nine records. The associated splitting criterion is *zip* = 500046. As a result, we split the records into two subsets, Records

ID	AGE	ZIP	CLASS
1	30	5600046	C1
2	25	5600046	C1
3	21	5600023	C2
4	43	5600046	C1
5	18	5600023	C2
6	33	5600023	C1
7	29	5600023	C1
8	55	5600046	C2
9	48	5600046	C1

Table 4.5   Training dataset for zip code and age

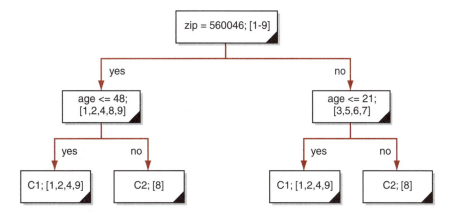

Figure 4.23   Decision tree for zip code and age

1, 2, 4, 8, and 9 are to the left child node and the remaining to the right node. This process is repeated at every node.

You may have noticed that the decision tree construction process is concerned with identifying the splitting attributes and splitting criteria at every level of the tree. The goal of the decision tree construction process is to generate simple, logical rules with high accuracy. Occasionally altering the tree through pruning and grafting can enhance the classification efficiency of the tree. These processes are activated after the decision tree is constructed. Some of the desired properties of decision tree generating methods should be able to handle both numerical and the categorical attributes and provide a clear indication of which fields are most important for prediction or classification.

Demerits of certain decision trees are that they can deal with only binary-valued target classes, and their development procedure is computationally expensive. At each node, each candidate splitting field is examined before the best split can be found.

We are now familiar with the basic features of decision trees. Next, we shall learn the techniques of constructing trees from a given training dataset. All the decision tree construction techniques are based on the principle of recursively partitioning the data set until homogeneity is achieved. The construction of the decision tree involves the following three major phases:

- *Construction phase.* This is where the initial decision tree is constructed on the entire training dataset. It requires recursively partitioning the training set into two or more subsets using a splitting criterion, until a stopping criterion is met.
- *Pruning phase.* The tree constructed in the previous phase may not result in the best possible set of rules due to overfitting. Pruning removes some of the lower branches and nodes to improve its performance.
- *Processing phase.* The pruned tree is further processed to improve understandability.

Though these three phases are common to most of the well-known algorithms, some algorithms attempt to integrate the first two phases into a single process.

The construction phase of many of the existing algorithms use *Hunt's method* as the essential notion. Let T be the training dataset with the class labels $\{C_1, C_2, ..., C_n\}$. The tree is built by repeatedly partitioning the training data, using criteria such as the goodness of the split. The process is continued until all the records in a partition belong to the same class.

T is homogeneous: T contains cases all belonging to a single class C_j. The decision tree for T is a leaf identifying class C_j.

T is not homogeneous: T contains cases that belong to a mixture of classes. A test is selected, based on a single attribute, that has one or more mutually exclusive outcomes $\{O_1, O_2, ..., O_n\}$. T is partitioned into the subsets $T_1, T_2, ..., T$, where T_j contains all those cases in T that have the outcome O_i of the chosen test. The decision tree for T consists of a decision node identifying the test and one branch for each possible outcome. The same tree building method is applied recursively to each subset of training cases. Most often, n is chosen to be 2, and therefore the algorithm generates a binary decision tree.

T is trivial: T contains no cases. The decision tree T is a leaf, but the class to be associated with the leaf must be determined from information other than T.

The basic algorithm of decision tree construction outlines the common principle used in all the algorithms. However, the subsequent features should be taken into consideration while learning a particular algorithm.

To build an optimal decision tree, it is necessary to select attributes that provide the best possible split. The main features during the tree building are as follows:

1. Evaluation of splits for each attribute and the selection of the best split, i.e., determination of the splitting attribute.

2. Determination of the splitting condition on the selected splitting attribute.

3. Partitioning the data using the best split.

The splitting depends on the domain of the attribute being numerical or categorical. The generic algorithm for the construction of decision trees assumes that the method to decide the splitting attribute at a node, as well as the splitting criteria, is known. The complexity lies in determining the best split for each attribute. The desirable feature of splitting is that it should do the best job of splitting at the given stage.

The first task is to decide which of the independent attributes makes the best splitter. The best split is defined as one that does the best job of separating the records into groups, where a single class predominates. To choose the best splitter at a node, we consider each independent attribute in turn.

Assuming that an attribute takes on multiple values, we sort it and then, using an evaluation function as the measure of goodness, evaluate each split. We compare the effectiveness of the split provided by the best splitter from each attribute. The winner is chosen as the splitter for the root node. How does one know which split is better than the other? We will study two distinct evaluation functions to decide the splitting attributes and the splitting criteria.

Entropy gives an information-theoretic approach to measure the goodness of a split. Let us suppose that there are n equally probable possible messages. The probability p of each message is $1/n$, and thus the information conveyed by a message is $-\log_2(p) = \log_2(n)$. If there are 16 messages, then because $\log_2(16) = 4$, we need 4 bits to identify each message. Hereafter, let us assume that all logarithms are to the base 2.

Definition 4.1 If we are given the probability distribution $P = (p_1, p_2, ..., p_n)$, then the information communicated by this distribution, called the entropy of P, is

$$Entropy(P) = -p_1 \log(p_1) - p_2 \log(p_2) - ... - p_n \log(p_n)$$

For example, if P is (0.5, 0.5), then $Entropy(P)$ is 1; if P is (0.67, 0.33), then $Entropy(P)$ is 0.92; if p is (1, 0), then $Entropy(P)$ is 0. That means, the more uniform the probability distribution, the greater is its entropy.

In the context of decision trees, if the outcome of a node is to classify the records into two classes, C_1 and C_2, the outcome can be viewed as a message that is being generated and the entropy gives the measure of information for the message to be C_1 or C_2. If a set of records T is partitioned into a set of disjoint exhaustive classes $C_1, C_2... ,C_n$ on the basis of the value of the class attribute, then the information needed to identify the class of an element of T is

$$Info(T) = Entropy(P),$$

where P is the probability distribution of the partition $C_1, C_2... ,C_n$. P is computed based on their relative frequencies; that is,

$$P = \left(\frac{|C_1|}{|T|}, \frac{|C_2|}{|T|}, ..., \frac{|C_n|}{|T|} \right)$$

Suppose that a dataset has three distinct classes, C_1, C_2, and C_3. Let these categories have 40, 30, and 30 objects respectively; thus, the value of the entropy of the whole dataset is

$$Info(T) = -\frac{40}{100} \log \frac{40}{100} - \frac{30}{100} \log \frac{30}{100} - \frac{30}{100} \log \frac{30}{100}$$

$$Info(T) = -0.4 \times -1.322 - 0.3 \times -1.737 - 0.3 \times -1.737$$

$$Info(T) = 1.57$$

If T is partitioned based on the value of the nonclass attribute X, into sets $T_1, T_2, ...T_n$, then the information needed to identify the class of an element of T becomes the weighted average of the information to identify the class of the element of T_i; that is, the weighted average of $Info(T_i)$.

$$Info(X, T) = \sum_{i=1}^{n} \frac{|T_i|}{|T|} Info(T_i)$$

Now let us consider splitting the dataset into two subsets, S_1, and S_2, with n_1 and n_2 number of records, respectively, where $n_1 + n_2 = n$. If we assume $n_1 = 60$ and $n_2 = 40$, the splitting can be given by

S_2	C_1	C_2	C_3
40	0	20	20

S_1	C_1	C_2	C_3
60	40	10	10

The entropy index value of the dataset after the segmentation is

$$\frac{40}{100}\left(-\frac{20}{40}\log\frac{20}{40}-\frac{20}{40}\log\frac{20}{40}\right)+\frac{60}{100}\left(-\frac{40}{60}\log\frac{40}{60}-\frac{10}{60}\log\frac{10}{60}-\frac{10}{60}\log\frac{10}{60}\right)$$

$$=\frac{40}{100}(0.5+0.5)+\frac{60}{100}(0.39+0.43+0.43)$$

$$=0.4+0.75=1.15$$

Definition 4.2 We define the *information gain* due to a split on attribute X as

$$Gain(X, T) = Info(T) - Info(X, T).$$

The information gain represents the difference between the information needed to identify an element of T and the information needed to identify an element of T after the value of attribute X is obtained.

In the previous example, splitting decreases the value of the entropy by 0.42. That means the gain is 0.42. Let us consider another splitting as follows:

S_2	C_1	C_2	C_3
40	20	10	10

S_1	C_1	C_2	C_3
60	20	20	20

In this case, the value of the associated entropy is 1.5596 and the gain is 0.0104. Thus, we can use this notion of gain to rank attributes and to build decision trees, where at each node the attribute with the greatest gain becomes the splitting attribute.

The concept of *gain* tends to support attributes that have a large number of values. For example, if we have an attribute X that has a distinct value for each record, then $Info(X,T)$ is 0, thus $Gain(X,T)$ is maximal. We noticed this for the attribute *humidity* in our golf example. To balance this, Quinlan proposes using the gain-ratio instead of gain:

$$Gain\_ratio(X,T) = \frac{Gain(X,T)}{Info(X,T)}.$$

One of its virtues relates to the low measure of diversity. There are several ways of calculating the index of diversity for a set of records. With all of them, a high index of diversity indicates that the set contains an even distribution of classes; while a low index means that members of a single class predominate. The best splitter is one that decreases the diversity of the record sets by the greatest amount. This means we want to maximize

$$diversity(before\ split) - (diversity(left\ child) + diversity(right\ child)).$$

The *gini* index is a diversity measure from economics. It can also be used to evaluate the virtue of a split.

Definition 4.3 If a dataset T contains n classes, then *gini(T)* is defined as

$$gini(T) = 1 - \sum p_i^2,$$

where p_i is the relative frequency of class j in T.

If the split divides T into T_1 and T_2, then the index of the divided data is given as

$$gini_{split}(T) = \frac{n_1}{n} gini(T_1) + \frac{n_2}{n} gini(T_2).$$

While determining the splitting attribute, we should also keep in mind the splitting criterion. For example, some algorithms generate only binary decision trees. These algorithms carry out only binary splits. This does not pose a problem if the domain of the splitting attribute is binary; but, if the attribute that is selected for splitting takes more than two values, takes continuous values, or is a categorical attribute, a binary split inevitably implies that we must determine the splitting criterion.

The numerical attributes are split by the binary split of the form $A \leq v$, where v is a real number. All the numerical attributes are sorted on the values of the attribute being considered for splitting. Let $A_1, A_2, ..., A_n$ be the sorted values of a numerical attribute A. Because any value between A_i and A_{i+1} divides the data into two subsets, we need to examine only $n - 1$ possible splits. The midpoint of A_i and A_{i+1} is taken as the split point; thus, while computing the splitting index, we take into account this candidate split points and determine the split points corresponding to the best split.

The splitting point for categorical attributes is different. Because we cannot have any ordering of the values of a categorical attribute, there cannot be a value n such that it splits the attribute into two. If $S(A)$ is the set of possible values of the categorical attribute A, then the split test is of the form $A \in S'$, where $S' \subset S$. For an attribute with n values, there are 2^n possible splits. If n is small, the split index value is found for all the possible combinations and the best split is taken. If n is large, then the split is made by some heuristics and the best split among them is found. The construction of an attribute list is similar to that of numerical attributes. But instead of having a class histogram, a count matrix is maintained for the categorical attribute.

To summarize, there are several algorithms proposed for decision tree construction. These algorithms relatively follow the principles discussed previously. However, they differ among themselves in the methods employed for selecting splitting attributes and splitting conditions. Quinlan introduced the Iterative Dichotomizer 3 (ID3) for constructing the decision trees from data. Here, each node corresponds to a splitting attribute, and each arc is a possible value of that attribute. At every node the splitting attribute is selected to be the most informative among the attributes not yet considered in the path from the root. Entropy is used to measure how informative a node is. The algorithm uses the criterion of information gain to determine the virtue of a split. The attribute with the largest information gain is selected as the splitting attribute, and the dataset is split for all distinct values of the attribute. This algorithm is extended to a version called C4.5, which accounts for unavailable values, continuous attribute value ranges, pruning of decision trees, and rule derivation.

4.3.1.1   Numerical Illustration

In Example 4.1 on golf playing, we had

$$Info(T) = Entropy\left(\frac{9}{14}, \frac{5}{14}\right) = -\frac{9}{14}\log\frac{9}{14} - \frac{5}{14}\log\frac{5}{14} = 0.94.$$

Let us consider the attribute *outlook*. It has three distinct values: sunny, overcast, and rain, with 5, 4, and 5 records, respectively. Among the five records that have *outlook = sunny*, two records are in the *play* class and three are in the *no play* class. Thus, these five records have a distribution (3/5, 2/5). Similarly, the distributions for *overcast* and *rain* are (1, 0) and (3/5, 2/5), respectively. Therefore,

$$Info(Outlook, T) = \sum_{i=1}^{3} \frac{|T_i|}{|T|} Info(T_i)$$

$$= \frac{5}{14} Info\left(\frac{3}{5}, \frac{2}{5}\right) + \frac{4}{14} Info(1,0) + \frac{5}{14} Info\left(\frac{3}{5}, \frac{2}{5}\right)$$

$$= \frac{5}{14}\left(-\frac{3}{5}\log\frac{3}{5} - \frac{2}{5}\log\frac{2}{5}\right) + \frac{4}{14} \times 0 + \frac{5}{14}\left(-\frac{3}{5}\log\frac{3}{5} - \frac{2}{5}\log\frac{2}{5}\right)$$

$$= 0.694$$

This means $Gain(outlook, T) = Info(T) - Info(outlook, T) = 0.94 - 0.694 = 0.246$.

Let us consider the attribute *humidity*. If we take all the distinct numeric values of this attribute, there are nine values such as 65, 70, 75, 78, 80, 85, 90, 95, and 96, with frequencies 1, 3, 1, 1, 3, 1, 2, 1, and 1, respectively. We ignore the values with zero frequencies, because the *Info* for them is zero. Thus,

$$Info(humidity, T) = \frac{3}{14}\left(-\frac{2}{3}\log\frac{2}{3} - \frac{1}{3}\log\frac{1}{3}\right) + \frac{3}{14}\left(-\frac{2}{3}\log\frac{2}{3} - \frac{1}{3}\log\frac{1}{3}\right)$$

$$+ \frac{2}{14}\left(-\frac{1}{2}\log\frac{1}{2} - \frac{1}{2}\log\frac{1}{2}\right)$$

$$= 0.5364$$

$$Gain(humidity, T) = Info(T) - Info(humidity, T) = 0.94 - 0.5364 = 0.4036.$$

The gain for *humidity* is higher than that for *outlook*; but the number of branches is high, and therefore is not practical.

Let us categorize these values into two sets, *high* and *low*, such that the value exceeding 75 is said to be of high humidity or else, it is of low humidity. There are nine records with high humidity, four of which are in the *no play* class and five are in the *play* class. Similarly, out of the five records with low humidity, one is in the *no play* class and the remaining four are in the *play* class. In such a situation, the gain is calculated as follows:

$$Info(humidity, T) = \frac{9}{14}\left(-\frac{4}{9}\log\frac{4}{9} - \frac{5}{9}\log\frac{5}{9}\right) + \frac{5}{14}\left(-\frac{4}{5}\log\frac{4}{5} - \frac{1}{5}\log\frac{1}{5}\right) = 0.89$$

Therefore, the gain is $0.94 - 0.89 = 0.05$.

For the attribute *windy*, we have the following expression:

$$Info(windy, T) = \frac{6}{14}\left(-\frac{3}{6}\log\frac{3}{6} - \frac{3}{6}\log\frac{3}{6}\right) + \frac{8}{14}\left(-\frac{6}{8}\log\frac{6}{8} - \frac{2}{8}\log\frac{2}{8}\right) = 0.89$$

Therefore, the gain is $0.94 - 0.89 = 0.05$.

Finally, for the attribute *temperature,* we have

$$Info(temp, T) = \frac{8}{14}\left(-\frac{5}{8}\log\frac{5}{8} - \frac{3}{8}\log\frac{3}{8}\right) + \frac{6}{14}\left(-\frac{4}{6}\log\frac{4}{6} - \frac{2}{6}\log\frac{2}{6}\right) = 0.93$$

So, the gain is $0.94 - 0.93 = 0.01$.

Splitting on the *outlook* attribute gives the maximum gain; therefore, the root node is expanded with three child nodes, one for each value of *outlook*. The dataset is also partitioned into three subsets, where one subset is associated with each child node. The algorithm proceeds recursively until the termination criterion is met.

Let us calculate the gain ratio for *outlook*:

$$Gain\_ratio(outlook, T) = \frac{Gain(outlook, T)}{Info(outlook, T)} = \frac{0.246}{0.694} = 0.3544$$

The *gini* index will then be:

$$gini(T) = 1 - \left[\frac{9}{14}\right]^2 - \left[\frac{5}{14}\right]^2 = 0.46.$$

Therefore, the *gini* index due to splitting on *outlook* is now

$$gini_{outlook}(T) = \frac{5}{14}\left[1 - \left[\frac{3}{5}\right]^2 - \left[\frac{2}{5}\right]^2\right] + \frac{4}{14}[1 - 1] + \frac{5}{14}\left[1 - \left[\frac{3}{5}\right]^2 - \left[\frac{2}{5}\right]^2\right] = 0.343$$

4.3.2 Rough Set Theory

Rough set theory is a useful means for studying delivery patterns, rules, and knowledge in data. The rough set is the estimate of a vague concept by a pair of specific concepts, called the lower and upper approximations. The classification model signifies our knowledge about the domain.

Let us assume that our set of interest is the set S, and we understand which sample elements are in S. We would like to define S in terms of the attributes. The membership of objects with respect to a random subset of the domain may not be definable. This fact gives rise to the definition of a set in terms of lower and upper approximations. The *lower approximation* is a type of the domain objects that are known with certainty to belong to the subset of interest. The *upper approximation* is a description of the objects that may perhaps belong to the subset. Any subset defined through its lower and upper approximations is called a *rough set*, if the boundary region is not empty. We present the formal definition of this concept in the following paragraph.

Suppose an equivalence relation, θ on U, is a binary relation that is transitive, reflexive, and symmetric. In rough set theory, an equivalence relation is known as an *indiscernibility relation*. The pair (U, θ) is called an approximation space. With each equivalence relation θ, there is a partition of U such that two elements x, y in U are in the same class in this partition, if and only if $x\theta y$. Let us represent a class in the partition due to θ, as $\theta_x = \{y \in U | x\theta y\}$. For a subset $X \subseteq U$, we say that

- $\underline{X} = \bigcup \{\theta_x | \theta_x \subseteq X\}$, is said to be the lower approximation or positive region of X.
- $\overline{X} = \bigcup \{\theta_x | x \in X\}$, is said to be the upper approximation or possible region of X.
- The *rough set* of X is the pair $(\underline{X}, \overline{X})$.
- $\underline{X} - \overline{X}$ is the area of uncertainty.
- $\underline{X} \cup (U - \overline{X})$ is said to be the region of certainty.

Figure 4.24 illustrates the concept of rough set theory pictorially.

We can describe rough set theory using a database T, which is a set of tuples. The set of attributes on these tuples is defined as $A = \{A_1, A_2, ..., A_m\}$. For a tuple $t \in T$, and for a subset $X \subseteq A, t[X]$ denotes the projection of the tuple t, on the set of attributes in X.

For a given subset of attributes Q, we define an equivalence relation on T as follows. For two tuples t_1, t_2, we say that $t_1 \theta t_2$ if $t_1[Q] = t_2[Q]$. Specifically, we say that two tuples t_1 and t_2 are imperceptible with respect to the attributes in Q. Further, we can determine the lower and upper approximation for any subset of tuples in T. We can say that a set of attributes Q is dependent on another set P, if the partition of the database with respect to P contains the partition with respect to Q. This will lead to efficient techniques of attribute elimination required for decision trees, association rules, and clustering.

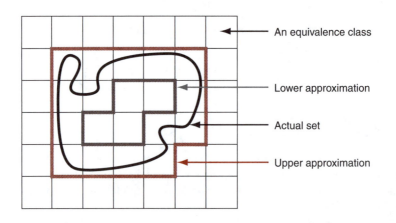

Figure 4.24   Lower and upper approximations of a rough set

Let us assume that the database T contains the following transactions: $\{a, b, c\}, \{a, b, d\}$, $\{a, c, d\}, \{a, c, e\}, \{a, d, e\}$, and $\{a, d, f\}$. Let us further assume that the items in the transaction are ordered.

We define an equivalence relation between transactions as having two common prefixes. In other words, two transactions are equivalent if their first two elements are the same. Now let us define the lower and upper approximations for X, which contains transactions $\{a, b, c\}, \{a, b, d\}$, and $\{a, c, d\}$. The lower approximation of X will be given by $\{\{a, b, c\}, \{a, b, d\}\}$. The upper approximation of X will be $\{\{a, b, c\}, \{a, b, d\}, \{a, c, d\}, \{a, c, e\}\}$.

The notion of the rough set was proposed in 1982 by Zdzislaw Pawlak, and has been found useful in the realms of knowledge acquisition and data mining. Many practical applications of this approach have been developed in recent years in areas such as medicine, pharmaceutical research, and process control. One of the primary applications of rough sets in artificial intelligence is for the purpose of knowledge analysis and discovery of data. The rough set framework has been used with success in several data mining applications. Some of these are

RSES System: The RSES system uses modern methods from the rough set theory. A maximum of 30,000 objects with 16,000 attributes can be processed for rule generation. The number of attributes poses few restraints, but the relatively low number of maximal objects prevents it from being used on large datasets. It was developed in Poland in 1997.

KDD-R System: This system is based on the Variable Precision Rough Set (VPRS) model. It carries out analysis of dependencies among attributes, elimination of superfluous attributes, and computation of rules from data.

LERS System: Learning from Examples based on Rough Sets is another system produced for rule induction. The system manages inconsistencies in datasets by following the principles of rough sets. These inconsistencies are not corrected, but instead the upper and lower approximation for each concept is calculated. Subsequently, deterministic and indeterministic rules are generated.

4.3.3 Classification Software CtreeinExcel

CtreeinExcel is a small Excel-based freeware to build Classification Trees. It uses the C4.5 algorithm. The software is very easy to learn and use, but has limited capability. It can be obtained from

http://www.geocities.com/adotsaha/CTree/CtreeinExcel.html

We have provided two files derived from the software in a folder `CTree`:

- `golf.xls`: Testing of the software for our golf example.
- `predictSpending.xls`: Application of the classification to Gazelle.com

Copy the folder `CTree` to your hard drive. In addition, download the original CTree.xls file from the website described previously to the same folder. By default, the level of macro security will forbid you from using the software. Before opening any of these files, set your macro security level to medium by launching Excel, choosing the options dialogue from the options menu, and then clicking on macro security (as shown in **Figure 4.25**). Now launch the original Excel file `CTree.xls`. You will see a warning sign as shown in **Figure 4.26** giving you an option of disabling or enabling the macros. Enable the macros in order to proceed. The ReadMe worksheet is the first worksheet you will see once the file is opened. It contains enough information to get started. We have copied the information from the worksheet in **Figures 4.27–4.29**. Figure 4.27 describes the first two steps: entering your data, setting up various options, and running the model. Steps 3 and 4, shown in Figure 4.28, tell us how to interpret the results. Additional tips are given in Figure 4.29.

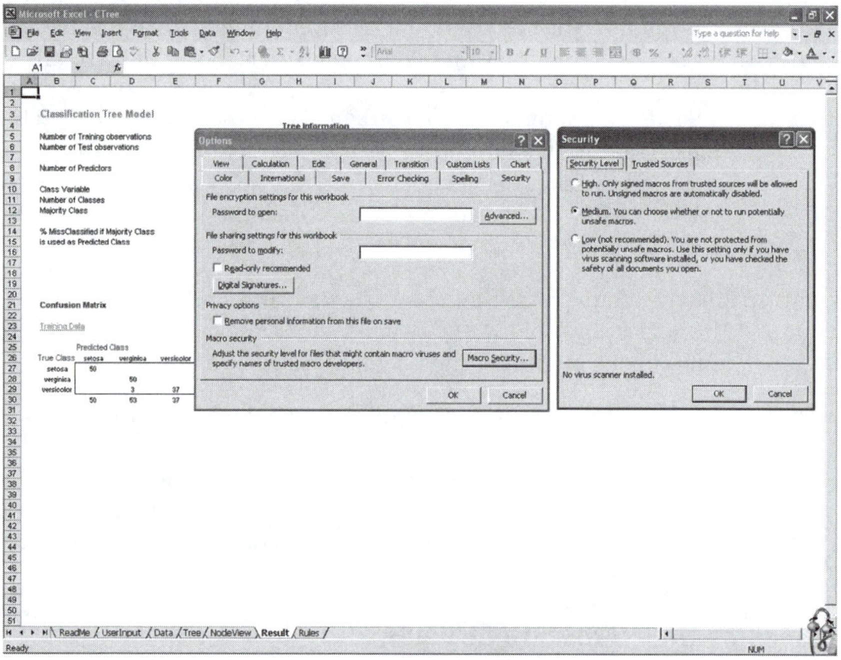

Figure 4.25 Setting Macro Security Level in Excel to Medium

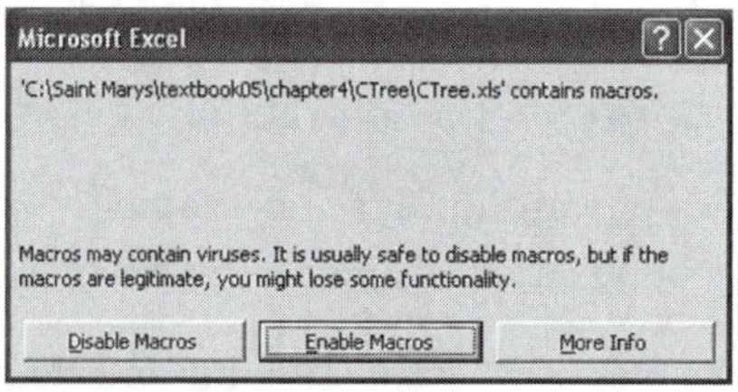

Figure 4.26 Enabling macros in Excel

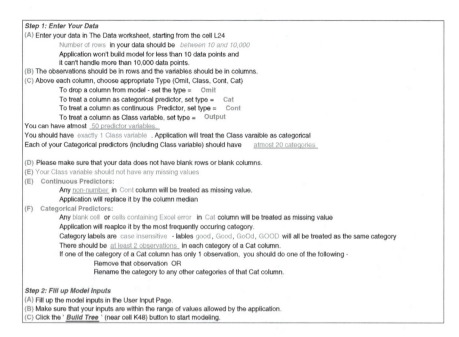

Figure 4.27 Steps 1 and 2 in creating decision trees using CtreeinExcel

Step 3: Results of Modeling
(A) When the run is over, the calssification tree can be seen in Tree sheet
  You can enter the values of predictors here and in cell H7 the class predicted by the tree is shown
(B) You can select a cell in any of the nodes and click the   _View Node_ button to see the
  details information on that node in NodeView Sheet
(C) In cell F7 of NodeView sheet you can enter any node number
  to see the class distribution and other information about that node

Step 4: Rule Generation
After the tree is grown, tree is further processed to generate Rules
Rule sets generated here are for viewing ONLY.   The tool does NOT have the capability of using these rules to classify new dat
Rule Summary Table tells you the quality of the individual rules.   Quality is measured by 3 different metrics explained below

For example, consider a rule :   IF Petal Width > **7** and Petal Length <= **70** THEN Species = **Setosa**
In context of the above rule, the quality metrics are explained as follows

 Support: % of training data for which the Left Hand Side (LHS) of the Rule (I.e. PetalWidth > 7 PetalLength <=70) is true
   If for a observation the LHS of the rule is true, we say that the rule   _APPLIES_ for that observation.
   This measures how widely applicable is the rule.

onfidence: Out of the training records for which the (LHS) of the Rule is true, % of records for which the Right Hand side is also true.
   In other words, for what % of the observations on which the rule applies, the rule is true.
   This measures the accuracy of the rule.

 Capture: What % of Setosa records is correctly captured by this rule.   This is more of a reflection of the structure of the probl
   If there is a rule with Capture close to 100%, that means, in the predictor space, all observations with this class
   sit closely to each other and the rule has been able to capture that part of the predictor space very well.

Suppose there are 150 observations in the training data, out of which 50 is Setosa.
Also assume that the above rule applies to 70 records and out of which 30 is Setosa

Then,
Support: 47% (=70 / 150)   **Confidence:** 43% (= 30/70)   **Capture:** 60% (= 30 / 50)

Figure 4.28 Steps 3 and 4 in creating decision trees using CtreeinExcel

(1) Adjust for # categories of a categorical predictor
    While growing the tree, child nodes are created by splitting parent nodes.
    Which predictor to use for this split is decided by certain crierion.
    This criterion has an inherent bias towards choosing predictors with more categories.
    This bias can be adjusted for by switching on this option.
(2) Minimum Node Size Criterion
    You may not select this.   However, if you select it then you should enter a valid minimum node size
    expressed as % of total observations.
    A valid minimum node size should be strictly greater than 0% and strictly less than 100%
    Higher the value of this, SMALLER will be the tree
(3) Maximum Purity Criterion
    You may not select this.   However, if you select it then you should enter a valid maximum purity
    which should be between 0% and 100%
    Higher the value of this, LARGER will be the tree
(4) Maximum Depth Criterion
    You may not select this.   However, if you select it then you should enter a valid maximum depth
    which should be an integer strictly greater than 1 and less than 20.
    Higher the value of this, LARGER will be the tree
(5) Pruning Option
    Ideally you should keep this option on by selecting YES
    This option is provided to let you study the effect of pruning
(6) Training and Test data
    You may like to use a subset of your data to build the model and the rest to study the performance of the model
    You may also use the whole data set as training data and may not use any test data
    If you want to use test data, you may either randomly select the test set or use last few rows as test set.
    If you are selecting the test set manually (Option 2), it is a good idea to check whether all the Class categories
    are present in both training as well as test data.
(6) Save Model Option
    If you choose YES here, application will save the model in a separate workbook.
    Since the worksheets in the application are protected, you will not be able to
    edit the tree. In such a case you should save the tree in a separate file and further experiment on it.

Figure 4.29   Additional tips for using CtreeinExcel

Let us apply the CtreeinExcel software to our golf example. Type the 14 records from the training set given in Table 4.3 and 10 test records from Table 4.4 in the *Data* worksheet, as shown in **Figure 4.30**. Either type these values yourself, or open the file `golf.xls`. We have designated *Outlook* and *Windy* as the categorical attributes, and *Humidity* and *Temperature* as the continuous attributes, while *Play* is the classification attribute. Take a moment to familiarize yourself with the various options. They are more or less self-explanatory, otherwise consult the explanation given in the ReadMe worksheet (Figures 4.27–4.29). We will make only one change to the default values from the *UserInput* worksheet in **Figure 4.31**. By default, the nodes are not split if the attribute has five or fewer records. Because we have only 14 training instances, we change the specification so that the nodes will continue to be split until they attain maximum purity or the number of records in the node is 1% of the total size of the training set (in our case that means 0). Note that we are keeping the default designation of the last 10 records as the test set. Click on the "Build Tree" button, and the macros will run the C4.5 algorithm to create a tree.

Figure 4.32 shows the decision tree generated by the CtreeinExcel software; it is identical to the one given in Figure 4.22, giving credence to the software. The NodeView worksheet (**Figure 4.33**) shows some statistics about the data, such as the fact that 64% of records were classified as "No Play" and 36% as "Play." More detailed statistics about the decision tree can be found in the Results worksheet, shown in **Figure 4.34**. Again, most of the information is self-explanatory. If you need more information, refer to the ReadMe worksheet or Figures 4.27–4.29. The confusion matrix tells how many actual "Play" instances were classified as

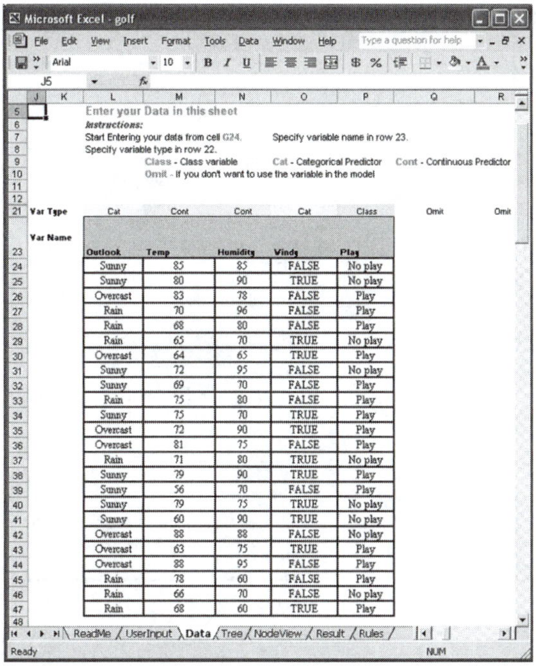

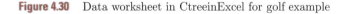

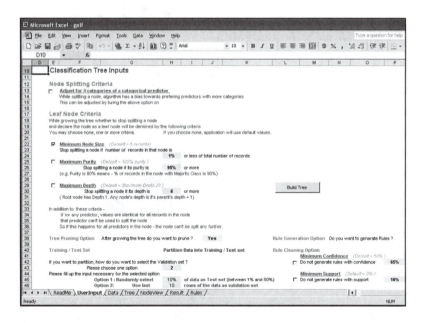

Figure 4.30   Data worksheet in CtreeinExcel for golf example

Figure 4.31   User input worksheet in CtreeinExcel for the golf example

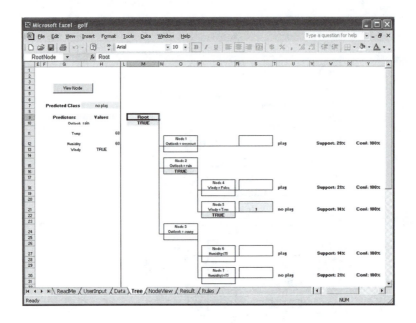

Figure 4.32 Tree worksheet in CtreeinExcel for golf example

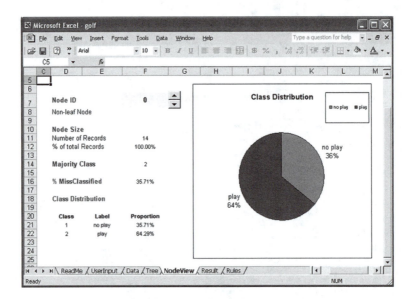

Figure 4.33 NodeView worksheet in CtreeinExcel for golf example

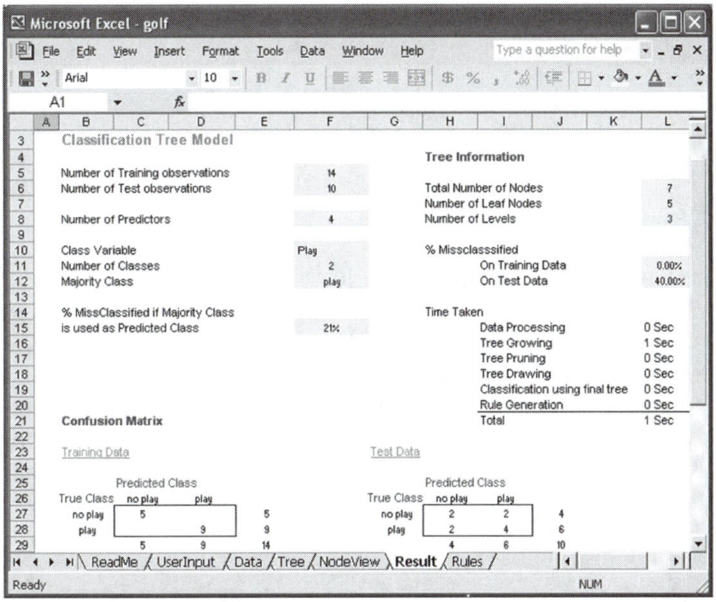

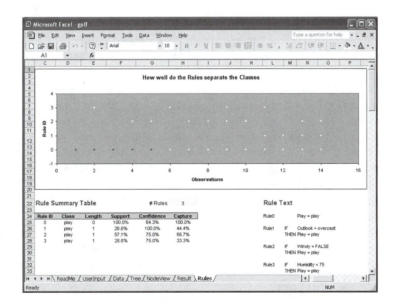

Figure 4.34 shows the Result worksheet in CtreeinExcel for golf example.

Figure 4.34 Result worksheet in CtreeinExcel for golf example

"Play" and "No Play," and vice versa. There are separate confusion matrices for training and test data. Finally, the rules from the decision tree are listed in the Rule worksheet (**Figure 4.35**).

Figure 4.35 Rules worksheet in CtreeinExcel for golf example

They seem to be a bit more generalized than the decision tree. For example, the decision tree suggests the rule

If Outlook = Rain and Windy = False Then Play

However, the rule in the "Rules" worksheet,

If Windy = False Then Play

is more generalized with higher Support and lower Confidence. The definition of Support, Confidence, and Capture is given in Figure 4.28 with an example. We will also revisit these definitions when we study association later in this chapter.

Readers are encouraged to change the options from the UserInput worksheet and analyze the regenerated decision tree (see Exercises). We have looked at the CtreeinExcel software with a small example that we studied in great theoretical detail. The original copy of `CTree.xls` contains an example that readers may want to study as well. In the following section, we are going to apply the CtreeinExcel software to our Gazelle.com dataset.

4.3.4   Classifying Customers from Gazelle.com Using CtreeinExcel

Let us recall the last query for our ORDERS database, which created a comma separated `csv` file that lists

- customer_id
- visits
- number of items bought
- spending

We will try to predict the spending of each customer based on visits and items. Because it is a classification problem, we will have to transform the spending attribute from continuous to a categorical attribute. We will create a new attribute called "Spending>25," which will have the values TRUE or FALSE. This step is called data transformation, which is necessary to make the data accessible to the data mining technique you are going to employ. Open `visitItemSpending.csv`, which was saved earlier using Excel. Also open `CTree.xls`. Copy the data from `visitItemSpending.csv` to the Data worksheet in `CTree.xls` as shown in Figure 4.36. "Spending>25" can be entered in the first record with the formula "=O24>25" and copying it down for the rest of the column. If you wish, you can skip the data copying and directly open the file `predictSpending.xls`.

We will change one of the default options from the UserInput worksheet by choosing Option 1 for selecting test data (Figure 4.37). Option 1 randomly selects 10% of the dataset for testing, as opposed to using the last ten records for testing. Click on the "Build Tree" button. Figure 4.38 shows the decision tree generated by the software. The first split is based on whether "Items<3". The following are some of the rules that can be deciphered from the decision tree:

If "Items<3" and "Visits<2" then Spending<=25.

If "Items<3" and "Visits>=2" then Spending>25.

Figure 4.36 Data worksheet in CtreeinExcel for the Gazelle.com data

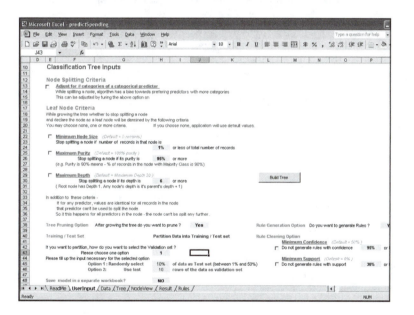

Figure 4.37 UserInput worksheet in CtreeinExcel for Gazelle.com data

Note that the rules can be simplified by using some simple mathematical logic. The Node-View worksheet (**Figure 4.39**) shows some statistics about the data, such as the fact that 81% of records were classified as "Spending <=25" and 19% as "Spending>25." More detailed statistics about the decision tree can be found in the Result worksheet shown in **Figure 4.40**.

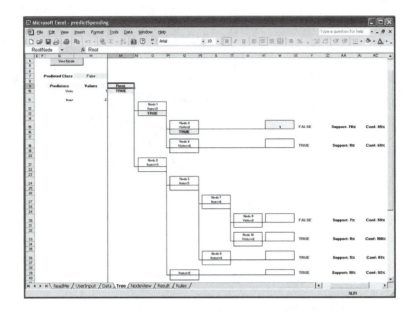

Figure 4.38   Tree worksheet in CtreeinExcel for Gazelle.com data

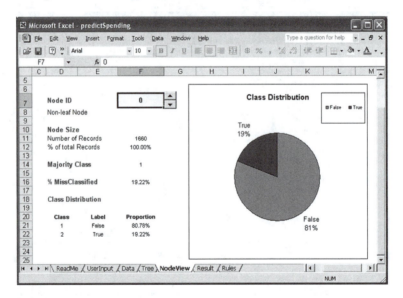

Figure 4.39   NodeView worksheet in CtreeinExcel for Gazelle.com data

If needed, refer to the ReadMe worksheet or Figures 4.27–4.29. The confusion matrix tells us how many actual "Spending>25" were classified as "Spending>25" and "Spending<=25," and vice versa. There are separate confusion matrices for training and test data. Finally, the rules from the decision tree are listed in the Rules worksheet (**Figure 4.41**). Notice again that

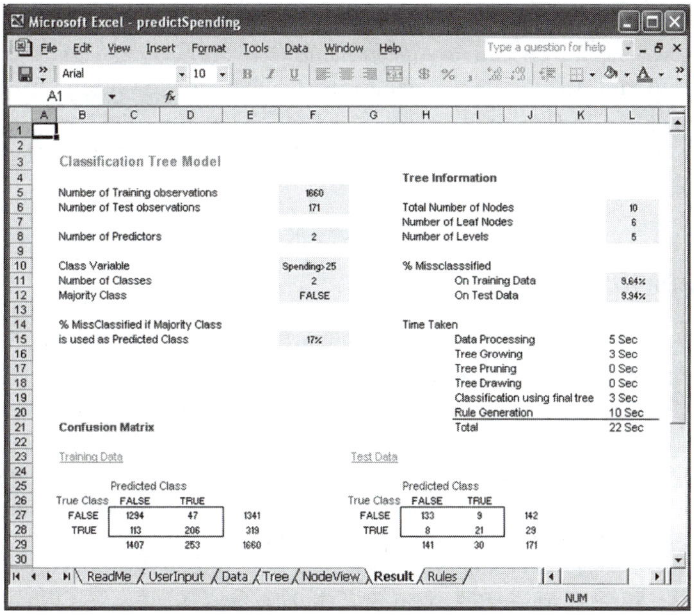

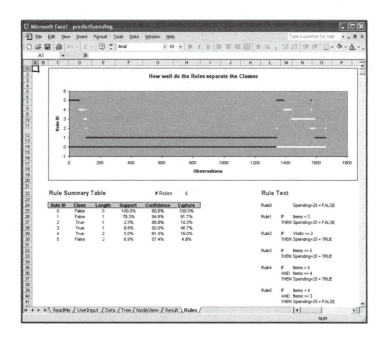

Figure 4.40 Result worksheet in CtreeinExcel for Gazelle.com data

Figure 4.41 Rules worksheet in CtreeinExcel for Gazelle.com data

the rules seem to be a bit more generalized than the decision tree to increase the support for a rule at the expense of confidence in the rule. Also note that this is probably not the best classification model. Readers are encouraged to change the options from the UserInput worksheet and analyze the regenerated decision tree. A good project will involve creating a larger database from the KDD Cup data and creating a more elaborate classification model (see Exercises).

4.4   Association

In data mining, the necessity of deriving associations from data has received considerable attention. The solution was formulated by Agrawal, Imielinski, and Swami (1993), and is well known as *market-basket analysis.* In this approach, we can think of a set of items and a large collection of transactions, which are subsets (baskets) of these items. The task is to find relationships between several items within these baskets. One can think of this type of data in terms of a matrix of p rows corresponding to baskets and q columns corresponding to items. Such a matrix can be very large. The notion of association rules was invented as a means to efficiently find simple patterns in such data.

There are many applications of data mining that fit into this context. The typical example from which the analysis gets its name is the shopping mall. In this situation, the objective is to analyze customers' buying habits by finding associations between the different items that they place in their shopping baskets. The discovery of such association rules can help the retailer develop marketing strategies by gaining insight into matters such as which items are most frequently purchased by customers. It also helps in inventory management and sales promotion strategies.

It is generally accepted that the discovery of association rules is dependent only on the discovery of frequent sets. The popular algorithms are thus concerned with determining the set of frequent itemsets in a given set of operation databases. The procedure is basically to compute the frequency of occurrences of each itemset in the database. As the total number of itemsets is exponential in terms of the number of items, it is not possible to count the frequencies of these sets by reading the database in just one pass; moreover a single pass will need numerous counters. Consequently, having multiple passes for generating all the frequent itemsets is unavoidable. Therefore, distinct algorithms for the discovery of association rules point at dropping the number of passes by generating candidate sets, which are probable frequent sets. The algorithms vary from one another in the method of handling the candidate sets and the method of reducing the number of database passes. However, there are some new methods that attempt to detect frequent sets without having to generate candidate sets.

In this perspective, we can see whether it is possible to generate association rules incrementally. The algorithms for discovering frequent sets are not directly suitable in the situation where the underlying database is incremented sporadically. The objective is to prevent computing the frequent sets again for the incremented set of data. The notion of border sets turns out to be very important in this perspective, because they can be determined without additional effort. Additionally, if no border set is eliminated by a database update, it is shown that the set of frequent sets can be found without having to search through the whole database.

In the real world, the number of frequent sets is enormous; thus the number of association rules is also too large to be useful. It turns out to be significant to generate only those association rules in which the user is interested. The user can state the constraint to specify which grouping of items is of his interest.

In this section, we will introduce the reader to the association rules and the *a priori* algorithm that can be used to discover such rules.

4.4.1 *a priori* Algorithm

Suppose that $A = \{l_1, l_2, ...l_m\}$ is a set of items and T is a set of transactions, where each transaction t is a set of items. Thus, t is a subset of A.

A transaction t is said to support an item l_i, if l_i is present in t. t is said to support a subset of items $X \subseteq A$, if t supports each item l_i in X. An itemset $X \subseteq A$ has a support in T, denoted by $s(X)_T$, if a certain percentage of transactions (e.g., 5%) in T supports X.

Support can be defined as a fractional support, denoting the proportion of transactions supporting X in T. It can also be discussed in terms of the absolute number of transactions supporting X in T. For ease, we will assume the support to be %-support. We will often drop the subscript T in the expression $s(X)_T$, when T is apparently implied.

Example 4.3 Consider the following set of transactions in a bookstore. We shall observe a set of only 6 transactions of book purchases. In the first transaction, purchases are made on books regarding Combinatorics, Data Mining, Theory of Algorithm, Computer Organization, and Numerical Analysis; we shall indicate these subjects by C, DM, TA, CO, and NA, respectively. So we describe the 6 transactions as follows:

$$t_1 := \{NA, C, TA, CO\}$$
$$t_2 := \{C, DM, CO\}$$
$$t_3 := \{NA, C, TA, CO\}$$
$$t_4 := \{NA, C, DM, CO\}$$
$$t_5 := \{NA, C, DM, TA, CO\}$$
$$t_6 := \{C, DM, TA\}.$$

So $A := \{NA, C, DM, TA, CO\}$ and $T := \{t_1, t_2, t_3, t_4, t_5, t_6\}$.

We can see that t supports the items C, DM, and CO. The item DM is supported by 4 out of 6 transactions in T. Thus, the support of DM is 66.6%.

Definition 4.4 For a given transaction database T, an association rule is an expression of the form $X \Rightarrow Y$, where X and Y are subsets of A. The rule $X \Rightarrow Y$ holds with *confidence* τ, if $\tau\%$ of transactions in D that support X also support Y. The rule $X \Rightarrow Y$ has *support* σ in the transaction set T if $\sigma\%$ of the transactions in T support $X \cup Y$.

Now once again consider the example of the bookstore (Example 4.3). We are looking for rules with $\sigma = 50\%$ and $\tau = 60\%$. Clearly, $NA \Rightarrow C$ holds. The confidence of this rule is 100%, because all the transactions that support NA also support C. $C \Rightarrow NA$ also holds but its confidence is a little lower at 66%.

The discovery of association rules is an important issue in data mining. Every algorithm for finding association rules assumes that the basic database is very large and requires multiple passes over it. The idea is to achieve all rules fulfilling prespecified frequency and accuracy criteria. In real datasets, there are relatively few frequent sets. For instance, generally customers will buy a small subset of the entire collection of products. If datasets are large enough, it will not fit into the main memory; therefore, one can aim at the procedures that read the data as few times as possible. Algorithms that obtain association rules from data usually divide the task into two parts: first, find the frequent itemsets and then form the rules from them. That means the problem of mining association rules can be divided into two subproblems:

1. Find itemsets whose support is greater than the user-specified minimum support, σ. Those itemsets are referred to as frequent itemsets.

2. Use the frequent itemsets to produce the desired rules. In general if $ABCD$ and AB are frequent itemsets, then we can determine if the rule $AB \Rightarrow CD$ holds by checking the following inequality

$$\frac{s(\{A, B, C, D\})}{s(\{A, B\})} \geq \tau$$

where $s(X)$ is the support of X in T.

Definition 4.5 Let T be the transaction database and σ be the user-specified minimum support. An itemset $X \subseteq A$ is said to be a *frequent itemset* in T with respect to σ, if

$$s(X) \geq \sigma.$$

Definition 4.6 A frequent set is a *maximal frequent set* if it is a frequent set and no superset of this is a frequent set.

Definition 4.7 An itemset is a *border set* if it is not a frequent set, but all its proper subsets are frequent sets. Furthermore, if X is an itemset that is not frequent, then it should have a subset that is a border set.

If we know the set of all maximal frequent sets of a given T with respect to a σ, then we can find the set of all frequent sets without any extra check of the database. Thus, the set of all maximal frequent sets can act as a compact representation of the set of all frequent sets. Though, if we need the frequent sets together with their relevant support values in T, then we have to make one more database pass to derive the support values, as the set of all maximal frequent sets is known.

A maximal frequent set may or may not be a proper subset of a border set. It is likely that a proper subset of a border set, of cardinality one less than the border set, is not necessarily maximal. Hence, it is difficult to determine an exact relationship between the set of maximal frequent sets and the set of border sets. Although, the set of all border sets and the maximal frequent sets, which are not proper subsets of any of the border sets, together propose enhanced representation of the set of frequent sets.

Example 4.4   Let us suppose $A = \{A_1, A_2, A_3, A_4, A_5, A_6, A_7, A_8, A_9\}$ and $\sigma = 20\%$. Consider the transaction database given in **Table 4.6**. Because T contains 15 records—an itemset supported by at least three transactions—it is a frequent set. This database is used for tracing the *a priori* algorithm.

1	0	0	0	1	1	0	1	0
0	1	0	1	0	0	0	1	0
0	0	0	1	1	0	1	0	0
0	1	1	0	0	0	0	0	0
0	0	0	0	1	1	1	0	0
0	1	1	1	0	0	0	0	0
0	1	0	0	0	1	1	0	1
0	0	0	0	1	0	0	0	0
0	0	0	0	0	0	0	1	0
0	0	1	0	1	0	1	0	0
0	0	1	0	1	0	1	0	0
0	0	0	0	1	1	0	1	0
0	1	0	1	0	1	1	0	0
1	0	1	0	1	0	1	0	0
0	1	1	0	0	0	0	0	1

Table 4.6   Sample transaction database

The number of transactions following some of the itemsets is given in **Table 4.7**. We are using index i for the item A_i. We shall use this notation from now on. Because $\{1\}$ is supported by only two transactions, it is not a frequent set with respect to σ; however, $\{3\}$ is supported by three transactions and hence is a frequent set.

Verification of $\{5, 6, 7\}$ as a border set is a rather easy task; $\{5, 6\}$ is a maximal frequent set, as is $\{2, 4\}$. However there is no border set having $\{2, 4\}$ as a proper subset. So $\{2, 4\}$

X	SUPPORT COUNT (Frequency)
1	2
2	6
3	6
4	4
5	8
6	5
7	7
8	4
9	2
5,6	3
5,7	5
6,7	3
5,6,7	1

Table 4.7   Frequency count for some itemsets

and $\{5, 6, 7\}$ together represent the set of all frequent sets of T with respect to σ. This is because we can generate all the frequent sets from these two itemsets. If we know the set of all maximal frequent sets, we can generate all the frequent sets. Instead, if we identify the set of border sets and the set of those maximal frequent sets, which are not subsets of any border set, then we will have all the frequent sets.

Agrawal and Srikant gave the *a priori* algorithm in 1994. It is also called the *level-wise* algorithm. It is the most accepted algorithm for finding all the frequent sets. It makes use of the downward closure property. The algorithm is a bottom-up search, progressing upward level-wise in the lattice; but the interesting fact about this method is that before reading the database at every level, it prunes many of the sets, which are unlikely to be frequent sets. In general, the algorithm works as follows:

- The first pass of the algorithm simply counts item occurrences to determine the frequent itemsets.
- A subsequent pass, say pass k, consists of two phases:

  a) The frequent itemsets L_{k-1} found in the $(k-1)^{th}$ pass are used to generate the candidate itemsets C_k, using the *a priori* candidate-generation procedure described in the following.

  b) The database is scanned and the support of candidates in C_k is counted.

For fast counting, one needs to efficiently determine the candidates in C_k contained in a given transaction t. The set of candidate itemsets is subjected to a pruning process to ensure that all the subsets of the candidate sets are already known to be frequent itemsets. The candidate-generation process and the pruning process are the very important parts of this algorithm.

$C_k = \{\}$

for all itemsets $l_1 \in L_{k-1}$

for all itemsets $l_2 \in L_{k-1}$

    if $l_1[1] = l_2[1] \wedge l_1[2] = l_2[2] \wedge ... \wedge l_1[k-1] < l_2[k-1]$

    then $c = l_1[1], l_1[2]...l_1[k-1], l_2[k-1]$

    $C_k = C_k \cup \{c\}$

Figure 4.42   *a priori* candidate-generation method

Consider L_{k-1}, the set of all frequent $(k-1)$-itemsets. We wish to create a superset of the set of all frequent k-itemsets. The insight behind the *a priori* candidate-generation procedure is that if an itemset X has minimum support, then consider all subsets of X.

Assume that the set of frequent 3-itemsets are $\{1, 2, 3\}$, $\{1, 2, 5\}$, $\{1, 3, 5\}$, $\{2, 3, 5\}$, $\{2, 3, 4\}$. Then the 4-itemsets that are generated as candidate itemsets are the supersets of these 3-itemsets. In addition, all the 3-itemset subsets of any candidate 4-itemset must be already known to be in L_3. The first part and portion of the second part is handled by the *a priori* candidate-generation method shown in **Figure 4.42**.

Using the *a priori* algorithm, $C_4 := \{\{1,2,3,5\}, \{2,3,4,5\}\}$ is obtained from $L_3 := \{\{1,2,3\}, \{1,2,5\}, \{1,3,5\}, \{2,3,5\}, \{2,3,4\}\}$. $\{1, 2, 3, 5\}$ is generated from $\{1, 2, 3\}$ and $\{1, 2, 5\}$. Similarly, $\{2, 3, 4, 5\}$ is generated from $\{2, 3, 4\}$ and $\{2, 3, 5\}$. No other pair of 3-itemsets satisfies the condition:

$$l_1[1] = l_2[1] \wedge l_1[2] = l_2[2] \wedge ... \wedge l_1[k-1] < l_2[k-1].$$

The following algorithm prunes some candidate sets that do not meet the second criterion. The pruning step eliminates the extensions of $(k-1)$-itemsets that are not found to be frequent, from being considered for counting support. For instance, the `itemset` $\{2, 3, 4, 5\}$ is pruned from C_4, because none of its 3-subsets are in L_3. The pruning algorithm is described in **Figure 4.43**. The *a priori* frequent itemset discovery algorithm uses these two functions at every iteration. It moves upward in the lattice starting from level 1 up to level k, where no candidate set remains after pruning. The *a priori* algorithm is given in **Figure 4.44**.

Prune(C_k)

For all $c \in C_k$

For all $(k-1)$-subsets d of c do

    If $d \notin L_{k-1}$

    Then $C_k = C_k \backslash \{c\}$

Figure 4.43   Pruning algorithm

Initialize: $k := 1, C_1$ all the $1 -$ itemsets;

read the database to count the support of C_1, to determine L_1

$L_1 := $ (frequent $1 -$ itemsets};

$k := 2; // k$ represents the pass number //

while $(L_{k-1} \neq \{\})$ do

begin

$\qquad C_k := $ gen_candidate_itemsets with the given L_{k-1}

$\qquad$ prune(C_k)

$\qquad$ for all transactions $t \in T$ do

$\qquad$ increment the count of all candidates in C_k that are contained in t;

$\qquad L_k := $ All candidates in C_k with minimum support;

$\qquad k := k + 1;$

end

Answer $:= \cup_k L_k;$

Figure 4.44 *a priori* Algorithm

Example 4.4 (continued) Let us illustrate how the algorithm discussed previously works.

$$k := 1$$

Read the database to count the support of 1-itemsets (itemsets with a single item) from Table 4.7. The frequent 1-itemsets and their support counts are given in the following:

$\qquad L_1 := \{\{2\} \to 6, \{3\} \to 6, \ \{4\} \to 4, \{5\} \to 8, \{6\} \to 5, \{7\} \to 7, \{8\} \to 4\}.$

$\qquad k := 2$

In the candidate-generation step, we get

$$C_2 := \{\{2,3\}, \{2,4\}, \{2,5\}, \{2,6\}, \{2,7\}, \{2,8\},$$
$$\{3,4\}, \{3,5\}, \{3,6\}, \{3,7\}, \{3,8\}, \{4,5\}, \{4,6\},$$
$$\{4,7\}, \{4,8\}, \{5,6\}, \{5,7\}, \{5,8\}, \{6,7\}, \{6,8\}, \{7,8\}\}$$

The pruning step does not change C_2.

Read the database to count the support of elements in C_2 to get

$$L_2 := \{\{2,3\} \to 3, \{2,4\} \to 3, \{3,5\} \to 3, \ \{3,7\} \to 3, \ \{5,6\} \to 3, \{5,7\} \to 5, \{6,7\} \to 3\}$$

In the candidate-generation step,

- from $\{2, 3\}$ and $\{2, 4\}$, we get $\{2, 3, 4\}$
- from $\{3, 5\}$ and $\{3, 7\}$, we get $\{3, 5, 7\}$, and likewise
- from $\{5, 6\}$ and $\{5, 7\}$, we get $\{5, 6, 7\}$.

$$C_3 := \{\{2,3,4\}, \{3,5,7\}, \{5,6,7\}\}.$$

The pruning step prunes $\{2, 3, 4\}$ as not all its subsets of size 2; that is, $\{2, 3\}$, $\{2, 4\}$, $\{3, 4\}$ are present in L_2.

The other two itemsets are reserved.

Thus, the pruned C_3 is $\{\{3, 5, 7\}, \{5, 6, 7\}\}$.

Read the database to count the support of the itemsets in C_3 to get

$$L_3 := \{\{3,5,7\} \rightarrow 3\}.$$
$$k := 4$$

Because L_3 contains only one element, C_4 is empty and the algorithm stops, *returning* the set of frequent sets along with their respective support values as

$$L := L_1 \cup L_2 \cup L_3.$$

4.4.2 Demonstration for an E-Commerce Application

Let us apply association mining to our data from the KDD Cup 2000. We would like to find the frequent sets for each session. The first step, of course, is to extract the products for each transaction. The following query

SELECT session_id, subassortment_id

FROM pawan.orders12

WHERE session_id != '?' and subassortment_id != '?';

gives us a list of products for each transaction. Export the data to a file called **subassortment. csv** using commas to separate fields and no character delimiter as done previously (Figure 4.21). We have provided the file **subassortment.csv** in the folder called "Support for KDD cup data" under Chapter 4.

There is a number of software programs available for finding the frequent sets, most of which require that the products per session be stored on a single line. For example, the session 101868 from our ORDERS database has the following entries in **subassortment.csv**:

101868	45711
101868	9193
101868	45711
101868	9193

The session should be represented on a single line as

$$45711\ 9193\ 45711\ 9193$$

We have written a small Java class called `CreateItemList.java` available under the `java folder` under Chapter 4. The compiled version `CreateItemList.class` is also available under the directory. The class can be run as follows:

```
java CreateItemList subassortment.csv
```
(Command 4.1)

You will have to ensure that the file `subassortment.csv` is in an appropriate folder. Redirect the output to another file called `subassortment.list`. We have also made the file `subassortment.list` available in the folder called "Support for KDD cup data" under Chapter 4.

Now we are ready to use one of the software programs for finding frequent item sets. One of the simplest and easiest ways to use packages is called PAFI (http://glaros.dtc.umn.edu/gkhome/pafi/overview). It is a software package that contains a set of programs that can be used to find frequent patterns in large and diverse databases.

The package includes three different pattern-discovery programs:

LPMiner: Finds patterns corresponding to itemsets in a transaction database.

SLPMiner: Finds patterns corresponding to subsequences in a sequential database.

FSG: Finds patterns corresponding to connected undirected subgraphs in an undirected graph database.

These programs can be used to mine a wide range of datasets arising in commercial information retrieval and scientific applications. We will restrict ourselves to the use of LPMiner. Unfortunately, the package supports only Linux and Sun OS platforms. We will assume familiarity with Linux. Download and unzip the file `pafi-1.0.1.zip`. You will see a file called `manual.pdf`, which gives detailed information about the program. The directory called Linux contains the executables. Copy the `subassortment.list` to the Linux directory. You should make all the files in the Linux directory executable by typing: `chmod +x *`. Run LPMiner by typing the following command:

```
lpminer subassortment.list
```
(Command 4.2)

However, notice that LPMiner produces a large number of frequent sets; therefore, we put a restriction that the minimum support must be 0.1 by using the "-s 0.1" option, and specifying that the minimum size of the frequent set should be at least 2 with "-m 2" option. The resulting command is as follows:

```
lpminer -s 0.1 -m 2 subassortment.list
```
(Command 4.3)

Figure 4.45 shows the log for (Command 4.3); it is divided into four sections. The first section tells us statistics about our input, such as the number of transactions, number of distinct items, and the average and maximum size of transaction sets. The second section describes the options used by the software. The third section describes the result summary. It tells us that there were 129 frequent sets with support greater than 0.1%: 117 with a length of 2, 11 with a length of 3, and 1 with a length equal to 4. The fourth section tells us the time required for these calculations.

The 129 frequent itemsets are in the file `subassortment.list.fp` (the file is also in the folder "Support for KDD cup data" under Chapter 4). **Figure 4.46** shows the last 29 lines from the file, containing 17 frequent itemsets of the size 2, 11 with a length of 3, and 1 with a length equal to 4. The first column in each row is pattern_id, which can be used for drawing pattern lattice (refer to `manual.pdf` from the `pafi-1.0.1` folder for more information). The second field tells how many transactions had the frequent itemset. The third column lists the support value. The rest of the row contains the actual frequent itemset. The most frequent itemset in the file is given by the entry "1-116 15 0.865 19859 19913." The frequent itemset was {19859, 19913}. It occurred 15 times with a support of 0.865. Readers are encouraged to experiment with the LPMiner (see Exercises).

```
****************************************************************************
lpminer (PAFI 1.0) Copyright 2003, Regents of the University of Minnesota

Transaction File Information ----------------------------------------------
  Transaction File Name:                    subassortment.list
  Number of Input Transactions:             1734
  Number of Distinct Items:                 170
  Average Number of Items In a Tran:        1.363
  Maximum Number of Items In a Tran:        11

Options -------------------------------------------------------------------
  Minimum Output Pattern Size:              2
  Maximum Output Pattern Size:              4294967295
  Constant Minimum Support:                 0.100000
  PC List File Generation:                  Skip
  Non-Maximal Frequent Pattern Pruning:     Skip

Solution ------------------------------------------------------------------
  Frequent Pattern File:                    subassortment.list.fp
  Number of Frequent Patterns:              129
  Number of Frequent Patterns[Length   2]   117
  Number of Frequent Patterns[Length   3]   11
  Number of Frequent Patterns[Length   4]   1

Timing Information --------------------------------------------------------
  Input File Transformation:                0.028 sec
  Generating Frequent Pattern File:         0.004 sec
****************************************************************************
```

Figure 4.45   Log from LPMiner

```
.................
1-100  4  0.231  12791  29725
1-101  3  0.173  19913  35895
1-102  3  0.173  19731  35895
1-103  5  0.288  35895  35931
1-104  8  0.461  19859  35895
1-105  2  0.115  19731  19859
1-106  3  0.173  19731  29725
1-107  6  0.346  19731  35931
1-108  3  0.173  11687  12295
1-109  3  0.173  12295  19913
1-110  4  0.231  11679  12295
1-111  2  0.115  9093   11667
1-112  2  0.115  9093   35931
1-113  4  0.231  19859  35931
1-114  4  0.231  19913  35931
1-115  3  0.173  9093   19859
1-116  15 0.865  19859  19913
2-0  2  0.115  33321  45691  45695
2-1  2  0.115  45687  45691  45695
2-2  2  0.115  10825  12295  19855
2-3  2  0.115  19859  33397  35895
2-4  2  0.115  19727  19859  35895
2-5  2  0.115  12543  19727  19859
2-6  2  0.115  12543  19727  35895
2-7  2  0.115  12791  20133  33393
2-8  2  0.115  12543  19859  35895
2-9  2  0.115  12791  20133  35887
2-10 3  0.173  19859  35895  35931
```

Figure 4.46   Partial output from LPMiner

EXERCISES

1. (Project) The Gazelle.com dataset given in `question3.data` contains many attributes not used in this chapter. Decompose the dataset into multiple tables based on functional dependencies. Create a new and more refined database.

2. (Project) Use the refined database from the previous project to develop a more accurate classification model to predict customers who spend more than $25. Write a report on your model.

3. Make changes to the options from `predictSpending.xls` and see if you can get a better prediction model. Write a report on your model.

4. Make changes to the options from `golf.xls` and see if you can get a better prediction model. Write a report on your model.

5. Define a frequent set and a border set.

6. Show that every subset of any itemset must contain either a frequent set or a border set.

7. Discuss the importance of discovering association rules.

8. Describe the essential features in a decision tree. How is it useful to classify data?

9. What is a splitting attribute? What is a splitting criterion? Are the splitting criteria different for numeric attributes and categorical attributes?

10. What are the disadvantages of the decision tree over other classification techniques?

11. Develop a table of training examples in some domain, such as classifying animals by species, and trace the construction of a decision tree by the ID3 algorithm.

12. (Project) Implement ID3 in a language of your choice, and run it on the examples discussed in this chapter.

Day	Outlook	Temperature	Humidity	Wind	PlayGolf
D1	Sunny	Hot	High	Weak	No
D2	Sunny	Hot	High	Strong	No
D3	Overcast	Hot	High	Weak	Yes
D4	Rain	Mild	High	Weak	Yes
D5	Rain	Cool	Normal	Weak	Yes
D6	Rain	Cool	Normal	Strong	No
D7	Overcast	Cool	Normal	Strong	Yes
D8	Sunny	Mild	High	Weak	No
D9	Sunny	Cool	Normal	Weak	Yes
D10	Rain	Mild	Normal	Weak	Yes
D11	Sunny	Mild	Normal	Strong	Yes
D12	Overcast	Mild	High	Strong	Yes
D13	Overcast	Hot	Normal	Weak	Yes
D14	Rain	Mild	High	Strong	No

Table 4.8 Training examples for target concept *PlayGolf*

13. Consider the data in **Table 4.8**. Here, the target attribute is *PlayGolf*, which draws a Boolean concept to be predicted based on other attributes. Using the provided information, illustrate how the ID3 algorithm works.

14. (Project) Implement the *a priori* algorithm in a language of your choice, and run it on the examples discussed in this chapter.

15. Experiment with the options from LPMiner, and write a report on the frequent-item sets obtained.

References

Agrawal R., T. Imielinski, and A. Swami. (1993): Mining associations between sets of items in massive databases. In *Proceedings of the ACM SIGMOD International Conference on Management of Data,* 207–16. Washington, DC.

Agrawal, R. and R. Srikant. (1994): Fast algorithms for mining association rules. In *Proceedings of the 20th International Conference on Very Large Databases,* Santiago, Chile.

Codd, E. F. (1970): A relational model of data for large shared data banks. Communications of the ACM, 13 (6): 377–87.

Date, C. J. (2004): *An introduction to the database systems. 8th* ed. Boston: Addison-Wesley.

Kohavi, R., C. Brodley, B. Frasca, L. Mason, and Z. Zheng. (2000): KDD-Cup 2000 organizers' report: Peeling the onion. *SIGKDD Explorations,* 2 (2): 86–98. http://robotics.stanford.edu/users/ronnyk/kddOrganizerReport.pdf.

Quinlan, R. (1986): Induction of decision tree. *Machine Learning* 1:81–106.

Wikipedia. (2006a): Database model. http://en.wikipedia.org/wiki/Database_model.

Wikipedia. (2006b): Database normalization. http://en.wikipedia.org/wiki/Database_normalization.

Wikipedia. (2006c): SQL. `http://en.wikipedia.org/wiki/SQL`

Wikipedia. (2006d): Decision tree. `http://en.wikipedia.org/wiki/Decision_tree`.

Further Reading

Adriaans, P. and Zantinge, D. (1996): Data Mining, Addison-Wesley.

Agrawal, R., Mannila H., Srikant R., Toivonen H., and Verkamo A. (1995): Fast discovery of association rules. Advances in Knowledge Discovery and Data Mining, Chapter 12, AAAI/MIT Press.

Banerjee M., and Chakraborty M. K. (1997): Rough Logics: A survey with further directions. In E. Orlowska (ed.) *Rough Set Analysis*, Physica-Verlag, Heidelberg.

Berry, M. and Linoff, G. (1997): Data Mining Techniques for Marketing, Sales and Customer Support, John Wiley & Sons, Inc.

Bigus, J.P. (1996): Data Mining with Neural networks: Solving Business Problems-from application development to decision support, McGraw Hill.

Brin S., Motwani R., Tsur D., and Ullman J., (1997): Dynamic Itemset Counting and Implication Rules for Market Basket Data. In *Proceedings of 1997 ACM SIGMOD*, Montreal, Canada.

Brin S., Motwani R., and Silverstein C., (1997): Beyond Market Basket: Generalizing Association Rules to Correlations. In *Proceedings of 1997 ACM SIGMOD*, Montreal, Canada.

Cabena, P., Hadjnian, P., Stadler, R., Verhees, J., and Zanasi, A. (Ed.) (1997): Discovering Data Mining from Concept to Implementation, Prentice Hall.

Dorian, P. (1999): Data Preparation for Data Mining, Morgan Kaufmann.

Fayyad, U. M., Piatetsky-Shapiro, G., Smyth, S., and Uthurusamy, R. (1996): Advances in Knowledge Discovery and Data Mining, M.I.T. Press.

Han, J. and Kamber, M. (2000): Data Mining: Concepts and Techniques, Morgan Kaufmann, San Francisco, CA.

Knowledge Discovery Nuggets: http://www.kdnuggets.com/

Liu, H. and Motoda, H. (1998): Feature Selection for Knowledge Discovery and Data Mining, Kluwer International.

Michalski, R., Brako, I., and Kubat, M. (1998): Machine Learning and Data Mining; Methods & Applications, John Wiley & Sons.

Mitchell, T. (1997): Machine Learning, Morgan Kaufmann.

Nguyen S., Hoa S., and Synak P. (1994): *Rough Sets in Data Mining: Approximate Description of Decision Classes.*

Nguyen, T. D. and Ho, T. B. (1999): "An Interactive-Graphic System for Decision Tree Induction", Journal of the Japanese Society for Artificial Intelligence, Vol. 14, N0. 1, 131–138.

Pujari A. (2001): Data Mining Techniques, Universities Press, India

Quinlan R. (1993): C4.5 Programs for Machine Learning, Morgan Kaufmann.

Weiss, S. M. and Kulikowski, C. A. (1991): Computer Systems That Learn: Classification and Prediction Methods from Statistics, Neural Nets, Machine Learning, and Expert Systems, Morgan Kaufmann.

Weiss, S. M. and Indurkhya, N. (1997): Predictive Data Mining: A Practical Guide, Morgan Kaufmann.

Westphal, C. and Blaxton, T. (1998): Data Mining Solutions: Methods and Tools for Real-World Problems, Wiley.

Clustering

5

5.1 Introduction

Clustering is a convenient method for discovering data distribution and patterns in underlying data. The primary goal of clustering is to learn the dense as well as the sparse regions in a dataset. Clustering can be considered the most important *unsupervised learning* problem, which means it deals with finding a structure in a collection of unlabeled data. The general definition of clustering can be stated as

Definition 5.1 The process of organizing objects into groups whose members are similar in some way.

Statistics, machine learning, and database researchers have studied data clustering with varied importance. The earlier approaches by researchers do not adequately consider the fact that a dataset can be too large to fit in the main memory or how to work with limited resources. The main emphasis was to cluster with the highest accuracy possible, even if the I/O costs are high. So instead of applying the classical clustering algorithms to data mining, we find it necessary to devise efficient algorithms that minimize the I/O operations.

In many datasets there are objects with categorical attributes that cannot be ordered. For instance, consider a market-basket database: the number of items and attributes in such a database is very large, while the size of an average transaction is less significant. Moreover, customers with similar buying patterns, who belong to a particular cluster, may buy a small subset of items from a much larger set that defines the cluster. In such cases, conventional clustering methods that handle only numeric data are not suitable.

This chapter will look into different clustering techniques for data mining by surveying various algorithms. There are two main approaches to clustering: partitioning clustering and hierarchical clustering. Clustering algorithms differ among themselves

- in their ability to handle different types of attributes (numeric and categorical),
- in accuracy of clustering, and
- in their ability to handle disk-resident data.

Partition-clustering techniques divide the database into a predefined number of clusters. They attempt to determine k partitions that optimize a certain criterion function. Partition-clustering algorithms are of two principal types: k-means and k-medoid; another type is the k-mode. We will concentrate on the k-means algorithm.

Hierarchical-clustering techniques do a sequence of partitions in which each partition is nested into the next partition of the sequence. It creates a hierarchy of clusters in ascending or descending orders. The hierarchical techniques fall into two types: *agglomerative* and *divisive*. The agglomerative technique starts with as many clusters as there are records, with each cluster having only one record. The pairs of clusters are sequentially merged until the number of clusters reduces to k. At each stage, the pairs of clusters that are merged are the ones nearest to each other. If the merging is continued, it terminates in a hierarchy of clusters, which is built with just a single cluster containing all the records, at the top of the hierarchy. Divisive clustering takes the opposite approach. It starts with all the records in one cluster and then tries to split that cluster into small slices.

Clustering can be carried out on both numerical data and categorical data. In numerical data, the inherent geometric properties can be used to define the distances between the points, whereas in categorical data, such a criterion does not exist. Many datasets consist of categorical attributes on which distance functions are not defined.

5.2   Statistical Methods

Thus far we have seen that clustering refers to the task of grouping objects into classes of similar objects. Clustering analysis has a long history both in statistics and machine learning. Clusters of related objects form one kind of information, which is revealed in data mining and can lead to new insights. There are many partitioning methods that construct partitions of a database of N objects into a set of k clusters. The construction involves determining the optimal partition with respect to an objective function. There are approximately $\frac{k^N}{k!}$ ways of partitioning a set of N data points into k-subsets. The partition-clustering algorithm normally adopts the iterative optimization paradigm, which begins with an initial partition and uses an iterative control strategy. It tries swapping data points to see if such a swapping enriches the quality of clustering. It locates a local optimal partition whenever swapping does not generate any progress in clustering. Furthermore, the quality of clustering is very sensitive to the initially selected partition.

In order to find clusters, the similarity or dissimilarity of objects needs to be measured. This is done with metrics on feature vectors such as Euclidean (or Minkowski or Manhattan) distance for real-valued features,

$$\rho(x, y) = \left(\sum_{i=1}^{d} (x_i - y_i^q) \right)^{1/q}$$

and simple matching for categorical features,

$$\rho(x, y) = |\{x_i | x_i \neq y_i\}|.$$

Frequently, the distances are normalized, or weighted differences are used.

In the next subsection, we will study the k-means algorithm, where each cluster is represented by the cluster's center of gravity.

5.2.1 The *k*–Means Algorithm

The *k*-means method of cluster detection is the most commonly used. It has many variations, but the form described here was the one first published by J. B. MacQueen in 1967. This algorithm has an input of predefined number of clusters, which is called *k*. "Means" stands for the average location of all the members of a single cluster. Assume that the data is represented as a relational table, with each row representing an object and each column representing an attribute. The value of every attribute from the table of data we are analyzing represents a distance from the origin along the attribute axes. Furthermore, to use this geometry, the values in the dataset must all be numeric. If they are categorical, then they should be normalized in order to allow adequate results of the overall distances in a multi-attribute space. The *k*-means algorithm is a straightforward iterative procedure in which a vital notion is *centroid*. A centroid is a point in the space of objects that represents an average position of a single cluster. The coordinates of this point are the averages of the attribute values of all objects that belong to the cluster. The iterative process of redefining centroids and reassigning data objects to clusters needs a small number of iterations to converge. The simple stepwise description of *k*-means can be given as

Step 1: Randomly select *k* points to be the starting points for the centroids of the *k* clusters.

Step 2: Assign each object to the centroid closest to the object, forming *k* exclusive clusters of examples.

Step 3: Calculate new centroids of the clusters. Take the average of all the attribute values of the objects belonging to the same cluster.

Step 4: Check if the cluster centroids have changed their coordinates. If yes, repeat from Step 2.

Step 5: If no, cluster detection is finished, and all objects have their cluster memberships defined.

Let us discuss the partitioning technique in detail.

The purpose of clustering is to obtain subsets that are more genuine than the initial set. This means their elements are much more similar on average than the elements of the original domain. A partition $T_1, T_2, ..., T_k$ is represented by the centroids $z_1, z_2, ..., z_k$ such that

$$x \in T_i \Leftrightarrow \rho(x, z_i) \le \rho(x, z_j), \quad i, j = 1, ...k$$

One can see that even though no information about the classes has been used in this case, the *k*-means algorithm is perfectly capable of finding the three main classes.

The centroids are used for estimates of an *impurity measure* of the form

$$J(z_1, z_2, ..., z_p) = \frac{1}{N}\sum_{i=1}^{k}\sum_{x^{(j)} \in T_i} \rho(x^{(j)}, z_i) = \frac{1}{N}\sum_{j=1}^{N} \min_{1 \le i \le k} \rho(x^{(j)}, z_i)$$

```
Select k arbitrary data points z₁, z₂, ..., zₖ.
repeat
   Tᵢ := {x⁽ʲ⁾ | ρ(x⁽ʲ⁾, zᵢ) ≤ ρ(x⁽ʲ⁾, zₛ),    s = 1, 2, ..., p}

          1
   zᵢ := ─────  Σ  x⁽ʲ⁾.
        | Tᵢ | x⁽ʲ⁾∈Tᵢ

until zᵢ do not change.
```

Figure 5.1 k-means algorithm

The algorithms for partitioning (i.e., k-means and k-medoid) vary in the manner that they estimate the centroids. In the k-means algorithm, the mean of the real-valued observations in the cluster T_i is calculated as

$$z_i = \frac{1}{N_i} \sum_{x^{(j)} \in T_i} x^{(j)},$$

where N_i denotes the number of data points in T_i.

We can observe an interesting property in that the k-means algorithm will not increase the function J. On the contrary, if any clusters are changed, J is reduced. As J is bounded from below, it converges, and as a consequence, the algorithm converges. It is also shown that the k-means will always converge to a local minimum.

The algorithm is presented in **Figure 5.1**. There are two key steps in the algorithm: the determination of the distances between all the points and the recalculation of the centroids.

Two disadvantages of the k-means method are that the mean may not be close to any data point at all, and the data is limited to real vectors.

An alternative algorithm is the k-medoid where the centroid is chosen to be the most central element of the set; that is, $z_i = x^{(s_i)}$ such that

$$\sum_{x^{(j)} \in T_i} \rho(x^{(j)}, x^{(s_i)}) \leq \sum_{x^{(j)} \in T_i} \rho(x^{(j)}, x^{(m)}) \text{ for all } x^{(m)} \in T_i.$$

5.2.1.1 Numerical Example

Consider a one-dimensional database with the attribute A, as shown in **Table 5.1**. Use the k-means algorithm to partition this database into $k = 2$ clusters. Start by selecting two random starting points, which will act as the centroids of the two clusters.

$$z_1 = 2$$
$$z_2 = 4$$

To form clusters, allocate each object in the database to the adjacent centroid. For instance, 10 is nearer to z_2 than to z_1. If an object is the same distance from two centroids, such as object 3, we make an arbitrary assignment. The new assignments are shown in **Table 5.2**.

A
2
4
10
12
3
20
30
11
25

Table 5.1   One-dimensional database

Clusters	A
T_1	2
T_2	4
T_2	10
T_2	12
T_1	3
T_2	20
T_2	30
T_2	11
T_2	25

Table 5.2   New cluster assignments

Once all objects have been assigned, recompute the means of the clusters.

$$\text{For cluster } T_1: \frac{2+3}{2} = 2.5$$

and for cluster T_2: $\dfrac{4 + 10 + 12 + 20 + 30 + 11 + 25}{7} = \dfrac{112}{7} = 16$

Then reassign each object to the two clusters based on the new calculations. This is given in the **Table 5.3**.

These steps are repeated until the means converge to their optimal values. In each iteration, the means are recomputed and all objects are reassigned. In this example, only one more iteration is necessary before the means converge. This can be given as

$$\text{For cluster } T_1: \frac{2+3+4}{3} = 3$$

$$\text{For cluster } T_2: \frac{10 + 12 + 20 + 30 + 11 + 25}{6} = \frac{108}{6} = 18$$

If we reassign the objects now, there will not be any change in the clusters. This signifies that the means have converged to their optimal values, and the algorithm terminates.

Clusters	A
T_1	2
T_1	4
T_2	10
T_2	12
T_1	3
T_2	20
T_2	30
T_2	11
T_2	25

Table 5.3   Reassignment of objects to two clusters

5.2.1.2   Implementation of the *k*-means Algorithm

Under Chapter 5 on the CD, you can see a link called java, which will take you to a directory/folder named `java`. Create a directory called `chapter5` on your hard disk, and copy the `java` subdirectory to it. The directory has a Java class called `Kmeans`, as well as a number of test files. The contents of the test file `test.txt` are shown in **Figure 5.2**. The file contains seven rows and seven columns. Each row corresponds to an object. Number these objects from 0 to 6. A seven-dimensional vector represents each object. For example, the 0th object has 1s in all the seven columns. A closer examination of Figure 5.2 shows that the objects can be grouped into two clusters. The objects 0, 2, and 6 seem to be closer to each other. Similarly, the objects 1, 3, 4, and 5 seem to belong to a single cluster. We can verify the clustering by running the Java class `Kmeans` as follows:

```
java Kmeans test.txt 7 7 2 10
```
(Command 5.1)

The first argument after the class name is the name of the file containing the data. The second and third arguments specify the number of rows and columns in the file. The third argument corresponds to the desired number of clusters. The number of iterations is given by the fourth argument. The output from (Command 5.1) is shown in **Figure 5.3**, which shows the objects from `test.txt` divided in the two clusters. The class `Kmeans` can work with any reasonable size matrix representing objects. The file `big2d.txt` in the same directory (`chapter5/java`)

```
1 1 1 1 1 1 1
2.5 2.5 1.5 2 2 2 2
1.5 1.5 1.5 1 1 1 1
2.5 2.5 1.5 2 2 2 2
1.5 1.5 1.5 2 2 2 2
2 2 2 2 2 2 2
1 1 1 1.5 1.5 1.5 1.5
```

Figure 5.2   Test data for clustering algorithms from file `test.txt`

```
Cluster #0 (Number of objects = 3)
 0 2 6
Cluster #1 (Number of objects = 4)
 1 3 4 5
```

Figure 5.3   Clustering for the test data from Figure 5.2

contains 252 objects represented using two dimensions. You can run the Java class `Kmeans` for this file as follows:

`java Kmeans big2d.txt 252 2 3 100`   (Command 5.2)

Here, we are grouping 252 objects (first argument) represented using 2 dimensions (second argument) into 3 clusters (third argument). The fourth argument specifies that the clustering algorithm should perform 100 iterations. The two-dimensional representation of objects helps us see the graphical representation of objects as shown in **Figure 5.4**. There are three clearly identifiable clusters. The algorithm, in fact, managed to assign all the objects to the appropriate clusters. The `Kmeans` class can work with fairly large matrices. (Try to run it for the file `superSize2D.txt`, which has 9627 rows and 2 columns. There should be three natural clusters for the data.)

Figure 5.5 shows the information about the constructor and methods of the `Kmeans` class. The class has only one constructor, which takes three parameters: number of rows, number of columns, and the desired number of clusters. The method `readObjects` reads the object matrix from a file supplied as a parameter of the type `String`. The method `makeClusters` runs the actual clustering. The only parameter to the method is the number of iterations to be used in

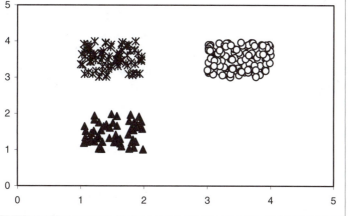

Figure 5.4   Graphical representation of clustering objects from `big2d.txt`

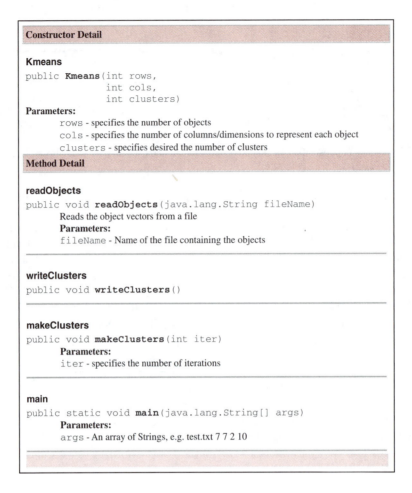

Figure 5.5 Methods from the Kmeans class (Suitable for Java programmers)

the algorithm. The method writeClusters simply writes out the formed clusters. The main program receives the four arguments as shown in (Command 5.1) and (Command 5.2). The complete source code for the class is available on the CD. The following are some of the salient features of the algorithm.

The class has three data members:

- double [ ][ ] objects: A two-dimensional array to store all the objects.
- double [ ][ ] centroids: A two-dimensional array to store all the centroids.
- Vector [ ] memberships: An array of Vectors. Each Vector stores the list of objects in a cluster.

Figure 5.6 shows a code snippet from the constructor of the class. The code shown in the figure essentially assigns a class randomly to one of the clusters. These assignments in the constructor are used to calculate the initial values of centroids.

```
for(int i = 0; i < objects.length; i++)
    memberships[(int)Math.round(Math.random()*(clusters-1))]
    .add(new Integer(i));
```

Figure 5.6 Code snippet from the constructor of the `Kmeans` class (Suitable for Java programmers)

The method `makeClusters`, shown in **Figure 5.7**, describes the progress of the k-means algorithm. The method `calculateCentroids` calculates centroid values. The method `findWinner` finds the centroid closest to an object, which is assigned to that cluster. The process is repeated for the specified number of iterations.

The method `calculateCentroids` is shown in **Figure 5.8**. The first loop in the function initializes all the centroid values to zero. The vectors corresponding to the objects that belong to a given cluster are added to its centroids in the nested loop. The third loop divides the accumulated centroid values by the size of each cluster to yield the average values.

```
public void makeClusters(int iter)
{
    for(int k = 0; k < iter; k++)
    {
        calculateCentroids();
        for(int i = 0; i < memberships.length; i++)
            memberships[i].clear();
        for(int i = 0; i < objects.length; i++)
        {
            memberships[findWinner(i)].add(new Integer(i));
        }
    }
}
```

Figure 5.7 `makeClusters` method from the `Kmeans` class (Suitable for Java programmers)

```
void calculateCentroids()
{
    for(int i = 0; i < centroids.length; i++)
        for(int j = 0; j < centroids[0].length; j++)
            centroids[i][j] = 0;

    for(int k = 0; k < memberships.length; k++)
        for(int i = 0; i < memberships[k].size(); i++)
        {
            int m = ((Integer)memberships[k].get(i)).intValue();
            for(int j = 0; j < centroids[0].length; j++)
                centroids[k][j] += objects[m][j];
        }

    for(int i = 0; i < memberships.length; i++)
        for(int j = 0; j < centroids[0].length; j++)
            centroids[i][j] /= memberships[i].size();
}
```

Figure 5.8 `calculateCentroids` method from the `Kmeans` class (Suitable for Java programmers)

```
int findWinner(int objectID)
{
     double min = dist(objectID,0);
     int minAT = 0;
     for(int j = 1; j < centroids.length; j++)
     {
          double temp = dist(objectID,j);
          if(temp < min)
          {
               min = temp;
               minAT = j;
          }
     }
     return minAT;
}
```

Figure 5.9   `findWinner` method from the **Kmeans** and **Kohonen** classes (Suitable for Java programmers)

```
double dist(int objectID, int centroidID)
{
     double d = 0;
     for(int j = 0; j < centroids[0].length; j++)
     {
          double o = objects[objectID][j];
          double c = centroids[centroidID][j];
          d += (c-o)*(c-o);
     }
     if(centroids[0].length == 0) return 0;
     return Math.sqrt(d)/centroids[0].length;
}
```

Figure 5.10   `dist` method from the **Kmeans** and **Kohonen** classes (Suitable for Java programmers)

Figure 5.9 shows the `findWinner` method, which finds the closest centroid for a given object. The distance between an object and a centroid is calculated using the method `dist` shown in **Figure 5.10**. The Euclidean distance is programmed in the function `dist`. It should be noted that it is possible to use other distance measures. For example, the inverse of similarity in the Vector Space Model (VSM) can also serve as distance. The readers are encouraged, in the Exercises section, to replace the existing `dist` function with the inverse of `sim` from the class **VSMranker** presented in Chapter 2.

The **Kmeans** class cannot be used for a Term Document Matrix (TDM) for even a moderate size document collection such as CACM. The resulting matrix would have 3204 rows (one for each document) and 6920 columns (one for each term). Readers are encouraged to use the basic algorithm given in **Kmeans.java** along with the **VSMranker** class from Chapter 2 to create an implementation of the k-means algorithm that will be able to cluster documents from a SMART collection. More complete descriptions of the clustering-related programming projects in this book appear in the Exercises section.

5.2.2 Other Methods

5.2.2.1 Probabilistic Clustering

There are some differences between partition-based clustering and probabilistic clustering. The idea for the partition-based algorithm is that if a point belongs to a cluster, it belongs exclusively to that cluster. Probabilistic clustering, on the other hand, permits a point x to have partial membership in a cluster.

The idea behind the partition-based algorithm does lead to some problems. In the graph in **Figure 5.11**, point x has the same distance from c_i and c_j, so it is unfair to let it belong exclusively to either c_i or c_j. One can tackle this situation using a probability function; that is, $p(c_i|x) = 0.50$ and $p(c_j|x) = 0.50$.

Now we are going to present one of the probabilistic clustering approaches, known as the *EM algorithm*, where E means Expectation and M means Maximization. It takes data as a combination of k-normal distribution, which is an important assumption of the algorithm. There are several unknown parameters $\mu_i, \sigma_i, \forall i = 1....k$, and $p(c_i), i = 1...k$, where μ_i, σ_i gives the mean and standard deviation of the cluster c_i respectively, and $p(c_i)$ is the prior probability of cluster c_i.

This is a four-step algorithm. The steps are explained here:

1. **Initialization:** Randomly select the parameters $\mu_{C_i}, \sigma_{C_i}, p(c_i), \forall i = 1....k$ for k clusters, so in total there are 3-k unknown parameters.

2. **Expectation Step**: Compute the probability of a point belonging to a cluster.

   Suppose that the model parameters $\mu_{c_i}, \sigma_{c_i}, p(c_i)$ are all known, and the objective is to compute $p(c_i|x), \forall x, \forall c_i$. Using the well-known Bayes rule, we get

   $$p(c_i|x) = \frac{p(x|c_i)p(c_i)}{p(x)},$$

   where $p(x) = p(x|c_1)p(c_1) + p(x|c_2)p(c_2) + ... + p(x|c_k)p(c_k)$.

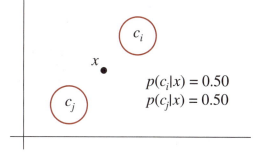

$$p(c_i|x) = 0.50$$
$$p(c_j|x) = 0.50$$

Figure 5.11   Depiction of probabilistic clustering

Further using the normal-distribution equation, we get

$$p(x|c_i) = f(x|\mu_{c_i}, \sigma_{c_i}) = \frac{1}{(\sigma_{c_i})\sqrt{2\pi}} e^{-\frac{(x-\mu_{c_i})^2}{2\sigma_{c_i}^2}}$$

3. **Maximization Step**: Compute the new parameters to accomplish a locally optimal result. Assume that $p(c_i|x)$ for all x and all c_i.

Let $w_i(x) = p(c_i|x), \forall x, \forall c_i$, which will be useful to compute the weighted parameter among all clusters, and reestimate the model parameters: $\mu_{c_i}^n, \sigma_{c_i}^n, p^n(c_i)$

$$\mu_{c_i}^n = \frac{\sum\limits_{j=1}^{N} x_j w_i(x_j)}{\sum\limits_{j=1}^{N} w_i(x_j)}$$

$$\left(\sigma_{c_i}^n\right)^2 = \frac{\sum\limits_{j=1}^{N} (x_j - \mu_{c_i}^n)^2 w_i(x_j)}{\sum\limits_{j=1}^{N} w_i(x_j)}$$

$$p^n(c_i) = \frac{\sum\limits_{j=1}^{N} w_i(x_j)}{\sum\limits_{i=1}^{k} \sum\limits_{j=1}^{N} w_i(x_j)}$$

4. Repeat Steps 2 and 3 until convergence; that is, there is little or no change in the model parameters.

The algorithm enhances the solution in each iteration. The major limitation of this algorithm is that it converges to only a local optima.

5.2.2.2 The Agglomerative Algorithm

Hierarchical algorithms create a hierarchical decomposition of the database. These algorithms iteratively split the database into smaller subsets until the termination condition is satisfied. The hierarchical algorithms do not need k (number of clusters) as an input parameter. This is an advantage over the partitioning algorithms. The disadvantage of the hierarchical algorithms is that the termination condition needs to be specified. The hierarchical decomposition can be represented as a bottom-up approach (which is termed as *agglomerative*) and a top-down approach. The general agglomerative algorithm works as follows:

- Initially, every object is placed in a unique cluster.
- For every pair of clusters, the value of dissimilarity and distance is calculated.
- Then at each step, the clusters with the minimum distances in the current clustering are merged.

- This is done until the whole dataset forms a single cluster.
- The termination criteria can be decided by fixing the critical distance D_{min} between the clusters.

5.2.2.3 Self-Organizing Maps

Self-organizing maps are a variant of neural networks, which have been used for several years in applications such as feature detection in two-dimensional images. More recently they have been applied successfully for more general clustering applications. We shall discuss self-organizing neural networks in the subsection 5.3.1 of this chapter.

5.3 Neural-Network-Based Approaches

Neural networks are another paradigm for computing that has its roots in neuroscience. The human brain consists of a network of neurons, each of which is made up of a number of nerve fibers called *dendrites,* connected to the *cell body* where the *cell nucleus* is located. The *axon* is a long, single fiber that originates from the cell body and branches near its end into a number of *strands.* At the ends of these strands are the transmitting ends of the *synapses,* which connect to other biological neurons through the receiving ends of the synapses found on the dendrites, as well as the cell body of biological neurons. A single axon normally makes thousands of synapses with other neurons. Transmission is a complex chemical process that, in fact, increases or decreases the electrical potential within the cell body of the receiving neuron. When this electrical potential reaches a threshold value, it enters its excitatory state and is said to *fire.* It is the connectivity of the neuron that gives these simple "devices" their real power.

Artificial neurons are basic or simplistic models of biological neurons. As in biological neurons, an artificial neuron has a number of inputs, a cell body that often consists of the summing node and the transfer function, and an output that can be connected to a number of other artificial neurons. Artificial neural networks are densely interconnected networks, together with a learning rule, to adjust the strength of connections between the units in response to externally supplied data.

The evolution of neural networks as a new computational model originates from the pioneering work of McCulloch and Pitts in 1943 (McCulloch and Pitts, 1943) They suggested a simple model of a neuron that computed the weighted sum of the inputs to the neuron and produced an output of 1 or 0, according to whether the sum was over a threshold value.

Consider a simple illustration of a single artificial neuron given in **Figure 5.12** The node has three inputs, $x = (x_1; x_2; x_3)$, that receive only binary signals (either 0 or 1). This node can receive 8 input patterns, as shown in **Table 5.4**.

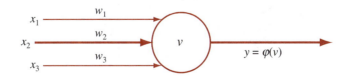

Figure 5.12   Single artificial neuron with three inputs

x_1	0	1	0	1	0	1	0	1
x_2	0	0	1	1	0	0	1	1
x_3	0	0	0	0	1	1	1	1

Table 5.4   All possible input patterns from Figure 5.12

For five inputs there will be 32 input patterns. Observe that $8 = 2^3$, $16 = 2^4$, and $32 = 2^5$ (for three, four, and five inputs). Therefore, the formula for the number of binary input patterns is 2^n, where n in the number of inputs. Furthermore, assume that the weights corresponding to the three inputs have the following values:

$$w_1 = 2,$$
$$w_2 = -4,$$
$$w_3 = 1.$$

A *combination function* is used to combine the input values and the weights. A *transfer function* calculates the output value, usually between 0 and 1. Together, the combination function and the transfer function make up the *activation function* of the node. We consider the activation of the neuron by the step function as

$$\varphi(v) = \begin{cases} 1 \text{ if } v \geq 0 \\ 0 \text{ otherwise} \end{cases}$$

Now we can find the output value y of the neuron for each pattern, as shown in **Table 5.5**. To do this, first we must calculate the weighted sum

$$v = \sum_i w_i x_i = w_1 x_1 + w_2 x_2 + w_3 x_3$$

Pattern	P1	P2	P3	P4
x_1	1	0	1	1
x_2	0	1	0	1
x_3	0	1	1	1

Table 5.5   Input patterns for the neural network

and apply the activation function to v. Thus, the computation of each input pattern will be given as

$$P_1 : v = 2 \times 1 - 4 \times 0 + 1 \times 0 = 2,$$
$$2 > 0, y = \varphi(2) = 1.$$
$$P_2 : v = 2 \times 0 - 4 \times 1 + 1 \times 1 = -3,$$
$$-3 < 0, y = \varphi(-3) = 0.$$
$$P_3 : v = 2 \times 1 - 4 \times 0 + 1 \times 1 = 3,$$
$$3 > 0, y = \varphi(3) = 1.$$
$$P_4 : v = 2 \times 1 - 4 \times 1 + 1 \times 1 = -1,$$
$$-1 < 0, y = \varphi(-1) = 0.$$

Here, the *training set* is a set of pairs of input patterns with corresponding desired-output patterns. Each pair represents how the network is supposed to respond to a particular input. The network is trained to respond correctly to each input pattern from the training set. Training algorithms that use training sets are called *supervised-learning algorithms*. Think of a supervised-learning algorithm as learning with a teacher, and the training set as a set of examples. During training, when presented with input patterns, the network gives "wrong" output. The error is used to adjust the weights in the network so that next time the error will be smaller. This procedure is repeated using many examples (pairs of inputs and desired outputs) from the training set until the error becomes sufficiently small.

The simple network, *perceptron*, is extended further to get multilayered, by which extra *hidden layers* (layers additional to the input and output layers, and not connected externally) are added. More than one hidden layer can be used. The network topology is constrained to be *feedforward* (loop free). Usually connections are allowed from the input layer to the first hidden layer; from the first hidden layer to the second, and so on, until the last hidden layer is connected to the output layer. The occurrence of these layers permits an artificial neural network to approximate a variety of nonlinear functions. The actual construction of a network, including the determination of the number of hidden layers and the determination of the overall number of units, is somewhat like a trial-and-error process. The transfer function is normally a sigmoid function yielding a value between 0 and 1.

5.3.1 Kohonen's Self-Organizing Maps

Simple perceptrons and multilayered networks are considered to be supervised networks. In an unsupervised form, the network adjusts solely in response to its inputs. These networks can learn to choose structures in their input. One of the most popular models in the unsupervised framework is the *self-organizing map* (SOM).

The self-organizing map was a neural network model developed by Teuvo Kohonen in 1979 (Kaski, et al., 1988; Kohonen, 1990, 1995, 1997; Lawrence, 1999). It is one of the most commonly used unsupervised neural-network models. A SOM uses competitive learning steps and consists of a layer of input units, each of which is fully connected to a set of output units, which are arranged in some topology (the most common choice is a two-dimensional grid). The input units, after receiving the input patterns x, propagate them to the output units. Each of the output units k is assigned a weight vector w_k. During the learning step, the unit c corresponding to the highest activity level with respect to a randomly selected input pattern x, is adapted in such a way that it exhibits an even higher activity level at a future presentation of x. Generally, the similarity metric is preferred to be the Euclidean distance. During the learning steps of the SOM, a set of units around the winner is tuned toward the currently presented input pattern, enabling a spatial arrangement of the input patterns, where similar inputs are mapped onto regions close to each other in the grid of output units. Hence, the training process of the SOM results in a topological organization of the input patterns. The process is similar to k-means clustering. Therefore, the SOM retains some of the topological ordering of the output. It also takes a high-dimensional input and clusters it. Subsequent to training, an input will cause some of the output units in some areas to become active. Such clustering is valuable as a preprocessing stage.

There are many different types of SOMs that exist today. The SOM defines a mapping from the input data space R^n onto a regular two-dimensional array of nodes. With every node i, a parametric reference vector $w_i \in R^n$ is associated. An input vector $x \in R^n$ is compared with the w_i, and the best match is defined as *response*: the input is thus mapped onto this location.

Each component plane of the array (the numerical values of the corresponding components of the w_i vectors) may also be displayed separately in the same format as the array, using a gray scale to illustrate the values of the components. One might say that the SOM is a *nonlinear projection* of the probability density function of the high-dimensional input data onto the two-dimensional display. Let $x \in R^n$ be an input-data vector. It may be compared with all the w_i in any metric; in practical applications, the smallest of the Euclidean distances $||x - w_i||$ is usually made to define the best-matching node, signified by the subscript c:

$$d_k = ||x - w_c||$$
$$c = \min_i d_k(t)$$

Thus, x is mapped onto the node c relative to the parameter values w_i. An optimal mapping technique would be one that maps the probability density function $p(x)$, trying to preserve at least the local structures of $p(x)$. The definition of such w_i values is far from trivial.

During learning, the nodes that are topographically close in the array will activate each other to learn from the same input. Without mathematical proof, we state that useful values of the m_i can be found as convergence limits of the following learning process, whereby the initial values of the $w_i(0)$ can be arbitrary; for example, random:

$$w_i(t+1) = w_i(t) + h_{ck}(t)[x(t) - w_i(t)], \tag{5.1}$$

where t is an integer, the discrete-time coordinate, and $h_{ck}(t)$ is the so-called neighborhood function. It is a function defined over the lattice points.

Normally, $h_{ck}(t) = h(||r_c - r_i||, t)$, where $r_c \in R^2$ and $r_i \in R^2$ are the radius vectors of nodes c and i, respectively, in the array. The basic SOM algorithm is shown in **Figure 5.13**.

Initialization: $w_i \in R^n$
    $t = 0$
    for period $= 1$ to N_{period} do
        interpolate new values for $\alpha(t)$ and $\sigma(t)$
        for record $= 1$ to *Nrecord* do
            $t = t + 1$
            for $k = 1$ to K do   //here K is the number of node
            compute distance, $d_k = ||x - w_k(t)||$
            endfor
            computer winning node, $c = \min_i d_k(t)$,
            for $k = 1$ to K do
                update weight vectors w_k using equation 5.1
            endfor
        endfor
    endfor

Figure 5.13   SOM algorithm

5.3.1.1 Numerical Demonstration

Consider the SOM given in **Figure 5.14**. The output layer of the SOM consists of six nodes: P, Q, R, S, T, and U, which are arranged into a two-dimensional lattice with neighbors connected by lines. Further, assume that every node has two inputs, say x_1 and x_2. Obviously every node will have two weights corresponding to the inputs. We call them w_1 and w_2.

Now suppose the values of the weights for every output in the SOM nodes are as in **Table 5.6**.

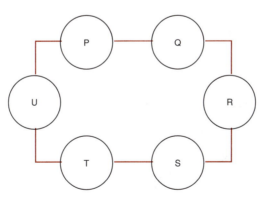

Figure 5.14 SOM

	P	Q	R	S	T	U
w_1	−1	0	3	−2	3	4
w_2	2	4	−2	−3	2	−1

Table 5.6 Values of the weights for SOM

Using Euclidean distance $||x-w|| = \sqrt{(x_1 - w_1)^2 + (x_2 - w_2)^2}$, we can find out the winner node for the input pattern $x = (x_1 = 2, x_2 = -4)$ as

$$||x - w_P|| = \sqrt{(2+1)^2 + (-4-2)^2} = \sqrt{45},$$
$$||x - w_Q|| = \sqrt{(2-0)^2 + (-4-4)^2} = \sqrt{68},$$
$$||x - w_R|| = \sqrt{(2-3)^2 + (-4+2)^2} = \sqrt{5},$$
$$||x - w_S|| = \sqrt{(2+2)^2 + (-4+3)^2} = \sqrt{17},$$
$$||x - w_T|| = \sqrt{(2-3)^2 + (-4-2)^2} = \sqrt{37},$$
$$||x - w_U|| = \sqrt{(2-4)^2 + (-4+1)^2} = \sqrt{13}.$$

Therefore, the winner node is R, because it has the smallest distance from x. As a next step, the weights of the nodes in the SOM must be adjusted using the formula given in Equation (5.1).

Let the neighborhood function be defined as

$$h_{ck}(t) = \begin{cases} 0.5 \text{ if node is the winner} \\ 0.25 \text{ if node is immediate neighbor of the winner} \\ 0 \text{ otherwise} \end{cases}$$

Begin with the winner node R.

The new weight of R will be

$$\begin{pmatrix} 3 \\ -2 \end{pmatrix} + 0.5 \left\{ \begin{pmatrix} 2 \\ -4 \end{pmatrix} - \begin{pmatrix} 3 \\ -2 \end{pmatrix} \right\} = \begin{pmatrix} 3 \\ -2 \end{pmatrix} + 0.5 \begin{pmatrix} -1 \\ -2 \end{pmatrix} = \begin{pmatrix} 2.5 \\ -3 \end{pmatrix}.$$

The immediate neighbors of R are Q and S, therefore new weights for Q and S are $\begin{pmatrix} 0.5 \\ 2 \end{pmatrix}$ and $\begin{pmatrix} -1 \\ -3.25 \end{pmatrix}$ respectively. Because other nodes in the given SOM have a neighborhood function value zero, their weights do not change.

5.3.1.2   Implementation of the Kohonen SOM

By now we will assume that you have created a directory called **chapter5** and copied the **java** subdirectory to that directory. The directory **chapter5/java** has a Java class called **Kohonen**. The **Kohonen** class runs the same way as the **Kmeans** class:

```
java Kohonen test.txt 7 7 2 10
```
(Command 5.3)

The first argument after the class name is the name of the file containing the data. The second and third arguments specify the number of rows and columns in the file. The third argument corresponds to the desired number of clusters. The number of iterations is given by the fourth argument. The output from (Command 5.3) is identical to the output from (Command 5.1) (shown in Figure 5.3). Readers should verify the clustering for the other two test data files: **big2d.txt** and **superSize2D.txt**.

There are many similarities between the Kohonen and Kmeans classes. **Figure 5.15** shows the information about the constructor and methods of the Kohonen class. The class has only one constructor, which takes four parameters: the number of rows, number of columns, desired number of clusters, and learning rate. The method readObjects reads the object matrix from a file supplied as a parameter of the type String. The method makeClusters runs the actual clustering. The only parameter to the method is the number of iterations to be used in the algorithm. The method writeClusters simply writes out the formed clusters. The main program receives the four arguments as shown in (Command 5.3). A learning rate is set at 0.01. Readers are welcome to experiment with different learning rates. The complete source code for the class is available on the CD. The following are some of the salient features of the class.

Constructor Detail

Kohonen
```
public Kohonen(int rows,
               int cols,
               int clusters,
               double initAlpha)
```
Parameters:
   rows - specifies the number of objects
   cols - specifies the number of columns/dimensions to represent each object
   clusters - specifies desired the number of clusters

Method Detail

readObjects
```
public void readObjects(java.lang.String fileName)
```
   Reads the object vectors from a file
   Parameters:
   fileName - Name of the file containing the objects

---

writeClusters
```
public void writeClusters()
```

---

makeClusters
```
public void makeClusters(int iter)
```
   Parameters:
   iter - specifies the number of iterations

---

main
```
public static void main(java.lang.String[] args)
```
   Parameters:
   args - An array of Strings, e.g. test.txt 7 7 2 10

Figure 5.15 Methods from Kohonen class (Suitable for Java programmers)

The class has four data members:

- double [][] objects: A two-dimensional array to store all the objects.
- double [][] weights: A two-dimensional array to store all the weights.
- Vector [] memberships: An array of **Vectors**. Each **Vector** stores the list of objects in a cluster.
- double alpha: The learning rate.

The method **makeClusters**, shown in **Figure 5.16**, describes the progress of the Kohonen algorithm. The method **initializeWeights** calculates initial weights. The method **findWinner** finds the centroid closest to an object. The method **update** updates the weights of the winner using the object. The process is repeated for the specified number of iterations. The **findWinner** (Figure 5.9) and **dist** (Figure 5.10) methods are identical to those from the Kmeans class. The method **initializeWeights** is shown in **Figure 5.17**. The method first assigns objects randomly to various clusters in the first loop (similar to the constructor from the

```
public void makeClusters(int iter)
{
    initializeWeights();
    for(int k = 0; k < iter; k++)
        for(int i = 0; i < objects.length; i++)
            update(findWinner(i), i);

    for(int i = 0; i < objects.length; i++)
        memberships[findWinner(i)].add(new Integer(i));
}
```

Figure 5.16 **makeClusters** method from the **Kohonen** class (Suitable for Java programmers)

```
void initializeWeights()
{
    //Initialize membership lists for each cluster
    for(int i = 0; i < objects.length; i++)
        memberships[(int)Math.round(Math.random()*
            (memberships.length-1))].add(new Integer(i));

    for(int i = 0; i < weights.length; i++)
        for(int j = 0; j < weights[0].length; j++)
            weights[i][j] = 0;

    for(int k = 0; k < memberships.length; k++)
        for(int i = 0; i < memberships[k].size(); i++)
        {
            int m = ((Integer)memberships[k].get(i)).intValue();
            for(int j = 0; j < weights[0].length; j++)
                weights[k][j] += objects[m][j];
        }

    for(int i = 0; i < memberships.length; i++)
        for(int j = 0; j < weights[0].length; j++)
            weights[i][j] /= memberships[i].size();
    //Don't need these random memberships anymore
    for(int i = 0; i < memberships.length; i++)
        memberships[i].clear();
}
```

Figure 5.17 **initializeWeights** method from **Kohonen** class (Suitable for Java programmers)

```
void update(int winner, int objectID)
{
    for(int j = 0; j < weights[winner].length; j++)
       weights[winner][j] =
       (1 - alpha)*weights[winner][j]
       + alpha*objects[objectID][j];
}
```

Figure 5.18   update method from the Kohonen class (Suitable for Java programmers)

Kmeans class). The second loop in the function initializes all the weight values to zero. The vectors corresponding to objects that belong to a given randomly created cluster are added to its weights in the nested loop. The third loop divides the accumulated weight values by the size of each randomly created cluster to yield the average values. The method update, shown in **Figure 5.18**, updates weights of the winners based on Equation (5.1).

5.3.2   Other Neural-Network-Based Approaches

5.3.2.1   Recurrent Back Propagation

Recurrent back propagation is a back-propagation network with feedback or recurrent connections. The feedback is restricted to either the hidden layer units or the output units. Adding feedback, in any configurations, from the activation of outputs from the previous pattern initiates a kind of memory to the process. Therefore, adding recurrent connections to a back-propagation network improves its ability to learn temporal sequences without altering the training process. Such networks are superior to standard back-propagation networks on time-series prediction problems.

5.3.2.2   Adaptive-Resonance Theory

Adaptive-resonance theory (ART) networks fall into a category of recurrent networks that can be used for clustering. Stephen Grossberg (Carpenter and Grossberg, 1988) introduced the notion of the ART networks. Input patterns are presented to the network, and an output unit is declared a winner in a process similar to the Kohonen feature maps. The feedback connections from the winner output encode the predictable input-pattern template. If the actual input pattern does not match the predictable connection weights to a sufficient degree, then the winner output is shut off. In such cases, the next closest output unit is declared the winner. This process resumes until one of the output unit's expectations is satisfied to within the requisite tolerance. If none of the output units win, then a new output unit is dedicated with the initial predictable pattern set to the current input pattern.

5.3.2.3   Probabilistic Neural Networks

Probabilistic neural networks (PNN) include feed-forward architecture and a supervised training algorithm similar to back propagation. Each training input pattern is used as connection weights to a new hidden unit, instead of altering the input-layer weights using the generalized delta rule. Each input pattern is incorporated into the PNN architecture. This technique is exceptionally fast because only one pass through the network is required to set the input-connection weights.

Probabilistic neural networks offer several advantages over back-propagation networks. Given enough input data, the PNN will converge to a Bayesian classifier. Probabilistic neural networks allow true incremental learning where new training data can be added at any time without requiring retraining of the entire network.

5.4 Evolutionary Computing

In 1975 Holland (1992) presented the concept of Genetic Algorithms (GA) as a class of computational models that mimic natural evolution in solving problems in a wide variety of domains. Genetic algorithms are mostly appropriate for solving complex optimization problems and also for applications that require adaptive problem-solving strategies. Genetic algorithms, which combine a Darwinian "survival of the fittest" approach with a structured information exchange, are search algorithms based on the mechanics of natural genetics. The advantage of the genetic approach of these algorithms is that they can search complex and large amounts of spaces well and trace near-optimal solutions quickly.

A GA maps strings of numbers to each potential solution. Each solution becomes an individual in the population, and each string becomes a representation of an individual. The GA subsequently manipulates the most promising strings in its search for an improved solution.

The algorithm operates through a simple cycle shown in **Figure 5.19**. Each cycle produces a new generation of possible solutions (individuals) for a given problem. At the first phase, a population of possible solutions is created as a starting point. Each individual in this population is encoded into a string (the chromosome) to be manipulated by the genetic operators. Then the individuals are evaluated. First, the individual is created from its string description (its chromosome), and then its performance in relation to the target response is evaluated. This evaluation process determines how fit the individual is in relation to the others in the population. Based on each individual's fitness, a selection mechanism chooses the best pairs for the genetic manipulation process. The selection policy is responsible for ensuring the survival of the fittest individuals. The manipulation process enables the genetic operators to produce a new population of individuals—the progeny—by manipulating the genetic information possessed by the pairs chosen to reproduce. This information is stored in the strings (chromosomes) that

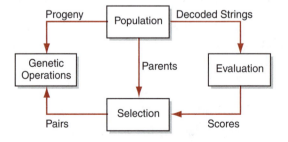

Figure 5.19   Genetic algorithm cycle

describe the individuals. Two operators are used: *Crossover* (used to recombine the population's genetic material) and *Mutation* (to introduce new genetic structures in the population by randomly changing some of its building blocks). The progeny generated by this process take the place of the older individual.

An application of the genetic algorithm in data mining is for *hypothesis testing and refinement,* whereby the user poses a hypothesis and the system first evaluates the hypothesis and then seeks to refine it. Seeding the system with the hypothesis and then allowing some or all parts of it to vary achieves hypothesis refinement. One can use a variety of evaluation functions to determine the fitness of a candidate refinement. The significant feature of the GA application is the encoding of the hypothesis and the evaluation function for the fitness.

One more application of the GA for data mining is to design hybrid techniques by blending one of the known techniques such as neural networks with the GA. For instance, it is possible to use the genetic algorithm for optimal decision-tree induction. As discussed in Chapter 4, we can take tests of a training dataset to build a decision tree. Thus, by randomly generating different samples, we can build many decision trees using any of the traditional techniques; but we are not sure if the constructed tree is optimal. At this stage, genetic algorithms are very useful in deciding on the optimal tree and optimal splitting attributes. Genetic algorithms also control the preference for one type of decision tree over another.

5.5 Application of Clustering to an E-Commerce Application

Let us apply our clustering programs to the data from Gazelle.com. We created a dataset called `visitItemSpend.csv` in Chapter 5 on the CD, which contains visits, items bought, and spending for each customer in the KDD-cup 2000 data. For convenience, we have copied the file in Chapter 5, under the directory `java`. Let us say we want to cluster the customers based on the three previous attributes. If we were to use the raw values of these variables, the spending attribute would dominate the clustering; therefore, we should normalize the values of these variables to be between 0 and 1. However, before we do that, let us have another look at the file `visitItemSpend.csv` by opening it using Microsoft Excel. The two highest values of spending are significantly higher than the rest, making them outliers. The last six lines have negative values, probably corresponding to returning merchandise. Delete the first two and last six lines, and then normalize each column by the maximum value of the variable. We will not store the `customer_id` either. The results are stored in a file called `gazelle.txt` in the directory `java`. There are 1823 records, and each one is represented by three variables. Assume that we want to partition them in four clusters. Run the k-means algorithm for 100 iterations by typing the following command:

```
java Kmeans gazelle.txt 1823 3 4 100
```
(Command 5.4)

Redirect the output to a file. Note that your results may not always be the same when you run the algorithm. **Figure 5.20** shows the values of the variables for the four clusters. Cluster C1 has maximum items and spending, followed by clusters C2, C3, and C4. The number of visits is the highest for cluster C2, followed by C1, C3, and C4. Cluster C1 has 10 customers, C2 has 27 customers, and C3 has 238 customers. Cluster C4 has 1548 customers. If we assume

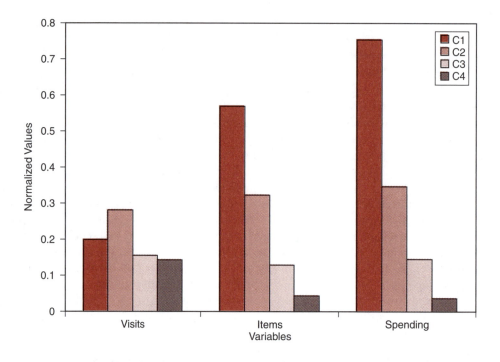

Figure 5.20   Results of clustering customers from Gazelle.com

that the items and spending is an indication of spending potential and visits as a measure of loyalty, we can label the clusters as follows:

C1: Semi-loyal, big spender

C2: Loyal, moderate spender

C3: Semi-loyal, moderate spender

C4: Infrequent, low spender

This analysis is based on limited data and analysis, and thus is not considered to be very meaningful. However, it gives us some insight into how clustering can be useful in an e-commerce environment. Readers are encouraged to modify the weighting scheme and see if they can come up with a more meaningful clustering scheme for the data from `visitItemSpend.csv`. A more interesting clustering exercise may include additional customer data from the KDD-cup site contained in `question3.data` (see Exercises section).

5.6   Text Clustering

Text clustering is very valuable in text mining. It can be done by using any of the clustering techniques discussed in this chapter. Initially, all features of unstructured text are identified or the structured data of the text is made available. Unstructured texts mean free documents such as news stories. One can use vectors of words to represent unstructured documents and extract different features from it. These features are extracted to convert the unstructured text to a structured one. A few important features are given here.

- **Latent semantic index**: It transforms the original text vectors to a lower dimensional space by analyzing the correlation structure of terms in the document.
- **Stop words**: This feature includes elimination of the case, punctuation, stop words, and so on.
- **Word Occurrences**: This vector representation takes single words found in the training corpus as features, ignoring the sequence in which the words occur. This is called Boolean, if we consider whether a word either occurs or does not occur in a document.
- **n-gram**: These are the word sequences of length up to n.
- **Part of speech**: Noun, verb, adjective, and adverb are common tags in the text. There can be 25 different values for the part-of-speech tags.
- **Stemming**: A process that reduces words to their morphological roots.
- **Higher-order features**: Features, such as phrases, named entities, locations, concept categories, are called higher-order features. Such features can be further reduced by applying other feature-selection techniques such as entropy, odds ratio, and information gain.

The text is represented as structured data after the aforementioned features are extracted and data-mining techniques can be applied. One of the most standard text clustering algorithms is *Ward's Minimum Variance*. It is an agglomerative hierarchical clustering method and has a tendency to create dense clusters.

One can use either the Hamming distance or Euclidean distance as the measure of dissimilarities between feature vectors. The clustering method starts with n clusters (one for each text). After a phase, two clusters are merged to generate a new cluster. The clusters, T_a and T_b, are merged to get a new cluster T_{ab} based on the following criterion:

$$V_{ab} = MIN_{i.j}V_{ij}$$

$$V_{ij} = \frac{||\bar{x}_i - \bar{x}_j||^2}{\frac{1}{n_i} + \frac{1}{n_j}},$$

where x_i is the mean value of the dissimilarity for the cluster T_i, and n_i is the number of elements in this cluster.

There is also a method of grouping the text using clustering techniques. It is called *scatter* or *gather interface*, and it uses text clustering taking into account similarities in their contents as a means to group texts. Each text here is represented by a list of topical terms. If the cluster has many documents, then the user can recluster the texts into smaller groups. Obviously, such reclustering tends to modify the sorts of themes of the clusters.

EXERCISES

1. What is clustering? Discuss various clustering techniques with their merits and demerits.

2. Why is it difficult to manage categorical data for clustering?

3. Discuss the suitability of the clustering algorithms for text clustering.

4. Use the k-means algorithm to carry out a cluster analysis for the following set of data points : $(1, 1), (1, 0.9), (0.9, 1), (1, -1), (0.9, -1), (1, -0.9), (-1, 1), (-0.9, 1), (-1, 0.9), (-1, -1), (-0.9, -1), (-1, 0.9), (0.1, 0.1)$, for $k = 4$. Repeat for $k = 5$ and $k = 6$. Display the data set and the cluster analysis results graphically.

5. Describe the suitability of neural computing to data mining.

6. Consider the SOM algorithm with one-dimensional topology and neighborhood that selects only the winner neuron. Does the output of this SOM algorithm depend on the order in which examples are selected during the execution?

7. Discuss the important features of the genetic algorithm.

8. How can a data-mining problem be an optimization problem?

9. (Project) Replace the `dist` function in the class `Kmeans` (or `Kohonen`) with the inverse of the `sim` function from the `VSMranker` class presented in Chapter 2. Test the modified `Kmeans` class for the two test datasets: `test.txt` and `big2d.txt`.

10. (Project) Implement the k-means algorithm (or Kohonen self-organizing maps) for clustering documents from a SMART collection. Use the `VSMranker` class from Chapter 2 to manage the document collection. You may also want to use the inverse of the `sim` function from the `VSMranker` as a distance measure. Try different numbers of clusters of documents for one of the SMART collections and test the effectiveness of the clustering. The cluster of documents may be compared with the relevance information. It is advisable to reduce the number of terms by eliminating those that appear in only one document.

11. (Project) Implement the k-means algorithm for clustering index terms from a SMART collection. The terms that appear in the same documents should be considered close to each other. You may want to reduce the number of terms by eliminating those that appear in only one document. Try different numbers of clusters of terms for one of the SMART collections and test the effectiveness of the clustering.

12. (Project) Change the weights of the variables in `visitItemSpend.csv` and redo the clustering. Analyze the resulting clusters.

13. (Project) We used only a small number of variables from the KDD-cup 2000 data. You can use a larger number of attributes for clustering the customers using the file `question3.data`.

References

Carpenter G.A. and Grossberg, S. (1988): The ART of Adaptive Pattern Recognition by a Self-Organizing Neural Network, Computer, Mar. 1988, pp. 77–88.

Holland J. H. (1992): *Adaptation in Natural and Artificial Systems* (2nd ed.), Prentice Hall.

Kaski, S., Lagus, K., Honkela, T., and Kohonen T. (1988): *Statistical aspects of the WEBSOM system in organizing document collections.* Computing Science and Statistics, 29:281–290. (Scott, D. W., ed.), Interface Foundation of North America, Inc.: Fairfax Station, VA.

Kohonen T. (1990): The self-organizing maps. In *Proceedings of the IEEE*, 78, no. 9, pp. 1464–1480.

Kohonen T. (1995): *Self-Organizing Maps*, Second Extended Edition, Springer Series in Information Sciences, Vol. 30, Springer, Berlin, Heidelberg, New York.

Kohonen T. (1997): *Exploration of very large databases by self-organizing maps.* In Proceedings of ICNN'97, International Conference on Neural Networks, IEEE Service Center, Piscataway, NJ pp. PL1–PL6.

Lawrence R. D., et al (1999): *A Scalable Parallel Algorithm for Self-Organizing Maps with Applications to Sparse Data Mining Problems*, Data Mining and Knowledge Discovery 3, Kluwer Academic Publishers, Netherlands, pp. 171–195.

MacQueen, J. (1967): Some methods for classification and analysis of multivariate observations. In the *Proceedings of the Fifth Berkeley Symposium on Mathematical Statistics and Probability,* 281–97. Berkeley, CA: Univ. of California Press.

McCulloch, W.S., Pitts, W. (1943): A Logical Calculus of the Ideas Immanent in Nervous Activity. Bulletin of Mathematical Biophysics, Vol 5, pp 115–133. Reprinted in Anderson & Rosenfeld, 1988, pp 18–28.

Further Reading

Adriaans, P. and Zantinge, D. (1996): *Data Mining*, Addison-Wesley.

Anderberg M. (1973): *Cluster Analysis for Applications.* Academic Press.

Berry, M. and Linoff, G. (1997): *Data Mining Techniques for Marketing, Sales and Customer Support,* John Wiley & Sons, Inc.

Bigus, J.P. (1996): *Data Mining with Neural networks: Solving Business Problems from application development to decision support*, McGraw Hill.

Cabena, P., Hadjnian, P., Stadler, R., Verhees, J., and Zanasi, A. (Ed.) (1997): *Discovering Data Mining from Concept to Implementation*, Prentice Hall.

Dorian, P. (1999): *Data Preparation for Data Mining*, Morgan Kaufmann.

Fayyad, U.M., Piatetsky-Shapiro, G., Smyth, S., and Uthurusamy, R. (1996): *Advances in Knowledge Discovery and Data Mining*, M.I.T. Press.

Jain A., and Dubes R. (1988): *Algorithms for Clustering Data.* Prentice-Hall, NJ.

Knowledge Discovery Nuggets: http://www.kdnuggets.com/

Liu, H. and Motoda, H. (1998): *Feature Selection for Knowledge Discovery and Data Mining*, Kluwer International.

Michalski, R., Brako, I., and Kubat, M. (1998): *Machine Learning and Data Mining; Methods & Applications*, John Wiley & Sons.

Mitchell, T. (1997): *Machine Learning*, Morgan Kaufmann.

Nguyen, T.D. and Ho, T.B. (1999): "An Interactive-Graphic System for Decision Tree Induction", Journal of the Japanese Society for Aritifical Intelligence, Vol. 14, N0. 1, 131–138.

Quinlan R. (1993): C4.5 *Programs for Machine Learning*, Morgan Kaufmann.

Weiss, S.M. and Kulikowski, C.A. (1991): Computer Systems That Learn: Classification and Prediction Methods from Statistics, Neural Nets, Machine Learning, and Expert Systems, Morgan Kaufmann.

Weiss, S.M. and Indurkhya, N. (1997): Predictive Data Mining: A Practical Guide, Morgan Kaufmann.

Westphal, C. and Blaxton, T. (1998): Data Mining Solutions: Methods and Tools for Real-World Problems, Wiley.

Web Usage Mining

6

6.1 Introduction to Web Mining

In Chapters 4 and 5 we discussed three major aspects of data mining: clustering, classification, and association. These techniques can be directly applied to transactions from e-commerce websites. Such analysis is not much different from traditional vendors who operate out of shops made of bricks and mortar. However, since all the interaction with an e-commerce site is recorded electronically, one can uncover many additional and potentially useful knowledge bits. This challenging area is termed web mining—data mining applied to web-data repositories, to enhance the analytical capabilities of known statistical tools (Ramadhan et al. 2005). Web mining is categorized into three areas (Cooley et al. 1997):

1. web-usage mining

2. web-structure mining

3. web-content mining

Web-content mining deals with primary data on the Web, meaning the actual content of the web documents. The objective of web-content mining is to extract information (information retrieval [IR]; see Chapters 2 and 3), which helps users locate and extract information relevant to their needs. However, our study was more or less limited to text. Web-content mining is composed of multiple data types: text, images, audio, and video. It also deals with an important aspect of information retrieval: crawling the Web and foraging for information. We will study additional aspects of web-content mining (other than information retrieval and the Semantic Web) in Chapter 7.

Web-structure mining, another type of web mining, is concerned with the topology of the Web. It focuses on data that organizes the content and facilitates navigation. The principal source of information in web-structure mining is hyperlinks, connecting one page to another. Chapter 8 presents web-structure mining.

Web-usage mining, which will be discussed in this chapter, does not deal with the contents of web documents. Instead, its goals are to determine how a website's visitors use web resources and to study their navigational patterns. The data used for web-usage mining is essentially secondary; it is generated by users' interaction with the Web. The data sources include web-server access logs, proxy-server logs, browser logs, user profiles, registration data, user sessions and transactions, cookies, user queries, bookmark data, mouse clicks, and scrolls (Kosala and Blockeel 2000).

6.2   Introduction to Web-Usage Mining

Web-usage mining applies data-mining techniques to discover usage patterns from web data in order to understand and better serve the needs of web-based applications. Although web-content mining and web-structure mining utilize the information found in web documents, web-usage mining uses secondary data generated by the users' interaction with the Web. The logs of web access available on most servers are good examples of the data sets used in web-usage mining. Other web-usage data may include browser logs, user profiles, registration files, user sessions or transactions, user queries, bookmark folders, as well as mouse clicks and scrolls (Kosala and Blockeel 2000). It should be noted that the transactions on an e-commerce site are usually not part of web-usage mining. A customer's basket can be analyzed by traditional data-mining techniques discussed in Chapters 4 and 5. Web-usage mining can supplement the knowledge obtained from mining a transaction database, by studying customer's interaction with the e-commerce site. Web-usage mining includes the creation of user profiles, user access patterns, and navigation paths. E-commerce companies can use the results of web-usage mining for tracking customer behavior on their sites; these results can then be used to reorganize services to improve the shopping experience. Just like any other data-mining activity, web-usage mining consists of three phases: preprocessing, pattern discovery, and pattern analysis. In this chapter we will discuss these three phases in the context of web-usage data.

6.3   Web-Log Processing

A general definition of a server log is a set of files consisting of the details of an activity performed by a server (Wikipedia 2006). Usually these files are automatically created and maintained by the server. The activity of a web server mainly consists of servicing the page requests; therefore, one of the important logs maintained by a web server is the history of page requests. The World Wide Web Consortium (W3C) has specified a standard format for web-server log files. In addition to the format specified by W3C, there are other proprietary formats for web-server logs. Most web logs contain information about the request, such as the IP address of the client making the request, date and time of the request, URL of the requested page, number of bytes sent to serve the request, user agent (program that is acting on behalf of the user such as a web browser or web crawler), and referrer (the URL that triggered the request). Server logs typically do not collect user-specific information. The logs of activities of a web server can all be stored in one file; however, a better alternative is to separate the log into different categories such as an access log, error log, and referrer log. An access log typically grows by more than 1 MB for every 10,000 requests (Apache 2006). This means that even on a moderately busy server, the log files tend to be fairly large. Consequently, it is usually necessary to periodically rotate the log files by moving or deleting the existing logs.

Depending on the duration of an analysis, it will be necessary to use data from multiple log files. On most servers, the log files are not accessible to general Internet users. Only the web-server administrators and system administrators have the necessary permissions to read, modify, and delete the log files. In some cases, users with an account on the system that hosts the web server may be able to read the access logs. These server logs contain a wealth of information that can be statistically analyzed to reveal potentially useful traffic patterns based on the time of the day or the day of the week. This information can be useful for planning system maintenance and load balancing. System maintenance could be scheduled during times when the server is in less demand. Similarly, elective computing jobs and network traffic emanating from the server could also be suspended during the peak times. Additionally, looking at traffic patterns based on referrer and user agents can also be useful for developing web strategies. For example, the look and feel of a website could be made more consistent with frequent referrer sites, and more visible links may also be placed on the referrer sites to further facilitate the navigation. The knowledge of frequent user agents could be helpful in optimizing the site for that user agent. For example, if most of the users use Mozilla Firefox, the web developers should ensure that their web pages are properly displayed in Mozilla Firefox. Thus, analysis of web logs can facilitate efficient website administration, scheduling of adequate hosting resources, and the fine-tuning of sales efforts.

A wide variety of tools is available for analyzing web server logs. It is important for marketing personnel from organizations that facilitate business through their website to understand these powerful tools. In this chapter we will discuss how these tools work and also look at the theoretical basis for them. The enclosed CD contains links to these three software packages. A detailed tutorial on the usage of three of these tools is also presented. Finally, we will see how the summary produced by these tools can be used to perform more sophisticated data mining to produce interesting knowledge nuggets.

6.3.1   Format of Web Logs

The common log format of records in web-server-log files is supported by most web servers. Similarly, a majority of log analyzers are designed to work with the common log-file format. **Figure 6.1** shows the general format of a common log file described on the W3C website. The

```
    remotehost rfc931 authuser [date] "request" status bytes
remotehost
        Remote hostname (or IP number if DNS hostname is not available, or if
        DNSLookup is Off.
rfc931
        The remote  logname of the user.
authuser
        The username as which the user has authenticated himself.
[date]
        Date and time of the request.
"request"
        The request line exactly as it came from the client.
status
        The HTTP status code returned to the client.
bytes
        The content-length of the document transferred.
```

Figure 6.1   Common log format (http://www.w3.org/Daemon/User/Config/Logging.html#common-logfile-format)

following are examples of an entry in the common log format:

```
140.14.6.11 - pawan [06/Sep/2001:10:46:07 -0300] "GET /s.htm HTTP/1.0" 200 2267
140.14.7.18 - raj [06/Sep/2001:11:23:53 -0300] "POST /s.cgi HTTP/1.0" 200 499
```

The first entry is a GET request that retrieves a file s.htm. The second request is a POST request that sends data to a program called s.cgi. Let us explore all the fields of the first request. The first field tells us that the request came from a computer (client machine) identified with the IP address of 140.14.6.11. The dash (-) for the second field tells us that the information for the field is unavailable. In this case, the missing information is the RFC 1413 identity of the client, which is determined by a program (daemon) called identd running on the client's machine. This information is highly unreliable and should almost never be used except on tightly controlled internal networks (Apache 2006). The third field tells us that the name or ID of the user is pawan. This ID is determined by HTTP authentication for documents that are password protected. This entry will be dash (-) for documents that are not password protected. The fourth entry provides the time of the request as [06/Sep/2001:10:46:07 -0300]. The first part of the time is rather obvious. The request came just after 10:46 a.m. on September 6, 2001. The -0300 tells us that the time zone is three hours behind the Greenwich Mean Time (GMT); in this case, it is the Atlantic Canadian Daylight Saving Time. The fifth field, given by "GET /s.htm HTTP/1.0", lists the request from the user. In this case, the request is to GET the document s.htm using the protocol HTTP/1.0. The sixth field is the status code that was sent back to the user by the server. The codes beginning with 2 mean that the request resulted in a successful response. In our example, the code is 200, which means the request was successfully served. The codes that start with 3 tell us that the request was redirected to another server. If the user makes an erroneous request (for example, requesting a nonexistent page), codes beginning in 4 will be returned to the user. Finally, an error in the server leads to codes starting with 5. The last field in the request indicates that 2267 bytes were transferred as a result of the request.

While the common log format is standard and supported by all the servers, information contained in these records is fixed and rather limited. Many web-server administrators find it necessary to record more information and thus create an extended log-file format. However, due to legislation related to the protection of websites, certain servers may want to omit certain data that may directly or indirectly make it possible to identify the users. In addition, the servers may need to change the field separator characters if the standard field separator occurs in their fields. The extended log-file format is designed to overcome some of the shortcomings of the common log format by providing the following features (Hallam-Baker and Behlendorf 1996):

- permit control over the data recorded
- support the needs of proxies, clients, and servers in a common format
- provide robust handling of character-escaping issues
- allow exchange of demographic data
- allow summary data to be expressed

The extended log-file format makes it possible to customize log files. Because the format of log files may vary from server to server, a header specifies the data types of each field at the start

```
#Version: 1.0

#Date: 14-Feb-2007

#Fields: time cs-method cs-uri bytes

10:46:07 GET /s.htm 3048

11:23:53 POST /s.cgi 4590

11:46:07 GET /p.htm 59684

12:23:53 POST /q.cgi 78726
```

Figure 6.2   An example of a log file in extended format

of the file. The format is readable by generic log-analysis tools. (We will discuss log-analysis tools later in this chapter.)

Hallam-Baker and Behlendorf (1996) describe the format of the extended log file in great detail. The following is a summary of their specifications. An extended log file contains a sequence of lines containing either a directive or an entry. **Figure 6.2** shows a simple example of an extended log file. The lines starting with a hash mark (#) are directives, while the rest are entries.

Directives record information about the logging process itself. The type of directives start with a hash mark (#) followed by the name of the directive. The type may be

#Version: version of the extended log file format used

#Fields: fields recorded in the log

#Software: software that generated the log

#Start-Date: date and time at which the log was started

#End-Date: date and time at which the log was finished

#Date: date and time at which the entry was added

#Remark: Comments that are ignored by analysis tools

The directives #Version and #Fields are mandatory and must appear before all the entries. Other directives are optional. The #Fields directive specifies the data recorded in the fields of each entry by providing the list of fields. Each field in the #Fields directive can be specified in one of the following ways:

- an identifier; for example, `time`
- an identifier with a prefix separated by a hyphen; for example, the method in the request sent by client to server is specified as `cs-method`

- a prefix following a header in parentheses; for example, the content type of the reply from the server to the client is given by `sc(Content-type)`

The prefixes can be one of the following:

`cs` client to server

`sc` server to client

`sr` server to remote server (this prefix is used by proxies)

`rs` remote server to server (this prefix is used by proxies)

`x`   application-specific identifier

The following is a list of identifiers that may not have a prefix:

`date`   date at which transaction was completed

`time`   time at which transaction was completed

`time-taken` time taken for the transaction to complete in seconds

`bytes`   bytes transferred

`cached`   records whether a cache hit occurred (1 means a cache hit and 0 indicates a cache miss)

The following identifiers must be used with a prefix:

`ip`   IP address and port

`dns`   DNS name

`status`   status code

`comment`   comment returned with status code

`method`   method

`uri`   URI

`uri-stem` stem portion alone of URI (omitting query)

`uri-query` query portion alone of URI

`host`   DNS hostname used

The entries in a log file consist of a sequence of fields as specified in the #Fields directive corresponding to a single HTTP transaction. Fields are separated by a whitespace, usually a tab. If information for a field is either unavailable or not applicable for a transaction, a dash (-) is used.

6.3.2 Web-Access Logs: Apache-Server Example

In the previous section we looked at the generic description of web-access log formats. Different web servers will have their own peculiarities in logging the HTTP requests. In this section, we will look at the web-logging process employed by one of the popular servers: Apache. A more detailed description of Apache can be found at http://httpd.apache.org/docs/2.2/logs.html.

For the Apache server, the LogFormat directive is used to specify the selection of fields in each entry. The format is specified using a string that is styled after the `printf` format strings in C. Let us recall an entry in the Common Log Format discussed earlier:

```
140.14.6.11 - pawan [06/Sep/2001:10:46:07 -0300] "GET /s.htm HTTP/1.0" 200 2267
```

The Common Log Format can be represented using the LogFile directive as

```
LogFormat "%h %l %u %t \"%or\" %>s %b" common
```

This directive defines the format of the log and associates it with the *nickname* "common." The format string consists of percent directives, which tell the server to log a particular piece of information. Literal characters in the format string will be copied directly into the log output. If we want the quote character (") to appear as a literal, it must be escaped by placing a backslash before it, so that it is not interpreted as the end of the format string. The format string may also contain the special control characters "\n" for new-line and "\t" for tab.

%h IP address of the client (remote host)

%l RFC 1413 identity of the client

%u userid of the person requesting the document

%t time when server finished processing the request

    [day/month/year:hour:minute:second zone]
     day = 2*digit
     month = 3*letter
     year = 4*digit
     hour = 2*digit
     minute = 2*digit
     second = 2*digit
     zone = ('+' | '-') 4*digit

\"%r\" request line from the client is given in double quotes

%>s status code that the server sent to the client

%b number of bytes returned to the client

Look at an example of another commonly used format, Combined Log Format:

```
140.14.6.11 - pawan [06/Sep/2001:10:46:07 -0300] "GET /s.htm HTTP/1.0" 200 2267
"http://cs.smu.ca/~csc/" "Mozilla/4.0 (compatible; MSIE 5.5; Windows NT 5.0)"
```

The corresponding format string is given by

```
LogFormat "%h %l %u %t \"%r\" %>s %b \"%{Referer}i\" \"%{User-agent}i\"" combined
```

The combined log format has two additional fields:

`\"%{Referer}i\"`   site that the client was referred from enclosed in quotes

`\"%{User-agent}i\"` software that made the request enclosed in quotes

In this example, the referrer is `http://cs.smu.ca/~csc/` and it has a link to the file `s.htm`. The software that was used for the request was `Mozilla/4.0 (compatible; MSIE 5.5; Windows NT 5.0)`; that is, the web browser, Microsoft Internet Explorer 5.5 for Windows NT 5.0.

The server configuration also specifies the location of the log file using the CustomLog directive. The path for the access log file is assumed to start from the Server Root unless it begins with a slash. For example,

```
CustomLog logs/access_log combined
```

The previous directive will store logs, in the **combined** log format, in a file called **access_log** under the subdirectory **logs** under the server root.

Apache (2006) cautions server administrators about the large sizes of access-log files, even on a moderately busy server. As mentioned before, an access-log file typically grows by 100 bytes per request; therefore, it is periodically necessary to rotate the log files by moving or deleting the existing logs.

6.4 Analyzing Web Logs

The formatting information about web-access logs in the previous section can be used to write programs to analyze the web usage for your website, as well as for running data-mining tools. However, prior to applying data-mining techniques, it is necessary to understand the data set. This is typically done by creating multiple summary reports and, if possible, using visual representations.

Before writing your own programs for analyzing web-access logs, you may want to consider one of the analysis tools already available. These tools may provide answers to most of your questions regarding usage of your website. **Figure 6.3** tabulates freeware and open-source web-access analysis tools listed on an Open Directory site (http://dmoz.org/). In addition to the freeware and open-source tools, you can also find a listing of commercial tools on the Open Directory site. In this section, we will discuss how to obtain summary reports, visualization of aggregate clickstream, as well as individual user sessions from web-access logs.

6.4.1 Summarization of Web-Access Logs

One of the more popular web-access-log-files analysis tools is called Analog (www.Analog.cx). The software is available for free and includes full C source code, as well as executables for

Analog	www.analog.cx
AWStats	awstats.sourceforge.net
BBClone	bbclone.de
The Big Brother Log Analyzer	bbla.sourceforge.net
BlibbleBlobble LogAnalyser	www.blibbleblobble.co.uk/Downloads/LogAnalyser
Dailystats	www.perlfect.com/freescripts/dailystats
GeoIP	www.maxmind.com/geoip
High Speed Merging	www.whurst.net/programming/hHSM/index.php
HitsLog Script	www.irnis.net/soft/hitslog
Http-Analyze	www.http-analyze.org
Kraken Reports	www.krakenreports.com
Logfile	www.ratrobot.com/programming/shell
LogFile Analyse	www.jan-winkler.de/dev
LogReport Foundation	logreport.org
MagicStats	www.nondot.org/MagicStats
Modlogan	www.modlogan.org
NedStat	www.nedstat.com
Pathalizer	pathalizer.bzzt.net
phpOpenTracker	www.phpopentracker.de
PowerPhlogger	pphlogger.phpee.com
RCounter	rcounter.noonet.ru
Realtracker Website Statistics	free.realtracker.com
Relax	ktmatu.com/software/relax
Report Magic for Analog	www.reportmagic.com
RobotStats	www.robotstats.com/en
Sevink Internet Advertising	www.sevink-2.demon.nl
Sherlog	sherlog.europeanservers.net
Snowhare's Utilities	www.nihongo.org/snowhare/utilities
Superstat	www.serversolved.com/superstat
VISITaTOR- a free web mining tool	visitator.fh54.de
Visitors	www.hping.org/visitors
WebLog	awsd.com/scripts/weblog
Webtrax Help	www.multicians.org/thvv/webtrax-help.html
W3Perl	www.w3perl.com/softs
Wwwstat	www.ics.uci.edu/pub/websoft/wwwstat
ZoomStats	zoomstats.sourceforge.net

Figure 6.3   Web access log analyzers (http://dmoz.org/Computers/Software/Internet/Site_Management/Log_Analysis/Freeware_and_Open_Source/)

Windows and Mac platforms. One should be able to compile it for almost any operating system. The website for Analog also has links to precompiled versions for a variety of other operating systems. The developers claim that it is designed to be fast and to produce accurate and attractive statistics. One can combine Analog with Report Magic (www.reportmagic.org) for better graphical analysis. Although Analog is free software, its distribution and modification are covered by the terms of the GNU General Public License. You are not required to accept this license, but nothing else gives you permission to modify or distribute the program (Turner 2006)

Under **Chapter 6** on the CD, there is a link to the Analog site (http://www.analog.cx/). The zipped version of Analog 6.0 for Windows can be downloaded from the site. Create a directory/folder on your hard drive called Chapter 6 and copy the zipped version to the newly created directory. If you right click on the zipped file and choose "Extract All," you will be able to access all the files. This should create a folder called **analog_60w32**. Double clicking on that folder will take you to another folder called **analog 6.0**, which has the Analog 6.0 package for Windows. The **docs** subfolder has all the documentation for the package. The best place to start is the **Readme.html** file, which can be opened using your web browser. This section provides an essential summary of the documentation and a tutorial.

In the previous section, we discussed the format and location of log files for the Apache web server. If you cannot easily locate these log files for your web server, you may wish to contact your administrator. In order to run Analog, you need read access to these logfiles. The Analog package comes with a small logfile called **logfile.log** with 50 HTTP requests. The file is located in the **Analog 6.0** folder. The file is too small for us to explore the real power of this analysis tool; hence, we have included another logfile from an educational site. The study data was obtained from the web-access logs of an introductory first-year course in Computing Science at Saint Mary's University over a sixteen-week period. The initial number of students in the course was 180. The number reduced over the course of the semester to 130–140 students. Certain areas of the website were protected, and users could access them using only their IDs and passwords. The activities in the restricted parts of the website consisted of submitting a user profile, changing a password, submitting assignments, viewing the submissions, accessing the discussion board, and viewing current class marks. The rest of the website was public, which consisted of viewing course information, a lab manual, class notes, class assignments, and lab assignments. If the users accessed only the public portion, their IDs would be unknown. For the rest of the entrants, the usernames were changed to "user" to protect their privacy. The zipped version of the log file is available under Chapter 6 on the CD as **classlog.zip**. Copy the file to the **Analog 6.0** folder and extract the log file. Make sure that the file is expanded in the **Analog 6.0** folder. The extracted file should have the name **classlog.txt**. Notice that the file is rather large (67 MB) and has 361,609 lines. It is in the combined log format, which was discussed in the previous section.

We are now ready to explore the power of Analog, which will involve the following three steps:

1. Edit **Analog.cfg**

2. Run Analog by double clicking on the icon (a DOS window flashes up).

3. Read **Report.html**

You can configure Analog by putting commands in the configuration file, `Analog.cfg`. This may seem a little tedious for users who prefer a graphical user interface (GUI); however, the package comes with a default configuration file that may simplify the process. Moreover, the configuration file allows users more flexibility than a GUI. You can edit `Analog.cfg` using any plain-text editor such as Notepad. First, copy the existing configuration file `Analog.cfg` to `origAnalog.cfg` for safe keeping/backup. Now we are ready to make changes to the configuration file `Analog.cfg`. Any text following a hash mark (#) until the end of line is ignored by Analog as a comment. One command you will need to change straight away is

```
LOGFILE logfilename     # to set where your logfile lives
```

The logfile must be stored locally on your computer, because Analog is not designed to use FTP or HTTP to fetch the logfile from the Internet. There's a sample logfile supplied with the program called `logfile.log`. As mentioned previously, the file consists of only 50 HTTP requests, and hence, may not help us realize the power of Analog; therefore, we will change the name of that file from `logfile.log` to our own logfile called `classlog.txt`. The rest of the configuration already contains many of the essential configuration commands to get us started. We will leave these commands unchanged and see what happens when we run Analog. Later on in this section, we will discuss the significance of these commands.

There are two ways to run Analog: either from Windows by double-clicking on its icon or from the DOS command prompt. If you run it from Windows, it will create a DOS window, which will flash on your screen momentarily during its execution (this usually takes a couple of seconds). When Analog is finished, it will produce an output file called `Report.html` and some graphics. A file called `errors.txt` will contain any errors that may have occurred during the analysis of the logfile.

If you run Analog from the DOS command prompt, you can specify the configuration-file commands via the command-line arguments. These are specified on the command line after the program name and are simply shortcuts for configuration-file commands. The use of command-line arguments may save you the trouble of editing the configuration file every time you want to change the nature of the reporting. The command-line arguments can also be specified from a batch file. Refer to the documentation in the `docs` folder to learn more about the command-line arguments.

Look at the `Report.html` file from the `Analog 6.0` folder by opening it using a web browser. If you double click on `Report.html`, Windows should open it using your default browser. If that does not work, you may want to open the file explicitly through your browser. The file `docs/reports.html` provides a list of all possible reports. Usually you will get only a subset of these reports, depending on what information is recorded in your logfile. Our report is divided into thirteen sections (Figures 6.4–6.16):

1. **General Summary**: contains overall statistics

2. **Monthly Report**: lists the activity in each month

3. **Daily Summary**: lists the total activity for each day of the week over all the weeks

4. **Hourly Summary**: lists the total activity for each hour of the day over all the days

5. **Domain Report**: lists the countries of the computers that requested files

6. **Organization Report**: lists the organizations of the computers that requested files

7. **Search-Word Report**: lists the words used in search engines to find the site

8. **Operating-System Report**: lists the operating systems used by the visitors

9. **Status-Code Report**: lists the HTTP status codes of all requests

10. **File-Size Report**: lists the sizes of files

11. **File-Type Report**: lists the extensions of files

12. **Directory Report**: lists the directories from which all files were requested

13. **Request Report**: lists the files on the site

The following are some definitions that will aide in understanding the reports obtained from `docs/defns.html`:

- The *host* is the computer that is making the request for information (also called the *client*). The request may be for a *page* or another file, such as an image. By default, filenames ending in `.html`, `.htm`, or `/` are considered pages. We can tell Analog to count other files as pages using the `PAGEINCLUDE` command.

- The *total requests* consist of all the files that were requested, including pages and graphics. Total requests corresponds to the traditional definition of number of hits. The *requests for pages* include only those files that are defined as pages.

- The *successful requests* are those with HTTP status codes in the 200s or with the code 304. Codes in the 200s correspond to requests in which the document was returned. The code 304 results when the document was requested but was not needed because it had not been recently modified, and the user could use a cached copy. You can configure the code 304 to be a redirected request instead of a successful request with the `304ISSUCCESS` command. *Successful requests for pages* are the subset of successful requests, limited to pages.

- *Redirected requests* are those with codes in the 300s with the exception of 304. These codes indicate that the user was directed to a different file. This may happen because of an explicit redirection. Another common cause is an incorrect request for a directory name without the trailing slash. Redirected requests may also result from their use as "click-thru" advertising banners.

- *Failed requests* are those with codes in the 400s (error in request) or 500s (server error). These failed requests generally occur when the requested file is not found or is not readable.

- The *requests returning informational status code* are those with status codes in the 100s. These status codes are rarely recorded at this time.

- The *corrupt logfile lines* are those that could not be parsed by Analog. It is possible to list all the corrupt lines by turning debugging on.

- There are a few other types of logfile lines not included in our example that may be listed in the General Summary. The term *Lines without status code* refers to those logfile lines without a status code. *Unwanted logfile entries* are entries that are explicitly excluded.

Successful requests: 303,511
Average successful requests per day: 2,285
Successful requests for pages: 101,655
Average successful requests for pages per day: 765
Failed requests: 24,571
Redirected requests: 33,495
Distinct files requested: 1,441
Distinct hosts served: 2,800
Corrupt logfile lines: 32
Data transferred: 2.09 gigabytes
Average data transferred per day: 16.15 megabytes

Figure 6.4   General Summary from Analog

Figure 6.4 shows the general summary for our `classlog.txt` file. Out of a total of 361,609 requests, there were 303,511 successful requests; that is, 84% of all requests were successful. Roughly one-third (101,655) of the successful requests were for pages. The average data transfer was a little over 16 MB per day. The average data transfer can be used to determine the bandwidth of connection to your server.

The general summary report can be turned on or off with the GENERAL command. The GENSUMLINES command controls which lines are included in the summary. The LASTSEVEN command can be used to include or exclude the figures for the last seven days.

The remaining 12 reports (other than the general summary) can be divided into 3 categories: time reports (Figure 6.5: monthly report), time summary report (Figures 6.6 and 6.7: daily and weekly summary) or non-time reports (Figures 6.8–6.16). Most of the following reports include only successful requests in calculating the number of requests, requests for pages, bytes, and last date, with the exception of reports on redirection or failure. You can control whether each report is included or not with the most appropriate ON or OFF command. You can control which columns are listed with the COLS commands.

The time reports describe the number of requests in each time period. They also identify the busiest time period. The monthly report given in **Figure 6.5**, which provides monthly statistics, is an example of a time report. The report shows the number of requests and how many of those were pages. The number of pages is also represented using a bar chart to make

Each unit (■) represents 1,000 requests for pages or part thereof.

month	reqs	pages	
Aug 2001	1974	904	▪
Sep 2001	67218	30136	
Oct 2001	111887	35054	
Nov 2001	96688	28603	
Dec 2001	25744	6958	

Busiest month: Oct 2001 (35,054 requests for pages).

Figure 6.5   Monthly report from Analog

it easier to compare. The month of August has the lowest traffic because classes do not start until September. The report lists October as the busiest month, which makes sense because that is when the midterm examination is held. There is a decline in traffic in November as the number of students in the course goes down after the midterm. The final examinations are over by the middle of December; therefore, December traffic is the second lowest.

In the time and time summary reports

- measurement for the bar charts and the "busiest" line can be changed using the `GRAPH` commands.
- the amount of rows displayed can be changed with the `ROWS` commands.
- lines can be displayed backward or forward in time by the `BACK` commands.
- the graphic used for the bar charts can be changed with the `BARSTYLE` command.
- the time zone is usually the server's local time. In some cases, it may be GMT. You can get Analog to report based on another time zone with the `LOGTIMEOFFSET` command.

Time-summary reports are different from time reports because a given time period may occur multiple times in a logfile. For example, there are multiple Sundays in our logfile; therefore, the daily report provides a sum of traffic for all the Sundays. The daily summary given in **Figure 6.6** is an example of a time-summary report. It specifies the total number of requests in each day of the week. From Figure 6.6, one can see that the highest traffic was on Tuesday, because classes and labs are held on those days. Thursday has the second highest traffic. Assignments are due on Monday, which explains traffic increase on Sunday and Monday. The hourly summary given in **Figure 6.7** describes the hourly variation in the traffic. The three peak hours—11 a.m., 2 p.m., and 7 p.m.—correspond to the laboratory times.

Now look at the non-time reports given in Figures 6.8–6.16. The domain report given in **Figure 6.8** is supposed to list all the domains that visited our site. Unfortunately, our report has very little useful information. All the domains are listed as "unresolved numerical addresses," which means that the domain server records only the numerical IP address of the hosts that contact you, not their names. Recording names of the hosts requires a time-consuming lookup process, which is why many server administrators choose to not record the domain names.

Each unit (■) represents 800 requests for pages or part thereof.

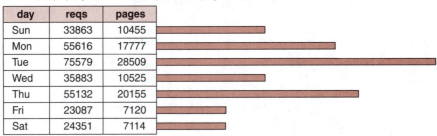

day	reqs	pages
Sun	33863	10455
Mon	55616	17777
Tue	75579	28509
Wed	35883	10525
Thu	55132	20155
Fri	23087	7120
Sat	24351	7114

Figure 6.6   Daily summary from Analog

Each unit (■) represents 250 requests for pages or part thereof.

hour	reqs	pages
0	6246	2143
1	4065	1143
2	1836	627
3	1115	413
4	599	267
5	473	143
6	1711	277
7	2986	718
8	10876	3648
9	12466	4439
10	10039	3070
11	26922	10236
12	21000	6990
13	13248	4318
14	27175	10176
15	22683	7719
16	19579	7227
17	15645	5204
18	19042	5773
19	24002	8315
20	18215	5823
21	18097	5208
22	14495	4332
23	10996	3446

Figure 6.7   Hourly summary from Analog

reqs	%bytes	domain
303511	100%	[unresolved numerical addresses]

Figure 6.8   Domain report from Analog

The organization report in **Figure 6.9** shows all the organizations that the host computers belong to. The organizations are identified by the first two numbers of their IP addresses. More than 62% of hosts are from Saint Mary's University (140.184). The next four listings correspond to IP numbers from cable and phone companies in Halifax and account for 32% of requests. The organization report not only tells us where our clientele comes from, but also gives us an opportunity to improve network connections for these organizations.

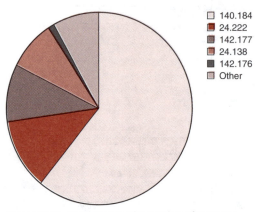

The wedges are plotted by the number of requests.

Listing the top 20 organizations by the number
of requests, sorted by the number of requests.

reqs	%bytes	organization
178914	62.54%	140.184
35737	12.22%	24.222
34127	9.99%	142.177
30520	8.49%	24.138
5489	1.25%	142.176
2333	0.45%	129.173
1949	0.34%	165.154
1895	0.70%	140.230
1500	0.20%	198.166
1391	0.46%	154.5
1283	0.22%	209.73
1273	0.44%	209.148
509	0.11%	216.239
429	0.19%	209.167
408	0.10%	209.226
372	0.16%	207.107
339	0.20%	64.10
322	0.03%	66.77
292	0.13%	172.149
248	0.06%	205.188
4181	1.72%	*

* [not listed: 211 organizations]

Figure 6.9 Organization report from Analog

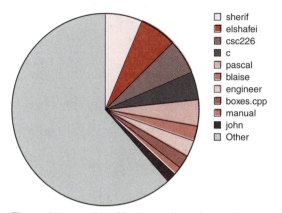

The wedges are plotted by the number of requests.

Listing the top 30 query words by the number
of requests, sorted by the number of requests.

reqs	search term
12	sherif
12	elshafei
11	csc226
9	c
8	pascal
5	blaise
5	engineer
4	boxes.cpp
...	...

Figure 6.10   Search-word report from Analog

The search-word report (**Figure 6.10**) tells us which words the user typed in a search engine to get to our site. Most of the traffic in the `classlog.txt` is from students registered in the class, who would typically bookmark the page instead of searching for it through a search engine; therefore, the search-word report is not very relevant in our case. However, for other organizations, it may reveal many interesting facts. If you look at the `Analog.cfg` file, you will notice the use of the `SEARCHENGINE` command to identify requests from search engines.

The operating-system report (**Figure 6.11**) tells us that most of the users came from Windows-based computers. It also lists the number of requests that came from robots. The `ROBOTINCLUDE` command in `Analog.cfg` is used to identify known robots.

The status-code report from **Figure 6.12** can be used to determine if the users are finding it difficult to navigate through the site, and the data from the report can be used as a means of improvement. If traffic from the site is unduly high, the file-size report (**Figure 6.13**) will allow us to determine if the problem is caused by many requests for small files or a small number of

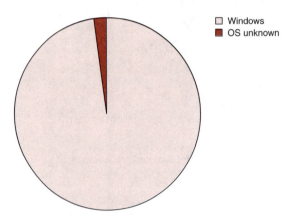

The wedges are plotted by the number of requests for pages.

Listing operating systems, sorted by the number of requests for pages.

no.	reqs	pages	OS
1	296266	99236	Windows
	157564	60126	Windows 2000
	70373	19427	Windows 98
	48870	13763	Windows ME
	8804	3085	Windows 95
	6682	1738	Windows XP
	2602	607	Windows NT
	1371	490	Unknown Windows
2	6867	2327	OS unknown
3	224	49	Macintosh
4	118	42	Unix
	74	26	Linux
	43	16	SunOS
	1	0	HP-UX

Figure 6.11 Operating-system report from Analog

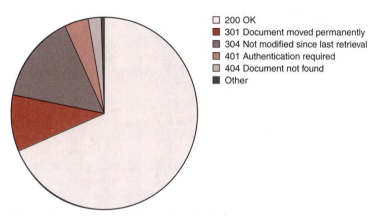

☐ 200 OK
■ 301 Document moved permanently
■ 304 Not modified since last retrieval
■ 401 Authentication required
☐ 404 Document not found
■ Other

The wedges are plotted by the number of requests.

Listing status codes, sorted numerically.

reqs	status code
237631	200 OK
1529	206 Partial content
33258	301 Document moved permanently
237	302 Document found elsewhere
54351	304 Not modified since last retrieval
6	400 Bad request
15174	401 Authentication required
466	403 Access forbidden
8428	404 Document not found
427	405 Method not allowed
21	408 Request timeout
5	416 Requested range not valid
44	500 Internal server error

Figure 6.12   Status-code report from Analog

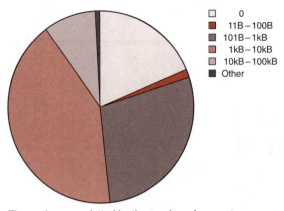

The wedges are plotted by the number of requests.

size	reqs	%bytes
0	56699	
1B–10B	117	
11B–100B	4576	0.01%
101B–1kB	86091	1.85%
1kB–10kB	126223	20.09%
10kB–100kB	27746	31.79%
100kB–1MB	2059	46.25%

Figure 6.13   File size report from Analog

requests for large files. Based on this report, one may start looking for the offending files. In our case, the largest frequency of requests is for files of fewer than 10 kilobytes.

Figure 6.14 shows the popular file types by number of requests and size. GIF (a type of image) files were most frequently requested. On the other hand, EXE (executable programs) files accounted for the largest amount of data transfer. This report can be useful in devising a strategy to reduce the data transfer; for example, if it were possible to reduce the size of EXE files, we could reduce the data transfer.

Figure 6.15 identifies two directories as the most popular ones in the directory report. The directory /~csc226/ corresponds to the root for the course, and /~pawan/ corresponds to the instructor for the course. A small portion of the request report is shown in **Figure 6.16**. In addition to the request for the homepage for the course (/~csc226/), the homepage for the bulletin board (/~csc226/cgi-bin/yabb.pl) is also a popular page.

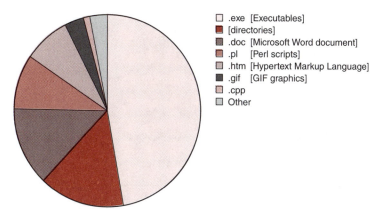

.exe [Executables]
[directories]
.doc [Microsoft Word document]
.pl   [Perl scripts]
.htm [Hypertext Markup Language]
.gif   [GIF graphics]
.cpp
Other

The wedges are plotted by the amount of traffic.

Listing extensions with at least 0.1% of the traffic,
sorted by the amount of traffic.

reqs	%bytes	extension
3040	47.49%	.exe [Executables]
82003	14.61%	[directories]
14440	13.39%	.doc [Microsoft Word document]
12908	9.17%	.pl [Perl scripts]
18907	8.19%	.htm [Hypertext Markup Language]
129170	3.32%	.gif [GIF graphics]
23231	1.03%	.cpp
745	0.81%	.html [Hypertext Markup Language]
349	0.66%	.zip [Zip archives]
2484	0.59%	.js [JavaScript code]
4976	0.43%	.php [PHP]
4618	0.13%	.cgi [CGI scripts]
6640	0.18%	[not listed: 8 extensions]

Figure 6.14   File type report from Analog

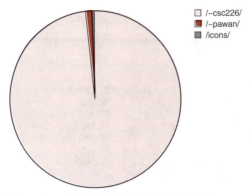

The wedges are plotted by the amount of traffic.

Listing directories with at least 0.01% of the traffic, sorted by the amount of traffic.

reqs	%bytes	directory
248972	98.56%	/~csc226/
2054	1.04%	/~pawan/
52460	0.40%	/icons/
25		[not listed: 4 directories]

Figure 6.15   Directory report from Analog

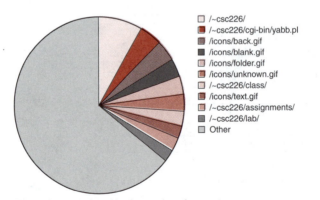

The wedges are plotted by the number of requests.

Listing files with at least 20 requests, sorted by the number of requests.

reqs	%bytes	last time	file
24304	9.25%	16/Dec/01 04:00	/~csc226/
11545	8.84%	15/Dec/01 22:47	/~csc226/cgi-bin/yabb.pl
1996	2.28	15/Dec/01 21:53	/~csc226/cgi-bin/yabb.pl?board=general
...	...	...	...

Figure 6.16   Request report from Analog

There are many commands that can change the non-time reports. You can

- control how many items are listed with the `FLOOR` commands.
- control whether to show charts and how the pie charts are plotted (if you choose to show them) with the `CHART` commands.
- list the time period covered by each report with the `REPORTSPAN` command.
- include or exclude individual items with the output `INCLUDE` and `EXCLUDE` commands.
- change the names of items in the reports with the output alias commands.
- control which files are linked in the reports by the `LINKINCLUDE` and `LINKEXCLUDE` commands.
- change the links by the `BASEURL` command.
- The "not listed" line at the bottom of the majority of non-time reports counts those items that did not get enough traffic to get above the `FLOOR` for the report. It does not include items that were explicitly excluded using various `EXCLUDE` commands in the configuration file.

6.4.2 Analysis of Clickstream: Studying Navigation Paths

In the previous section we studied various summarizations of web-access logs, which can be used to get an insight into the web usage for a particular site. In this section, we will use the same logs to study how users navigate through the site. There are a number of commercial and free software packages available for studying navigation on the site. We will look at a free software called Pathalizer for this section.

Pathalizer (2006a) is a visualization tool that shows the paths most users take when browsing a website. This information can be useful for improving the navigation within a site. In conjunction with the summarization of web logs, the visual representation of navigation can also be used to determine which parts of the site need most attention. Pathalizer generates a weighted directed graph from a web-access log in the combined format favored by Apache servers; however, it can be configured to analyze web-access logs in other formats.

The software can be downloaded from http://pathalizer.sourceforge.net/ (Pathalizer 2006b). The software usage is subject to standard GNU Public License (GPL). It is written in C++ and can be compiled using a GNU C++ compiler (g++) for any platform; however, end users may want to download the graphical user interface (GUI) versions for Linux, Windows, or Mac. Under `chapter 6` on the CD, there are links to two software packages: GraphViz and Pathalizer. Install GraphViz before running the Pathalizer. GraphViz (also subject to GPL) is used to create graphical versions of navigation graphs. We will assume that you have already created a folder called `chapter 6` on the hard drive. Create another folder under `chapter 6` called `Pathalizer`. Download `graphViz-2.8.exe` from (http://www.graphviz.org/Download_windows.php) and `pathalize.exe` from http://pathalizer.sourceforge.net/ to the `Pathalizer` folder. Double click on the `graphViz-2.8.exe` to install GraphViz. Once installed, we are ready to run `pathalize.exe`.

Double clicking on `pathalize.exe` will launch Pathalizer. The top window in **Figure 6.17** shows the screenshot of what you will see when you launch Pathalizer. (If you wander around, you can come back to this screen by clicking on "Input" in the left panel.) Under the box for

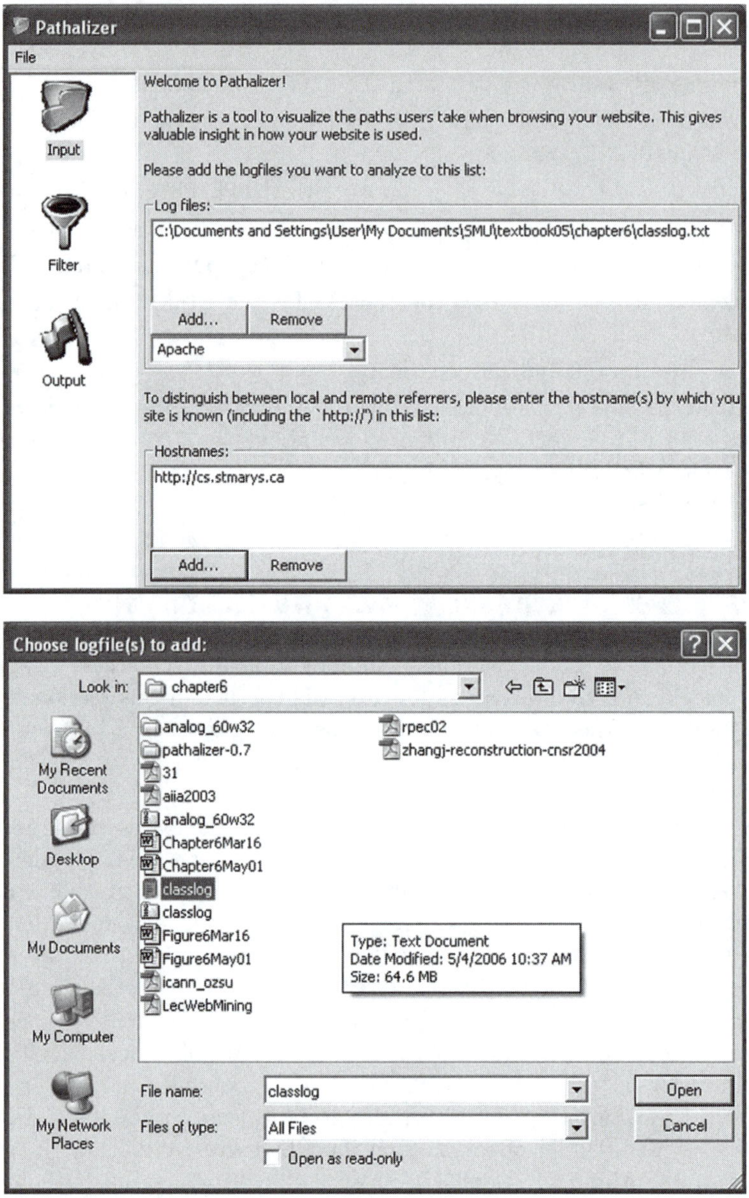

Figure 6.17 Choosing the logfile for Pathalizer

"Log files:", click on the "Add ... " button, and you will see the window shown at the bottom of Figure 6.17 for choosing the logfile. Go up one level to select the file `classlog.txt`. You will have to pick "All files" from "Files of type:" to see the files that do not have the ".`log`" extension. You may also want to click on the "Add ... " button under the "Hostnames:"

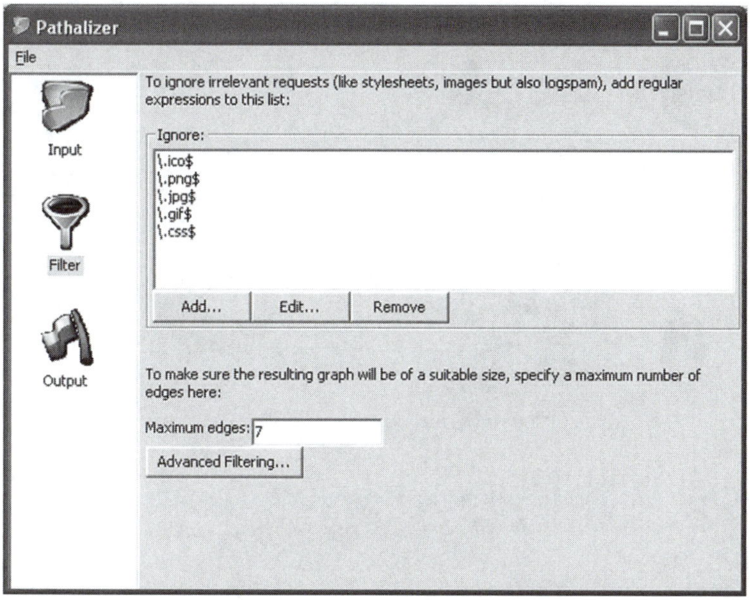

Figure 6.18 Specifying filters for Pathalizer

box to add the domain name "http://cs.stmarys.ca". This addition of hostname simplifies the output by not explicitly listing the prefix http://cs.stmarys.ca.

Now, click on "Filter" in the left panel to specify display criteria. If you choose to see every link in the logfile, you will get a cluttered graph; therefore, specify a reasonable number of links to be displayed. The default is 20, but change it to 7 as shown in **Figure 6.18**. (Pathalizer always displays one more edge than what is specified.)

Clicking on the "Output" in the left panel will bring up the top window shown in **Figure 6.19**. Choose an appropriate file type. We have chosen the "png" file type. Under "Action:", click on "Save as … " and choose a filename as shown in the bottom window in Figure 6.19. Note that we have to explicitly mention the extension ".png" in the filename. Now that we have all the essential information, click on the "Start!" button, and wait for Pathalizer to finish its computation. Generally, there is a barely perceptible flashing of the window to signify computing. You can then go to the directory where you asked Pathalizer to store the file, and launch it by double clicking on it. **Figure 6.20** shows the output. The following is an explanation of the graph drawn by Pathalizer:

- Every node is a page. The path/URL for the page and the number of hits on the page are listed inside these shapes.
- Although all the nodes in our figure are rectangles, nodes can have various shapes:
  - Ellipse: default.
  - Rectangle: it was the first node of a session at least once (all the nodes in Figure 6.20 fall into this category).
  - Diamond: it was the last node of a session.

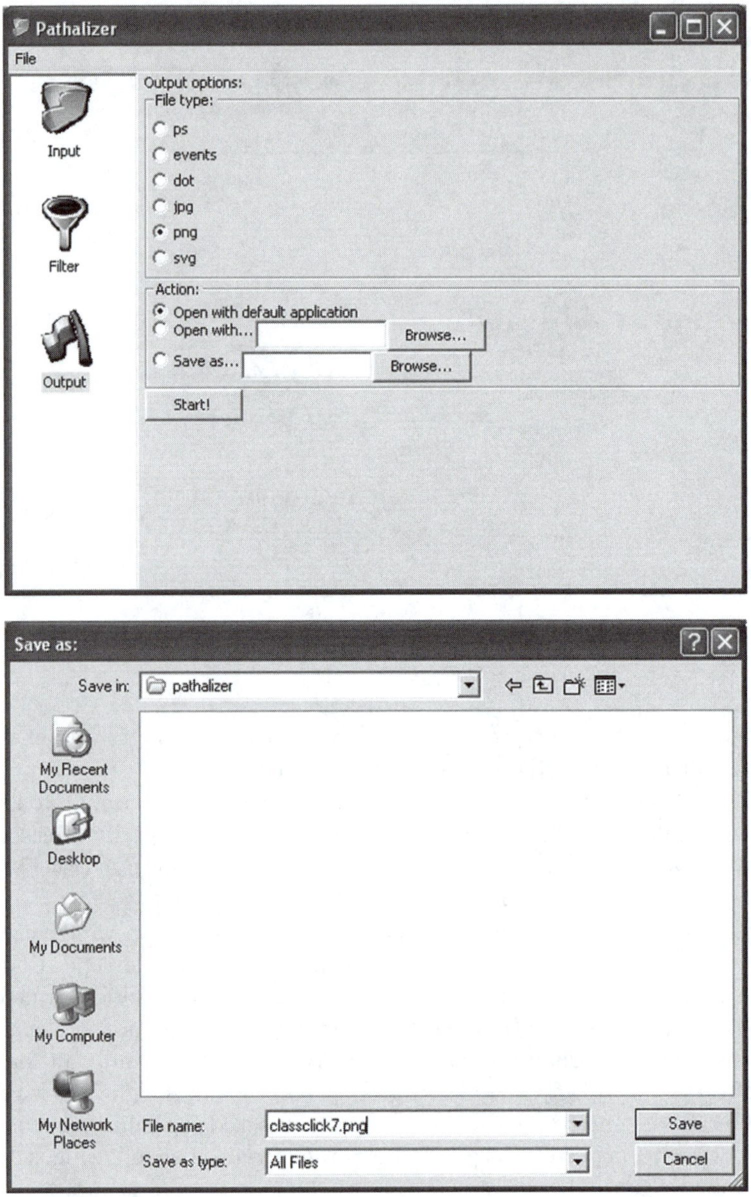

Figure 6.19   Specifying output format and file for Pathalizer

- Octagon: it was both a start-node and an end-node at least once.

- Every arrow represents a user visiting those 2 pages in succession. The width and the number associated with the arrow represent the number of times that path was taken (the thicker the arrow, the bigger the frequency).

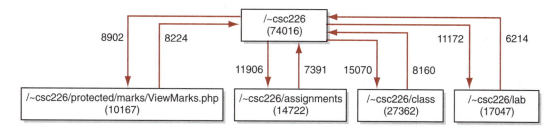

Figure 6.20 Clickstream using Pathalizer with seven link specification

Figure 6.20 tells us that one or more visitors went directly to all five pages shown. The homepage for the course was the most frequently visited page, and the link from the homepage to the class directory was the most frequently taken. The link from the homepage to the assignment page was the second-most popular path, followed by the link from the homepage to the lab folder. This knowledge of popular pages and links tells us that every page should have a link to the homepage, and that links to the class folder, assignment, and lab folder should be prominently displayed on the homepage.

The specification of seven links to Pathalizer gave us only a birds-eye view of the website. If we wish to have a more detailed analysis, we need to increase the number of edges in the filter section. **Figure 6.21** shows a more detailed analysis with 20 edge specifications. As the number of edges increases, it is difficult to read the graph because of the large amount of information

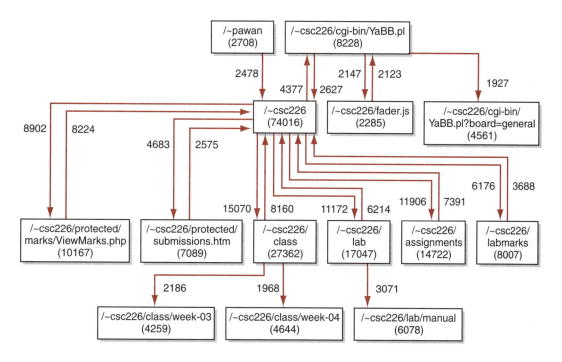

Figure 6.21 Clickstream using Pathalizer with twenty link specification

as well as the smaller text size. You may want to experiment with different output-file types to determine the best type for your usage. We found the use of postscript file (converted to pdf) makes it possible to view as many as 100 edges easily. These pdf files are available in the folder Pathalizer under chapter 6 on the CD. The filenames are `classclick7.pdf`, `classclick20.pdf`, and `classclick100.pdf`. It will be necessary to magnify and then analyze the graph in pieces by scrolling horizontally and vertically. The graph in Figure 6.21 uncovers additional important pages (such as the bulletin board, submissions page), and links (such as ~pawan→~csc226, lab page→ manual). This information can be used to design other pages on the site.

Now that we have some idea of what Pathalizer does, let us see how it works. The computation of paths is based on a list of hits with referrer fields. Consider two requests from a user session (from the same computer in a reasonably short time interval):

Requested URL: /~csc226/class/ **Referer URL**: /~csc226/

Requested URL: /~csc226/class/week-03/ **Referer URL**: /~csc226/class/

Clearly, we should have the following edges:

/~csc226/→/~csc226/class/, and

/~csc226/class/→/~csc226/class/ week-03/.

The following case uses a bit of heuristics to model user behavior:

Requested URL: /~csc226/class/ **Referer URL**: /~csc226/

Requested URL: /~csc226/assignment/ **Referer URL**: /~csc226/

Again, assume that it is the same user making these two requests. In this case, it is reasonable to assume that the user used the Back button from /~csc226/class/ to /~csc226/ after the first request, before making the second request. Therefore, Pathalizer creates three edges:

/~csc226/→/~csc226/class/,

/~csc226/class/→/~csc226/, and

/~csc226/→/~csc226//assignment/

6.4.3 Visualizing Individual User Sessions

In the previous two sections, we looked at two different aggregate web-usage analytical techniques. The first one (Analog) created a variety of reports on web usage. The second (Pathalizer) provided a visualization of pages that are in high demand as well as being the most popular paths. It is possible to also look at individual user's interaction with a website. Because a site will have a large number of visitors, it will be practically impossible to analyze each one of them in great detail; but one can randomly pick sessions of various sizes to study how individual visitors traverse through a site. Such an analysis should always be a precursor to the application of a data-mining technique. Sometimes such a visualization process may also be conducted after uncovering interesting navigational patterns from the data-mining exercise. For example, if one notices a certain category of users aborting their sale, the site manager may pick a session from a list of such preemptive users and study the visual representation of their navigation pattern.

Again, there are a number of commercial and free software programs that can help track individual user sessions. We will look at free software that is available under the MIT license (http://www.opensource.org/licenses/mit-license.php). The software is available from http://sourceforge.net/projects/StatViz/. The description of the software can be found at http://StatViz.sourceforge.net/. The software is written in php.

The installation of StatViz requires a fair bit of computing experience. The description is based on the assumption that you will be running the software under a UNIX system with access to the system administrator. The compressed version of StatViz can be downloaded using the link from the CD (under **chapter 6: http://statviz.sourceforge.net/**) as a tar+gzip file: **statViz-0.5.tgz**. The folder consists of two files: **statViz.php** and **example.conf**. You should edit the first line in the **statViz.php**:

```
#!/usr/local/php/bin/php -d output_buffering=0
```

and change the directory to where your php is located. You should further edit the **example.conf** file and consider changing the input and output locations:

```
LogFilePath=./testlogfile.log
OutputDir=./StatViz-output
```

Once you have made these changes, you are ready to run the StatViz by typing the following command:

```
statViz.php --config example.conf
```

If the program does not run successfully, you may want to visit:

```
http://ctotodevelopers.blogspot.com/2006/01/clickstream-analysis-tool.html
```

There are a couple of commonly noted problems and possible solutions (you will need to consult your system administrator to fix these):

1. Config.h not found: You will need the PEAR:Config package (http://pear.php.net/package/Config/). Once you have downloaded the package, uncompress/untar it. The easiest thing to do is move the Config.php and the Config dir to /usr/share/pear (your system may use a different path).

2. Low memory: StatViz takes up a lot of memory, so you may need to increase the memory_limit configuration parameter in your /etc/php.ini (your system may use a different path). Even after increasing the limit, you may want to limit the number of records in your file. For example, 56MB will process 275,000 records.

If the program runs successfully, it will create DOT files. These files can be converted to any graphics format using the GraphViz package that we installed in the previous section. We will not get into the details of converting DOT files to graphics. The use of GraphViz is fairly intuitive.

The software StatViz produces two types of output: an aggregate clickstream analysis similar to Pathalizer and an individual session track. Because we have already looked at the aggregate clickstream analysis using Pathalizer, we will look only at the individual session tracks.

StatViz keeps track of the movements from pages to pages within an individual session stored in the logfile. A session is simply associated with an IP address. That means all the requests from a given computer are considered to be for the same session. This is not a good assumption, especially for a public computer. The developer indicates that it is possible to configure the definition of a session. You can easily configure StatViz to use a different column as the "unique session ID." The unique session IDs can be obtained from mod_usertrack or a custom session id logged via the Apache notes mechanism.

The session-track reporter from StatViz graphs the exact clickstream for the longest sessions in the log. The number of clicks, not time, determines the length of the session. The configuration file is used to specify how many sessions should be graphed. The session-track reporter will produce one graph per session. Each graph is designed to give a good sampling of how visitors move around the site.

Tracking individual sessions is a computationally intensive activity. Moreover, it is difficult to study all the user sessions individually; therefore, we selected a 1.25-hour snapshot from our `classlog.txt`. The time period that was chosen was from 11:30 a.m. to 12:45 p.m. on a Tuesday (October 9, 2001). Usually, this time reports fairly intensive activity on the course website, because it follows the class, and there are two labs scheduled in parallel during that time. We picked three sessions of different lengths, which are shown in Figures 6.22–6.24.

The following is a brief explanation of a StatViz "session tracks" graph (StatViz 2006):

- The graph shows movement through the website as links from one page to another. Each node is a web page; each solid line is a "click" from one page to the other as indicated by the arrow.
- Each line has a number next to it representing the number of that particular "click" in the session track. The time of the "click" is also shown next to the number.
- In some cases you will also see a dashed line with the same number as another click. These "BACK" links indicate that the visitor went back to that page using the Back button before proceeding.
- Pages that are not on our site (external referrers) are shown as brown ovals.
- The "entry" page is colored green. The "exit" page is colored red. If the entry and exit pages are the same, that page will be red.

Graphical display of individual session tracks allows us to understand how people successfully or unsuccessfully navigate through the site. Studying them will not only help us understand the information needs of our visitors but also provide insight into how we could better present information on the site to facilitate easier navigation. Let us try to interpret the StatViz graphs from Figures 6.22–6.24.

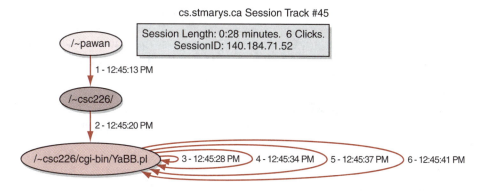

Figure 6.22 A brief on-campus session identified by StatViz that browses the bulletin board

The session #45 depicted in **Figure 6.22** lasted less than half a minute and involved six clicks. The user came from the instructor's home page, /~pawan/, to the home page for the class, /~csc226/, and immediately proceeded to the bulletin board. He quickly looked at various messages posted on the board and exited from the bulletin board. It is clear that he knew exactly what information he was looking for and did not waste any time wandering around. The IP number starts with 140.184, which means it was an on-campus computer.

Figure 6.23 shows an off-campus session (#31), which was equally brief, lasting a little over 1.5 minutes. The IP number starting with 142.177 tells us that the user comes from an Internet

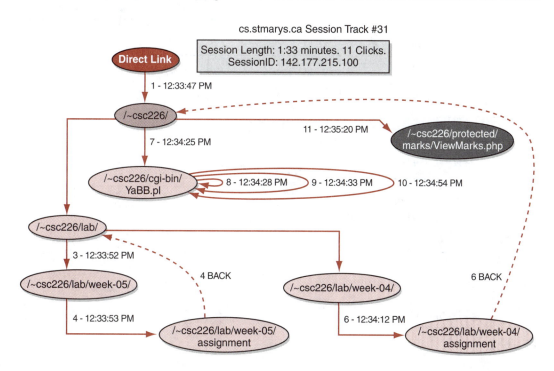

Figure 6.23 A brief off-campus session identified by StatViz with three distinct activities

service provided by the local phone company. Again, the user seemed to know what she was looking for. She either used a bookmark or typed the URL directly to get to the entry page, /~csc226/. She then proceeded with three clicks to look at the assignment for week-05, came back to the lab folder with the Back button, and used two clicks to look at the assignment from the previous week (week-04). She then used the Back button to get to the course homepage. Clicks 7–10 were used to browse the bulletin board. Finally, she checked the marks and then exited the site. Similar to the previous user (Figure 6.22), this user also knew the structure of the site very well. That is why she managed to conduct three separate activities in a relatively short period of time:

- view two lab assignments
- browse bulletin board
- view marks

The third session (#9), depicted in **Figure 6.24**, is a little more leisurely than the previous two, lasting almost half an hour. (It is possible that this in fact is a combination of two distinct sessions.) While the user accesses the lab manual for sample programs, he does not seem to be directly working on the lab assignment, because he is not looking at any lab assignment. There is a flurry of activity from 11:45 to 11:50 a.m., when he looks at two programs `fileio.cpp`

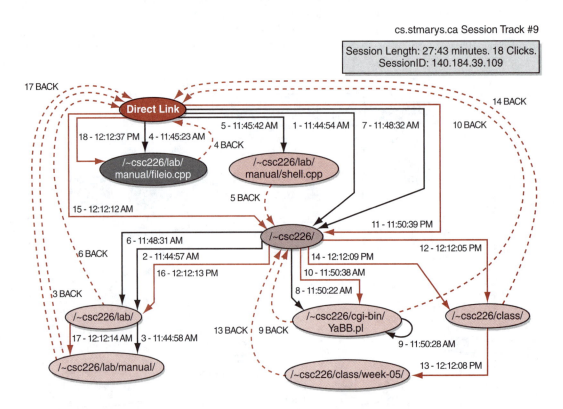

Figure 6.24   A long on-campus session identified by StatViz with multiple activities

and `shell.cpp` from the lab manual, and checks the bulletin board. Presumably he uses the information to do some course-related activity, such as an assignment. The activity picks up again after about 20 minutes (12:12 p.m.) as the user looks at the class folder and has another look at the two sample programs before exiting. There are two possible explanations to these two distinct sets of activities. One possibility is that the last bit of activity involves double-checking the work that was done in the previous 20 minutes. Another possibility is that the graph is representing two distinct visits. They may very well be from the same user or from two different users, because the IP address corresponds to an on-campus public-access computer. This discussion underscores the difficulties in interpreting web-access logs. The next section articulates these difficulties in greater detail.

6.4.4   Caution in Interpreting Web-Access Logs

In the previous three sections, we discussed how information in web-access logs could help us learn about the usage of a website. While the information in these logs can be very useful, the developer of Analog throws cold water on our excitement by pointing out many pitfalls in an optimistic interpretation of web-access logs (Turner 2004). This section provides an essential summary of Turner's arguments. Sometimes his arguments are copied verbatim, in order to avoid misinterpretation.

Web-access logs record information such as the date and time of page requests, the requested page, the Internet address (IP number) of the user's computer, which page referred the user to the site, and the make and model of the user's browser. Unless specifically programmed, the user's name and email address are not recorded. In addition to the web page, the browser will generate additional requests unbeknownst to the user for any graphics on the page. If a page has 10 pictures, there will be 11 requests. In reality, the user asked for only one page.

Turner (2004) points out that the reality is not as simple as described above due to caching. There are two major types of caching. First, the browser automatically caches files when they are downloaded. This means that if the same user revisits the page, there is no need to download the whole page again. Depending on the settings, the browser may check with the server that the page has not changed. If such a check is made, the server will know and record the page access. If the browser is set to not check with the server, the access log will have no entry of the page reuse.

The other type of cache is implemented by Internet Service Providers (ISPs). The ISP proxy server will not forward a request to a server if some other user from the same ISP has already downloaded the page, because the ISP proxy server will cache it. The user browser settings cannot overrule the proxy server caching. That means even though the server served and recorded the page request only once, many people can read the same page. With web-access logs, the only information we know for certain is the number of requests made to our server, when they were made, which files were asked for, and which host asked for them. We also know what browsers were used and what the referring pages were. However, Turner cautions about the browser and referrer information. Many browsers deliberately lie about what sort of browser they are, or even let users configure the browser name (Turner 2004). Moreover, some proponents of protection of privacy use "anonymizers" to deliberately send false browser and referrer information.

Turner (2004) emphasizes that you do not know the following:

Identity of readers: Unless you explicitly program the server to receive the identity.

Number of visitors: The number of distinct hosts is not always a good measure because

- ISP proxy server caching will not show some of the requests.
- many users may use the same IP number.
- the same user may appear to connect from many different hosts. For example, AOL allocates a different hostname for every request. This means if an AOL user downloads a page with 10 pictures, the server may think that there were 11 visitors.

Number of visits: Programs that count visits define a visit as a sequence of requests from the same host until there is a significant gap between requests. This assumption may not always be true. Some sites try to count their visitors by using cookies, which may provide better estimates. However, in order for the cookies to be effective, you will have to mandate that users accept them and assume that they don't delete them.

User's navigation path through the site: The use of the Back button and caching gives only a partial picture. Programs will have to use the kind of heuristics employed by Pathalizer to guess the complete path.

Entry point and referral: If the home page was retrieved from the cache, the first request may actually be somewhere in the middle of the true visit.

How users left the site or where they went next: There is no way to know the next request made by the user after leaving the site.

How long people spent reading each page: After downloading a page, they might read some (unrecorded) cached pages before a new request is recorded. They might step out of the site and come back later with a new request to the site.

How long people spent on the site: In addition to the problems with recording time for each page, there is no way to tell the time spent on the final page. In most cases, the final page may take the majority of the time of the visit, because the user has finally found what he or she was looking for, but there is no way to verify.

We end this section with the following quote (Turner 2004):

> *I've presented a somewhat negative view here, emphasizing what you can't find out. Web statistics are still informative: it's just important not to slip from "this page has received 30,000 requests" to "30,000 people have read this page." In some sense these problems are not really new to the web—they are present just as much in print media too. For example, you only know how many magazines you've sold, not how many people have read them. In print media we have learnt to live with these issues, using the data which are available, and it would be better if we did on the Web too, rather than making up spurious numbers.*

6.5 Web-Usage Mining Applications

Thus far, we have seen an example of data available for web-usage mining. We have also looked at a summarization of web usage, as well as aggregate and individual session visualization. Now it is time to apply data-mining techniques to this data and discover more interesting nuggets of knowledge. The discussion will start by using our web-access log to group users into different clusters. Later on we will see how classification and association have been used in the web-usage-mining context. Finally, a dataset from msnbc.com will be used to demonstrate the analysis of sequential patterns of web access.

6.5.1 Clustering of Web Users

Chapter 5 promised that we would see an application of clustering to real web data. In this section, we will apply the `Kmeans` class to the web-access log of a first-year computing-science course. We have already used the web-access log from the course to study various analysis tools in the previous sections.

The students in this course come from a wide variety of backgrounds, such as computing-science major hopefuls, students taking the course as a required science course, and students taking the course as a science or general elective. As is common in a first-year course, students' attitudes toward the course also vary a great deal. It is hoped that the profile of visits will reflect some of the distinctions between the students. For the initial analysis, we will hypothesize that the visitors could fall into one of the following three categories:

Workers: These visitors are mostly working on class or lab assignments or accessing the discussion board.

Studious: These visitors download the current set of notes. Because they download a limited/current set of notes, they probably study class notes on a regular basis.

Crammers: These visitors download a large set of notes. This indicates that they have stayed away from the class notes for a long period of time. They are planning for pretest cramming.

Note that we are not classifying individual students into one of these categories. It is possible that a student could be a worker during one visit and a crammer in another visit (especially when it is close to exam time). We are simply trying to guess the objective of a visit. The descriptions of these clusters are just speculation; hopefully, it is an educated guess. Usually such a hypothesis is based on subjective knowledge of the application domain and preliminary analysis of the data. The preliminary analysis will be done using data summarization and visualization tools discussed in the previous section. The hypothesis is useful because it provides us with an objective. Now we know what kind of user characteristics we should focus on in order to achieve our desired grouping of web users. The next step is to manipulate the web-access logs to create an appropriate representation of web users.

6.5.1.1 Data Preparation for Clustering

The first step in preparing data for clustering is to determine which variables will help us distinguish the behavior described previously. A list of variables consisting of the number of web accesses, types of documents downloaded, and time of day seems to be a good choice. We will now try to create an appropriate representation of a visit. The first problem is to determine what constitutes a visit.

Let us review the nature of our educational website. The fact that certain areas of the website were protected and users could access them using only their IDs and passwords can be used to identify a visit. However, only some of the activities were in the restricted parts of the site: submitting a user profile, changing a password, submission of assignments, viewing the submissions, accessing the discussion board, and viewing current class marks. The rest of the website was public, which consisted of views of course information, the lab manual, class notes, class assignments, and lab assignments. If the users accessed only the public site, their IDs were unknown; therefore, the web users are identified based on their IP addresses. This also assures that the user's privacy is protected. In any case, we have replaced all the usernames in the log to a generic value of "user" so privacy will be protected in the restricted parts of the website as well.

While we note the objections raised by Turner (2004), we will track a visit by studying the time interval between visits from the same IP address. A visit starts when the first request is made from an IP address. The visit continues as long as the consecutive requests from the IP address have a sufficiently small delay. Assume that a delay longer than 10 minutes means a new visit. This is a fair assumption because even if it is the same user that comes back after staying away for 10 minutes, he or she is most likely coming back to the website with a new objective.

The web logs were preprocessed to create an appropriate representation of each user corresponding to a visit. The abstract representation of a web user is a critical step that requires a good knowledge of the application domain. Previous personal experience with the students in the course suggested that some of them printed preliminary notes just before a class and an updated copy after the class. Some students view the notes online on a regular basis. Some students print all the notes around important days such as midterm and final examinations. In addition, there are many accesses on Tuesdays and Thursdays, when the in-laboratory assignments are due. On- and off-campus points of access can also provide some indication of a user's objectives for the visit. Based on some of these observations, it was decided to use the following attributes for representing each visitor:

1. On-campus/off-campus access.

2. Daytime/nighttime access: 8 a.m. to 8 p.m. was considered to be the daytime.

3. Access during lab/class days or non-lab/class days: All the labs and classes were held on Tuesday and Thursday. The visitors on these days were more likely to be workers.

4. Number of hits.

5. Number of class notes downloaded.

The first three attributes will have binary values of 0 or 1. The last two values may have much higher values than the first three variables. For example, the number of hits can be as high as 350, and the number of class notes downloaded can be as high as 100. The last two variables will dominate the clustering process, so we will have to normalize them, while maintaining their importance in the representation. Because the class notes are the focus of the clustering, the last variable should probably be assigned a higher importance. We will discuss the normalization process a little later after studying the distribution of the actual values of these variables.

Under `chapter 6` on the CD, there is a folder called `BigBrother`, which has all the relevant files that will be used in the clustering process. Copy this folder to your hard drive under the Chapter 6 directory. We have taken the original logfile with 361,609 records and removed the visits by the web crawlers. The remaining 343,188 records were used to create a database of visits.

This highlighted paragraph describes a C++ program that was used to create the database of visits.

C++ files for creating the two programs in the folder `BigBrother` were written by Jonathan Sharkey as part of a research project. Both of these programs are designed to work with the Apache combined log format. The first program, called `sort.cpp`, is designed to change the ordering of http requests. (The original logfile is chronologically ordered.) The program `sort.cpp` can sort a logfile based on the IP addresses as the primary key and the time of request as the secondary key. Compile and link the program with your favorite C++ compiler. It has been tested with the GNU C++ compiler. The input is taken from standard input, and output is directed to standard output. You will have to use I/O redirection for file I/O.

The second program consists of five files: `Visit.h`, `Visit.cpp`, `BigBrother.h`, `BigBrother.cpp`, and `run.cpp`. The program reads from standard input and writes to standard output. Use I/O redirection for file I/O. The input to the program is web-access logs sorted according to the IP address as the primary key and the time of request as the secondary key. The output will be a database of visits. If you run the program with the access log given in the file `classlog.txt,` you will get slightly different results, because the file consists of the hits from the web crawlers. You may want to use utilities such as `grep` to remove all requests from web crawlers. We will leave that as an exercise for more experienced programmers.

The file `allVisits.txt` in the `BigBrother` folder shows all the visits identified by our preprocessing. The file consists of 21,637 visits. A majority of these visits did not download any class notes; therefore, we separated the file into two categories: visits with no class notes were stored in a file called `zeroDocVisits.txt`, and visits with at least one downloaded class note were stored in `docVisits.txt`. The `zeroDocVisits.txt` has 13,561 records, while `docVisits.txt` has 8,076 records.

All three files have the same format. **Figure 6.25** shows the first 10 lines of the file `docVisits. txt`. The first line is the header explaining each column. The first column is the visit number. The reason the visit number jumped from 1 to 17 is that visits 2–16 did not download any class notes. The second column gives the IP address of the computer used by the visitor. The date and time is given in the third and fourth columns. The fifth column tells us whether the visit was from a Saint Mary's University (SMU) computer or external access. A value of 1 means SMU computer, and a value of 0 means external access. As an additional note, any IP number starting with 140.184 is an SMU computer. The sixth column tells us whether the visit was during the day (value of 1) or night (value of 0). A value of 1 in the seventh column tells us that the access was either on a Tuesday or Thursday (lab day), and 0 means any other day of

```
Visit   IP              DATE          TIME    SMU   D/N   TuTH   REQS   DOC-REQS
    1   24.165.7.57     05-08-2001    15:48   0     1     0      2      1
   17   140.184.44.130  08-08-2001    17:06   1     1     0      14     1
   22   140.184.37.121  08-08-2001    22:33   1     0     0      2      1
   27   140.184.20.68   09-08-2001    16:48   1     1     1      40     6
   28   24.138.46.172   09-08-2001    20:46   0     0     1      45     1
   31   140.184.37.103  10-08-2001    00:49   1     0     0      28     2
   32   164.106.225.116 10-08-2001    11:15   0     1     0      1      1
   34   129.173.1.66    10-08-2001    12:54   0     1     0      9      1
   40   24.222.171.0    11-08-2001    17:40   0     1     0      39     5
```

Figure 6.25   First ten lines of the file `docVisits.txt`

Location	Frequency
External	5820
Campus	7741

(a) Location

Time	Frequency
Night	3672
Day	9889

(b) Time of day

Day	Frequency
Other	7985
Tue or Thu	5576

(c) Day of week

Table 6.1   Frequency of binary attributes of visitors with no class-notes downloads

the week. The eighth column reports the number of hits, and a count of number of class notes downloaded is shown in the ninth column.

Before applying the clustering technique, we should study the distribution of various variables. Table 6.1 shows the frequency distribution for the three binary variables for visitors with no class notes. Table 6.1(a) tells us that 5,820 or 43% of the visits come from off-campus locations. The remaining 57% of visits are from campus computers. The day accesses exceed night accesses 73% to 27%. While Tuesday or Thursday accesses make up only 41% of the visits, one should note that each of these two days receive 20% of visits as opposed to 12% for each of the rest of the days. Table 6.2 shows the frequency distribution for the hits by visitors

Hits	Frequency	Cumulative %
1-20	11606	85.58%
21-40	998	92.94%
41-60	556	97.04%
61-80	181	98.38%
81-100	105	99.15%
101-120	56	99.56%
121-140	25	99.75%
141-160	9	99.82%
161-180	5	99.85%
181-200	2	99.87%
200-350	18	100.00%

Table 6.2   Frequency of hits by visitors with no class-notes downloads

who did not download any class notes. As expected, 86% of these visitors have 20 or fewer requests. A surprising 18 visitors made more than 200 requests without downloading any class notes.

Table 6.3 shows the frequency distribution for the three binary variables for visitors who downloaded at least one set of class notes. Table 6.3(a) tells us that 2,688 or 33% of visits come from off-campus locations. The corresponding number for visits with no class notes was 43%. Day accesses exceed night accesses 75% to 25%, which was similar to the visits with no class notes. Tuesday or Thursday accesses were somewhat higher when the visit involved class notes downloading, at 48%. **Table 6.4** shows the frequency distribution for the hits by visitors who did not download any class notes. The numbers of hits in Table 6.4 were higher when there were class notes downloaded as opposed to Table 6.2 with no class notes downloaded. For example, only 64% of visits had fewer than 20 hits, while the corresponding number was 85% in Table 6.2. **Table 6.5** shows the distribution of number of class notes. More than 90% of visitors downloaded fewer than 10 class notes. At the same time, there were three visitors who downloaded more than 100 class notes.

It would be interesting to get a visual impression of some of these class-notes downloads. We have already seen a visual representation of some of the visits in Figures 6.22–6.24. These visits were relatively short, especially if Figure 6.24, in fact, represents two distinct visits. These visits seem to fit the descriptions of workers (described earlier). In order to get visual displays of studious and crammers, we will have to look at visits with a large number of

Location	Frequency
External	2688
Campus	5388

(a) Location

Time	Frequency
Night	2015
Day	6061

(b) Time of day

Day	Frequency
Other	4235
Tue or Thu	3841

(c) Day of week

Table 6.3   Frequency of binary attributes of visitors with class-notes downloads

Hits	Frequency	Cumulative %
1-20	5169	64.00%
21-40	1874	87.21%
41-60	580	94.39%
61-80	244	97.41%
81-100	98	98.63%
101-120	43	99.16%
121-140	28	99.50%
141-160	19	99.74%
161-180	7	99.83%
181-200	7	99.91%
200-350	7	100.00%

Table 6.4   Frequency of hits by visitors who downloaded class notes

Documents	Frequency	Cumulative %
1-10	7385	91.44%
11-20	514	97.81%
21-30	101	99.06%
31-40	33	99.47%
41-50	13	99.63%
51-60	13	99.79%
61-70	8	99.89%
71-80	3	99.93%
81-90	3	99.96%
91-100	0	99.96%
101-110	3	100.00%

Table 6.5   Frequency distribution of class notes

hits and class notes downloaded. Unfortunately, it is difficult to produce a visualization of visits with even as many as 18 class notes downloaded on a normal book page, because the labels will be too small to be legible. Let us look at a representative visit with 18 class notes downloaded. We have included 18doclog.txt, which provides all the requests and a pdf file called 18docVisual.pdf under the folder BigBrother. The file can be viewed using an Acrobat pdf viewer. You will need to magnify and use horizontal scrolling for a better view. The visit depicted in 18docVisual.pdf was from a computer served by the local phone company. It lasted only 1.5 minutes involving 26 clicks. The user clearly knew what he or she was looking for. Most of the class notes were from weeks 4, 5, and 6; there were two from the lab manual. Based on our hypothesis, such a user probably corresponds to either the studious or crammer category, someone who probably neglected to download class notes for a couple of weeks.

It is not possible to easily plot a visit with more than 100 class notes. The requests from a visit that downloaded 104 are listed in a file called 104doclog.txt in the folder BigBrother. If you edit the file or use some pattern-matching tool such as grep, you can find out more information about the visit. There are only 145 requests in the list, 104 of which are for class notes. The visit comes from an on-campus location. If you list the class notes, you will notice that it has cpp and doc files from every one of the 12 weeks when the classes were held. There are no class notes downloaded from the lab folder, indicating a focus on class material. Moreover, the visit was on December 10, just before the final examination. This visitor may very well be the definition of a crammer.

The previous analysis of individuals seems to support our hypothesis that there are three types of visitors: workers, studious, and crammers. We should now conduct the actual clustering of these visitors. We have defined workers as those who download very few, if any, class notes. Therefore, we can categorize all the visits with no class notes as workers. We will apply clustering to the visits that included class notes. The frequency analyses from Tables 6.1 to 6.4 tell us that the workers who do not download class notes are more likely to come from campus locations during Tuesdays or Thursdays. We will see if the clustering of visitors with class notes supports this observation as well.

6.5.1.2 Clustering of Visitors to Course Site

For convenience, the Java class `Kmeans.class` is copied from `chapter 5` to the `BigBrother` folder. Use the data from the database of visitors who downloaded class notes stored in the file `docVisits.txt`. We have extracted the five variables that will be used from the file into `v8076toCluster5D.txt`. The high values of hits and class notes downloaded will essentially dwarf the effect of the binary variables; therefore, we normalized the values of hits to be in the range 0 to 5. The numbers of class notes are given a higher importance, and they are normalized to be in the range 0 to 10. These normalizations are somewhat arbitrary. Different normalizations will give us different results.

We can cluster the records in `v8076toCluster5D.txt` using the following command:

`java Kmeans v8076toCluster5D.txt 8076 5 3 100`   (Command 6.1)

Review what (Command 6.1) achieves. We are running the Java class called `Kmeans`. The first argument, `v8076toCluster5D.txt`, is the input file. The following arguments tell the class that

- there are 8,076 records,
- 5 columns per record,
- these records should be grouped into 3 clusters, and
- the algorithm should run for 100 iterations.

The output from the command is given in the file `cluster8076out5D.txt`. and is rather long. Focus on some of the salient features shown in **Table 6.6**. The values are also graphically represented in **Figure 6.26**. The graphical representation makes it easier to compare the three clusters. Both the table and figure show the average values of all five variables and the sizes for the three clusters. Cluster 1 has the greatest number of visitors, 4,841, as shown in the last column in Table 6.6. The second column tells us that most of them came from campus locations and during the day (third column). The significant majority came on Tuesday or Thursday, indicated by a value of 0.7178 in the fourth column. The number of hits (column 5) and class notes downloaded (column 6) are modest. We normalized the values of hits and

Cluster	Campus External	Day Night	TTh Other	Hits	Class-notes	Size
1 (Workers)	0.9236	0.9322	0.7178	0.2938 (20)*	0.2853 (3)*	4841
2 (Studious)	0.2307	0.4370	0.0863	0.2692 (18)*	0.3040 (3)*	2792
3 (Crammers)	0.6163	0.7404	0.2822	0.9558 (66)*	2.2128 (23)*	443

*Values in parentheses for hits and documents are after reversing the normalization

Table 6.6   Clustering at a glance with five variables

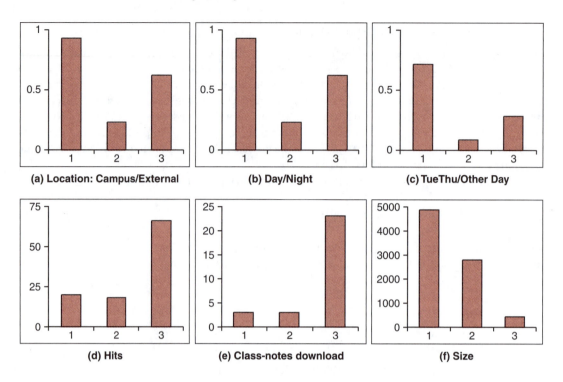

Figure 6.26 Attributes of three clusters obtained with five variables

class notes. The values in parentheses in columns 5 and 6 are the actual values obtained after reversing the normalization and rounding off.

The hits and class notes for the first two clusters are approximately the same. The third cluster has a significantly larger number of hits (average of 66) and class notes (average of 23). We can safely label the third cluster as crammers. Incidentally, the size of the cluster of crammers is the smallest. This is expected because crammer visits tend to be concentrated over a short period around examinations.

It is not easy to distinguish between the first two clusters based on hits and class notes. We can see that Cluster 2 has slightly fewer hits and more class notes, which would indicate fewer workers and more studious; however, the binary variables are the real distinguishing factors. The workers are more likely to visit from campus locations, during the daytime, and during laboratory days (Tuesdays and Thursdays). These are essential characteristics of the first cluster. We can see that the values for these three variables for Cluster 2 are significantly lower than Cluster 1. Readers may want to look at Figure 6.26 (a, b, and c) for a visual representation of the difference. Therefore, it makes sense to label Cluster 1 as worker and Cluster 2 as studious. It is also worth noting that this description of a worker is similar to characteristics of visitors who did not download any class notes.

The previous discussion is just an example of how to cluster web users and interpret the results. A different choice of variables and weighting schemes can give us different answers. In fact, let us experiment a little by clustering the visitors based only on the number of hits and

Cluster	Hits	Class-notes	Size
1	0.2495	0.2397	7024
(Workers)	(17)*	(3)*	
2	0.7595	1.2087	981
(Studious)	(52)*	(13)*	
3	1.4031	4.7955	71
(Crammers)	(96)*	(50)*	

*Values in parentheses for hits and documents are after reversing the normalization

Table 6.7   Clustering at a glance with two variables

class notes. The file `v8076toCluster2D.txt` has the corresponding records. We can cluster the records in `v8076toCluster2D.txt` using the following command:

```
java Kmeans v8076toCluster2D.txt 8076 2 3 100
```
(Command 6.2)

In addition to changing the name of the input file, we have also changed the number of variables in (Command 6.2) from five to two. The output from the command is available in the file `cluster8076out2D.txt`. The summary of the output can be found in **Table 6.7** and as a graph in **Figure 6.27**. The interpretation of results in this particular case is fairly straightforward. The workers have the lowest number of hits and class notes downloaded, followed by the studious visitors. Crammers have a significantly higher number of hits and class notes downloaded. It is also interesting to note that the size of the workers cluster is 100 times more than the crammers. The clustering with five variables seems to be a little more interesting than the one with two variables, because it allows us to consider different aspects of user behavior. The clustering obtained using two variables seems to simply segment the user population into a low, medium, and high number of hits and class notes. Readers are encouraged to experiment with different combinations of weighting schemes and variables (see Exercise section).

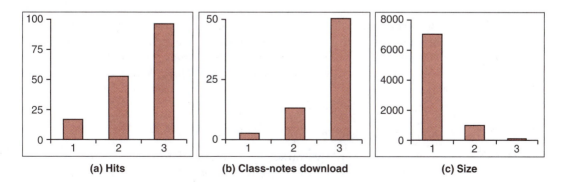

(a) Hits   (b) Class-notes download   (c) Size

Figure 6.27   Attributes of three clusters obtained with two variables

6.5.2   Classification Modeling of Web Users

Classification is another data-mining technique that can contribute to web-usage mining. Web personalization (Dai and Mobasher 2003) is a common application of such a classification exercise. The interest in web personalization can be traced back to the Firefly system (no longer available URL: www.firefly.com), which was used to suggest music CDs that match the user's interests. Similar attempts can also be seen on Amazon.com. When a user requests information about a book, the system provides a list of additional books. The list consists of books purchased by people who bought the book the user is interested in. Attempts at web personalization are increasing at a rapid rate. The increased interest is also leading to more formal frameworks for web personalization (Perkowitz and Etzioni 1997). Joachim and colleagues (1995) proposed the use of a tour-guide approach. Perkowitz and Etzioni (1997) attempted to formalize the concept of adaptive websites, which were defined as those that automatically improve their organization and presentation by learning from visitor-access patterns. They suggested that much of the earlier work was focused on fairly simple adaptations such as automatically creating shortcuts on the site and customization of a website to suit the needs of each individual user. Perkowitz and Etzioni proposed the use of sophisticated adaptations of websites to users' needs, and the aggregation of information gleaned from the user population to improve the navigation for a large number of users.

In this section, we will discuss a web-personalization project called ClickWorld (Baglioni et al. 2003), which uses classification as the main underlying technique. The project is aimed at extracting models of the navigational behavior of users. The study involved analysis of five months worth of access logs from an Italian web portal, vivacity.it. The portal includes web contents of national interest (www.vivacity.it) such as news, forums, and a humor section. In addition, the portal contains more than 30 websites that serve the interests of local areas. For example, www.roma.vivacity.it serves the interests of users from Rome. The local city-specific information includes local news, restaurant addresses, theater programming, and a bus timetable. The overall scope of the ClickWorld project includes applications of various data-mining techniques, including clustering, classification, association, and sequential pattern analysis, to extract useful information for a proactive personalization of websites. Baglioni (2003) conducted two sets of classification experiments. The first created a classification model to identify the gender of a user based on the set of web pages visited. The second consisted of a classification model that would predict if a particular user is likely to visit a given category of pages such as sports or finance. The first experiment had limited success due to a lack of sufficient data. The second experiment, however, did find some success. We will study the second model-building process in this section. The model building involved the traditional data-mining steps: collection of data, preparation of data for mining, and application of data-mining techniques. We will briefly review these three steps. More details can be found in (Baglioni et al. 2003).

6.5.2.1   Collection and Preprocessing of Data for the Italian Web Portal

The available data consisted of user registration data, information about the web contents, and information about the web-access logs. Because registration is not mandatory, registration data was available for only a subset of users who chose to register. For a registered user, the system records the following information: gender, city, province, civil status, and birth date.

This personal information is not guaranteed to be accurate. During the preprocessing stage, improbable data such as a birth date in the future was eliminated. Similarly, if values of all the fields corresponded to the default values in the form, it was assumed that the user did not enter any information; hence, it was deleted as well. The web portal uses cookies to save the users the trouble of entering login information for every visit. If a cookie exists on the user's computer, authentication is not required. Otherwise, after authentication, a new cookie is sent to the user. This way, it is possible to track a user as long as the cookies are not deleted from the system. Cross-referencing of cookies and registration information was also used to eliminate robot accesses.

The information regarding web contents was obtained by analyzing the URLs of the documents. The URLs for the web portal are designed to facilitate fast server processing. For example, consider a URL, such as

`http://roma.vivacity.it/speciali/EditColonnaSpeciale/1,3478,|DX,00.html`

These URLs are not very meaningful in terms of identifying the semantic contents of the document. Further processing of the URLs was required to extract additional information from the URLs as follows (Baglioni et al. 2003):

- Spatial information about user interests using the name of the server, such as www.roma. vivacity.
- First-level classification of URLs into 24 types. Examples of these categories include *home, news, finance, photo galleries, jokes, shopping, forum,* and *pubs.*
- Second-level classification of URLs dependent on the first-level one. For example, URLs classified as *shopping* may be further classified as *book shopping* or *PC shopping.*
- Third-level classification of URLs dependent on the second-level one. For example, *book shopping* may be further classified as *programming book shopping* or *narrative book shopping.*
- Further information about the three level classifications; for example, URLs classified as *programming book shopping* may have the ISBN book code as a parameter.
- The depth of the classification; that is, 1 if the URL has only a first-level classification, 2 if the URL has first and second-level classification, and 3 if it has complete three-level classification.

The web-access logs were processed to create a database of visits or sessions. The database consisted of the following derived attributes:

- **SessionID** is a unique identifier of the user session. We will discuss how *users* and *user sessions* were identified a little later.
- **Last** counts how long in the past the same URL was requested. The count is absolute; that is, it considers the number of requests. Last is set to a large constant if there is no previous request.
- **Next** counts how long into the future the same URL will be requested. Next is set to a large constant if there is no further request.
- **PageDelay** is the distance in milliseconds of a request from the previous request by the same user. PageDelay is set to a large constant for the very first request from a user.

As we saw in the previous experiment with an educational website, the identification of a session can be a little tricky. The registration information in this case was not very useful, because the majority of requests came from unregistered users. The cookies were often deleted, or web browsers were set to not accept cookies. Semantically, a user session could be defined as the set of URLs accessed by a user for a particular purpose; however, it is not possible to guess the purpose a user has in mind. Baglioni and colleagues used heuristics based on what they called a *reference length* approach, which is based on the assumption that the amount of time a user spends examining a document is related to the interest in its contents. A model for user sessions is obtained by distinguishing the *navigational* pages from the *content* pages. Navigational pages contain links interesting only to the user. The content pages were those that had the information the user was looking for. The distinction between navigational and content accesses is related to the distance (in time) between two successive requests. If the time delay between two accesses (A and B) is greater than a given threshold, then A can be considered a content URL; otherwise, it was a navigational URL. A user session is defined as a sequence of navigational URLs followed by one content URL. Starting from PageDelay, a SessionID was assigned to each URL request by grouping requests whose distance is below a given threshold.

6.5.2.2 Predicting Interests of Users by Means of a Classification Model

Baglioni used the classification algorithm C4.5 to develop a model to predict whether a user might be interested in visiting a section of a website based on the sections the user had already visited. The knowledge of the sections of interest make it possible to create a personalized view of the website by using on-the-fly menu or page reorganization.

The vivacity.it website includes channels such as news, sports, shopping, finance, jokes, and restaurants. Channels can usually be described using the second-level classification described earlier. Our classification problem can be restated as predicting whether a user session includes access to a channel based on the accesses to the other channels. Such a model can be used to predict the potential interest of a new user in a channel he or she has not visited yet, based on the channels visited in the last or current session (Baglioni et al. 2003). The model can use these predictions to suggest another channel of interest to new users. Using information on the user sessions that first accessed the new channel, the model could suggest which other users may be interested in the new channel. The website could then prominently display the new channel to these possibly interested users.

The data consisted of more than 215,000 user sessions. For each channel chosen in a session, Baglioni created a record as follows:

- The chosen channel is the output or class attribute.
- The other channels chosen in the session are input variables.
- Each attribute has a binary value.

Two-thirds of the records were used in the training set for building the model. The remaining one-third of records was set aside in the test set to examine the quality of predictions. The accuracy of predictions was evaluated using the precision and recall measures we studied in information retrieval (Chapter 2). The definitions were adapted to the classification. Let

Channel	Recall	Precision
Finance	44.3%	98.27%
Health	52.3%	89.66%
Market	49.1%	83.34%
News	44.1%	89.27%
Shopping	31.5%	91.31%
Specials	60.2%	92.86%
Sport	50.0%	91.93%
Surveys	21.9%	92.66%
Theatre	54.8%	94.63%

Table 6.8 Precision and recall for predicting user's interest in channels (Baglioni, et al., 2003)

RET be the set of records that have been predicted as *yes*, and *REL* be the set of records that actually belong to the class *yes*.

$$precision = \frac{|RET \cap REL|}{|RET|}$$

$$recall = \frac{|RET \cap REL|}{|REL|}$$

Precision measures what proportion of predictions is correct. Recall tells us what percentage of channels the user is interested in, which is identified as such by the classification model. **Table 6.8** shows the precision and recall values for a select list of channels. The precision values are consistently high, ranging from 83% to 98%, with a majority of them above 90%. This means when the model predicts that a user will be interested in a channel, it is almost always correct. The recall values vary from 22% to 60%. The lower values of recall suggest that the model is not able to identify all the channels a user may be interested in. If the model were fine-tuned to increase the recall, the precision would likely go down (as we have seen in IR). Increasing recall at the cost of reducing precision may lead to a cluttered personalized home page, with many channel links that may not be interesting to the user. In this case, one would rather err on the side of higher precision than higher recall.

There is a subtle difference between the classification model described in this section and association mining. In applying association mining, we would find pairs of channels that are accessed during the same session. The model developed by Baglioni (2003), on the other hand, takes a list of channels of user interest and predicts the likelihood of the user accessing a given channel. In the next section, we will see how association mining can be applied for similar purposes.

6.5.3   Association Mining of Web Usage

In this section, we will look at an application of association mining to web usage conducted by Batista and Silva (2002). Publico On-Line is a daily online newspaper in Portugal. Like on many newspaper sites, the newspaper staff enters articles into a system, which then creates the online edition using these articles. The process includes formatting the articles and generating a navigable web structure. The articles are grouped based on themes into sections such as society, local news, international news, culture, and education.

6.5.3.1   Data Preparation for Publico On-Line

The data used from the newspaper site consists of web-access logs. The first step in the data preparation involves removing erroneous requests as well as requests for images. The next step is session identification. Similar to the clustering experiment for our educational site, the sessions were determined by grouping all requests for viewing articles from a given IP address until there was a significant gap between requests. A 30-minute or longer gap was considered to be significant enough and by that point, the session was considered to be over. For each valid request for a news article, the corresponding news section was recorded. The news section or the page could be easily identified using the site-structure information present in the page's URL. Each article was associated with one and only one section, although a visitor could request one or more articles during a session. Batista and Silva called the sessions identified by the aforementioned process short sessions. If a user's browser was set to accept cookies, a long session was defined for that user as a series of short sessions that shared the same cookie.

The session data collected was represented in a table. There was a column corresponding to each news section, and each row corresponded to a session. Thus, each matrix cell contained the number of articles requested on each (session, section) pair. The matrices were sparse; that is, a significant number of cells had zero values. As a part of the preliminary data analysis, Batista and Silva studied the maximum, minimum, mean, and standard deviation of requests for each news section. These values are shown in **Table 6.9**. Note that the cells with zero values were not included in the calculations in the table. Inspection of individual rows shows that each session contained requests for a small number of articles from an even smaller number of sections. For example, 83% of the sessions did not request any article from the Science section. Even in the remaining 17% of the sessions, there was an average of only 2.3 requests for science articles. The Science and Education sections were probably tied for the least popular sections. The maximum values seem to be rather high compared with the average values. There is a likelihood that these maximum values may be outliers; for example, resulting from web crawler's visits. Batista and Silva did not report that they eliminated requests from web crawlers.

After the data preparation and preliminary analysis, we are ready to look at association mining on the data. For association mining, the actual numerical values of the number of articles requested were not necessary. Therefore, Batista and Silva created the Boolean version of the data matrix such that every nonzero value was converted to 1, and zero values were left unchanged.

News Section	Minimum Requests	Maximum Requests	Mean Requests	Standard Deviation
Science	1	97	2.3034	2.8184
Culture	1	208	3.7878	5.9742
Sports	1	318	5.6985	10.8360
Economics	1	258	3.9335	7.2341
International	1	208	3.3823	5.5540
Local Lisbon	1	460	5.6883	11.5650
Local Port	1	256	7.5984	13.2351
Politics	1	208	3.3577	5.4101
Society	1	367	4.2673	7.9853
Education	1	90	2.6496	3.29090

Table 6.9 Summary statistics of requests to the Publico On-line newspaper (Courtesy of P. Batista and M. Silva, 2002)

6.5.3.2 Association Mining for Publico On-Line

The association mining conducted by Batista and Silva (2002) addressed essentially the same question as the one answered by the classification exercise reported in Baglioni and colleagues (2003); that is, which category of articles are requested by the same visitor? Batista and Silva's approach falls into the classical *Market-Basket Analysis* problem (Berry and Linoff 1997).

The aim of market-basket analysis is to find groups of items that are frequently referred together. In this case, a transaction is the web request and the item is the news section that the article is from. Groups of items that occur frequently together in the same visit are called frequent itemsets (Agrawal and Srikant 1994). A typical association-mining process needs guidance for restricting the search space, usually in terms of a support threshold. The algorithms then find the itemsets that satisfy this minimum support threshold. Batista and Silva defined weak associations as those below 5% of the total number of occurrences, and heavy associations as those above 10%. The association-mining results showed strong associations between the following pairs:

- Politics and Society
- Politics and International News
- Politics and Sports
- Society and International News
- Society and Local Lisbon
- Society and Sports
- Society and Culture
- Sports and International News

Because the long sessions were just a concatenation of the short sessions, the strong associations from the short sessions were also present in the long sessions.

6.5.4   Sequence-Pattern Analysis of Web Logs

The data in web-access logs are intrinsically sequential. We used data-visualization techniques to look at aggregate navigation using Pathalizer as well as navigation in individual sessions using StatViz. Applying data-mining techniques to analyze sequences of web requests is an important area of research (Cadez et al. 2000; Iváncsy and Vajk 2006). Many of the techniques involved are at an experimental stage and contain sophisticated mathematical analysis. In this section, we will first look at some preliminary analytical techniques and review some of the more esoteric ones.

Cadez (2000) presented msnbc.com (2000) anonymous web data, which can be downloaded from http://kdd.ics.uci.edu/databases/msnbc/msnbc.html. It is also available on the CD under Chapter 6 in a folder called msnbc. Copy the folder to your hard drive under the folder for Chapter 6. The file `msnbc990928.seq` contains the original data, which comes from the web-access logs of msnbc.com and news portions of msn.com for the 24-hour period on September, 28, 1999. There was a total of 989,818 user sessions. The data is anonymized, so we have no knowledge of the login details of the users. The first 20 lines of the file `msnbc990928.seq` are shown in **Figure 6.28**. (Note that the third line wraps around twice, so it looks like there are 22 lines.) The first seven lines give us information about the data. The third line lists various news categories on the site. These categories are referred to in the data as numbers.

Table 6.10 shows the categories and corresponding numeric code. The data consists of a sequence of numbers starting at line 8. Each sequence in the dataset corresponds to a user's web request. We know the only category of the web page that was requested by the user; we do not know the name of the actual page. The reporting of categories of the pages as opposed

```
% Different categories found in input file:

frontpage news tech local opinion on-air misc weather
msn-news health living business· msn-sports sports
summary bbs travel

% Sequences:

1 1
2
3 2 2 4 2 2 2 3 3
5
1
6
1 1
6
6 7 7 7 6 6 8 8 8 8
6 9 4 4 4 10 3 10 5 10 4 4 4
1 1 1 11 1 1 1
12 12
1 1
```

Figure 6.28   First twenty lines of msnbc.com data (Note: The third line wraps around twice) http://kdd.ics.uci.edu/databases/msnbc/msnbc.html

Category	Number
frontpage	1
news	2
tech	3
local	4
opinion	5
on-air	6
misc	7
weather	8
msn-news	9
health	10
living	11
business	12
msn-sports	13
sports	14
summary	15
bbs	16
travel	17

Table 6.10 Categories and corresponding numbers for msnbc.com data

to the actual pages, in fact, simplifies our job. There are anywhere from 10 to 5,000 pages per category. It would be difficult to keep track of each one of these pages. Average length of the sequences is 5.7. As with any other web-access logs, any page request served via a caching mechanism could not be recorded in the data.

One of the most useful pieces of information in the web-access logs is the sequence in which users access pages. This information can be used to provide appropriate links to simplify the navigation. One can do a frequency analysis of all the category pairs, such as (1,1), (1,2), (1,3), ..., (17,1), (17,2), ..., (17,3). In total, there are 289 pairs. The sequence of category numbers in a pair is important for two reasons:

- The links are always between a pair of pages. Thus, knowing which pages are requested from a given page is the most relevant information needed in order to determine the navigational links.
- The pairs of sequences will have the highest frequency. For example, a sequence (i, j, k) cannot have a higher frequency than either of the pairs, (i, j) or (j, k).

Moreover, the number of pairs is much smaller than any longer sequence. We can use pattern-matching programs such as `grep` (available for various platforms including UNIX and DOS) to look for sequences of pairs.

The regular expression that will help us search for a pair (i, j) in the msnbc.com data is "\bi j\b". For a more specific example, the pair (7, 4) would be "\b7 4\b". The '\b' on both ends of the pair makes sure that the expression does not pick up additional patterns such as "17 4". If you have access to the UNIX utility for word count called wc, you can combine the pattern matching and word counting to get the number of sessions containing a given pair:

grep ''\b7 4\b'' msnbc990928.seq | wc 1   (Command 6.3)

If you produce a similar command as (Command 6.3) for every pair using a program, you will be able to get the values for all the pairs. You can also repeat the same process for triplets. For example, if you were looking for the triplet (1, 4, 7), you could run the following command:

grep \b1 4 7\b msnbc990928.seq | wc 1   (Command 6.4)

Again, (Command 6.3) and (Command 6.4) can be automatically generated for all the triplets using a simple program (see Exercises).

In the folder msnbc, you will find two files: freq2.txt and sortedfreq2.txt. The first 10 and last 10 lines from freq2.txt are shown in **Figure 6.29**. The second and third columns in the figure represent the pair (divided), and the first column shows the number of users who

```
138441   1       1
56768    1       2
20840    1.      3
22492    1       4
6481     1       5
24930    1       6
20793    1       7
5929     1       8
2593     1       9
16821    1       10
......
......
......
......
142      17      8
65       17      9
264      17      10
1344     17      11
268      17      12
17       17      13
242      17      14
143      17      15
2        17      16
2334     17      17
```

Figure 6.29   First and last ten lines of freq2.txt

followed the sequence given by the pair. For example, 138,441 users first accessed a page from Category 1, followed by another page in the same category. Similarly, 2 users first read an article from Category 17 and then moved to a page from Category 16. There are a total of 289 paired sequences listed in file `freq2.txt`. It may be a little difficult to analyze all the pairs; therefore, `sortedfreq2.txt` lists these sequences in descending order of accesses. The sequences that were followed by the most users are at the top and those sequences that were followed by the least number of users are at the bottom.

Figure 6.30 shows some of the lines from the `sortedfreq2.txt`. The pairs that stay within the same category—such as the top four sequences, (1, 1), (2, 2), (14, 14), (8, 8)—tend to have higher frequencies. This seems reasonable because once a user starts reading an article from one category, he or she is likely to access another article from the same category. Usually such sequences would be well served by the web structure because the site is likely to provide reasonable navigation between articles within the same category. The pairs wherein one of the categories is 1 (corresponding to front page) tend to have higher frequencies. (The fifth-highest frequency is for the pair (1, 2).) This sequence probably corresponds to users first coming to the front page and then following links to other categories. The website will also better serve these sequences because the front page will have links to other categories. The pair (6, 7) with a frequency of 25,106 is the first pair with two distinct categories, neither of which is front page. Category 6 is "on-air" and Category 7 is "misc." The high frequency for this pair suggests that the site should provide easy navigation from "on-air" to "misc." The last five

```
138441    1         1
76927     2         2
68312     14        14
65036     8         8
56768     1         2
......
......
......
25106     6         7
24930     1         6
24896     1         11
......
......
......
8         9         16
8         16        13
2         17        16
2         16        17
2         13        17
```

Figure 6.30   A sample of lines from `sortedfreq2.txt`

lines in Figure 6.30 show very little movement between some of the categories. There are three possible explanations for such a lack of migration:

- These categories have limited contents, and hence very few visitors. For example, only 2,032 users accessed a page from Category 16 (bbs).
- These categories attract different types of readers.
- The link structure does not make it possible to easily navigate between these categories. The web administrator may consider improving the navigational structure.

The previous discussion shows how one can interpret paired sequences of web usage to study the web structure. One can extend such an analysis to longer sequences. The frequency of sequences that are three-events long can be found in the files: `freq3.txt` and `sortedfreq3.txt`. The `sortedfreq3.txt` file shows triplets ordered based on the frequency with which users followed those sequences. There are a total of $17 \times 17 \times 17 = 4913$ triplets. Some of the lines from `sortedfreq3.txt` are shown in **Figure 6.31**. Similar to the paired sequences, the triplets where all three pages are from the same category tend to have higher frequencies. The triplets where the three categories are not distinct do not provide any additional knowledge about user behavior than the one gathered from paired sequences; therefore, we will focus only on triplets where all three categories are distinct. The first such pair is (1, 7, 4) as shown in Figure 6.31, which corresponds to frontpage-misc-local. This information could probably be used to put the links to Categories 7 and 4 next to each other on pages from Category 1.

One could extend the analysis to longer sequences; however, it should be noted that 635

```
64107    1    1    1
49723    8    8    8
44921   14   14   14
42129    2    2    2
29871    7    7    7
29444    4    4    4
26295    1    2    2
.......
.......
.......
 4379    1    7    4
 4331    7    1    7
 4279    9    7    9
.......
.......
.......
    0    1   16   17
    0    1   16   13
    0    1   13    5
    0    1   13   17
```

Figure 6.31 A sample of lines from `sortedfreq3.txt`

of the triplets had a frequency of 0. The longer sequences with distinct categories would have smaller and smaller frequencies, because the average length of sequences is only 5.3. Another possible analysis could include compressing the sequences by replacing multiple sequential articles from the same categories and then analyzing the resulting sequences. For example, a sequence "3 2 2 4 2 2 2 3 3" could be represented as "3 2 4 2 3", which shows how a user migrates from one category to the next. Such an analysis is left as an exercise (see Exercises).

The msnbc.com data has been subject to more sophisticated analysis by a number of researchers. Cadez and colleagues (2000) partitioned users from msnbc.com into clusters based on similarity in their navigation paths through the site. The clustering approach is model-based (as opposed to the distance-based approaches we have seen thus far); it partitions users according to the order in which they request web pages. Cadez and colleagues use a mixture of first-order Markov models using the Expectation-Maximization algorithm. They display aggregate paths for each cluster. As expected from our earlier analysis, the larger clusters tend to have a navigation path that seems to navigate within a given category.

Iváncsy and Vajk (2006) show how the automata theory can be used for discovering frequent web-navigation patterns from the msnbc.com data. The SM-Tree algorithm discovers the frequent page sequences using finite state machines. The navigation patterns are rarely sequential. Sometimes users use the Back button to go back one level and then traverse to the next page. Such navigation is best represented using a tree. Iváncsy and Vajk show how the PDTree algorithm based on pushdown automaton can be used to identify the tree-like web navigation patterns.

6.6 Concluding Remarks

One of the primary questions all website developers are wondering is: What do users want? In this chapter we used web-access logs to study user behavior and try to answer this enduring question. We studied the format of the data, as well as various tools to summarize and visualize it. We also discussed how various data-mining techniques could be applied to discover more knowledge about web usage. This is an ongoing area of research, and it will be interesting to follow new developments in the coming years. In the meantime, we will see how web-usage data can be used for making a website better in the following two chapters, Web Content Mining and Web Structure Mining.

EXERCISES

1. Specify the `#FIELDS` directive for the common log format.

2. Find out where the web-access log files are stored on your server. Download the access-log file from the previous week, and run Analog for your web-access log. Study and write a report on the web usage. The chances are that the logfile is very large. You may want to use a pattern-matching utility such as `grep` to select a subset of the logfile and then do the analysis.

3. Extract one day's worth of data from the logfile in the previous exercise and analyze it using Pathalizer. Report your findings.

4. If you have installed StatViz, run it for a small portion of the logfile from the previous exercise and report your findings.

5. Use the Kohonen algorithm for clustering the data from `V8076Cluster5D.txt`, and compare the results with those obtained using the k-Means algorithm.

6. Experiment with various weighting schemes in the file `V8076Cluster5D.txt`, and run the clustering class again. You may also want to use different combinations of variables. Write a report on the results.

7. The database in the file `V8076Cluster5D.txt` can also be used for classification and predictions. For example, we may be interested in finding out if a visitor is likely to come from an off-campus location, based on the values of hits and class notes. Or we may want to predict the number of class notes based on the location, time of the day, and day of the week. Describe the objectives of such a classification or prediction experiment, and apply an appropriate technique from Chapter 4. Write a report on your findings.

8. The web-access logs in `classlog.txt` can be used to create an innovative database for mining. For example, you may want to create a data-mining exercise that predicts the amount of bytes that will be requested by a visitor or find associations between different types of files. Describe the objectives of such a classification or prediction experiment and apply an appropriate technique from Chapter 4. Write a report on your findings. The C++ programs from the `BigBrother` folder may be helpful for data processing.

9. Write a program that generates a series of commands similar to (Command 6.3) and (Command 6.4). Use the generated commands to produce a frequency of occurrence of various pairs and triplets for msnbc.com.

10. Compress the sequences in msnbc.com by replacing multiple sequential articles from the same categories. For example, a sequence "3 2 2 4 2 2 2 3 3" could be represented as "3 2 4 2 3", which shows how a user migrates from one category to next. Analyze the resulting compressed sequences. Compare the differences in frequencies.

References

Agrawal, R., and R. Srikant. (1994): Fast algorithms for mining association rules. In *Proceedings of the 20th VLDB Conference*, 487–99. Santiago, Chile.

Apache. (2006): Log files. http://httpd.apache.org/docs/2.2/logs.html.

Baglioni, M., U. Ferrara, A. Romei, S. Ruggieri, and F. Turini. (2003): Preprocessing and mining Web log data for Web personalization. In *Proceedings of the 8th National Conference of the Italian Association for Artificial Intelligence (AI-IA 2003)*. Pisa, Italy.

Batista, P., and M.J. Silva. (2002): Mining Web access logs of an on-line newspaper. In *Proceedings of the 2nd International Workshop on Recommendation and Personalization in eCommerce (RPeC'02)*. Spain: Univ. of Malaga.

Berry, M., and G. Linoff. (1997): *Data mining techniques for marketing, sales and customer support*. New York: John Wiley & Sons.

Cadez, I., D. Heckerman, C. Meek, P. Smyth, and S. White. (2000): Model-based clustering and visualization of navigation patterns on a Web site. *Technical Report, MSR-TR-00-18*, Microsoft Research. Redmond, Washington.

Cooley, R., B. Mobasher, and J. Srivastava. (1997): Web mining: Information and pattern discovery on the World Wide Web. In *Proceedings of the International Conference on Tools with Artificial Intelligence*. 558–67.

Dai H., and B. Mobasher. (2003): A road map to more effective Web personalization: Integrating domain knowledge with Web-usage mining. In *Proceedings of the International Conference on Internet Computing 2003 (IC03)*.

Hallam-Baker, P.M., and B. Behlendorf. (1996): Extended log file format. http://www.w3.org/pub/WWW/TR/WD-logfile-960221.html.

Iváncsy, R., and I. Vajk. (2006): Frequent pattern mining in Web log data. Acta Polytechnica Hungarica, *Journal of Applied Science*. 3 (1): 77–90. Budapest Tech Hungary.

Joachims, T., R. Armstrong, D. Freitag, and T. Mitchell. (1995): Webwatcher: A learning apprentice for the World Wide Web. In *Proceedings of AAAI Spring Symposium on Information Gathering from Heterogeneous, Distributed Environments*. Stanford Univ.

Kosala, R., and H. Blockeel. (2000): Web mining research: A survey. *SIG KDD Explorations*, 2 (15): 1–15.

msnbc.com. (2000): msnbc.com Anonymous Web data, http://kdd.ics.uci.edu/databases/msnbc/msnbc.html.

Pathalizer (2006a): Project details for Pathalizer. http://freshmeat.net/projects/pathalizer/.

Pathalizer (2006b): Pathalizer download, http://pathalizer.sourceforge.net/

Perkowitz, M., and O. Etzioni, (1997): Adaptive Web sites: An AI challenge. In *Proceedings of the Fifteenth International Joint Conference on Artificial Intelligence*.

Ramadhan, H., M. Hatem, Z. Al-Khanjri, and S. Kutti. (2005): A Classification of techniques for Web usage analysis. *Journal of Computer Science,* 1 (3): 413–18.

StatViz. (2006): StatViz—Graphical clickstream/path analysis of Web traffic. http://statviz.sourceforge.net/.

Turner, S. (2006): Analog, http://www.Analog.cx

Turner, S. (2004): How the Web works. http://www.Analog.cx/docs/Webworks.html.

Wikipedia. (2006): Server logs. http://en.wikipedia.org/wiki/Server_log.

Web Content Mining

7

7.1 Introduction

Web-content mining techniques (Liu, B.; Chang, K., 2004) are used to discover useful information from content on the Web. The Web contains a variety of information such as documents from digital libraries, government sites providing information about services and regulations, and business services providing information about products, as well as an ability to conduct e-commerce. Web content (Hand, D.; Mannila H.; and Smyth P, 2001) can be textual, audio, video, still images, metadata, or hyperlinks. Some web content is generated dynamically using queries to database management systems, while other content may be hidden from general users.

There are various methods that can be used to search the Internet. The most common approach is through search engines, most of which are keyword based. Traditional search engines have crawlers to search the Web and collect useful information, indexing techniques to store the information, and query-processing support to offer exact information to users. Web-content mining goes beyond the traditional IR technology.

There are two approaches to web-content mining: agent-based and database oriented. In the agent-based approach, software agents perform the content mining, whereas database-oriented approaches view the data as belonging to a database. Several mining efforts have centered on methods to summarize the accumulated information. We have already discussed keyword-based IR in Chapter 2 and semantic search in Chapter 3. In this chapter, we will discuss web crawlers and search engines, including implementation issues.

7.2 Data Collection

7.2.1 Web Crawlers

A crawler is a computer program that navigates the hypertext structure of the Web. Crawlers are used to ease the formation of indexes used by search engines. The page(s) that the crawler begins with are called the *seed URLs*. Here, every link from the first page is recorded and saved in a queue. The crawler builds an index of the number of visits to a page, replacing the current index. Such a crawler is known as *periodic* because it is activated periodically.

Focused crawlers are generally recommended for use due to the huge size of the Web. A focused crawler visits pages related to topics of interest. The advantage of focused crawling is that if a page is not pertinent, the entire set of possible pages below it is pruned. The focused crawler structure consists of two major parts: the distiller and the hypertext classifier. A distiller verifies which pages contain links to other relevant pages, which are called *hub* pages; these can play a vital role in the ongoing search. A hypertext classifier establishes a resource rating to estimate how advantageous it would be for the crawler to pursue the links to that page. The classifier connects a significant score for each document with respect to the crawl theme. The pages that the crawler visits are selected using a priority-based structure managed by the priority associated with pages by the classifier and the distiller.

To use a focused crawler, the user first identifies sample documents that are of interest. These are then classified based on a hierarchical classification tree, and nodes in the tree are marked as good, thus indicating that they have associated document(s) that are of interest. These documents are then used as the seed documents to begin the focused crawling. As relevant documents are found during the crawling phase, whether or not to follow the links from these documents is determined. Each document is classified into a leaf node of the taxonomy tree. One proposed approach, called hard focus, follows links if there is an ancestor of this node that has been marked as good. Another technique, soft focus, identifies the probability that a page, d, is relevant as follows:

$$R(d) = \sum_{good(c)} P(c|d),$$

where c is a node in the tree (thus a page) and $good(c)$ is the indication that it has been labeled as being of interest. The priority of visiting a page that has not yet been visited is the maximum of the relevance of pages that have been visited and that point to it.

More recent work on focused crawling proposed the use of context graphs, which in turn created the context-focused crawler (CFC), which crawls in two phases. In the first phase, context graphs and classifiers are constructed using a set of seed documents as a training set. In the second phase, the crawling is performed using the classifiers as a guide. In addition, the context graphs are updated during the crawl. This is a major difference from the focused crawler, wherein the classifier is static after the learning phase. The CFC approach is designed to overcome many problems associated with previous crawlers, such as

- some pages that may not be relevant but have links to relevant pages. The links from these documents should be followed.
- relevant pages that may actually have links into an existing relevant page, but no links into them from relevant pages. However, crawling can only follow the links out of a page. It would be nice to identify pages that point to the current page. A type of backward crawling to determine these pages would be beneficial.

The CFC approach uses a context graph, which is a rooted graph in which the root represents a seed document and nodes at each level represent pages that have links to a node at the next-higher level. A context graph is used to gather information about topics that are related to the topic being explored. The user determines the number of levels in a context graph. **Figure 7.1** contains three levels. A node in the graph with a path of length n to the seed-document node represents a document that has links indirectly to the seed document through a path of length n. The number of back links followed is chosen as input to the algorithm. At this point, n is called the depth of the context graph. The context graphs created for all seed documents are merged.

Backward crawling finds pages that are not pointed to by relevant documents but are themselves relevant. These types of pages may be new and not yet discovered and linked to

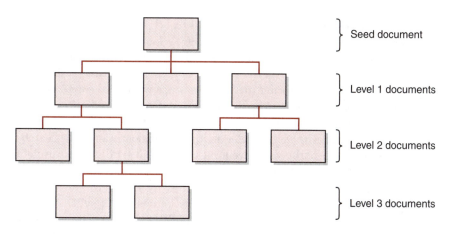

Figure 7.1 Context graph

from other pages. Although backward links do not really exist on the Web, a backward crawl can be performed without difficulty because most search engines already maintain information about the back links. This type of information is similar to the information often used by commercial citation servers, which find documents that cite a given document. The value of the Science Citation Index in performing traditional literature searches is well known. The use of backlinks on the Web can provide similar benefits.

The CFC performs classification using a term frequency–inverse document frequency (TF-IDF) technique. The vocabulary used is formed from the documents in the seed set and is shown in the merged context graph. Each document is represented by a TF-IDF vector representation and is assigned to a particular level in the merged context graph.

Recent research has looked at how to use an incremental crawler. Traditional crawlers usually replace the entire index. An incremental crawler selectively searches the Web and only updates the index incrementally as opposed to replacing it.

7.2.2 Implementation of a Web Crawler

A wide variety of freeware, shareware, and commercial robots for traversing and downloading documents is available for web developers. This section first describes one of the most popular freeware programs, Wget, and an associated graphical user interface. A simple implementation of a web crawler in Java is used to illustrate the development of a web crawler. Readers can get additional information on these crawlers at http://www.robotstxt.org/.

7.2.2.1 Wget

Wget is a freely available GNU utility that makes it possible to retrieve web documents. Wget supports two of the most widely used Internet protocols: HTTP (HyperText Transfer Protocol) and FTP (File Transfer Protocol).

Unlike web browsers that require constant user intervention in order to download documents, Wget's noninteractive nature allows a user to run it in the background even when not logged on. Wget can recursively browse through the structure of HTML documents and FTP directory trees. It can make a local copy of the directory hierarchy, similar to the one on the remote server. Wildcard matching of file names as well as recursive mirroring of directories are available when retrieving via FTP. Wget is capable of reading the time stamp of documents from HTTP and FTP servers and storing these time stamps with local copies. This means that Wget can keep track of changes to remote files since last retrieval and automatically retrieve the new versions. These capabilities make Wget an ideal utility for creating mirror archives.

Wget can also be used as a web crawler in the implementation of a search utility; it understands and respects the norobots convention (which will be discussed in detail later in this chapter), which is used by website developers to restrict robots access to their sites.

Wget accommodates slow and unstable connections by trying to get a document until it is fully retrieved or a user-specified retry count is surpassed. It will try to resume the download from the point of interruption. Wget supports PROXY servers as well as passive FTP downloading. Wget's features can be configured through command-line options or on a UNIX system by creating an initialization file called ".wgetrc". Chapter 7 on the CD included with this textbook contains a link to the detailed introduction to the use of Wget from the command line as well as a setup file for Windows (http://gnuwin32.sourceforge.net/packages/wget.htm). Here, we will provide a basic introduction to the command-line use of Wget through some examples. The command-line Wget utility is available on most UNIX systems. Download the setup file from the website, which will also install a graphical user interface (GUI) and documentation for the use under Windows. The command-line description will assume that the user is working on a UNIX system. The description of the GUI interface will assume a Windows user.

Wget can be invoked on the command line by typing "wget" followed by the URL as follows:

```
wget http://www.gnu.org
```
(Command 7.1)

(Command 7.1) will retrieve the `index.html` file from http://www.gnu.org. If you do not specify the protocol such as " http://", the HTTP protocol is assumed. For more sophisticated use of this command, one needs to use options. **Figure 7.2** shows a summary of some more commonly used options. If the attempt at retrieving the file fails, (Command 7.1) will retry 20 times by default. One can change the default number of tries to 40 using the –t option as

```
wget -t 40 http://www.gnu.org
```
(Command 7.2)

Retrieving files from an ftp server is similar:

```
wget ftp://prep.ai.mit.edu/pub/gnu/acm.README
```
(Command 7.3)

If we specify a directory name, Wget will convert the directory listing to an HTML file, called index.html. Try

```
wget ftp://prep.ai.mit.edu/pub/gnu/
```
(Command 7.4)

The messages can be directed to a log file (called log in this example) using the –o option as

```
wget -o log ftp://prep.ai.mit.edu/pub/gnu/
```
(Command 7.5)

-a *logfile*	append messages to *logfile*
-d	print debug output
-h	help
-i *file*	download URLs found in *file*
-l *depth*	maximum recursion depth (inf or 0 for infinite, default 5)
-nc	do not clobber existing files
-o *logfile*	log messages to *logfile*
-q	quiet (no output)
-r	recursive download
-t *num*	set number of retries to *num* (0 or *inf* for infinite retrying)
-v	verbose output
-np	don't ascend to the parent directory
-m	mirror a site

Figure 7.2   Some of the commonly used options for wget

The use of the ampersand "&" at the end of the command will allow the user to run the command in the background. The output can be suppressed using the –q option:

```
wget -q log ftp://prep.ai.mit.edu/pub/gnu/
```
(Command 7.6)

Thus far we have retrieved only one file at a time. It is possible to retrieve multiple files from a hierarchical structure using the –r option for recursive retrieval. Caution should be exercised while using the –r option, however, because it will recurse for four levels by default, which can retrieve a potentially large number of files. One can change the number of levels using the –l option as illustrated in the following command:

```
wget -r -l1 www.gnu.org
```
(Command 7.7)

Here, the number of levels was restricted to just one, which at the time of writing this section retrieved 85 files. Another way to restrict the number of files is by using the –np option, which prevents ascensions to the parent directory. One can mirror a website using the option –m. Additional examples and options can be found in the Wget manual. You can also explore additional options by either using the –h option for help or retrieving the manual entry using the command "man wget" under UNIX.

The setup file for the Windows platform will install both the Wget utility as well as a graphical user interface (GUI) on a Windows system. **Figure 7.3** shows a screenshot of Wget GUI for Windows. The *Jobs* menu will allow us to add a new job. The dialogue box for adding a job is shown in **Figure 7.4**. Various tabs in the lower half of the panel allow you to select various options. The top text field allows us to provide a name for the job. The text field marked Address is used to provide the URL. The rest of the fields correspond to various options for the Wget command. The option and a meaningful name appear next to each field. If a mouse is left hovering over any of the fields, more information will pop up. Readers are welcome to

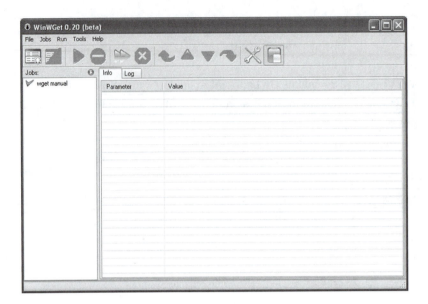

Figure 7.3 Wget GUI

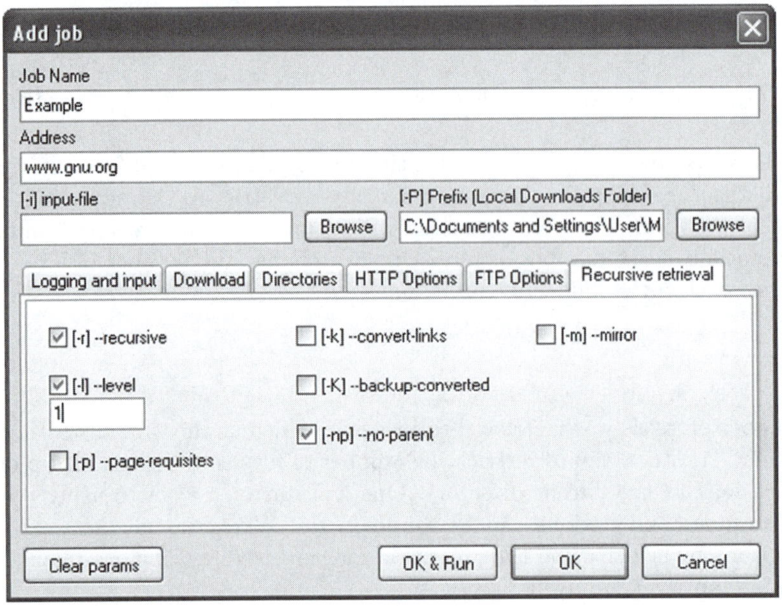

Figure 7.4 Creating a new download job with Wget GUI

enter the information as shown in Figure 7.4 and click OK. Note that you will have to click on the "Recursive retrieval" tab to see the lower panel from Figure 7.4. You can get information on the job that you have created by going back to the main screen of the GUI and clicking

[WinWGet 0.20 (beta) screenshot showing job details with Parameter/Value columns]

Parameter	Value
Job status	Ready
Job Date	1/14/2006 1:25:14 PM
Last Started	
Local File	
Progress	0 KB [0%]
Current Speed	0 KB/s
Address	cs.smu.ca
Prefix	C:\Documents and Settings\User\My Documents\SMU\textbook05\chapter7\wgetManual
Continue	True
Recursive	True
Depth level	1
Command line	"cs.smu.ca" -P "C:\Documents and Settings\User\My Documents\SMU\textbook05\chapter7\wgetManual" -c -r -l 1

Figure 7.5 Details of a job created with Wget GUI

on the job. The additional information includes the corresponding command-line parameters as shown in **Figure 7.5**. Because the Wget GUI provides the command-line parameters for the retrieval job that you have created, it can also be used as a tool to learn or construct Wget commands.

7.2.2.2 A Simple Implementation of a Web Crawler in Java

The more recent programming languages such as Java and C# as well as many scripting languages provide built-in functionality for downloading web pages. These languages also provide powerful tools for processing strings of text. We will use such web-page downloading and string-manipulation utilities from Java to construct a simple web crawler, which is modeled after the WebCrawler class written by Thom Blum, Doug Keislar, Jim Wheaton, and Erling Wold of Muscle Fish, LLC. For a detailed description of the original implementation, please see

http://java.sun.com/developer/technicalArticles/ThirdParty/WebCrawler/

The Java class called `Crawl`, included on the CD, can be run using the following command:

```
java Crawl http://java.sun.com
```
(Command 7.8)

(Command 7.8) runs the class called `Crawl` with one parameter, which is the URL of the page. In this case, the URL is http://java.sun.com. The output of the program is a list of all the links in the page given by the URL. At the time of writing this section, (Command 7.8) listed 116 links from the web page http://java.sun.com. Readers are encouraged to try the program with other websites.

The link `javadoc` under Chapter 7 provides documentation for all the Java classes used in Chapter 7. **Figure 7.6** shows the information about the constructor and methods of the `Crawl` class. The main method takes one parameter: the URL to be searched as a String. In addition

---

Method Detail

readContent

```
public java.lang.String readContent(java.net.URL url)
```
> **Parameters:**
> url - URL of the web page passed of the type URL
> **Returns:**
> Contents from the web page as a string

---

extractURL

```
public java.util.Vector extractURL(java.net.URL url,
                                     java.lang.String content)
```
> **Parameters:**
> url - URL of the web page of the type URL
> content - Contents of the web page of the type String
> **Returns:**
> A vector of links, each link is of the type URL

---

main

```
public static void main(java.lang.String[] args)
```
> **Parameters:**
> args - An array of Strings, e.g. http://www.sun.com

Figure 7.6   Methods for Crawl class (Suitable for Java programmers)

to the main, the class has two public methods: readContent and extractURL. The method readContent takes one parameter, which is the URL, and returns the contents of the web page as a String. The method extractURL takes the URL as well as the contents of the web page and returns a Vector of URLs from that page. Figures 7.7–7.9 show the code for the Crawl class. The code for the main given in **Figure 7.7** illustrates the use of the class. The first argument to the program (args[0]) is the URL represented as a string. The string version of the URL is used to create an object of the type URL. This object is passed to the method readContent to retrieve the contents of the web page as a string. The URL and contents are passed to the extractURL method to extract links from the web page. The URL needs to be passed again, so that it can be used as the base URL, if necessary, while constructing the URLs from the web page. **Figure 7.8** shows the code for the method readContent. The method first creates an object of the type InputStream from the URL. The rest of the code reads the contents of the page using the function read, and appending the newly read string to the existing string. **Figure 7.9** contains the code for the extractURL method. The method first converts the contents to lowercase and then uses the method getStartOfLink to look for "<a href =". Once that pattern is found, the actual link is located using the class StringTokenizer. Once the complete link is retrieved in the form of a String, it is combined with the original URL to create the new URL, which is then added to the Vector of URLs. The Java class Crawl can be used to write your own web crawler. See Exercise 5 at the end of the chapter.

```
public static void main (String [] args)
{
    if(args.length < 1)
    {
        System.err.println("Usage: java Crawl URL");
        return;
    }
    try
    {
        Crawl c = new Crawl();
        URL url = new URL(args[0]);
        String doc = c.readContent(url);
        Vector urlList = c.extractURL(url,doc);
        for(int i = 0; i < urlList.size(); i++)
            System.out.println(urlList.get(i));
    }
    catch(Exception e)
    {
        System.err.println(e);
    }
}
```

Figure 7.7 Code from the main of Crawl class (Suitable for Java programmers)

```
public String readContent(URL url)
{
    try
    {
        if (url.getProtocol().compareTo("http") != 0)
            return "";
        InputStream urlStream = url.openStream();
        byte b[] = new byte[1000];
        int numRead = urlStream.read(b);
        String content="";
        if(numRead != -1)
            content = new String(b, 0, numRead);
        while (numRead != -1)
        {
            numRead = urlStream.read(b);
            if (numRead != -1)
            {
                String newContent = new String(b, 0, numRead);
                content += newContent;
            }
        }
        urlStream.close();
        return content;
    }
    catch(Exception e)
    {
        System.err.println(e);
        return "";
    }
}
```

Figure 7.8 Code from the **readContent** method of Crawl class (Suitable for Java programmers)

```
int getStartOfLink(String lowerCaseContent, int index)
{
    if ((index = lowerCaseContent.indexOf("<a", index)) == -1)
        return -1;
    if ((index = lowerCaseContent.indexOf("href", index)) == -1)
        return -1;
    if ((index = lowerCaseContent.indexOf("=", index)) == -1)
        return -1;
    return index;
}
public Vector extractURL(URL url, String content)
{
    Vector urlList = new Vector();
    String lowerCaseContent = content.toLowerCase();
    int index = 0;
    try
    {
        while ((index = getStartOfLink(lowerCaseContent, index)) != -1)
        {
            index++;
            String remaining = content.substring(index);
            StringTokenizer st
                = new StringTokenizer(remaining, "\t\n\r\">#");
            String strLink = st.nextToken();
            urlList.add(new URL(url,strLink));
        }
    }
    catch(MalformedURLException e)
    {
        System.err.println(e);
    }
    return urlList;
}
```

Figure 7.9   Code for extracting links from Crawl class (Suitable for Java programmers)

7.2.3   Multiple-Layered Database

One technique to manage the large amounts of somewhat unstructured data on the Web is to create a multiple-layered database (MLDB) on top of the data on the Web. In a MLDB, every layer of the database is more generalized than the layer below it. Unlike the lowest level, the upper levels are structured and can be mined by an SQL-like query language. This database is huge and scattered. The MLDB provides an abstracted view of a fraction of the Web. A view of the MLDB, which is called a Virtual Web View (VWV), can be constructed. The indexing approach used by MLDB does not require the use of spiders. The technique used is to have the web servers themselves dispatch their indexes to the site(s) where indexing is being performed. This process is triggered when changes to the sites are made. Each layer of the index is smaller than that below it and to which it points. Both extraction and translation tools are proposed to assist in the formation of the first layer of the MLDB. Translation tools are used to convert web documents to XML, while extraction tools extract the desired information from the web pages and insert it into the first layer of the MLDB. Web documents that use XML and follow a standard format do not need any tools to create the layers.

The higher levels of the database become less dispersed and more summarized as the hierarchy is ascended. Also, concept hierarchies are used to help in the generalization process for constructing the higher levels of the MLDB. These hierarchies can be created using the WordNet Semantic Network, a database of the English language. Nouns, adjectives, verbs, and adverbs are divided into groups of synonyms and linked together using both lexical and semantic relationships.

WebML, which is a web data-mining query language specifically designed to provide data-mining operations on the MLDB, is an extension of the Data-Mining Query Language (DMQL). Documents are accessed using data-mining operations and lists of keywords. A key characteristic of WebML is the four primitive operations based on the use of concept hierarchies for the keywords (Zaiane 1999):

1. COVERS: One concept covers another if it is higher (ancestor) in the hierarchy.

2. COVERED BY: This is the reverse of COVERS in that it reverses to descendents.

3. LIKE: The concept is a synonym.

4. CLOSE TO: One concept is close to another if it is a sibling in the hierarchy. This is extended to include synonyms.

The following example illustrates WebML.

Example 7.1 The query finds all documents at the level of "www.smu.ca" that have a keyword that covers the keyword "ran":

```
SELECT *
FROM document in www.smu.ca
WHERE ONE OF keywords COVERS ran
```

In WebML, the `WHERE` clause indicates selection based on the links found in the page, keywords for the page, and information about the domain where the document is found.

7.3 Search Engines

7.3.1 Introduction to Search Engines

The objective of a search engine is to let an Internet user locate any information, websites, or other resources. "Search Engine" is a synonym for both real search engines and directories. Search engines use a spider or crawler that crawls the Web hunting for new or updated pages to store in an index. The information stored in the index of a directory is submitted manually. There are also *hybrid* search engines that possess the characteristics of both search engines and directories. A search engine usually receives one or more keywords as a list of arguments; it then searches an index for information containing these keywords. Once the search engine has a list of results, it can be formatted and presented to the user. A search engine can be

Figure 7.10   Search engine

accessed via an HTML form, and the results are returned to the user in an ordered list in HTML format.

Three basic components to a search engine are

- the *spider*, which gathers new or updated information on Internet websites;
- the *index*, which is used to store information about several websites;
- the *search software*, which searches through the huge index in an effort to generate an ordered list of useful results.

Figure 7.10 shows how a user would interact with a search engine. A user types one or more words into the text field and clicks the search button. The search engine then presents the results in a list format. There are many search engines on the Internet; one can compare them in order to understand their characteristics.

The search engine mechanism (see **Figure 7.11**) shows the inputs and outputs of a generic search engine. In order to understand the concept, we have shown the index as a separate entity. A search engine receives a query from a user, and results are returned. The user's search terms are converted into a Boolean query, and then every entry in the index is searched and compared to the query. All those index entries that meet the terms of the query are returned to the user as a list of results. Typically, results include several documents, ostensibly ranked in order of relevance.

The index in a search engine is automatically built-up over time. To insert a new document reference in the index, the URL of the page must be submitted along with a "comment" to the search engine website. Google.com operates in this manner. When the crawler searches through the Internet, it will visit the newly submitted URLs, read the contents of the entire website, and add an index entry in the appropriate index category.

Even though the generic structure of all search engines is basically the same, the search results differ from engine to engine for the same search terms; this is because the structure of the index can make a difference in the relevance of the results and also because most search

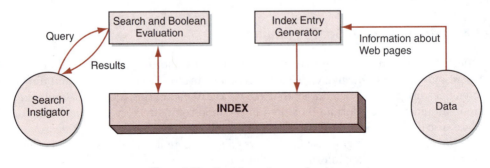

Figure 7.11   Search engine mechanism

engines have different search software. The software compares an entry in the index with the user query. It also handles any special Boolean or parsing rules. Some search engines share indexes and use the same search software.

7.3.2 Query Types

The system for the mechanical analysis and retrieval of text (SMART), developed by Gerard Salton and his group at Cornell University, was the first illustration of a Vector Space IR Model. We discussed an implementation of the VSM in detail in Chapter 2. Query matching within a VSM can be different from conventional item matching. Upon submitting the query, the search engine will retrieve the cluster of documents and terms whose word-usage pattern reflects that of the query. Boolean methods—connected by AND or OR—are the most common techniques used in searching terms.

Query binding is a general term relating the three-tier process of translating the user's need into a search engine query. The first level involves the user formulating the information need into a question or a list of terms using her experiences and vocabulary and entering it into the search engine. On the next level, the search engine must translate the words with possible spelling errors, such as *manga* instead of *mango*, into processing tokens. On the final level, the search engine must use the processing tokens to search the document database and retrieve the appropriate documents (see **Figure 7.12**).

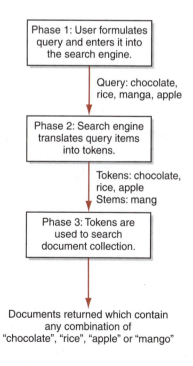

Figure 7.12 diagram:

Phase 1: User formulates query and enters it into the search engine.

Query: chocolate, rice, manga, apple

Phase 2: Search engine translates query items into tokens.

Tokens: chocolate, rice, apple
Stems: mang

Phase 3: Tokens are used to search document collection.

Documents returned which contain any combination of "chocolate", "rice", "apple" or "mango"

Figure 7.12   Three phases of query binding

In reality, users may enter their query in a variety of ways: as a Boolean statement, as a question (natural-language query), as a list of terms with proximity operators and contiguous word phrases, or with the use of a thesaurus. Problems therefore arise when search engines cannot accept all types of queries. A query that uses a Boolean operator such as AND or OR has to be processed in a different way than a natural-language query. Building a search engine to accept a certain type of query eventually forces the user to learn how to enter queries in that manner.

There are many types of queries, each of which should be assessed with respect to how the user enters it, what is anticipated in return, its strengths and limitations, and its compatibility with the search engine design. There are no hard and fast rules when discussing query/search engine compatibility. Consider the following list to illustrate different queries.

1. `Rima is a housewife,`

2. `Who wanted to buy some stuff in an online shop.`

3. `She put ''chocolate'' and ''rice'' in her basket`

4. `Along with ''apples'' and ''mango'',`

5. `She did not want ''pears'' or ''wheat.''`

6. `Other than chocolate, rice, or mango,`

7. `She wanted to have ''cookies'' or ''donuts.''`

8. `But the shop had no bakery products.`

9. `Thus Rima was unhappy.`

Boolean Queries: Boolean logic queries connect words in the search using operators such as AND or OR. If the searcher wishes the document that contains the words `rice OR cookies`, then documents three, six, and seven would be dragged. If the searcher wanted `rice AND cookies,` no documents would have been displayed because none of the lines of the list contain both the words `rice` and `cookies.` One drawback of Boolean queries is that there does not appear to be a better mode to measure significance. A term is either present or absent. For systems based on a Vector Space IR Model, Boolean operators are known as stop words, and therefore are unseen.

Natural-Language Queries: In natural-language queries, the user frames a question or a statement. For instance, a feasible natural-language query might be "Which documents have information on bakery products?"

To process a natural-language query, the search engine should extract every indexed term to begin the search. Some words in the query will be removed by the use of stop lists. In this case, the context of the word is lost. When a word has multiple meanings, the effect of deleting stop words can be much more pronounced.

Thesaurus Queries: In a thesaurus query, the user selects the term from a preceding set of terms predetermined by the retrieval system. The disadvantage of this type of query is that the searcher is bound to the thesaurus term even if he does not think the term is the best choice. In addition, the meaning of a word may be different depending upon the context.

Fuzzy Queries: Fuzzy queries reflect no specificity. They can be observed in two ways. The fuzziness in a search system refers to the capability of handling the misspelling or variations of the same words. By using our list, a fuzzy query, which misspelled the word *mango* as *manga*, would even return documents on mangoes, as the word stem (root) *mang* would be the same for both words. Fuzzy queries can be observed in terms of the sets of retrieved documents.

Term Searches: The most common type of query on the Web is that in which a user provides a few words or phrases for the search. In order for systems to support proximity operators and contiguous phrases, the inversion list must trace not only which terms appear in which documents but also the arrangement of those terms in the documents. This requires more storage and processing capabilities.

Normally, users have a tendency to type in just two or three terms. This would be all right if the system were more match oriented or based on the Boolean OR operator. However, if the IR system is based on a VSM, the user may have more success with more terms. In this context, more terms means more vectors to synthesize and construct the final query vector.

Probabilistic Queries: Probabilistic queries refer to the way in which the IR system retrieves documents according to relevancy. The basis for this type of search is that for a given document and query, it should be possible to compute a probability of relevancy for the document with respect to the query.

7.4 Robot Exclusion

In Section 7.2 we discussed the creation of web crawlers or robots to retrieve pages. While most web developers welcome automatic indexing of their contents that will be advertised to the wider population, there are a variety of reasons why the developers may prefer to exclude robots from parts of their sites. For example, we may not want robots to index and advertise internal data and program files that are used to dynamically create web pages, because these files may provide very little information to legitimate users. However, wider advertisement of the existence of such files may compromise the integrity of the site. Moreover, automatic downloading of large data files that may be of little relevance to the users will unnecessarily clog the bandwidth. In this section, we will discuss the exclusion protocols that are observed by most robots. We will study an essential summary of the information. A more detailed description about robot exclusion can be found at http://www.robotstxt.org.

Knowledge of the robot-exclusion protocol is essential for two reasons: we need to follow the protocol during the development of web crawlers or robots. We may also need to know the protocol in order to indicate restricted parts of the site to visiting robots. Website administrators and content providers can limit robot activity through two mechanisms:

1. **The Robots Exclusion Protocol** is used by website administrators to specify which parts of the site a robot should not visit, by providing a file called `robots.txt` on their

site. For example, if a robot visits a site called http://www.myweb.ca/, it should first check for http://www.myweb.ca/robots.txt. If this document exists, the robot should parse it looking for records such as

```
User-agent: *
Disallow: /
```

These records indicate if robots are allowed to retrieve all documents from the website. A site can have only a single "/robots.txt" file. Moreover, the file cannot be in any of the user directories. A robot will never look for `robots.txt` appearing anywhere except at the root of a web document hierarchy, such as http://www.myweb.ca/robots.txt. If individual users want to create their own "robots.txt" file, the system administrator will have to merge all the individual `robots.txt` files into a single "/robots.txt" file. For a large number of users who dynamically change their robot access requirements, this is not a feasible solution. In that case individual users might want to use the robots META tag as an alternative.

2. **The Robots META Tag** is a special html META tag that can be used in any web page to indicate whether that page should be indexed, or parsed for links. Unlike the Robots Exclusion Protocol, the use of the Robots META Tag does not require any server administrator action; therefore, any individual web-page authors can use it. Consider a simple example of the Robots META Tag:

```
<META NAME="ROBOTS" CONTENT="NOINDEX, NOFOLLOW">
```

If a web page contains the previous tag, a robot should not index this document (indicated by the word NOINDEX) or parse it for links (specified using NOFOLLOW). Although this META tag is a useful technique available for any web author, currently only a few robots implement it.

In the rest of this section, we will study these two mechanisms in greater detail. However, it should be noted that these methods assume cooperation from the robots. An unscrupulously or carelessly implemented robot may ignore these safeguards. A stronger protection from robots and other agents will have to be implemented using alternative methods such as password protection.

7.4.1 Robots Exclusion Protocol

This section is based on the information at http://www.robotstxt.org/wc/exclusion-admin. html, from which many of the examples in this section are adapted. The description is written more in the form of a guide for web administrators and robot developers. For details and formal syntax and definitions, go to http://www.robotstxt.org/wc/norobots.html.

When a web robot that complies with the exclusion protocol visits a site, it first checks for a "/robots.txt" URL on the site. If such a URL exists, the robot parses the file for instructions on which parts of the site should not be visited. A web-server administrator can create directives that make sense for the site. As mentioned before, there can be only one `robots.txt` file on a site, which appears at the root of the web document hierarchy. The exact location of the file depends on the server software and configuration. For most servers, the file will be created in the top-level server directory. On a UNIX machine, the path for the file may be /usr/local/etc/httpd/htdocs/robots.txt. Only the system administrator has write access to this file. If individual users want to add their own restrictions for the robots, they must contact their administrator. The system administrator then may enter individual user restrictions in the single `robots.txt` file for the site. In this context, a site is defined as a HTTP server running on a given host and port number. The same host may have a different site for different port numbers. Some of the valid `robots.txt` URLs in our example are shown in **Table 7.1**. On the other hand, **Table 7.2** provides examples of URLs containing `robots.txt` files that are pointless, because a robot will ignore these. It should be noted that the name of the file must be in lower case.

The following is an example of a record in the "/robots.txt" file:

```
User-agent: *
Disallow: /cgi-bin/
Disallow: /tmp/
Disallow: /~joe/
```

The first line indicates that this record is applicable to all the robots. The next three lines indicate the three directories that are to be excluded by all records: /cgi-bin, /tmp, and the HTML directory for the user, joe. It is necessary to specify a separate "Disallow" line for every URL prefix; for example, it is not possible to specify two URLs such as "Disallow: /cgi-bin/ /tmp/". The /robots.txt file may contain multiple records, each of which usually spans several lines. A blank line separates two records. There should not be blank lines in a record, because blank lines are used to separate multiple records.

Site URL	Corresponding Robots.txt URL
http://www.myweb.ca/	http://www.myweb.ca/robots.txt
http://www.myweb.ca:80/	http://www.myweb.ca:80/robots.txt
http://www.myweb.ca:1234/	http://www.myweb.ca:1234/robots.txt
http://myweb.ca/	http://myweb.ca/robots.txt

Table 7.1 Sites and corresponding valid URLs for `robots.txt`

URL	Reason for ignoring the instructions from the file
http://www.myweb.ca/adm/robots.txt	The file is not at the root of the web document hierarchy.
http://www.myweb.ca/ pl/robots.txt	The file appears in a user directory.
ftp://ftp.myweb.ca/robots.txt	The exclusion protocol is only defined for the http protocol not for the ftp protocol.

Table 7.2 URLs for `robots.txt` that will be ignored by robots

The asterisk (*) is used only in the User-agent field indicating any robot. It cannot be used as a wild card to specify multiple files; for example, ~~Disallow: *.gif~~ is not acceptable. Similarly, any other form of regular expression is not supported. The type of files one would disallow will depend on the site and application. Anything that is not explicitly disallowed is considered to be eligible for retrieval. The following are some examples from http://www.robotstxt.org/wc/exclusion-admin.html:

To exclude all robots from the entire server

```
User-agent: *
Disallow: /
```

To allow all robots complete access

```
User-agent: *
Disallow:
```

Or create an empty "/robots.txt" file.

To exclude all robots from a part of the server

```
User-agent: *
Disallow: /cgi-bin/
Disallow: /tmp/
Disallow: /private/
```

To exclude a single robot

```
User-agent: BadBot
Disallow: /
```

To allow a single robot

```
User-agent: WebCrawler
Disallow:

User-agent: *
Disallow: /
```

To exclude all files except one

This particular protocol does not provide an "Allow" field. Therefore, a longwinded way of achieving this would be to disallow every other file using a record such as

```
User-agent: *
Disallow: /~joe/private.html
Disallow: /~joe/foo.html
Disallow: /~joe/bar.html
```

Reorganizing the directory structure may be a better solution. Let us say we wanted to allow access only to a single file called ok.html. We can create a subdirectory called docs. All the files except ok.html may then be moved to the subdirectory docs, leaving the file ok.html in the level above docs. The following record will then provide us with the necessary restriction:

```
User-agent: *
Disallow: /~joe/docs/
```

7.4.2 Robots META Tag

The robot-exclusion protocol can be implemented only by the web-server administrator, which can cause inconvenience. On many servers, individual users do not have easy access to the administrator and cannot dynamically change their specifications for robot access through the /robots.txt file. The Robots META tag is a simple mechanism for individual web page authors to let visiting web robots know whether a page should be indexed, or the links on the page be followed. One of the main drawbacks of this alternative is that currently only a few robots are designed to read robots META tags. The examples and description in this section are from http://www.robotstxt.org/wc/meta-user.html. Similar to other meta tags, the robots META tag is placed in the HEAD section of an HTML page; for example,

```
<html>
<head>
<meta name="robots" content="noindex,nofollow">
...
<title>...</title>
</head>
<body>
...
```

The "robots" name of the tag and the content are case insensitive. The content field contains a comma-separated list of terms. There are six possible terms that may be included in the list: ALL, NONE, INDEX, NOINDEX, FOLLOW, NOFOLLOW. The INDEX/NOINDEX directives specify whether an indexing robot should or should not index the page. The FOLLOW and NOFOLLOW directives specify if a robot is to follow or not follow links on the page. The default values are INDEX and FOLLOW. The values ALL and NONE set all directives either on or off: that is, ALL is equivalent to the list INDEX,FOLLOW, while NONE is the same as saying NOINDEX,NOFOLLOW.

The following is a list of all the meaningful combinations:

```
<meta name="robots" content="index,follow">
<meta name="robots" content="noindex,follow">
<meta name="robots" content="index,nofollow">
<meta name="robots" content="noindex,nofollow">
```

The first combination is equivalent to

```
<meta name="robots" content="all">
```

and the fourth combination is equivalent to

```
<meta name="robots" content="none">
```

Any other combination will either provide contradictory or repetitive specifications and should be avoided. For example, the following is not acceptable:

```
meta name="robots"
     content="index,noindex,nofollow,follow,follow">
```

7.5   Personalization of Web Content

Various *personalization* techniques can be used to modify the contents of a web page as per the needs of a user (Hand, D.; Mannila H.; and Smyth P, 2001). This may involve essentially building web pages exclusively for each user. There are three basic types of web page personalization:

(a) *Collaborative filtering*: This achieves personalization by suggesting web pages that have earlier been given high ratings from similar users.

(b) *Manual techniques*: They perform personalization via the use of rules that are used to classify individuals based on profiles or demographics.

(c) *Content-based filtering*: This retrieves pages based on the similarity with user profiles.

Example 7.2   Assume that advertisements for an Online Shop, to be sent to a prospective customer, are selected based on knowledge about the customer. In this case, personalization may be achieved on the target web page. This technique may entice the customer into purchasing something she may not have thought about buying. Personalization is in some sense the opposite of targeting. When a person visits a website, the advertising can be designed exclusively (personalized) for that person. In the case of targeting, companies exhibit their advertisements at different sites visited by their users. For instance, when a customer logs in using his ID to shop online, he goes directly to pages containing the groceries he is interested in purchasing, and at the same time, the site shows a banner advertisement about a special sale on products that the customer buys frequently from the shop.

Personalization can be regarded as a form of clustering, classification, or prediction problem. With classification, the needs of a user are determined based on those for the class. Prediction is used to predict what the user really wants to see. With clustering, the needs are determined based on those users to which he or she is determined to be similar.

7.6   Multimedia Information Retrieval

Retrieval by content can be fascinating due to the large number of images and videos. It is tough to retrieve images manually because it is time-consuming, subjective, and may neglect specific characteristics of the image.

Finding images that are similar to each other is somewhat the same as solving the general image-understanding problem; that is, the problem of extracting semantic content from image data. The performance of humans in visual understanding and recognition is exceptionally tough to imitate with computer algorithms. For example, a baby can learn to classify animals such as cats of all sizes, colors, and shapes. Such recognition is beyond the competence of any existing vision algorithm. This capability to extract semantic content from raw-image data is rather unique to the human brain. There is considerable rationale for building interactive systems that allow a user to issue queries such as "find the p images that tally the given set of image properties." There can be various applications of such systems: searching for similar diagnostic images in radiology, finding pertinent stock records for advertising, and cataloging applications in a field of study.

For retrieval purposes, the original pixel data in an image can be abstracted to a feature representation. The features are typically expressed in terms of primitives such as color and texture. As with text documents, the original images are converted into a more standard data-matrix format where each row represents a particular image, and each column represents an image feature. Such feature representations are typically more robust with regard to changes in scale and translation than the direct pixel measurements. Typically the features for the images in the image database are precomputed and stored for use in retrieval; therefore, distance calculations and the retrieval are carried out in multi-dimensional feature space. As with text, the original pixel data is reduced to a standard $n \times p$ data matrix, where each image is now represented as a p-dimensional vector in feature space.

Spatial information can be introduced in a coarse manner by computing features in localized subregions of an image. For example, we could compute color information in each 32×32 subregion of a $1,024 \times 1,024$ pixel image. This allows coarse spatial constraints to be specified in image queries, such as "Find images that are primarily red in the center and blue around the edges."

In addition to regular $m \times n$ pixel images of scenes, an image database can also contain specific images of objects, such as objects on a constant background. One can extract primitive properties that are object specific: color, size, and shape of the object. Video images signify more of a generalization of image data, where images are linked sequentially over time.

A recognized commercial case of retrieval-by-content system for images is the Query by Image Content (QBIC) system, which was developed by IBM researchers in 1990. The QBIC system uses diverse features, and an associated distance measures for retrieval:

- A three-dimensional color feature vector. Here distance measure is a simple Euclidean distance.
- K-dimensional color histograms, where the bins of the histogram can be chosen by a partition-based clustering algorithm, for instance, k-means.
- A three-dimensional texture vector consisting of features that measure scale, directionality, and contrast. Distance is computed as a weighted Euclidean distance measure, where the default weights are inverse variances of the individual features.

Image queries can be expressed in two simple forms. In query by example, we provide a sample image of what we are looking for, or sketch the shape of the object of interest. Features are then computed for the example image, and the computed feature vector of the query is then matched to the precomputed database of feature vectors.

On the other hand, the query can be expressed directly in terms of the feature representation itself; for instance, "Find images that are 40% blue in color and contain a texture with a specific coarseness property." If the query is presented in terms of a subset of the features, for instance, color features, only that subset of features is used in the distance calculations.

Obviously one can generalize to relatively complex queries, allowing various Boolean combinations of query terms. For image data, the query language can also be specialized to allow queries that take advantage of spatial relations, such as "Find images with object 5 above object 9."

For retrieval-by-content with images, it is important to keep in mind that we can practically work only with a restricted notion of semantic content, based on relatively simple "low-level" measurements, such as color, texture, and simple geometric properties of objects. There are numerous regular distortions in visual data: translations, rotations, scale variability, nonlinear distortions, and so on. The human visual system is competent to manage certain distortions without difficulty.

7.6.1   Demonstration of a Multimedia Information Retrieval System

IBM's Query By Image Content (QBIC) search technology helps you locate artwork using visual tools at the website of the State Hermitage (www.hermitagemuseum.org/html_En/index.html), which occupies six magnificent buildings situated along the embankment of the River Neva, right in the heart of St. Petersburg, Russia. By using the URL www.hermitage museum.org/fcgi-bin/db2www/browse.mac/category?selLang=English you can find artwork by selecting colors from a palette or by sketching shapes on a canvas. Requesting all artwork with comparable visual attributes can further refine the existing search results.

The image information retrieval system allows you to conduct tasks such as finding a Gauguin masterpiece simply by recalling the organization of his subjects or locating a Da Vinci painting by searching for its predominant colors. You can visually search for artwork using tools that an artist would use. Due to copyright restrictions placed by Hermitage, we cannot include the images from the website here. For an overview of the QBIC searches, take a look at the animated demonstrations at www.hermitagemuseum.org/fcgi-bin/db2www/qbicSearch.mac/qbic?selLang=English.

The QBIC Color Search allows us to specify colors and locates two-dimensional artwork in the Digital Collection that match. The colors are selected from a palette that contains a spectrum of colors. The search can then be executed after defining the proportions. Visit the QBIC Color Search Demo to view a step-by-step demonstration of this search at www.hermitage museum.org/fcgi-bin/db2www/qbicColor.mac/qbic?selLang=English.

In addition, you can use the QBIC Layout Search for specifying geometric shapes. Using geometric shapes, you can arrange areas of colors on a virtual canvas to approximate the visual layout of the work of art that you are looking for. QBIC interprets the virtual canvas as a grid of colored areas. This grid is then matched to other images stored in the database. A QBIC Layout Search Demo that illustrates a step-by-step demonstration of this search can be found at www.hermitagemuseum.org/fcgi-bin/db2www/qbicLayout.mac/qbic?selLang=English.

EXERCISES

1. (Project) Perform the same keyword searches using three different search engines. Describe the number of documents retrieved. Combine the top ten documents into a document collection, go through these documents and mark them as relevant or nonrelevant. Calculate precision and recall for the search results. Compare the differences of the top ten pages found by each. Envisage why such differences exist.

2. Describe two different approaches used by Web sites to perform personalization.

3. Write a short note on search-result mining.

4. (Project) Use the Java class `Crawl` to create a new class that recursively retrieves pages from links extracted from the initial URL. The class should accept two parameters: the first being the initial URL, and the second being the depth of recursion. For example, if the initial URL is http://java.sun.com and the depth of recursion is 1, then the file http://java.sun.com/index.html is retrieved, as well as all the files that are linked from the http://java.sun.com/index.html. If the level of recursion is 2, then in addition to the aforementioned files, the files that are linked from the files that are linked from the http://java.sun.com/index.html are retrieved as well. A level value of 0 can be used to suppress recursive retrieval.

5. (Project) Visit the State Hermitage Web site described in the chapter. Experiment with the image retrieval facility, and write a report on your experience.

References

Hand, D., Mannila H., and Smyth P, (2001): Principles of Data Mining, Prentice Hall of India.

Liu, B., and Chang, K. (2004): "Editorial: Special Issue on Web Content Mining" SIGKDD Explorations special issue on Web Content Mining, Dec.

Zaiane, O. (1999): Resource and knowledge discovery from the Internet and multimedia repositories. PhD diss., Simon Frazer University.

Further Reading

Agrawal, R., and Srikant R. (1994): Fast algorithm for mining association rules. VLDB-94.

Agrawal, R., and Srikant R. (2001): On integrating catalogs. WWW-01.

Agrawal, R., Rajagopalan, S., Srikant, R., Xu, Y. (2003): Mining newsgroups using networks arising from social behavior. WWW-03.

Arasu, A., and Garcia-Molina, H. (2003): Extracting Structured Data from Web Pages. SIGMOD-03.

Baeza-Yates, R. (1989): Algorithms for string matching: A survey. ACM SIGIR Forum, 23(3-4): 34–58.

Barton, G., and Sternberg, M. (1987): A strategy for the rapid multiple alignment of protein sequences: confidence levels from tertiary structure comparisons. J. Mol. Biol.; 327–337.

Bar-Yossef, Z., and Rajagopalan, S. (2002): Template Detection via Data Mining and its Applications, WWW-02.

Brill, E. (1994): Some advances in rule-based part of speech tagging. AAAI-94.

Broder, A., Glassman, S., Manasse, M., Zweig, G. (1997): Syntactic Clustering of the Web. WWW-6.

Bunescu, R., and Mooney, R. (2004): Collective Information Extraction with Relational Markov Networks. ACL-04.

Buttler, D., Liu, L., Pu, C. (2001): A fully automated extraction system for the World Wide Web. IEEE ICDCS-21.

Cai, D., Yu, S., Wen, J-R., Ma, W-Y. (2003): Extracting Content Structure for Web Pages based on Visual Representation, Fifth Asia Pacific Web Conference (APWeb-03).

Cai, D., Yu, S., Wen, J.-R., Ma, W.-Y. (2004): Block-based web search. SIGIR-04.

Chakrabarti, S. (2002): Mining the Web: Discovering Knowledge from Hypertext Data. Morgan Kaufmann Publishers.

Chang, C., and Lui, S-L. (2001): IEPAD: Information extraction based on pattern discovery. WWW-10.

Chen, W. (2001): New algorithm for ordered tree-to-tree correction problem. Journal of Algorithms, 40:135.158.

Chriisment, C., Dousset, B., Karouach, S., Mothe, J. (2004): Information mining: extracting, exploring and visualising geo-referenced information. SIGIR-04 Workshop on Geographic information retrieval.

Cimiano, P., Handschuh, S., Staab, S. (2004): Towards the self-annotating Web. WWW-04.

Cohen, W., Hurst, M., Jensen, L. (2002): A flexible learning system for wrapping tables and lists in HTML documents. WWW-02.

Crescenzi, V., Mecca, G., Merialdo, P. (2001): Roadrunner: Towards automatic data extraction from large web sites. VLDB-01.

Cui, H., Kan M-Y, Chua, T-S. (2004): Unsupervised Learning of Soft Patterns for Definitional Question Answering, Proceedings of the Thirteenth World Wide Web conference (WWW 2004), New York, May 17-22, pp. 90–99.

Das, S., and Chen, M. (2001): Yahoo! for Amazon: Extracting market sentiment from stock message boards. APFA-01.

Dave, K., Lawrence, S., Pennock, D. (2003): Mining the Peanut Gallery: Opinion Extraction and Semantic Classification of Product Reviews. WWW-03.

Doan, A., and Halevy, A. (2005): Semantic Integration Research in the Database Community: A Brief Survey. AI magazine.

Doan, A., Madhavan, J., Domingos, P., Halevy, A. (2002): Learning to map between ontologies on the semantic web. WWW-02.

Embley, D., Jiang, Y., Ng, Y. (1999): Record-boundary discovery in Web documents. SIGMOD-99.

Etzioni, O., Cafarella, M., Downey, D., Kok, S., Popescu, A., Shaked, T., Soderland, S., Weld, S. (2004): Web-Scale Information Extraction in KnowItAll. WWW-2004.

Fellbaum, C. (1998): WordNet: an Electronic Lexical Database, MIT Press.

Freitag, D., and McCallum A. (2000): Information extraction with HMM structures learned by stochastic optimization. AAAI-00.

Gruhl, D., Guha, R., Liben-Nowell, D., Tomkins, A. (2004): Information diffusion through blogspace. WWW-04.

Guha, R., Kumar, R., Raghavan, P., Tomkins, A. (2004): Propagation of trust and distrust. WWW-04.

Gupta, S., Kaiser, G., Neistadt, D., Grimm, P. (2003): DOM based Content Extraction of HTML Documents, WWW-03.

Gusfield, D. (1997): Algorithms on strings, tree, and sequence, Cambridge.

Hatzivassiloglou, V., and McKeown, K. (1997): Predicting the Semantic Orientation of Adjectives. ACL-97.

Hatzivassiloglou, V., and Wiebe, J. (2000): Effects of adjective orientation and gradability on sentence subjectivity. COLING-00.

He, B., and Chang, K. (2003): Statistical Schema Matching across Web Query Interfaces. SIGMOD-03.

He, B., Chang, K., Han, J. (2004): Discovering complex matching across web query interfaces: a correlation mining approach. KDD-04.

Hearst, M. (1992): Automatic acquisition of hyponyms from large text corpora. In Proceedings of the 14th International Conference on Computational Linguistics, pages 539–545.

Hogeweg, P., and Hesper, B. (1984): The alignment of sets of sequences and the construction of phylogenetic trees: An integrated method. J. Mol. Evol.; 20, 175–186.

Hogue, A., Karger, D. Thresher (2005): Automating the unwrapping of semantic content from the World Wide Web.. WWW-05.

Hsu, C.-N., and Dung, M.-T. (1998): Generating finite-state transducers for semi-structured data extraction from the Web. Information Systems. 23(8): 521–538.

Hu, M., and Liu, B. (2004): Mining and summarizing customer reviews. KDD-04.

Kummamuru, K., Lotlikar, R., Roy, S., Singal, K., Krishnapuram, R. (2004): A hierarchical monothetic document clustering algorithm for summarization and browsing search results. WWW-04.

Kushmerick, N., Weld, D., Doorenbos, R. (1997): Wrapper induction for information extraction. IJCAI-97.

Kushmerick, N. (2000): Wrapper Verification. WWW Journal 3.

Kushmerick, N. (1999): Regression testing for wrapper maintenance. AAAI-99, pp. 74–79.

Kushmerick, N. (2000): Wrapper induction: efficiency and expressiveness. Artificial Intelligence, 118:15–68.

Lafferty, J., McCallum, A., Pereira, F. (2001): Conditional random fields: probabilistic models for segmenting and labeling of sequence data. ICML-01.

Lerman, K., Minton, S., Knoblock, C. (2003): Wrapper Maintenance: A Machine Learning Approach. J. Artif. Intell. Res. (JAIR) 18: 149–181.

Lerman, K., Getoor L., Minton, S., Knoblock, C. (2004): Using the Structure of Web Sites for Automatic Segmentation of Tables. SIGMOD-04.

Leuski, A., and Allan, J. (2000): Improving interactive retrieval by combining ranked lists and clustering. In Proceedings of RIAO-2000, pages 665–681, Paris, France.

Li, X., Liu, B., Phang, T., Hu, M. (2002): "Using Micro Information Unit for Internet Search," CIKM-2002, McLean, VA, Nov 5–9.

Lin, S., and Ho, J. (2002): Discovering informative content blocks from Web documents. KDD-02.

Liu, B., Chin, C., Ng, H. (2003): "Mining Topic-Specific Concepts and Definitions on the Web." WWW-03.

Liu, B., Grossman, R., Zhai, Y. (2003): "Mining Data Records in Web Pages." KDD-03.

Liu, B., and Zhai, Y. (2005): "NET–A System for Extracting Web Data from Flat and Nested Data Records." WISE-05.

Liu, B., Hsu, W., Ma, Y. (1998): Integrating Classification and Association Rule Mining. KDD-98.

Liu, B., Hu, M., Cheng, J. (2005): "Opinion Observer: Analyzing and comparing opinions on the Web" WWW-05, May 10-14, in Chiba, Japan.

Liu, B., Ma, Y., Yu, P. (2001): "Discovering unexpected information from your competitors' Web sites." KDD-01, San Francisco, CA; Aug 20–23.

Liu, B., Zhao, K., Yi, L. (2002): "Visualizing Web site comparisons." WWW-02. Honolulu, Hawaii, USA.

Maedche, A., Staab, S. (2001): Ontology Learning for the Semantic Web. IEEE Intelligent Systems 16(2): 72–79.

Meng, X., Lu, H., Wang, H., Gu, M. (2002): Schema-guided wrapper generator. ICDE-02.

Mooney, R., and Bunescu, R. (2005): Mining Knowledge from Text Using Information Extraction. To appear in a special issue of SIGKDD Explorations on Text Mining and Natural Language Processing.

Morinaga, S., Yamanishi, K., Tateishi, K., Fukushima, T. (2002): Mining Product Reputations on the Web. KDD-02.

Muslea, I., Minton, S., Knoblock, C. (1999): Active Learning for Hierarchical Wrapper Induction. AAAI-99, 975.

Muslea, I., Minton, S., Knoblock, C. (2000): Selective Sampling with Co-Testing: Preliminary Results. AAAI-00.

Muslea, I., Minton, S., Knoblock, C. (1999): A hierarchical approach to wrapper induction.. Agents-99.

Nasukawa, T., and Yi, J. (2003): Sentiment analysis: Capturing favorability using natural language processing. Proceedings of the 2nd Intl. Conf. on Knowledge Capture (K-CA-03).

Nigam, K., and Hurst, M. (2004): Towards a Robust Metric of Opinion. AAAI Spring Symposium on Exploring Attitude and Affect in Text.

NLProcessor. Text Analysis Toolkit. (2000): http://www.infogistics.com/textanalysis.html

Noy, N., and Musen, M. (2000): PROMPT: Algorithm and Tool for Automated Ontology Merging and Alignment. AAAI-00.

Pang, B., Lee, L., Vaithyanathan, S. (2002): Thumbs up? Sentiment Classification Using Machine Learning Techniques. EMNLP-02.

Pinto, D., McCallum, A., Wei, X., Bruce, W. (2003): Table Extraction Using Conditional Random Fields. SIGIR-03.

Ramaswamy, L., Ivengar, A., Liu, L., Douglis, F. (2004): Automatic detection of fragments in dynamically generated Web pages. WWW-04.

Reis, D., Golgher, P., Silva, A., Laender, A. (2004): Automatic Web news extraction using tree edit distance, WWW-04.

Riloff, E., and Wiebe, J. (2003): Learning extraction patterns for subjective expressions. EMNLP-03.

Rosenfeld, B., Feldman, R., Aumann, Y. (2002): Structural extraction from visual layout of documents. CIKM-02.

Song, R., Liu, H., Wen, J-R., Ma, W-Y. (2004): Learning block importance models for Web pages. WWW-04.

Tai, K. (1979): The tree-to-tree correction problem. J. ACM, 26(3):422–433.

Tong, R. (2001): An Operational System for Detecting and Tracking Opinions in on-line discussion. SIGIR 2001 Workshop on Operational Text Classification.

Vaithyanathan, S., Dom, B. (1999): Model Selection in Unsupervised Learning with Applications To Document Clustering. ICML-99.

Wang, J., Wen, J-R., Lochovsky, F., Ma, W-Y. (2004): Instance-based Schema Matching for Web Databases by Domain-specific Query Probing. VLDB-04.

Wang, J., and Lochovsky, F. (2003): Data extraction and label assignment for Web databases. WWW-03.

Wang, Y., Hu, J. (2002): A machine learning based approach for table detection on the Web. WWW-02.

Wiebe, J., Bruce, R., O'Hara, T. (1999): Development and Use of a Gold Standard Data Set for Subjectivity Classifications. ACL-99.

Wu, W., Yu, C., Doan, A., Meng, W. (2004): An Interactive Clustering-based Approach to Integrating Source Query interfaces on the Deep Web. SIGMOD-04.

Yi, L., Liu, B., Li, X. (2003): "Eliminating Noisy Information in Web Pages for Data Mining." KDD-2003, Washington, DC, USA, August 24 - 27.

Zamir, O., and Etzioni, O. (1999): Grouper: A Dynamic Clustering Interface to Web Search Results. WWW8.

Zeng, H-J., He, Q-C., Chen, Z., Ma, W-Y., Ma, J. (2004): Learning to cluster web search results. SIGIR-04.

Zhai, Y., and Liu, B. (2005): Web data extraction based on partial tree alignment. WWW-05.

Zhai, Y., and Liu, B. (2005): Extracting Web Data Using Instance-Based Learning. WISE-05.

Zhang, D., and Lee, W-S. (2004): Web taxonomy integration using support vector machines. WWW-04.

Zhao, H., Meng, W., Wu, Z., Raghavan, V., Yu, C. (2005): Fully automatic wrapper generation for search engines. WWW-05.

Web Structure Mining

8.1 Introduction

To deal with the treasure of accessible information on the World Wide Web, users need to rely on intelligent tools that support them in finding and categorizing the information. Just as data mining aims at discovering valuable information that is hidden in conventional databases, web mining aims at finding and extracting relevant information that is hidden in web-related data; in particular, in text documents that are published on the Web. Like data mining, web mining is a multidisciplinary effort that draws techniques from fields such as information retrieval, statistics, machine learning, and natural language processing.

Web-structure mining is one of the three active research areas of web mining. It deals mainly with discovering the model underlying the link structure of the Web, and also with the topology of hyperlinks with or without the description of the links. This model can be used to classify web pages and is helpful in creating information such as the similarity and relationship between different websites. Web-structure mining is a suitable tool for discovering authority sites and overview sites for the subjects. Authority sites contain information about the subject, while overview sites point to many authority sites. We have seen in an earlier chapter that web-content mining attempts to explore the structure within a document; but structure mining studies the citation relationship of documents within the Web itself.

Consider the graph terminology used to understand the concept of web-structure mining (Kleinberg 1998). We can consider any collection, V, of hyperlinked pages as a directed graph $G = (V, E)$ where the nodes correspond to the pages, and a directed edge $(p, q) \in E$ specifies the occurrence of a link from p to q. We know from graph theory that the *out-degree* of a node p is the number of nodes to which it has links, and the *in-degree* of p is the number of nodes that have links to it. If $W \subseteq V$ is a subset of the pages, we use $G[W]$ to denote the graph induced on W; that is, its nodes are the pages in W, and its edges correspond to all the links between the pages in W.

A number of algorithms have been suggested to model web topology. In 1998 Jon Kleinberg of Cornell University formalized the approach with the hyperlink-induced topic search (HITS) algorithm. This takes into account the Web's social network. The advantage of the HITS algorithm for web queries is that the user receives two lists of results: a set of authoritative pages he seeks and a set of link pages that can give a more comprehensive look at the information that is available. The major disadvantage of the HITS algorithm is that the computations are made after the query is made; therefore time to create the lists would be unacceptable to some users. Another approach is the PageRank algorithm developed by the founders of Google, Larry Page and Sergey Brin. Google looks not only at the number of links to a website, but also at the importance of those referring links. This is computed before the user ever types the query. As soon as the query comes, the results are returned based on these intricate page-rank values.

We will discuss some of the techniques that are useful in modeling web topology in subsequent sections.

8.2   Modeling Web Topology

We have seen that in information retrieval, we usually rank documents as a function of frequencies of query terms within the document and across all documents. This method works very well if most queries are long and well specified. Moreover, the documents in a single collection such as CISI or MEDLAR are coherent, well authored, and are mostly about one topic. We can also assume that the vocabulary contained in these documents is small and relatively well understood.

The World Wide Web poses a new challenge to information retrieval: the documents range widely in terms of language, quality, and duplication; the vocabulary in these documents is huge; and there is intentional misinformation on the Web. This creates significant difficulty in discerning which web document contains useful information from documents that do not. As a result, search engines such as Google rank documents as a function of *both* the query terms, which is very small in size, and the hyperlink structure of the Web.

The use of text on pages that have a hyperlink pointing to the target might put forward the following issues:

- **Redundancy:** The situation of more than one page pointing to a single page on the Web can be observed frequently. If we combine various independent sources of information together, we may improve their classification accuracy.

- **Sparse text:** It is possible that a web page contains mostly images and very little text. Sometimes web developers even put text in the form of images, to ensure their display properties are not changed. The predecessor pages may provide more information about a page than the page itself.

- **Variety of languages:** Although English is the main language of the Web, documents in other languages also exist. The text on the page may be written in a non-English language, but there may be links coming from pages that are written in English. In many cases, this allows a text classifier based on English vocabulary to infer a bit about the contents of the page.

- **Individual encoding:** The predecessor pages come from several distinct authors, each of whom would have a varying vocabulary; therefore, the information will be less sensitive to the vocabulary used by a single author.

- **Irrelevant or misleading text:** A lot of web pages contain irrelevant text. Many pages attempt to incorporate many keywords into comments or invisible parts of the text in order to expand the breadth of their indexing for word-based search engines.

A good discussion on PageRank and web search information can be found in Page and Brin (1998). This section is mostly based on material from various sources (Berry, Dumais, and O'Brien 1995; Bharat and Broder 1998; Henzinger et al. 1999; Henzinger et al. 2000; Kleinberg 1998; Licamele et al. 2005; Page et al. 1999; Page and Brin 1998; Page et al., 1998; Rogers 2006; Ullman 2006; Wilf 2006; Xing and Ghorbani 2006).

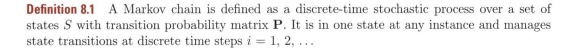

Let us discuss a statistical concept of Markov chains, which will help us in understanding some of the algorithmic techniques used in web-structure mining.

Definition 8.1   A Markov chain is defined as a discrete-time stochastic process over a set of states S with transition probability matrix $\mathbf{P}$. It is in one state at any instance and manages state transitions at discrete time steps $i = 1, 2, \ldots$

We define P_{ij} as the probability of heading for state j while at state i, and $\mathbf{q}^{(t)}$ as the row vector where the ith component represents the probability that the chain is in state i at time t. The initial state is taken as per some probability distribution $\mathbf{q}^{(0)}$ over S.

Then,

$$\mathbf{q}^{(t+1)} = \mathbf{q}^{(t)}\mathbf{P}$$
$$\mathbf{q}^{(t)} = \mathbf{q}^{(0)}\mathbf{P}^t,$$

where $\mathbf{P}^t$ is the tth power of $\mathbf{P}$

Example 8.1   We consider a two-state Markov chain such as $P_{00} = P_{01} = P_{10} = P_{11} = 1/2$. This is the Markov chain generated by a random walk on the graph with two nodes and edges $(0, 0)$, $(0, 1)$, $(1, 0)$, and $(1, 1)$. Solving $\mathbf{q} \times \mathbf{P} = 1 \times \mathbf{q}$, gives $l \times (l - 1) = 0$, with result $1_0 = 1$ and $1_1 = 0$. The corresponding eigenvectors are $\mathbf{e}^{(0)} = (1/2, 1/2)$ and $e^{(1)} = (1/2, -1/2)$. Furthermore, we take $\mathbf{q}^{(0)} = (0, 1)$ and find $\mathbf{q}^{(0)} = \mathbf{e}^{(0)} - \mathbf{e}^{(1)}$; therefore $\mathbf{q}^{(t)} = \mathbf{e}^{(0)}$, for all $t > 0$; that is, the final state is reached in a single step. This holds for any starting state because any $\mathbf{q}^{(0)}$ can be written as $\mathbf{q}^{(0)} = \mathbf{e}^{(0)} + x\mathbf{e}^{(1)}$, for some $-1 \le x \le 1$.

A stationary distribution is a probability distribution $\mathbf{q}_{stat}$ such that

$$\mathbf{q} \times \mathbf{P} = 1 \times \mathbf{q},$$
$$\mathbf{q}_{stat} = \mathbf{q}_{stat}\mathbf{P}.$$
$$\mathbf{q}_{stat} = \mathbf{q}_{stat}\mathbf{P}.$$

In certain conditions, there exists a unique stationary distribution $\mathbf{q}$, with $q_i > 0$ for all i. Suppose $N(i, t)$ represents the number of times the Markov chain visits state i in t steps. Then, the *Markov chain theorem* states that

$$\lim_{t \to \infty} \frac{N(i, t)}{t} = q_i$$

A Markov chain is irreducible, finite, and aperiodic when respectively its basic graph consists of a single strong component, S is finite, and no state is periodic.

Example 8.2   A random walk on a graph.

Let us assume that the set of states S refers to the set of vertices in a graph, and the transitional probability matrix $\mathbf{P}$, depends on the edges and nodes in the graph.

Consider an undirected graph $G = (V, E)$ with n nodes and m edges. If, for instance, the transition probability P_{ij} is defined as

$$P_{ij} = \begin{cases} degree(i)^{-1} & (i,j) \in E \\ 0 & (i,j) \notin E \end{cases}$$

Then

$$q_i = \frac{degree(i)}{2m}$$

Markov chains represent a probabilistic distribution over a graph that ultimately starts on a given node and picks a random edge at each time step.

In the web perspective, a page is defined recursively as *important* if important pages link to it. We can create a stochastic matrix of the Web, with the assumption that each page has one unit of importance. Every page allocates the importance it has among its successors and also collects new importance from its predecessors. The importance of a page reaches a limit at a particular juncture, which is called the component of the page in the principal eigenvector of the matrix. The importance is the probability that a web surfer reaches the required page following a series of links, using a random walk.

Example 8.3   (Wilf 2006) Consider a matrix

$$\begin{pmatrix} 0 & 1 & 0 & 0 & 1 & 0 \\ 1 & 0 & 0 & 0 & 1 & 0 \\ 0 & 0 & 0 & 1 & 0 & 0 \\ 1 & 0 & 1 & 0 & 1 & 1 \\ 1 & 1 & 1 & 0 & 0 & 1 \\ 1 & 1 & 0 & 0 & 1 & 0 \end{pmatrix}$$

that signifies six baseball teams, where Team 1 defeated Teams 2 and 5, Team 2 defeated Teams 1 and 5, and so on. The eigenvector of this matrix is $(0.31, 0.31, 0.22, 0.57, 0.50, 0.43)$. The finest team, according to this ranking system, is Team 4, followed by Teams 5, 6, 1, 2, and 3. Teams 4 and 5 each defeated four other teams; however the technique chose Team 4 over Team 5 because Team 4 beat superior teams when compared with Team 5.

Example 8.4 Assume that the Web consists of only three pages: a, b, and c. The links among these pages are given in **Figure 8.1**.

Let $[a, b, c]$ be the vector of importance for these pages in a given order. The subsequent matrix equation gives the values of these variables.

$$\begin{pmatrix} a \\ b \\ c \end{pmatrix} = \begin{pmatrix} 1/2 & 0 & 1/2 \\ 0 & 0 & 1/2 \\ 1/2 & 1 & 0 \end{pmatrix} \begin{pmatrix} a \\ b \\ c \end{pmatrix}$$

The first column of the matrix indicates that a divides its importance between itself and c. The second column indicates that b gives its importance to c. To solve the matrix equation, we assume $a = b = c = 1$, and apply the matrix to the existing estimate of these values continually. We can get the following estimates after the first four iterations:

Iteration 1:
$$\begin{pmatrix} a \\ b \\ c \end{pmatrix} = \begin{pmatrix} 1/2 & 0 & 1/2 \\ 0 & 0 & 1/2 \\ 1/2 & 1 & 0 \end{pmatrix} \begin{pmatrix} 1 \\ 1 \\ 1 \end{pmatrix} = \begin{pmatrix} 1 \\ 1/2 \\ 3/2 \end{pmatrix}$$

Iteration 2:
$$\begin{pmatrix} a \\ b \\ c \end{pmatrix} = \begin{pmatrix} 1/2 & 0 & 1/2 \\ 0 & 0 & 1/2 \\ 1/2 & 1 & 0 \end{pmatrix} \begin{pmatrix} 1 \\ 1/2 \\ 3/2 \end{pmatrix} = \begin{pmatrix} 5/4 \\ 3/4 \\ 1 \end{pmatrix}$$

Iteration 3:
$$\begin{pmatrix} a \\ b \\ c \end{pmatrix} = \begin{pmatrix} 1/2 & 0 & 1/2 \\ 0 & 0 & 1/2 \\ 1/2 & 1 & 0 \end{pmatrix} \begin{pmatrix} 5/4 \\ 3/4 \\ 1 \end{pmatrix} = \begin{pmatrix} 9/8 \\ 1/2 \\ 11/8 \end{pmatrix}$$

Iteration 4:
$$\begin{pmatrix} a \\ b \\ c \end{pmatrix} = \begin{pmatrix} 1/2 & 0 & 1/2 \\ 0 & 0 & 1/2 \\ 1/2 & 1 & 0 \end{pmatrix} \begin{pmatrix} 9/8 \\ 1/2 \\ 11/8 \end{pmatrix} = \begin{pmatrix} 5/4 \\ 11/16 \\ 17/16 \end{pmatrix}$$

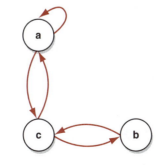

Figure 8.1 Representation of Web as a graph

If we continue the process, eventually the solution will be $a = c = 6/5$ and $b = 3/5$. Thus, web pages a and c have the same importance, which is double the importance of b.

8.2.1   PageRank Algorithm

The PageRank algorithm is convenient for finding important pages on the Web. The basic motivation for research in this area is from academic citation literature, where the importance of a document is measured by counting citations or backlinks to a given document.

The PageRank algorithm asserts that if a page has important links pointing to it, then its links to other pages are also important. Consequently, PageRank takes the backlinks into consideration and transmits the ranking through links. A page has a high rank if the sum of the ranks of its backlinks is high. **Figure 8.2** shows an example of backlinks. In the example, page A is a backlink of page B and page C, while page B and page C are backlinks of page D.

The PageRank algorithm presents an estimation of a document's importance or quality. This concept can be extended to web pages. A page can have a high PageRank if there are many pages that point to it, or if there are some pages that point to it that have high PageRanks. In short, pages that are well cited from many places around the Web are worth looking at. Furthermore, pages that have only one citation from some high-ranking web page like the Google Homepage are also worth looking at. PageRank handles both cases and everything in between by recursively propagating weights through the link structure of the Web.

The PageRank method was developed in 1998 as part of the Google prototype search engine. Google makes extensive use of this structure present in hypertext.

Within a website, two or more pages might link to each other to develop a loop. Assume that these pages do not link to other web pages outside the loop; however, they are linked from different web pages that are outside the loop. In that case, they would collect rank but never circulate any rank. This situation is called a *rank sink*.

One can monitor the users' activities to work out the rank-sink problem. In practice, users do not just follow existing links like a web crawler. For instance, after viewing page A, some

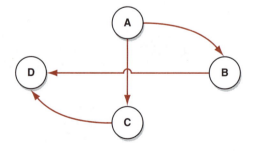

Figure 8.2   An example of backlinks

users may not choose to track the existing links but go to page B, which is not directly linked to page A, by typing its URL in the URL text field of their browsers. Some information on page A may lead users to make this transition to page B. It is also possible that information on page A may trigger a search that will lead to page B. In this situation, the rank of page B should be affected by page A, even though these two pages are not explicitly linked; therefore, there is no absolute rank sink. However, it is difficult to incorporate such implicit links between pages while calculating PageRanks.

Definition 8.2 (*PageRank*) The web-page scoring approach called PageRank produces ranking independent of a user's query. The number of other important web pages that are pointing to that page and the number of out-links from other web pages determine the importance of a web page. The PageRank of a page u is computed as follows:

$$PageRank\,(u) = (1-d) + d \sum_{(v,u) \in E} \frac{PageRank\,(v)}{OutDegree\,(v)}$$

where, $OutDegree(v)$ represents the number of links going out of the page v and parameter d be a damping factor, which can be a real number between 0 and 1. The value of d is generally taken as 0.85.

We can elaborate on this technique: Assume an infinite random walk in which the surfer starts from a random page and proceeds to a randomly chosen web page with probability d and a randomly chosen successor of the current page with probability $1 - d$. Then the PageRank of a page u is defined as the fraction of steps the surfer spends at u in the limit. This is equal to the stationary probability for the Markov chain, in which the set of states corresponds to the set of vertices in the web graph, and the transition probability is as previously defined.

The PageRank of a page can be considered as a summary of the *Web opinion* of the page's importance. By itself, it cannot be used for web-structure mining, as it is query independent.

The PageRank presents models of user behavior. Assume a surfer starts from a web page at random and keeps clicking links without hitting "Back," but ultimately he gets frustrated and switches to another random page. The probability that the surfer visits a page is its page rank. The damping factor d is used to model the probability that at each page the surfer will become unhappy with the links and request another random page.

8.2.1.1 PageRank Toolbar

PageRank can be displayed on the toolbar of your Web browser if you have installed the Google toolbar (http://toolbar.google.com/). The PageRank tool displays a score for a website based on encoded criteria established by Google. Key features that are used to calculate a website's

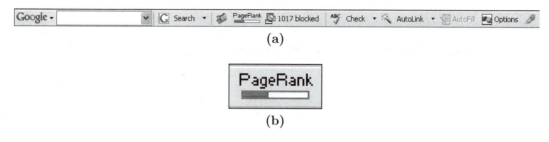

(a)

(b)

Figure 8.3   The PageRank toolbar

PageRank include traffic volume, returning traffic, the site's structure, and the number of links pointing to it. The PageRank bar within the Toolbar is shown in **Figures 8.3(a)** and **8.3(b)**.

The green bar shows the value of the page bar. If your mouse hovers around the PageRank bar, you will see a message resembling "**PageRank is Google's measure of the importance of this page (5/10).**" Here, the first number in the parentheses signifies the score of the web page. The second number, which is always 10, signifies the highest possible score. The higher the score means that the site gets crawled recurrently. Some sample scores with their meaning are as follows

0/10:	The site or page is probably new.
3/10:	The site is perhaps new, small in size, and has very little or no worthwhile arriving links. The page gets very little traffic.
5/10:	The site has a fair amount of worthwhile arriving links and traffic volume. The site might be larger in size and gets a good amount of steady traffic with some return visitors.
8/10:	The site has many arriving links, probably from other high-PageRank pages. The site perhaps contains a lot of information and has a higher traffic flow and return visitor rate.
10/10:	The website is large, popular, and has an extremely high number of links pointing to it.

The PageRank toolbar moves from 0 to 10 and looks like a logarithmic scale as shown in **Table 8.1**.

(log base 10)	Real PageRank
0	0–10
1	100–1,000
2	1,000–10,000
3	10,000–100,000
4	...

Table 8.1   Toolbar PageRank and corresponding real PageRank

8.2.1.2   An Algorithm: The Power Method

A link from page u to page v can be seen as evidence that v is an important page. The total importance bestowed on v by u is proportional to the importance of u and inversely proportional to the number of pages u points to. While the importance of u itself is unknown, calculating the importance for every page involves an iterative fixed-point computation. In their paper "Extrapolation Methods for Accelerating PageRank Computations," S.D. Kamvar and colleagues (2003) discussed the fast computation of PageRank. Although the analysis discussed in this subsection is based on convergence properties of the linear system used in PageRank, we will refer to part of Kamvar's paper.

Consider a random walk on the directed web graph G. Let $u \rightarrow v$ denote the existence of an edge from u to v in G. Let $OutDegree(u)$ be the $OutDegree$ of page u in G. Consider a random surfer visiting page u at time k. In the next time step, the surfer chooses a node v from among u's out-neighbors uniformly at random, thus at time $k + 1$, the surfer lands at node v with probability $1/OutDegree(u)$.

The PageRank of a page i is defined as the probability that at some particular time step k, the surfer is at page i. Consider the Markov chain derived from the random walk on G. The stochastic transition matrix showing the transition from j to i is given by $\mathbf{P}$ with $P_{ji} = 1/OutDegree(j)$. Let $\mathbf{M}$ be the transpose matrix, where $\mathbf{M} = \mathbf{P}^T$, thus the transition probability distribution for a surfer at node i is given by row i of $\mathbf{P}$ and column i of $\mathbf{M}$.

The transpose matrix $\mathbf{M}$ can be converted into a valid transition matrix by adding a complete set of outgoing transitions to pages with $OutDegree$ of 0. Now we define the new matrix $\mathbf{M}'$ where all states have at least one outgoing transition.

Let n be the number of nodes in the web graph and $\vec{p}$ be the n-dimensional column vector with a uniform probability distribution over all nodes:

$$\vec{p} = \left[\frac{1}{n} \right]_{n \times 1}$$

Let $\vec{d}$ be the n-dimensional column vector identifying the nodes with $OutDegree$ of 0:

$$d_i = \begin{cases} 1 & if \ \deg(j) = 0 \\ 0 & otherwise \end{cases}$$

So, we get $\mathbf{M}'$ as follows:

$$\mathbf{D} = \vec{p} \times \vec{d}^{\,T}$$
$$\mathbf{M}' = \mathbf{M} + \mathbf{D}$$

In random walk notation, the $\mathbf{D}$ is used to modify the transition probabilities with the intention that a surfer visiting a page with no out links randomly goes to another page, using the distribution given by $\vec{p}$ in the next time step.

Consider the Markov chain defined by $\mathbf{M}'$. It has a unique stationary probability distribution if $\mathbf{M}'$ is aperiodic and irreducible. We create the irreducible Markov matrix $\mathbf{A}$ as follows:

$$\mathbf{A} = c\mathbf{M}' + (1 - c)\mathbf{E}$$

In random walk notion, with probability $(1 - c)$, a surfer visiting some node will jump to a random web page at each time step. The target of the random jump is preferred according to the probability distribution given in $\vec{p}$.

Next we can introduce the matrix-vector multiplication $\vec{y} = \mathbf{A}\vec{x}$ as

$$\vec{y} = c\mathbf{M}\vec{x};$$
$$w = \|\vec{x}\|_1 - \|\vec{y}\|_1;$$
$$\vec{y} = \vec{y} + w\vec{p};$$

Suppose that the probability distribution over the surfer's place at time 0 is given by $\vec{x}^{(0)}$. Then the probability distribution for the surfer's place at time k is given by

$$\vec{x}^{(k)} = \mathbf{A}^k \vec{x}^{(0)}.$$

Further, the unique stationary distribution of the Markov chain is defined as

$$\lim_{k \to \infty} \mathbf{x}^{(k)} = \lim_{k \to \infty} \mathbf{A}^k \mathbf{x}^{(0)}.$$

It is the principal eigenvector of the Markov matrix $\mathbf{A}$, which is exactly the PageRank vector that is independent of the initial distribution $\vec{x}^{(0)}$.

Now the Power Method for computing PageRank can be written as shown in **Figure 8.4**.

Remark 8.1 Imagine that the vector $\vec{x}^{(0)}$ lies in the subspace spanned by the eigenvectors of $\mathbf{A}$. Then $\vec{x}^{(0)}$ can be taken as a linear combination of the eigenvectors of $\mathbf{A}$:

$$\vec{x}^{(0)} = \vec{u}_1 + \alpha_2 \vec{u}_2 + ... + \alpha_m \vec{u}_m$$

Because the first eigenvalue of a Markov matrix $\lambda_1 = 1$,

$$\vec{x}^{(1)} = \mathbf{A}\vec{x}^{(0)} = \vec{u}_1 + \alpha_2 \lambda_2 \vec{u}_2 + ... + \alpha_m \lambda_m \vec{u}_m$$

and subsequently,

$$\vec{x}^{(n)} = \mathbf{A}^n \vec{x}^{(0)} = \vec{u}_1 + \alpha_2 \lambda_2^n \vec{u}_2 + ... + \alpha_m \lambda_m^n \vec{u}_m,$$

```
function x̄ⁿ = PowerMethod( )
{
        x̄⁽⁰⁾ = p̄;
    repeat
            x̄ᵏ⁺¹ = Ax̄ᵏ;
            δ = ||t⁽ᵏ⁺¹⁾ − tᵏ||¹;
        until δ < ε;
}
```

Figure 8.4   The Power method for computing PageRank

PageRank Algorithm: Assume that there are n linked pages. Let $S_\sigma = (V, E)$. (V = set of pages, E = set of hyperlinks between pages.)

Repeat until *PageRank* vector converges (i.e., stabilize or do not change):

For all pages $u \in V$

$$PageRank(u) = (1 - d) + d \sum_{(v,u) \in E} \frac{PageRank(v)}{OutDegree(v)}$$

Return *PageRank* vector

Figure 8.5   PageRank algorithm

where $\lambda_n \;\; \le ... \le \;\; \lambda_2 < 1$. $\mathbf{A}^{(n)}\vec{x}^{(0)}$ approaches $\vec{u}_1$ as n increases. Consequently, the Power Method converges to the principal eigenvector of the Markov matrix $\mathbf{A}$.

The essence of the previous mathematical formulation tells us that the PageRank of each page depends on the PageRank of the pages pointing to it. But we cannot guess what Page-Rank those pages have until the pages pointing to them have their PageRank calculated. So, let us start with randomly chosen initial values of PageRanks, which are used to calculate a page's PageRank. The newly calculated values of PageRanks replace the initial guesses. The calculations are repeated several times until the numbers stop altering. The PageRank algorithm can be written as presented in **Figure 8.5**.

Example 8.5   (This example is taken from Rogers 2006. Courtesy of Ian Rogers, 2006.) Consider the simple graph of two pages, each pointing to the other, as shown in **Figure 8.6**.

Each page has one outgoing link (the outgoing count is 1; i.e., OutDegree(A) = 1 and OutDegree(B) = 1). Here we do not know what their PageRanks should be to begin with, so we can take a guess at 1.0 and perform the following calculations:

$$d = 0.85$$
$$PageRank(A) = (1 - d) + d(PageRank(B)/1)$$
$$PageRank(B) = (1 - d) + d(PageRank(A)/1)$$

Figure 8.6   A simple network of pages

that is,

$$\text{PageRank}(A) = 0.15 + 0.85 * 1$$
$$= 1$$
$$\text{PageRank}(B) = 0.15 + 0.85 * 1$$
$$= 1$$

We calculated that the PageRank of A and B is 1. Now, we plug in 0 as the guess and perform the calculations again:

$$\text{PageRank}(A) = 0.15 + 0.85 * 0$$
$$= 0.15$$
$$\text{PageRank}(B) = 0.15 + 0.85 * 0.15$$
$$= 0.2775$$

We have now another guess for PageRank(A), so we use it to calculate PageRank(B) and continue:

$$\text{PageRank}(A) = 0.15 + 0.85 * 0.2775$$
$$= 0.3859$$
$$\text{PageRank}(B) = 0.15 + 0.85 * 0.3859$$
$$= 0.4780$$

Repeating the calculations, we get

$$\text{PageRank}(A) = 0.15 + 0.85 * 0.4780$$
$$= 0.5563$$
$$\text{PageRank}(B) = 0.15 + 0.85 * 0.5663$$
$$= 0.6229$$

If we repeat the calculations, eventually the PageRanks for both the pages converge to 1.

Example 8.6   In this example, three pages are given: A, B, and C, as shown in **Figure 8.7**. There is a link between page A to both B and C. Also there is a link from pages B and C to A.

Begin with initial values of PageRanks as 0, after the first iteration the results are

Document $= A$ PageRank $= 0.15$
Document $= B$ PageRank $= 0.21$
Document $= C$ PageRank $= 0.21$

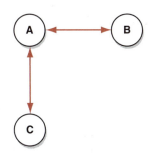

Figure 8.7   Web Graph used in Example 8.6

Iteration 2:

      Document $= A$ PageRank $= 0.51$

      Document $= B$ PageRank $= 0.37$

      Document $= C$ PageRank $= 0.37$

Iteration 3:

      Document $= A$ PageRank $= 0.78$

      Document $= B$ PageRank $= 0.48$

      Document $= C$ PageRank $= 0.48$

Iteration 4:

      Document $= A$ PageRank $= 0.97$

      Document $= B$ PageRank $= 0.56$

      Document $= C$ PageRank $= 0.56$

Iteration 5:

      Document $= A$ PageRank $= 1.10$

      Document $= B$ PageRank $= 0.62$

      Document $= C$ PageRank $= 0.62$

Iteration 6:

      Document $= A$ PageRank $= 1.20$

      Document $= B$ PageRank $= 0.66$

      Document $= C$ PageRank $= 0.66$

The PageRanks converge after 20 iterations to

Document = A PageRank = 1.46

Document = B PageRank = 0.77

Document = C PageRank = 0.77

In these iterations, the total PageRank within the entire site (sum of all the PageRanks) is 3. Also you can see that page A has a much larger proportion of the PageRank than the other two pages. This is because pages B and C are passing PageRank to A and not to any other pages.

Here are some remarks on the PageRank algorithm:

- Because initially the arbitrary value of 0 was assigned to every page, we always get ratios but never get absolute values for pages A, B, and C.
- A page with no successors has no scope to send its importance. As well, a group of pages that have no links out of the group will eventually collect all the importance of the Web.

8.2.1.3 Implementation of the PageRank Algorithm

Under Chapter 8 on the CD, you will be able to see a link called `java`, which will take you to a directory/folder named `java`. Create a directory called `chapter8` on your hard disk. Copy the `java` subdirectory to the newly created directory `chapter8`. The directory has a Java class called `PageRank`. The directory also contains a number of test files, including one called `figure8.8`. The contents of the file are shown in **Figure 8.8**. The format of the file uses the conventions from the SMART document collections. The fields are indicated by a period in the first column of a line followed by a letter. The only relevant fields for the PageRank algorithm are ".I" and ".X". The ID of the documentation appears on the same line as ".I". Lines following ".X" provide a list of document IDs linked from the current document. The file `figure8.8` (shown in Figure 8.8) in fact corresponds to the network shown in Figure 8.6. The first line in Figure 8.8 is ".I A", indicating that the current document ID is "A". The line after ".X" is "B", which means the current document "A" has a link to document "B". The next document in the file is signified by the line ".I B" corresponding to document B. The line following ".X" is "A", which tells us that there is a link from the current document "B" to "A". We can run the Java class `PageRank` as follows:

```
java PageRank figure8.8 0.85 20
```
(Command 8.1)

The first argument after the class name is the name of the file containing the data. The second argument specifies the damping factor. The number of iterations is given by the third argument. The output from (Command 8.1) is shown in **Figure 8.9**, which indicates the PageRank for each document. Readers can verify that the calculations progress as discussed in Section 8.2.1 by varying the values of number of iterations from 1, 2, ... , 20. Try the class for a little more complicated network, given by **Figure 8.10**. The file is helpfully called `figure8.10` in the directory `chapter8/java`. Readers are encouraged to draw the corresponding network. Run

```
.I A
.X
B
.I B
.X
A
```

Figure 8.8   Test data for graph from Figure 8.6

```
Document = A    PageRank = 1.00
Document = B    PageRank = 1.00
```

Figure 8.9   PageRanks for data from Figure 8.8

```
.I homepage
.X
about
product
links
.I about
.X
homepage
.I product
.X
homepage
.I links
.X
homepage
externSiteA
externSiteB
externSiteC
.I externSiteA
.I externSiteB
.I externSiteC
```

Figure 8.10   Additional test data for the PageRank algorithm

the **PageRank** class with a damping factor of 0.85 and a number of iterations equal to 10 using the command

```
java PageRank figure8.10 0.85 10
```
(Command 8.2)

The output is shown in **Figure 8.11**. Readers are invited to see the progress of the PageRank algorithm for Figure 8.10 by varying the number of iterations from 1, ... , 10. By studying the corresponding network, readers may want to satisfy themselves of the reasonability of the PageRanks shown in Figure 8.11. The class **PageRank** can work with any reasonably sized network. The **wget** utility and Java class **Crawl** discussed in Chapter 7 can be used to create a network file for a small collection of websites. Such a real network of web documents can be run through the PageRank class (see Exercise 14).

```
Document = about          PageRank = 0.42
Document = externSiteA     PageRank = 0.24
Document = externSiteB     PageRank = 0.24
Document = externSiteC     PageRank = 0.24
Document = homepage        PageRank = 0.95
Document = links           PageRank = 0.42
Document = product         PageRank = 0.42
```

Figure 8.11   PageRanks for data from Figure 8.10

Complete documentation for all the Java classes described in this chapter is available through the link `javadoc` under `chapter8` on the enclosed CD. **Figure 8.12** shows the information about the methods of the `PageRank` class. The method `readStructure` reads the document IDs and

Method Detail

getDocMap

```
public java.util.TreeMap getDocMap()
```
   Returns:
   A collection of PRdoc indexed using ID
   See Also:
   PRdoc

readStructure

```
public void readStructure(java.lang.String fileName)
```
   Function to read the ID and links from a file
   Parameters:
   fileName - Name of the file containing the document collection.

rank

```
public void rank(double damp,
                 int iter)
```
   The function that claculates the Page Rank
   Parameters:
   damp - The damping factor used in the page rank algorithm
   iter - Number of iterations

main

```
public static void main(java.lang.String[] args)
```
   Parameters:
   args - An array of Strings, e.g. figure8.15 0.85 20

Figure 8.12   Methods from the PageRank class (Suitable for Java programmers)

links from the documents from a file supplied as a parameter of the type `String`. The method is modeled after the `SMARTparser` class from Chapter 2. The method `rank` runs the actual PageRank algorithm. The first parameter to `rank` specifies the damping factor, and the second parameter supplies the number of iterations to be used in the algorithm. The main program receives three arguments as shown in (Command 8.1) and (Command 8.2). The complete source code for the class is available on the CD. The following are some of the salient features of the algorithm.

The class has one data member called `docMap,` which is a collection (Java class `TreeMap`) of documents of the type `PRdoc` indexed by the document IDs.

The class `PRdoc` is used to store the document ID, links emanating from the document, and its PageRank. The class `PRdoc` has three fields:

- `ID`: A `String` representing document IDs
- `links`: A set (Java class `TreeSet`) to store document IDs linked from the current document
- `pageRank`: A `double` value indicating the PageRank of the document.

The method `rank`, shown in **Figure 8.13**, describes the progress of the PageRank algorithm. For each iteration, the algorithm goes through every document and accumulates the proportional PageRank from the documents that are pointing to the current document, as given in Section 8.2.1.

```java
public void rank(double damp, int iter)
{
    for(int i = 0; i < iter; i++)
    {
        Iterator keys1 = docMap.keySet().iterator();
        while(keys1.hasNext())
        {
            PRdoc prd1 = (PRdoc)docMap.get(keys1.next());
            double sum = 0.0;
            Iterator keys2 = docMap.keySet().iterator();
            while(keys2.hasNext())
            {
                PRdoc prd2 = (PRdoc)docMap.get(keys2.next());
                if(prd2.links.contains(prd1.ID))
                {
                    sum += prd2.pageRank/prd2.links.size();
                }
            }
            prd1.pageRank = (1-damp) + damp*sum;
        }
    }
}
```

Figure 8.13   `rank` method from the PageRank class (Suitable for Java programmers)

The taxonomy of different types of hyperlinks that can be found on the Web was suggested around 1997. The fruitful research outcome of the study was the understanding of the popularity and the importance of a page and its correlation to the number of incoming links. One can use this information to sort the query results of a search engine. The in-degree alone is a poor measure of importance because many pages are frequently pointed to without being connected to the contents of the referring page.

Kleinberg described a method for web information retrieval using the concepts of *hubs* and *authorities* (Kleinberg 1998, 1998a). This is a detailed evaluation of the importance of web pages using a variant of the eigenvector calculation used for PageRank. He described hubs as web pages with good sources of links and authorities as web pages with good sources of content. For instance, the authorities are your course home pages, whereas the hub is your college course-listing page. Hubs and authorities exhibit a mutually reinforcing relationship. A good hub is one that points to many good authorities and a good authority is one that is pointed to from many good hubs.

Given any topic query specified by a query string σ, we can decide on authoritative pages by an analysis of the link structure, but we must initially determine the subgraph of the WWW on which the algorithm will operate. We would like to have the subgraph somewhat small, rich in relevant pages, and containing several of the strongest authorities.

We can construct a *root set* R_σ of the World Wide Web by accumulating the t highest-ranked pages for the query σ from a text-based search engine such as Google or Yahoo for a particular parameter t. This set of pages is somewhat small and rich in relevant pages, but does not consistently contain several of the strongest authorities. Even though a strong authority for the query topic might not be in the root set R_σ, it is likely to be *pointed to* by at least one page in R_σ. We can expand this root set R_σ to produce a set of pages S_σ that fulfills the criteria by taking any Web pages pointed to by a page in R_σ.

Now, we correlate a non-negative authority weight $AUTH^{(p)}$ and a non-negative hub weight $HUB^{(p)}$ with each page p. The weights are normalized so that

$$\sum_{p \in S_\sigma} (AUTH^{(p)})^2 = 1$$

$$\sum_{p \in S_\sigma} (HUB^{(p)})^2 = 1$$

The normalization can be accomplished by dividing the $AUTH$ and HUB values by the square root of the sum of their squares,

$$normalizedAUTH^{(p)} = \frac{AUTH^{(p)}}{\sqrt{\sum_{u \in S_\sigma} \left(AUTH^{(u)}\right)^2}}$$

Then pages with larger $AUTH$ and HUB values are viewed as "better" authorities and hubs respectively. This can be done using the iterative algorithm shown in **Figure 8.14**.

HITS Algorithm: Assume that there are n linked pages.

Let $S_\sigma = (V, E)$. (V = set of pages, E = set of hyperlinks between pages)

Initialize $\vec{HUB} = \vec{AUTH} = (1, 1, \ldots, 1) \in \mathbb{R}^n$

Repeat until $\vec{HUB}$ and $\vec{AUTH}$ converge (i.e., stabilize or do not change);

Normalize $\vec{HUB}$ and $\vec{AUTH}$.

For all pages $p \in V$,

$$HUB^{(p)} = \sum_{q:(p,q)\in E} AUTH^{(q)}$$

$$AUTH^{(p)} = \sum_{q:(q,p)\in E} HUB^{(q)}$$

Return $\vec{HUB}$ and $\vec{AUTH}$

Figure 8.14   HITS algorithm

Example 8.7   Apply the previous algorithm to the network from **Figure 8.15**.
   After initializing the $\vec{HUB}$ and $\vec{AUTH}$ uniformly to 1 and normalizing the two vectors, we get the following values:

Document = A HUB = 0.58 AUTH = 0.58

Document = B HUB = 0.58 AUTH = 0.58

Document = C HUB = 0.58 AUTH = 0.58

The new HUB value of document A will be the sum of AUTH values of B and C: 1.16.
   The new HUB values of both B and C will be equal to 0, because they are not pointing to any page.
   The new AUTH values of A will be 0, because no page is pointing to it.
   The new AUTH values of both B and C will be equal to the HUB value of A: 0.58.

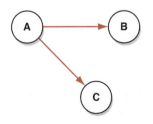

Figure 8.15   Web graph used in Example 8.7

After normalization we get

Document = A HUB = 1.00 AUTH = 0.00

Document = B HUB = 0.00 AUTH = 0.71

Document = C HUB = 0.00 AUTH = 0.71

Recalculating the values of HUB and AUTH and normalizing the two vectors will give us

Document = A HUB = 1.00 AUTH = 0.00

Document = B HUB = 0.00 AUTH = 0.71

Document = C HUB = 0.00 AUTH = 0.71

Because the values are unchanged, we stop there. As we can see from Figure 8.15, page A is clearly the hub, and pages B and C share the honor of being authorities, a fact confirmed by the HITS algorithm.

Kleinberg proved that the vectors $\vec{HUB}$ and $\vec{AUTH}$ do converge to the limits h* and a* respectively, in which h* denotes the principal eigenvector of $\mathbf{A}^T\mathbf{A}$, a* denotes the principal eigenvector of $\mathbf{A}\mathbf{A}^T$, and $\mathbf{A}$ denotes the adjacency matrix of the subgraph S_σ. This is due to the assumption that the principal eigenvalue of matrix $\mathbf{A}$ is *unique*.

Example 8.8   Consider the web pages a, b, and c as given in **Figure 8.16**.
The relevant matrix representations are

$$
\mathbf{A} = \begin{pmatrix} 1 & 1 & 1 \\ 0 & 0 & 1 \\ 1 & 1 & 0 \end{pmatrix} \quad
\mathbf{A}^T = \begin{pmatrix} 1 & 0 & 1 \\ 1 & 0 & 1 \\ 1 & 1 & 0 \end{pmatrix} \quad
\mathbf{A}\mathbf{A}^T = \begin{pmatrix} 3 & 1 & 2 \\ 1 & 1 & 0 \\ 2 & 0 & 2 \end{pmatrix} \quad
\mathbf{A}^T\mathbf{A} = \begin{pmatrix} 2 & 2 & 1 \\ 2 & 2 & 1 \\ 1 & 1 & 2 \end{pmatrix}
$$

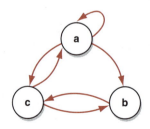

Figure 8.16   Web graph used in Example 8.8

Assume that the value of scaling factors is 1 and the vectors

$$H\vec{U}B = \left[HUB^{(a)}, HUB^{(c)}, HUB^{(b)}\right]$$

and

$$A\vec{U}TH = \begin{array}{l} \left[AUTH^{(a)}, AUTH^{(c)}, AUTH^{(b)}\right] \\ AUTH^{(a)} = AUTH^{(c)} \\ 1 + \sqrt{3} : 2 \end{array}$$

are each initially $[1, 1, 1]$.

After the first iteration, the equations for $A\vec{U}TH$ and $H\vec{U}B$ are $[5, 5, 4]$ and $[6, 2, 4]$.

Following the second iteration, $A\vec{U}TH$ and $H\vec{U}B$ are $[24, 24, 18]$ and $[28, 8, 20]$, and after the third iteration, the equations of $A\vec{U}TH$ and $H\vec{U}B$ are $[114, 114, 84]$ and $[132, 36, 96]$.

This information shows that the vector $A\vec{U}TH$ will converge to a vector where $AUTH^{(a)} = AUTH^{(c)}$, and each of these is greater than $AUTH^{(b)}$ in the ratio $1 + \sqrt{3} : 2$.

We now present a proof of convergence (Tsaparas et al. 2006).

Theorem 8.1   The sequence $A\vec{U}TH$ provided by the HITS algorithm converges to an authority vector, and this authority vector is a non-negative eigenvector of the largest eigenvalue of $\mathbf{A}^T\mathbf{A}$. Similarly, $H\vec{U}B$ converges to a hub vector that is a non-negative eigenvector of the largest eigenvalue of $\mathbf{A}^T\mathbf{A}$.

Proof of Theorem 8.1: We know that the eigenvalues of $\mathbf{A}^T\mathbf{A}$ are real and non-negative. Furthermore, all other eigenvalues have a strictly smaller modulus, as the eigenvalue of the largest modulus is being repeated. Because $\mathbf{A}^T\mathbf{A}$ is symmetric, the eigenspaces are orthogonal.

The dot product of $H\vec{U}B$ with the non-negative vector is positive, because $H\vec{U}B$ is positive; hence, $H\vec{U}B$ has a nontrivial component in the eigenspaces of a principal eigenvalue. This guarantees that the algorithm converges to an eigenvector of the largest eigenvalue. Even if the algorithm converges, it could converge to any non-negative, normalized vector in the eigenspaces of the dominant eigenvalue λ_1, depending on the initial choice of $H\vec{U}B$.

The same argument applies to the HITS authority vector. $\square$

The Kleinberg Algorithm converges naturally to the principal eigenvector of the associated matrix; that is, to the eigenvector that corresponds to the largest eigenvalue (Tsaparas et al. 2006). Kleinberg makes a remarkable assertion about the secondary (i.e., nonprincipal) eigenvectors (or their positive and negative components) being related to secondary or opposing communities of web pages.

Next we present a simple example to illustrate the idea that such secondary eigenvectors sometimes are (but sometimes are not) indicative of secondary communities.

Example 8.9 We consider a sequence of two-digit numbers: Each number represents a link, with the first digit being the hub number and the second digit being the authority number. For instance, the numbers 23, 24, and 34 indicate that there are links between the second hub and third authority, second hub and fourth authority, and third hub and fourth authority, respectively. Assume that the example has fewer than 10 hubs and fewer than 10 authorities.

Assume that the links are 11, 21, 31, 41, 52, 62, 53, and 63. Then the corresponding matrix of transitions of authority weights is shown as

$$\mathbf{AA}^T = \begin{pmatrix} 4 & 0 & 0 \\ 0 & 2 & 2 \\ 0 & 2 & 2 \end{pmatrix}.$$

The eigenvalues of the matrix are 4, 4, and 0. Here, the equality of two eigenvalues shows that we have a wide choice of representative eigenvalues. One choice for eigenvectors is $(0, 1, 1)$, $(1, 0, 0)$, $(0, 1, -1)$. You will notice a correlation between eigenvectors and communities. However, if eigenvectors are chosen to be $(1, 1, 1)$, $(2, 1, 1)$, $(0, 1, -1)$, there is no correlation between eigenvectors and communities.

The main drawback of the HITS algorithm is that the hub's and authority's scores must be calculated iteratively from the query result. This does not meet the real-time constraints of an online search engine. Nevertheless, the implementation of a similar idea in the Google search engine resulted in a step forward in search engine technology. Another limitation of standard HITS is that it assumes that all links pointing to a page are of equal weight and fails to recognize that some links might be more important than others.

8.2.2.1 Implementation of the HITS Algorithm

We will assume that you have copied the `java` subdirectory from Chapter 8 on the CD to your directory `chapter8`, as suggested in Section 8.2.2. The directory has a Java class called `HITS`, which can work with the same test files as the class `PageRank`. We can run the Java class `HITS` for the test file `figure8.8` as follows:

```
java HITS figure8.8 10                                    (Command 8.3)
```

The first argument after the class name is the name of the file containing the data. The number of iterations is given by the second argument. The output from (Command 8.3) is shown in **Figure 8.17**, which indicates the HUB and AUTH values for each document. Readers can verify

```
Document = A     HUB = 0.71      AUTH = 0.71
Document = B     HUB = 0.71      AUTH = 0.71
```

Figure 8.17 HUB and AUTH values for data from Figure 8.8

```
Document = about       HUB = 0.33    AUTH = 0.00
Document = externSiteA  HUB = 0.00    AUTH = 0.41
Document = externSiteB  HUB = 0.00    AUTH = 0.41
Document = externSiteC  HUB = 0.00    AUTH = 0.41
Document = homepage     HUB = 0.00    AUTH = 0.71
Document = links        HUB = 0.89    AUTH = 0.00
Document = product      HUB = 0.33    AUTH = 0.00
```

Figure 8.18   HUB and AUTH values for data from Figure 8.10

that the calculations progress as discussed in Section 8.2.3 by varying the values of number of iterations from 1, 2, ... , 10. Try the class for a little more complicated network given by Figure 8.10. The HUB and AUTH values for this file do not stabilize until about 25 iterations. Run the HITS class with a number of iterations equal to 25 using the command

```
java HITS figure8.10 25
```
(Command 8.4)

The output is shown in **Figure 8.18**. Readers are invited to see the progress of the HITS algorithm for Figure 8.10 by varying the number of iterations from 1, ... , 25. By studying the corresponding network, readers may want to satisfy themselves about the reasonability of the HUB and AUTH values shown in Figure 8.18. Similar to the class PageRank, HITS can work with any reasonably sized network. Readers may want to put these two classes to a real-world test using the wget utility and Crawl class discussed in Chapter 7 (see Exercise 14).

Complete documentation for all the Java classes described in this chapter is available through the link javadoc under chapter8 on the CD. **Figure 8.19** shows the information about the methods of the HITS class. The method readStructure is identical to the corresponding method from the PageRank class, which reads the document IDs and links from the documents. The method calcHubAuth runs the actual HITS algorithm. The only parameter to calcHubAuth specifies the number of iterations to be used in the algorithm. The main program receives two arguments as shown in (Command 8.4) and (Command 8.5). The complete source code for the class is available on the CD. The following are some of the salient features of the HITS algorithm:

The class has one data member called docMap, which is a collection (Java class TreeMap) of documents of the type HITSdoc indexed by the document IDs.

The class HITSdoc is used to store the document ID and links emanating from the document, as well as the new and old HUB and AUTH values. The class PRdoc has three fields:

- ID: A String representing document IDs
- links: A set (Java class TreeSet) to store document IDs linked from the current document
- HUB: A double value indicating the HUB value for the document.
- AUTH: A double value indicating the AUTH value for the document.
- newHUB: A double value for intermediate storage of the HUB value for the document.
- newAUTH: A double value for intermediate storage of the AUTH value for the document.

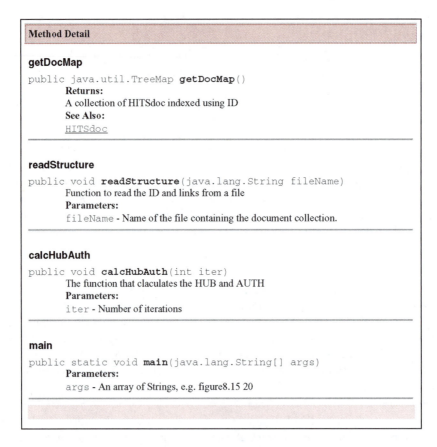

Figure 8.19   Methods from the HITS class (Suitable for Java programmers)

The method `calcHubAuth`, shown in **Figure 8.20**, describes the progress of the HITS Algorithm. For each iteration, the algorithm goes through every document to accumulate the AUTH values from the documents that are pointed at by the current document as the new HUB values and accumulates the HUB values from the documents that are pointing to the current document as the new AUTH values.

The new values of HUB and AUTH are normalized using the method `normalize` given in **Figure 8.21**. Both the methods `calcHubAuth` and `normalize` follow the algorithm description given in Section 8.2.2.

```
public void calcHubAuth(int iter)
{
    Iterator keys1 = docMap.keySet().iterator();
    while(keys1.hasNext())
    {
        HITSdoc hitsd1 = (HITSdoc)docMap.get(keys1.next());
        hitsd1.newAUTH = 1.0;
        hitsd1.newHUB = 1.0;
    }
    normalize();

    for(int i = 0; i < iter; i++)
    {
        keys1 = docMap.keySet().iterator();
        while(keys1.hasNext())
        {
            HITSdoc hitsd1 = (HITSdoc)docMap.get(keys1.next());

            // HUB of hitsd1 is AUTH of all the docuemtns that
            // hitsd1 points to
            hitsd1.newHUB = 0;
            Iterator keys2 = hitsd1.links.iterator();
            while(keys2.hasNext())
            {
                HITSdoc hitsd2 = (HITSdoc)docMap.get(keys2.next());
                hitsd1.newHUB += hitsd2.AUTH;
            }

            // AUTH of hitsd1 is HUB of all the docuemtns that
            // are pointing to hitsd1
            hitsd1.newAUTH = 0;
            keys2 = docMap.keySet().iterator();
            while(keys2.hasNext())
            {
                HITSdoc hitsd2 = (HITSdoc)docMap.get(keys2.next());
                if(hitsd2.links.contains(hitsd1.ID))
                {
                    hitsd1.newAUTH += hitsd2.HUB;
                }
            }
        }
        normalize();
    }
}
```

Figure 8.20   `calcHubAuth` method from the HITS class (Suitable for Java programmers)

8.2.2.2   Extended HITS Algorithm

The CLEVER algorithm is an extension of standard HITS. CLEVER allocates a weight to each link based on the terms of the queries and end points of the link. It also splits large hub pages into smaller units, so each hub page is focused on as a single topic. In the case of a large number of pages from a single domain, it scales down the weights of pages to reduce the probabilities of overhead weights.

In the ARC algorithm (proposed by Chakrabarti et al. 1998b), the root set was expanded by 2 links instead of 1 link (i.e., expand S by all pages that are a 2-link distance away from S). Bharat and Henzinger used weights to improve the performance of HITS (K. Bharat and M. Henzinger, 1998). The edge weights essentially normalize the contribution of authorship

```
void normalize()
{
    double sumHub = 0.0;
    double sumAuth = 0.0;
    Iterator keys = docMap.keySet().iterator();
    while(keys.hasNext())
    {
        HITSdoc hitsd = (HITSdoc)docMap.get(keys.next());
        sumHub += (hitsd.newHUB*hitsd.newHUB);
        sumAuth += (hitsd.newAUTH*hitsd.newAUTH);
    }
    sumHub = Math.sqrt(sumHub);
    sumAuth = Math.sqrt(sumAuth);
    keys = docMap.keySet().iterator();
    while(keys.hasNext())
    {
        HITSdoc hitsd = (HITSdoc)docMap.get(keys.next());
        hitsd.HUB = hitsd.newHUB / sumHub;
        hitsd.AUTH = hitsd.newAUTH / sumAuth;
    }

}
```

Figure 8.21   `normalize` method from the HITS class (Suitable for Java programmers)

by dividing the contribution of each page by the number of pages created by the same author. The HITS formulas are modified as follows:

$$HUB^{(p)} = \sum_{q:(p,q)\in E} AUTH^{(q)} HUB\_WT(p, q)$$

$$AUTH^{(p)} = \sum_{q:(q,p)\in E} HUB^{(q)} AUTH\_WT(q, p)$$

In these equations, $AUTH\_WT(q, p)$ is $1/m$ for page q, whose host has m documents pointing to p, and $HUB\_WT(p, q)$ is $1/n$ for page q, which is pointed to by n documents from the host of p.

8.2.3 Comparison of PageRank and HITS

In this subsection we compare the two web-structure-mining algorithms: PageRank and HITS.

1. **Computation:** PageRank is computationally less intensive than HITS. The PageRank for all the web documents needs to be computed only once. The computed PageRank can be used for a specific time period until the PageRank values become outdated. In the case of HITS, the authority and hub weights calculations need to be carried out for each query.

2. **Query dependency:** PageRank is query independent, meaning the PageRank of a particular page is not determined by the user query. The PageRank needs to be combined

with some query-dependent criteria. However, the set of pages used in the HITS algorithm is generated from a text search based on the query.

3. **Search Results:** PageRank, with some query-dependent criteria, returns the top authoritative sources. The HITS algorithm also returns the top authoritative sources, as well as the top hubs.

4. **Rank stability:** Neither PageRank nor HITS are rank stable, which means constant $O(1)$ changes in the graph structure can result in $O(N^2)$ changes in the order relations, where N denotes the number of pages in the web graph.

5. **Value stability:** PageRank is "value stable." This means that a change in k nodes with corresponding PageRank values $(p_1, p_2, \ldots, p_k)$ results in $p*$ such that

$$||p * -p|| \leq 2 \sum_{j=1}^{k} \frac{p_j}{\epsilon}$$

On the other hand, the value stability of the HITS algorithm depends on the gap g between the largest and the second-largest eigenvector.

8.2.4   Random Walks on the Web

8.2.4.1   Index Quality of Search Engines

In the 1999 paper "Measuring Index Quality using Random Walks on the Web," Henzinger and colleagues argue that the quality of pages in a search engine's index is one of the important measures of search engine effectiveness.

There is no established method for choosing a web page uniformly at random. Thus, a random walk on the web graph with an equilibrium distribution analogous to the PageRank measure is not possible. Instead of jumping to a random page, the walk rarely chooses a host uniformly at random from the set of hosts encountered on the walk. It then jumps to a page chosen uniformly at random from the set of pages discovered on that host.

The equilibrium distribution of such a finite walk does not harmonize the PageRank distribution; it gives only an approximation of the PageRank. Pages that have not already been visited cannot be chosen. Moreover, the pages on hosts with a small number of pages are more likely to be chosen than the pages on hosts with a large number of pages. On the other hand, experimental results have revealed that such bias does not stop the random walk from approximating a good quality metric that acts similar to PageRank.

During experimentation, two long random walks with $d = 1/7$ were performed, starting at www.yahoo.com. The first walk took 18 hours, during which time the crawler attempted to download 2,867,466 pages; 1,393,265 of the successfully downloaded pages were HTML pages, and 509,279 were unique.

The second walk took 54 hours, during which time the crawler attempted to download 6,219,704 pages; 2,940,794 of the successfully downloaded pages were HTML pages, while 1,002,745 were different. Furthermore, the average in-degree of pages with an in-degree less than 1000 was high. It was 53 in the first walk and 60 in the second walk. This is better than the in-degree of an average web page, signifying the random walk often visits pages with higher

Page	Freq. Walk2	Freq. Walk1	Rank Walk1
www.microsoft.com/	3172	1600	1
www/microsoft.com/windows/ie/default.htm	2064	1045	3
www.netscape.com	1991	876	6
www.microsoft.com/ie/	1982	1017	4
www.microsoft.com/windows/ie/download/	1915	943	5
www.microsoft.com/windows/ie/download/all.htm	1696	830	7
www.adobe.com/prodindex/acrobat/readstep.html	1634	780	8
home.netscape.com	1581	695	10
www.linkexchange.com/	1574	763	9
www.yahoo.com/	1527	1132	2

Table 8.2   Most frequently visited pages (Copyright 1999 Hewlett-Packard Development Company, L. P. Reproduced with Permission)

Site	Frequency Walk2	Frequency Walk1	Rank Walk1
www.microsoft.com	32452	16917	1
home.netscape.com	23329	11084	2
www.adobe.com	10884	5539	3
www.amazon.com	10146	5182	4
www.netscape.com	4862	2307	10
excite.netscape.com	4714	2372	9
www.real.com	4494	2777	5
www.lycos.com	4448	2645	6
www.zdnet.com	4038	2562	8
www.linkexchange.com	3738	1940	12
www.yahoo.com	3461	2595	7

Table 8.3   Most frequently visited hosts (Copyright 1999 Hewlett-Packard Development Company, L. P. Reproduced with Permission)

quality. **Table 8.2** shows the most frequently visited web pages over the two random walks. **Table 8.3** shows the most frequently visited hosts over the two random walks.

The following process shows a means to estimate the quality of the index of the search engines:

- Choose a sample of pages according to PageRank distribution.
- Check if the pages are in a search engine index S (Exact match and Host match).
- Estimate the quality of S as the percentage of sampled pages that are in S.

The outcomes of estimating the index quality of a search engine based on the technique explained previously are shown in **Figures 8.22** and **8.23**. These two figures show that although the

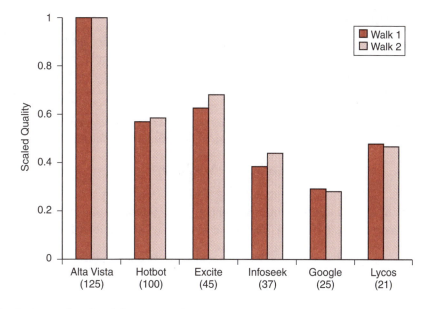

Figure 8.22   Index quality for different search engines (Copyright 1999 Hewlett-Packard Development Company, L. P. Reproduced with Permission)

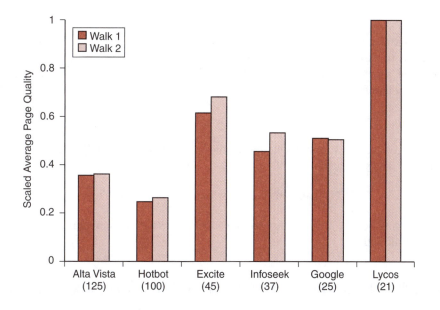

Figure 8.23   Index quality per page for different search engines (Copyright 1999 Hewlett-Packard Development Company, L. P. Reproduced with Permission)

index quality for a search engine with large index counts is normally higher, the index quality per page for a large search engine is sometimes higher as well. For instance, Altavista does better than Hotbot in both the quality and quantity of pages. This means the search methods used by a search engine for crawling or indexing can significantly influence the quality of the search engine.

8.2.4.2   Uniform URL Sampling

In the paper "On Near-Uniform URL Sampling" (2000), Henzinger and her colleagues introduced another sampling approach. It provides a *nearly uniform* sample of the Web. The ability to choose a URL uniformly at random allows us to estimate some web properties. These properties include the percentage of pages in a domain, the percentage of pages on a topic, and the comparison of the index size of various search engines.

Research in uniform URL sampling involves random walks over a sample of well-connected pages. The method is based on the Bayes Rule, which states that for any events A and B,

$$P(A|B) = P(A \cap B)/P(B).$$

Here, P(A|B) is the conditional probability of A, given the fact that B is true. P(A ∩ B) is the probability of both A and B being true, and P(B) is the probability of B being true.

The Henzinger method of uniform URL sampling can be described formally as follows:

$$P(p \text{ is crawled and sampled}) = P(p \text{ is crawled}) \times P(p \text{ is sampled} \mid p \text{ is crawled})$$

The fraction of time that each page is visited in equilibrium is proportional to its Page-Rank:

$$E(\text{number of times } p \text{ is visited}) \approx L \times \text{PageRank}(p),$$

where L denotes the length of the random walk.

Assuming the web graph consists essentially of well-connected pages, we can extend the approximation to short walks of order $O(n^{1/2})$ steps, where n is the number of pages in the web graph. For short walks of the order of $O(n^{1/2})$ steps, most pages are expected to appear at most once. Therefore, with short walks,

$$\mathbf{P}(p \text{ is crawled}) \approx E(\text{number of times } p \text{ is visited}) \approx L \times \text{PageRank}(p)$$

Consequently, to get a uniform sampling such that $\mathbf{P}(p \text{ is sampled})$ is uniformly constant, we can sample pages such that

$$\mathbf{P}(p \text{ is sampled} \mid p \text{ is crawled}) \propto 1 \,/\, \text{PageRank}(p).$$

For additional fine points on the Henzinger method, refer to "On near-uniform URL sampling" (Henzinger et al. 2000).

8.3   Other Approaches to Studying the Web-Link Structure

8.3.1   Social Networks

Social-network analysis (Licamele et al. 2005) is an alternative means of studying the web-link structure of a web page. The social-network theory was created on the work of Stanley Milgram, who performed several experiments related to this subject. In one experiment from 1967, he asked several subjects in Omaha, Nebraska, to convey a letter to a Boston colleague of his. However, the subjects from Omaha could send the letter only to someone they knew on a first-name basis, who in turn could forward the letter only to people they knew on a first-name basis. The entire exercise was intended to get the letter to Milgram's colleague in the least number of "hops." Milgram realized that the median number of hops along the path of effectively handed-over letters was six. He concluded that any two people in the United States are linked in a social network that consists of *six degrees* of separation.

Definition 8.3   A *social network* is a map of the relationships between individuals; the analysis of a social network involves a study of these relationships.

Web-structure mining can apply social-network analysis to model the link structure of the Web. The social network studies ways to assess the relative standing or significance of individuals in a network. An identical process can be mapped to study the link structures of the web pages. The fundamental assumption is that if a web page points a link to another web page, then the former is endorsing the importance of the latter. In this network, links will have different weights, corresponding to the strength of endorsement.

A social network can be characterized by its relational structure. The core graph structure of the network states the structural properties, such as the density of the graph and average degree of the nodes to the measure of information flow. Most research in social networks focuses on the structural aspects of the networks. Social networking services collect details about users' social contacts, construct a large interconnected social network, and disclose to users how they are connected to others in the network.

Social networks on the Web are relatively new. Kautz, Selman, and Shah (1997) proposed a measure of standing of a web page based on path counting, and carried out social-network analysis to model the network of artificial intelligence researchers. The standing of a web page can be given as follows:

Definition 8.4   For pages p and q, let $P_{pq}(r)$ denote the number of paths of length r from p to q. Let $b < 1$ be a constant considered to be small enough so that $Q_{pq} = \sum_r b^r P_{pq}(r)$ converges. We can view b^r as a damping factor that varies with the length of the path. Here the *standing* of the page q, σ_q is defined as $\sum_p Q_{pq}$.

The social network exhibits the *small-world phenomenon* if any two individuals in the network are likely to be connected through a short sequence of intermediate acquaintances.

Kleinberg presented a heuristic technique of assigning weight to links. A link is called *transverse* if it is between pages with different domain names and *intrinsic* if it is between pages with the same domain name, where the domain name is the first level in the URL string associated with a web page. Intrinsic links convey less information than transverse links in terms of the importance of the web pages to which they point. This is because the majority of intrinsic links simply exist to navigate the infrastructure of a website. Kleinberg suggested a deletion of every intrinsic link from the graph, keeping only the edges corresponding to transverse links for further analysis; therefore, the intrinsic links need not be taken into consideration in computing the PageRank or standing of a page.

The hierarchical network model of Watts assumes that individuals belong to groups that are hierarchically well established into larger groups. In this context, the word *group* means the set of individuals linked by a well-defined set of social characteristics. For instance, an individual could be a part of a software laboratory that is part of a school of computing science, which is part of a university. The probability that two individuals have a social link to one another is proportional to $e^{-\alpha h}$, where h is the height of their lowest common branching point in the hierarchy, and α is the decay parameter. The decay in linking probability means that two people in the same software laboratory are more likely to know one another than two people from the same school but different laboratories.

8.3.2   Reference and Index Pages

There is another method of ranking pages that introduces the notion of a *reference page* and an *index page* (Kleinberg 1998, 1998a).

Definition 8.5   A *reference page* is a page whose in-degree is notably greater than the average in-degree of the graph.

Definition 8.6   An *index page* is a page whose out-degree is notably greater than the average out-degree of the graph.

In order to cluster web documents based on web structure, we have to identify the influential pages that are referred by a substantially larger number of pages. Then we can create a soft cluster around each of the influential pages based on citation count. The pages are then assigned to the soft cluster if they are co-cited with the influential page.

Definition 8.7   For a pair of pages, say p and q, the *co-citation* is the number of pages that point to both p and q.

Once the soft clusters are created, the similarities between them are calculated. Some of them are merged based on the values of the similarity measures. If the similarity between two soft clusters is high, they will be merged to form a single cluster.

To determine the set of influential pages, it is necessary to define a threshold λ and identify the pages whose degree exceeds the value λ. There are variations to this approach. We can calculate the out-degree and in-degree, or we can calculate either the transverse or intrinsic degrees. To construct a soft cluster around an influential page v, we detect all other pages x, such that there is at least one page y that cites both x and v. We may have to consider similarity functions such as bibliographic and co-citation couplings.

Definition 8.8   For a pair of pages, say p and q, the *bibliographic coupling* is equal to the number of pages that have links from both p and q.

The similarity measure between two sub-clusters S_x and S_y can be computed as $\dfrac{|S_x \cap S_y|}{|S_x \cup S_y|}$.

EXERCISES

1. How is web-structure mining different from web-usage mining and web-content mining?

2. What is PageRank? How is it computed?

3. What are the drawbacks of the PageRank and HITS Algorithms?

4. How does the HITS Algorithm calculate the principal eigenvector, and what was the corresponding calculation in the Google paper?

5. Explain the "sampling step" of the HITS algorithm. Is this a plausible way of creating the root and base sets? Explain why or why not.

6. What is the difference between an "authoritative" page and a "hub" page? How are these two types related, and how do they affect the weighting of a page?

7. What is a social network? How is it related to web-structure mining?

8. If page A links once to page B and 3 times to page C, does page C receive 3/4 of page A's shareable PageRank? Justify your answer.

9. Verify that the HITS Algorithm works. To verify, do a search engine search on specific terms and use the first N documents as your basis set. Next, form an enlarged set by collecting

    i) all pages pointed to by the basis set

    ii) all pages pointing to the basis set

Recall that the enlarged set has a size limit (Kleinberg used 2000), so if required, add pages only from ii up to the prespecified limit. Create a directed graph of this extended set and determine the authorities and hubs. A nice way to implement this project would be to automate the entire process. This would require writing a crawler using the `Crawl` class from Chapter 7. To find the pages that point "to" the basis set, one could use the "link" option in a Google set. This problem would probably require you to consider smaller sets than those that Kleinberg used (try a basis-set size of 20 and an extended-set size of 100). Remember that the algorithm calls for deletion of URLs from the same domain.

10. In PageRank, when a page links to itself, is the link counted? Is it reasonable to assume that a page cannot vote for itself and that such links are not counted?

11. Apply the HITS algorithm on the web graph shown in **Figure 8.24**.

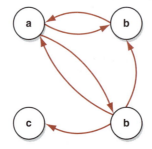

Figure 8.24   Web graph for Exercise 11

12. Apply the PageRank algorithm, discussed in this chapter, on the web graph given in **Figure 8.25**.

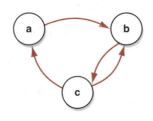

Figure 8.25   Web graph for Exercise 12

13. Draw the network for the data file from Figure 8.10.

14. Use the `wget` utility discussed in Chapter 7 to collect web pages from a website. Use the `crawl` class from Chapter 7 to extract links from these web pages. Use the extracted links to create a network file. Obtain PageRank, HUB, and AUTH values for each of the pages using the `PageRank` and `HITS` classes.

15. Implement the modified `HITS` Algorithm.

References

Berry, M.W., S.T. Dumais, and G.W. O'Brien. (1995): Using linear algebra for intelligent information retrieval. *SIAM Review* 37: 573–95.

Bharat, K., and A. Broder. (1998): A technique for measuring the relative size and overlap of public Web search engines. *Computer Networks* 30 (1): 107–17.

Bharat, K. and M. Henzinger, (1998): Improved algorithms for topic distillation in hyperlinked environments, in: Proc. of the 21st International ACM SIGIR Conference on Research and Development in Information Retrieval (SIGIR'98), pp. 104t111.

Chakrabarti, S., Dom, B., Raghavan, P., Rajagopalan, S., Gibson, D., Kleinberg, J. (1998b): Automatic resource compilation by analyzing hyperlink structure and associated text. Computer Networks, 30(1–7), pp. 65–74.

Henzinger, M.R., A. Heydon, M. Mitzenmacher, and Marc Najork. (1999): *Measuring index quality using random walks on the Web.* WWW8. http://www8.org/w8-papers/2c-search-discover/measuring/measuring.html. http://www8.org/w8-papers/2c-search-discover/measuring/measuring.html

Henzinger, M.R., A. Heydon, M. Mitzenmacher, and Marc Najork. (2000): On near-uniform URL sampling. In *WWW9*. Amsterdam. http://www9.org/w9cdrom/88/88.html.

Kamvar, S.D., T.H. Haveliwala, C.D. Manning, and G.H. Golub. (2003): Extrapolation methods for accelerating PageRank computations. Stanford University Technical Report.

Kautz, H., B. Selman, and M. Shah. (1997): The hidden Web. *AI Magazine* 18 (2): 27–36.

Kleinberg, J. (1998): Authoritative sources in a hyperlinked environment. Proceedings of the 9th ACM-SIAM Symposium on Discrete Algorithms.

Kleinberg, J. (1998a): Authoritative sources in a hyperlinked environment, *SODA 1998.*

Licamele, L., M. Bilgic, L. Getoor, and N. Roussopoulos. (2005): Capital and benefit in social networks. *LinkKDD'05.*

Page, L., and L. Brin. (1998): *The anatomy of a large-scale hypertextual Web search engine.* Proc. 7th International World Wide Web Conference.

Page, L., S. Brin, R. Motwani, and T. Winograd. (1998): What can you do with a Web in your pocket? *Bulletin of the Technical Committee on Data Engineering*, 21: 37–47.

Page, L., S. Brin, R. Motwani, and T. Winograd. (1999): The PageRank citation ranking: Bringing order to the Web. *Technical Report SIDL-WP-1999-0120,* Stanford Digital Libraries.

Rogers, I. (2006): The Google PageRank algorithm and how it works. http://www.iprcom.com/papers/pagerank/. http://www.innrogers.net/google-page-rank

Tsaparas, P., A. Borodin, G. Roberts, and J. Rosenthal. (2006): Finding authorities and hubs from the link structures on World Wide Web. In the Proceedings of the 10th International World Wide Web Conference.

Ullman, J. (2006): Web mining lecture notes. Stanford University. http://infolab.stanford.edu/~ullman/mining/pdf/pagerank.pdf.

Wilf, H. (2006): Searching the Web with eigenvectors. http://www.math.upenn.edu/~wilf/website/KendallWei.pdf.

Xing W., and A. Ghorbani. (2006): Weighted PageRank algorithm. http://glass.cs.unb.ca/ias/papers/xingw_weighted.pdf.

Further Reading

Albert, R., Jeong, H., Barab'asi, A.-L. (1999): Diameter of the world-wide Web. Nature, 401, pp. 130–131.

Broder, A., Kumar, R., Maghoul, F., Raghavan, P., Rajagopalan, S., Stata, R., Tomkins, A., Wiener, J. (2000): Graph structure in the Web. Computer Networks, 33(1–6), pp. 309–320.

Chakrabarti, S. (2000): Data mining for hypertext: A tutorial survey. SIGKDD explorations, 1(2), pp. 1–11.

Chakrabarti, S., Dom, B., Indyk P. (1998a): Enhanced hypertext categorization using hyperlinks. In Proc. of the ACM SIGMOD International Conference on Management on Data, pp. 307–318, Seattle, WA.

Chang, G., Healy, M. J., McHugh, J. A. M., Wang J. T. L. (2001): Mining the World Wide Web: An Information Search Approach. Kluwer Academic Publishers.

Dean, J., and Henzinger, M. R. (1999): Finding related pages in the World Wide Web. In A. Mendelzon, editor, Proceedings of the 8th International World Wide Web Conference (WWW-8), pp. 389–401, Toronto, Canada.

Fürnkranz, J. (1999): Exploiting structural information for text classification on the WWW. In D. Hand, J. N. Kok, and M. Berthold, (eds), Advances in Intelligent Data Analysis: Proc. of the 3rd International Symposium (IDA-99), pp. 487–497, Springer-Verlag.

Jeh G., and Widom, J. (2002): Scaling Pesonalized Web Search. *http://www-db.stanford.edu/~glenj/spws.ps.*

Index